THE
EXCUSE
FACTORY

*How Employment Law
Is Paralyzing
The American Workplace*

WALTER OLSON

MARTIN KESSLER BOOKS

THE FREE PRESS

New York   London   Toronto   Sydney   Singapore

THE FREE PRESS
A Division of Simon & Schuster Inc.
1230 Avenue of the Americas
New York, NY 10020

Manufactured in the United States of America

10   9   8   7   6   5   4   3   2   1

Library of Congress Cataloging-in-Publication Data

Olson, Walter K.
   The excuse factory: how employment law is paralyzing the
American workplace / Walter Olson.
      p. cm.
   Includes bibliographical references and index.
   1. Labor laws and legislation—United States.   2. Discrimination
in employment—Law and legislation—United States.   3. Industrial
relations—United States—Case studies.   4. Labor productivity—
United States—Case studies.   I. Title.
KF3457.044   1997
344.7301—dc21   97–7114
                                           CIP

ISBN 0-684-82732-8

To Anne Brunsdale

CONTENTS

INTRODUCTION

- Many companies forbid employees to browse the Internet from their work stations, even at lunchtime or after hours, because they fear that letting them visit bawdy sites might prompt charges of a "hostile working environment" from some offended co-worker. Other firms reserve for managers the right to post messages on water-cooler bulletin boards or coffee-room refrigerators, having been advised by their lawyers that they could be held liable if someone posts a vulgar piece of "photocopier humor."

- The *Wall Street Journal* has reported a boom in seminars on how to fire problem employees. The American Management Association alone holds more than 150 how-to-sack sessions a year, each drawing about seventy managers at $145 a pop. One such panel was entitled "How to Legally Fire Employees with Attitude Problems"— though the class leader quickly disappointed many attendees when he pointed out that attitude problems don't necessarily count any more as legal grounds to fire someone. Even with good luck and careful work, it might take months to oust the underperforming or insubordinate jobholder.

- Managers are often amazed at the questions they're not supposed to ask any more at job interviews. Don't ask whether an applicant grew up in the area; his answer might reveal his national origin. If he mentions that he attended a local college, don't ask *when* he was there; that would suggest interest in his age, another forbidden category. Asking where he lives might suggest a wish to evade a ban on considering applicants' credit records. If you learn that he's a war veteran, don't ask which war (his age and Vietnam-era status are none of your business). "Don't ask a woman if she wants to be called Miss, Mrs., or Ms., don't talk about 'mother tongue,' and don't ask where an applicant was born," add the managers' guidelines of a store chain in the Midwest.

- Employees have begun citing a wide range of physical, mental, and emotional deficits, from bad backs to learning disabilities, as reason why they should be excused from job functions or given easier schedules as an accommodation under the Americans with Disabilities Act of 1990. "Traditional" disabled groups—the deaf, blind, and paraplegic—now account for only a small share of ADA job complaints. One federal court ruled that an employee dismissed for stealing money from co-workers and bringing a loaded gun to work could sue for failure to accommodate his "chemical imbalance," while another ruled that to accommodate an employee with narcolepsy—the tendency to fall asleep at inappropriate times—a federal agency should expect to "tolerate an occasional nap."

- Fewer than 5 percent of personnel managers at the nation's biggest firms say they'd be "very candid" in giving a written reference about a former employee; in fact, most have formal policies prohibiting the release of information about such employees beyond name, position, and dates worked. "The whole thing has broken down," one told the *New York Times*. "People don't bother to check references. It's not worth it. If you call, you won't get information. And this is true everywhere."

INTRODUCTION

Since the mid-1960s the American workplace has been transformed by a series of powerful new laws. Lawmakers have long attempted to control what goes on in the workplace, but the new laws differ greatly from what came before.

To begin with, they are vast in the scope of their ambition. They aim to regulate not just a few readily measured dimensions of working life—such as pay scales, hours worked, or the conditions under which employers must recognize unions—but a wide range of personal interactions that includes job assignments, employee evaluations, benefit packages, and working conditions. And the latter very much includes the intangible elements of workplace life: what gets said in casual conversations, the tones in managers' voices and the looks on their faces, and other intimate details of daily interaction among workers. Unlike most previous laws, the new ones tend to avoid giving employers definite rules to obey but instead lay out sweeping if vague aspirations that are given the force of law. Thus employers are expected to refrain from "wrongful" firings, to give disabled workers "reasonable" accommodation, and to shelter employees from profanity or pointed criticism that reaches the point of creating a "hostile environment." No one really knows where these concepts begin and leave off; all employers know is that if they guess wrong some future jury or judge may decide that they have broken the law. Finally, and not least, the new laws draw their clout from a distinctive method of enforcement: individual workers can take their employers to court in lawsuits, often for very rich damages.

Together these laws have led to the rise of a thriving new sector of the legal system, called *employment law* (to distinguish it from *labor law*, the earlier law of collective bargaining and the like). A Chicago attorney terms employment suits "currently the fastest growing area of litigation in the country"; they're "without question the number one growing field" for claims against governments, concurs a Nebraska official. The litigation is "phenomenal," says a New York City official. "It has caught everybody by surprise." Employee claims are "by far" the leading source of legal trouble for members of nonprofit boards, a survey finds. Job-bias suits in federal courts have risen more than twentyfold since the mid-1970s, while age complaints have doubled since the late 1980s. Wrongful-discharge claims under state law and privacy and harassment suits have seen explosive growth as well, with the latter nearly tripling in the five years to 1994. One specialist estimates the overall field is expanding by 10 or 15 percent a year, which implies that it will double every six years or so.

For lawyers, this is good news. In its 1996 career guide, *U. S. News & World Report* lists employment law among its "20 hot job tracks," quoting a New York legal headhunter who's seen a tripling in requests for such lawyers (with an average partner compensation of $173,000-$191,000) in a year. The article points out that the Americans with Disabilities Act alone has generated fifty thousand new filings of discrimination charges with the Equal Employment Opportunity Commission, ensuring "more jobs for lawyers on both sides of the courtroom." The representation of plaintiffs, commonly for a percentage of the proceeds, has become an industry with its own Washington presence and a National Employment Lawyers Association to look out for its interests. On the management side, too, billions are spent on direct legal representation, negotiations, and "defensive" personnel practice.

———

Most central in the new bustle of legal activity are *discrimination laws.* Originally introduced as a drastic and unusual measure impelled by the hope of overcoming the nation's legacy of racial oppression, they have been relentlessly expanded to cover slights based not only on religion, sex and national origin but on age, disability, pregnancy, veteran status, and much more. The disabled category alone has added protection for tens of millions who display major physical, mental, emotional, and behavioral differences from the norm; court interpretations soon expanded ADA coverage to obesity-as-disability. Another federal law bars discrimination against aliens who are working in this country legally—that is, bias in favor of U.S. citizens.

Employment discrimination law has assumed an iconic role in American public discussion that is curiously hard to reconcile with what little can be observed of its actual results. On the one hand, it's come to symbolize the organized aspirations of a long series of groups that present ever more dubious analogies to the situation of blacks in the Jim Crow South: the elderly, the mentally ill, the paralyzed, mothers trying to juggle child care with careers, legal aliens, gays, and more. Some of these groups had already been doing extremely well in the job market; some had been disadvantaged but were making great strides in the job market in the absence of such legal protection; some had seen employer preferences more often aimed in their favor than against them; and still others suffered woes that seemed at best tangentially related to the hiring biases of employers. Yet many members of all these groups began to fix their hopes for collective advancement on job bias law, thus implicitly blaming their earlier troubles (if any) on the collective ill will or benightedness of the nation's employers.

In practice there has been no consistent pattern of improvement in the relative job situations of these groups. No amount of practical experience, though, seems to shake the faith in employment discrimination law as an act of group uplift. If you are for it, then you are for the success of the groups it covers, and vice versa—and a similar logic seems to operate to call into question the good faith of those who oppose such laws.

From the main line of discrimination law have branched off various other new areas of legal obligation for employers, each vast in itself. Disabled workers can demand *accommodation* of their individual needs. *Harassment* law, perhaps the fastest-growing area for complaints, began with cases where bosses had pressured women for sexual favors but soon grew to encompass a sweeping new right to be free of a *hostile working environment* as conveyed by co-workers' jokes, political and religious discussions, or artwork or photos posted on the wall. *Age discrimination* law has made unlawful the practice, previously common at large employers, of automatic retirement at a given age.

In recent years state courts have invented entirely separate new doctrines of common law that allow fired workers to sue on the basis of *wrongful discharge,* even when there are no allegations of bias. Old lawsuit theories such as defamation, infliction of emotional distress, and even false imprisonment have been creatively adapted to the workplace context, and new laws of *employee privacy* can sometimes be invoked as well. *Retaliation* law adds further grounds for suit when workers already locked in a dispute with their employers suffer adverse consequences on the job.

As the new body of law grew, virtually every decision employers made became the subject of a potential lawsuit. Salaries, benefits, bonus and incentive pay, pensions, vacation and leave policies all might serve as grist for legal challenges. The employment lawyer on the attack will pick and choose theories depending on what is available: wrongful firing, an age claim if the client is over forty, defamation because the employer has impugned his competence, maybe failure to accommodate if it has not made an effort to work around his weak points. A consistent theme is that talk was dangerous—a favorite method by which lawyers assemble cases is to sift through files or clients' recollections of everything supervisors have said or put in memos for years and pick out the most inflammatory phrase here and sentence there. Chicago lawyer Michael Leech is blunt in advising employers: "Every time you open your mouth or write something down, you're opening yourself up to potential liability."

———

The new laws exemplify a wider trend.

For most of American history, as a legal matter, and at least in the North, most jobs were "at will": either side could end the relation on short notice or none, much as we are free to stop dealing with a local tradesman if we grow dissatisfied with his service. Courts might intervene in some circumstances, of course, as when an employer refused to pay someone the agreed wages for work done. But hardly ever would they dictate that a working relationship be continued indefinitely against one side's will.

Obviously this hands-off attitude harmonized with widely shared ideas of the importance of keeping things voluntary in a private economy. But it had another, perhaps less apparent advantage: it tended to keep everyone out of court. And this country, like other countries, until fairly recently went to some lengths to avoid lawsuits. Slow, messy, and phenomenally expensive, legal disputes stirred up acrimony, invaded privacy, and ruined reputations; their outcomes were highly uncertain if not random, and they invited underhanded behavior. People might be forced to turn to them as a last resort, but they were hardly a method society would deliberately use to accomplish anything important.

With the decline of laissez-faire in the first decades of this century, lawmakers began to prescribe many terms of the employment relationship. They passed new laws requiring employers to take part in worker's compensation and unemployment insurance programs; they set minimum wages and maximum hours; and they regulated safety in mines, on ships, and on railways. In what was by far the most complicated set of laws, Franklin Roosevelt's New Deal legislation required employers to bargain with unions if a majority of their workers so wished. These laws were often quite burdensome to employers; but they still did not bring about any great rush of litigation between individual workers and those employers. One of the most notable reform programs, workers' compensation, was considered a success in part because it actually reduced litigation in one of the few areas where it had been common before.

By the late 1960s, however, our legal establishment had begun to see things in an entirely new light. Lawyers and courts suddenly seemed like a potential vanguard of social progress. Litigation wasn't a miserable and costly last resort at all, but really a positive thing for society; nothing seemed more natural than to apply its many benefits to the workplace. We can all recall many instances from personal experience in which managers have treated subordinates callously, arbitrarily, or unfairly. The results can be quite damaging to the victims, since everyone needs a job. Why not just *force* employers to be fair?

A great movement resulted, led in the law schools and among the public-interest litigation projects that seemed to be springing up everywhere. New laws laid out vague but sweeping rights to sue for damages, and old laws already on the books were reworked to reflect the new ideas. Both Republicans and Democrats signed on to support those ideas, which indeed met with little resistance. Progress in creating new rights to sue continued unabated through the reputedly conservative 1980s, and then took two further leaps forward when President George Bush signed into law the Americans with Disabilities

Act of 1990 and the Civil Rights Restoration Act of 1991. By this point, legal academics were proclaiming that the old general rule of at-will employment was on its way out for good: the new rule that would replace it would guarantee workers continued tenure in their jobs unless employers could show cause otherwise.

This movement, it is worth repeating, was a sharp departure from the road taken by previous labor advocates. Through the Progressive and New Deal eras, these advocates generally were at pains to minimize occasions for litigation, in part because they nursed unpleasant memories of the courts' longstanding role as a guardian of property rights and owners' interests. Nor did labor activists in other countries have much use for the deliberate building of litigation into their systems; European countries shared the presumption against lawsuits. It was hardly that any of these groups could be considered soft on employers: antagonism between capital and labor had run deep in the politics of the twentieth century, on every continent and in every decade. The results of these conflicts had ranged from strikes to sabotage and from bureaucratic stultification to (in the self-proclaimed "workers' states") mass murder. But although labor advocates had at times pursued almost every other proposed method of bringing the boss to heel—quietly appealing to his conscience, sending in government inspectors to harass him and eat out his substance, barricading his gates, occupying his plants, or even stringing him up from a sour apple tree—it had seldom occurred to anyone to make it a high priority to *sue* him.

———

"Defensive" personnel management aimed at keeping employers in compliance with the law and out of the worst scrapes has become an industry in itself, spawning hundreds of management manuals, newsletters, hotlines, and sensitivity seminars. Managers could easily spend their time doing nothing but keeping up with this literature, and yet never master the half of it. Whether unwittingly or not, in any case, employers constantly break the new laws. A Virginia attorney who uses a wheelchair told *Training* magazine that during her job search nearly every interviewer had asked her unlawful questions—

no small matter, since she'd been looking for work at law firms, many of which specialized in employment and discrimination law. Deliberate flouting of the law is common enough, but so is simple confusion. One recruiting firm asked 200 company managers which of a dozen questions they thought were legally okay to ask at interviews. In fact the list was composed entirely of unsafe questions, but 70 percent thought at least five were permissible, with the wrong guesses varying from one respondent to the next.

At the same time, a vast and popular self-help literature attempts to bring workers the happy news about all their new options. Age bias awards can be "rather substantial," says a New York lawyer, advising magazine readers who feel they have a case to "go for it . . . it's worth it to take the risk." The author of *Every Employee's Guide to the Law* writes that "if you can prove that clearly discriminatory remarks were made, there is a jury award out there with your name on it." A third attorney straightforwardly entitles his volume *Sue Your Boss,* proffering an "invitation" to take advantage of laws that are "very much in your favor" and just "waiting to be used." "Vast sums" can be on the table, he tells readers, presumably capturing the attention of even those who were only half awake. "Money—lots of it—has been changing hands."

A 1992 cover story in *New York* magazine shows how to get some of that money. "The potential costs for an employer are substantial—far greater than any severance package you could possibly ask for," explain the authors. Win or lose, the cost of defending a suit to trial is likely to exceed $100,000, and even cases settled early in the process can easily cost tens of thousands. Sexual harassment charges, which require more elaborate investigations than most other kinds, are especially expensive: a leading New York attorney has estimated that the cost just of pursuing the in-house investigation of a substantiated charge can run $200,000.

The authors proceed to offer cheerfully amoral advice, based on extensive interviews with practicing lawyers, on how to shake one's boss by the ankles until coins roll out. Your "leverage" in negotiating a severance "is your agreement not to sue the employer. Only by withholding it can you hope to up the ante." As a result, your lawyer's first job is to "determine exactly how much legal leverage you have" and "how much your former employer will be willing to pay to get you to give it up." Trial lawyers often argue that they have no incentive to take on clients with weak cases since they get nothing if the case fails at trial, the hidden assumption being that poor cases never get settlement offers before that point. The *New York* authors, however, seem unaware of this theory: "In examining your legal leverage, you're not so much weighing the odds of a *victory* in court as you are deciding whether or not you have grounds to *file* a lawsuit" (emphasis added).

————

Surveys report differing numbers on median or average awards in the various branches of employment law. One widely cited survey found that median sex and handicap discrimination cases were bringing roughly $100,000, race discrimination $150,000, and age discrimination $200,000. A 1988 survey found employees winning an average of $375,000 on claims of privacy invasion, sexual harassment, and defamation. Common-law theories in the more liberal states seem to bring higher sums. Individual wrongful-firing cases filed under common law have been reported to run more than half a million dollars nationally, and reached an astounding $1.5 million in one survey of cases in California, often seen as the most liberal state in this respect. And although judges often reduce verdicts substantially in later proceedings—one study found only about half the money voted at the jury level made its way into eventual payouts—even half of a zillion dollars is enough to get anyone's attention.

One scholar found the top awards in employment verdicts around the country often exceeded the top payout in the same states' Lotto games. A jury voted $7 million to an American Airlines manager at New York's La Guardia Airport after her promotion didn't come through, only to be topped by a California jury that voted $20 million to a Texaco employee who lost out on a promised upgrade to credit manager. A fired Colorado garbage driver won $1.4 million, while a handyman at New York's Off-Track Betting Corporation was awarded $2.5 million. But managers and supervisors themselves typically make out best in employment suits: they sue more often, they win more often when they sue, and they get far more money when they win than do rank-and-file workers.

Why do managers do so well as employment plaintiffs? Some of their advantage derives from the fact that they earned higher salaries in the first place, leading to higher awards for "back pay" and the like. Their solid personal background and articulate manner often impresses juries, and they are more likely to know "how to sue"—pocketing the right kinds of company documents, and provoking higher-ups into the right kind of damaging statements. Whatever the reasons, all sides seem to agree that age bias and common-law wrongful termination cases, both typically filed by affluent males at the middle-manager level and up, do much better than race and sex discrimination cases. It's as ironic as anyone could wish—employment law is largely the law of employment discrimination, yet its biggest financial rewards go to complainants who are neither minority nor female. Call it the revenge of the white males.

But everyone can take a spin at the wheel: a shrewd lawyer increasingly can find some grounds or other for suit in almost every case. "Few who are fired do not have some kind of claim," a Washington D.C., employment lawyer assured *Consumers Reports* in what may have been cheerful tones. As time goes on, the results may come to resemble the situation in a unionized workplace or civil service system, where contractual grievance arbitration processes or civil service rules allow individual workers to challenge whether a dismissal, discipline, or other "adverse action" has occurred for good cause. By what appears to be an underlying logic of these systems, seemingly moderate restrictions on management prerogatives can lead to pronounced entrenchment as managers find it advisable to work around the limitations of a problem employee, perhaps trying to get him transferred to another department. Indeed, there are signs of similar developments under the new employment law even in private nonunion workplaces.

The new law is the subject of a huge but strangely lopsided professional and academic commentary. The vast majority of this output, both from the law schools and from academia, takes an admiring view of the new law—especially the portions that travel under a civil rights banner—commonly accepting at face value its aspiration to make life in the workplace fairer. Ten thousand contributions to the literature of identity politics and victimology refer to the laws approvingly as part of their discourses on race and sex, speech and power.

Most of this literature spends little time examining what the cumulative effects of the new laws may be on the nature of the employment relationship. Even less often does it tend to acknowledge the differences between the official version of how the law is intended to work—a simple model in which employees sue purely in reaction to egregious acts of employer misbehavior—and the grubbier realities on the ground, where the law is readily pressed into service for settling scores, digging in, and maneuvering tactically for a maximum buyout.

To be sure, one aspect of the new law has drawn critical fire almost from the start: namely, the law's official encouragement of preferences, numerical goals, and quotas for favored groups. There's no doubt the preference issue is one of crucial importance, well worth the public debate. And yet quotas and preferences are far from the top item on most practicing managers' worry list, nor are they by any means the main ball game in the courts. If official encouragement for preferences were withdrawn tomorrow, the great bulk of litigation would continue, and so would most of the managerial headaches.

This book is a broad critical overview of the new employment law, written for the simple reason that no one else had written the book I wanted to read. Of necessity it examines the development of legal doctrine in courts, in agencies such as the Equal Employment Opportunity Commission, in Congress, and elsewhere. At the same time it makes no apology for illustrating the legal trends with stories that put a human face on the abstractions; hundreds of other stories had to be left on the cutting-room floor, and I hope that those that did make it in serve to illuminate general principles as well as convey shock value. To me, it is hard to spend much time among the documents that employment law leaves behind—the case reports, hearings, and press summaries of actual lawsuits—without being struck by the volume of spectacular injustice and irrationality the law has produced. More

INTRODUCTION

than one reader of early drafts of this book suggested I include frequent disclaimers that I really wasn't making it up.

Other consequences have followed on the heels of injustice. This book will also try to show that in its zeal to provide a remedy for everything it perceives as wrong at work, our law has too often undercut the quest for competence and excellence. Those concepts, too, are not mere abstractions; among other things, they determine whether lives and livelihoods will be saved or lost on the front lines of medicine, transportation, and public safety. Nor does the new law live up to its promises to foster gentler, more considerate dealings between employer and employee. As the management of a working relationship falls into the hands of lawyers on both sides, it becomes not more humane and harmonious but more artificial and adversarial. Evidence is mounting that as employers adjust, the law is backfiring so as to make many of its intended beneficiaries less rather than more secure. Rather than bringing a new liberation to our working hours, it has begun to stifle free expression, curb the sense of limitless possibility that characterizes the best jobs, and (with its clumsy one-size-fits-all methods) actually subtract from the pleasing "diversity" of which we hear so much today.

I expect that this book will help make the contentious world of employment law even more contentious in the short run; in the long run, I hope less so.

Part I

TENURE TRACK

Chapter 1

HIRING HELL

When Martin K. joined the Boston police force, the application form included a question about whether he'd ever been admitted to a hospital. He declared under oath that he had not, which was quite a whopper: actually, he'd been admitted five times to Veterans Administration facilities for psychiatric inpatient care. When it learned of the untruth, the city fired him. Aside from whether someone with his medical history should be toting a gun in the name of the citizenry, it figured Martin's lie in a sworn statement was disqualification enough for a job where he would frequently be asked to give credible testimony under oath.

The state high court ruled against the city and ordered him reinstated with back pay and damages for emotional distress. It said Massachusetts handicap-rights law prohibited employers from taking into account job applicants' medical history, including mental health treatment; would-be cops were no exception. Since the city had no business taking past hospitalization into account, it had no business asking about it. And since it had no business asking about it, it also had no right to act on the basis of responses to its question—a sort of employment-law analogue to the exclusionary rule in criminal law.

The case was no fluke. In many other cases, lawyers were succeeding in advancing the notion that if a question is improper, a job applicant needn't answer it truthfully; it's known as the "right to lie."

———

The hiring and interview process is the place everyday managers are most likely to encounter the new employment law. And the new law—especially as applied by the federal Equal Employment Opportunity Commission—has made the regulation of hiring one of its special missions. The result has been to give not only managers, but also applicants, a lot of new things to be nervous about.

The legal hazards begin with the classified ad. Statements such as "recent grads," "young office," "beginner," and "ideal for retiree" have all set companies up for age-bias suits. On the other hand, "career prospects," "possible long-term situation," and the like have been seized on as grounds for claims that the employer was implicitly promising tenure and thus forfeiting its right to fire later without "good cause." Employers have also been targeted by complaints for buying ads in the big local newspaper without advertising in smaller publications catering to black or foreign-language readers. (Many such publications, aware of the captive ad base, charge rates quite a few times higher than their circulation would otherwise seem to justify.) The EEOC has said some employers may even violate the law if they run a classified ad that gives only a voice telephone number, without an address or teletype number for the convenience of deaf applicants.

The interviewing of job applicants comes under remarkably intense legal pressure, with any number of everyday questions considered off-limits. One consultant describes it as hazardous to ask whether an applicant has friends at the company, since white males might have more. If a question is forbidden by itself, of course, it's also generally forbidden as a follow-up to an applicant's puzzling or unsatisfactory statement or résumé entry. Many managers try to guess age from dates in personal history; another common ploy is to toss the ball into the applicant's court by asking open-ended questions in the hope he'll volunteer information that couldn't be probed for directly.

Inappropriate interview questions can serve as a basis for cash damages all by themselves, even if an applicant would not have been offered a job. Managers at the Community Coffee Co. of Baton Rouge, Louisiana, allegedly asked insensitive questions of a sales applicant whose handicaps included facial disfigurement as well as visual and hearing problems; a jury agreed he wouldn't have landed the job but voted him $15,000 anyway for his emotional distress, plus $30,000 in punitive damages to teach the company a lesson.

Other careless comments pose a danger of giving a later complainant something to seize on as a binding promise of tenure. Attorney Alan Koral notes that "it is probably safe to say that 'this is a nice place to work' or 'we want our employees to be happy with their jobs.'"

———

What about reference-checking? That runs into its own problems. Until the 1980s or so American courts largely shielded employers from defamation suits arising from bad references or other comments on employee performance. Quite suddenly, though, a series of decisions knocked down the old "qualified privilege." A New York court ruled that describing a former employee as having been fired "for cause" was reason enough to send a defamation case to a jury. "Malice" could be shown, courts decided, if a company showed "conscious indifference" to the impact of its words on the former employee. Invasion of privacy and infliction of emotional distress are among other newly popular theories; the Ninth Circuit in 1989 upheld a $1.4 million award against a railroad for "intentional interference" with an ex-worker's prospects. Mentions of a former employee's proclivity toward alcohol or drug abuse—or bad behavior linked to such abuse—are especially dangerous, running afoul of privacy and disabled-rights concerns as well as the rest.

Where managers have tried to dispense largely positive evaluations interspersed with a caveat here and there, lawyers have interpreted it as an attack on their clients that is all the more damaging for being coded. Giving references only where one can be enthusiastic, and keeping mum otherwise, has run into claims that silence about one former worker under such circumstances is tantamount to a negative comment. And even giving positive references to everyone is dangerous. "An employer who fires you but gives you a positive reference . . . is just begging to be hit with a wrongful discrimination suit," writes attorney Lewin Joel. "After all, if you were such a good employee, what was the real reason you were fired?"

Some commentators have pointed out that relatively few reference suits make it to trial or win big awards. But the reason is hardly a mystery; the point of this kind of legal weaponry is to serve as a threat rather than to have to be carried through—and the threat works very well. The giving of references is for the most part a volunteer activity carried on from a sense of public spirit, and it is easy to pull back once a liability risk appears. Most big employers soon retreated, therefore, to an almost wholly uninformative name-rank-and-serial-number recitation of dates worked and titles. In other cases, the wording of a reference is set in exit negotiations with a worker's lawyer. Some courts even order employers to provide favorable references to workers who have sued them, in what might seem a remarkable example of compulsory insincere speech for the purpose of fooling blameless third parties.

Though some state legislatures have heeded a business outcry by passing laws intended to restore limited immunity for giving references, it has not proved easy to restore confidence overnight, especially as ingenious lawyers start looking for ways around the limits. The atmosphere remains unrecognizably different from that of a generation ago. "Regarding character, we are wandering in a wasteland," Cleveland recruiter Alan Schonberg told the *New York Times*.

Reference-giving was also the subject of one of the EEOC's most exotic crusades over the years. The commission has insisted that the entire process of checking references has "adverse impact" on blacks, who allegedly will receive poorer references than others. Hence, it has held, employers should not be permitted to check references unless they have carried out elaborate studies to validate the use of the practice in their particular circumstances. The commission spent years in court suing the National Academy of Sciences on behalf of one black applicant whom the NAS had decided not to hire after her reference came in negative. (The bad reference was itself conceded as not unfair or racially motivated.) The prospective employer finally won after hiring two academics who conducted elaborate analyses of its personnel records and showed that aside from the single case at issue, its policy of checking references had not worked to reduce the number of blacks hired; in fact, few applicants of either race had received bad references. Though it lost that case, the commission has apparently never given up on its wider view that reference-checking is to be held legally suspect.

———

The EEOC's view that reference-checking is inherently unfair to minorities is just one of the countless applications of its famous doctrine of "disparate impact," approved by the Supreme Court in the celebrated case of *Griggs* v. *Duke Power,* laid out in the Uniform Guidelines on Employee Selection Procedures more than two decades ago, and minutely analyzed in flume-jamming flows of legal commentary ever since. The doctrine essentially provides that any employee selection procedure with adverse impact against any protected group will be unlawful unless an employer is willing on demand to validate its business necessity. Almost every phrase in the preceding sentence might better be enclosed in quotation marks, since each is an ambitiously broad term of art:

- *Employee selection procedure* means virtually any screening method an employer might use to choose among applicants: education or experience requirements, consideration of standardized test results, typing speeds, height, possession of a driver's license, and so on.

- *Adverse impact* occurs when members of some protected group fail to make it through the process in numbers proportional to their share of (1) the general population, (2) the workforce, (3) the pool of workers who are in some sense qualified for the particular job, or (4) those who in fact applied. Complainants have used all these theories, depending on which comes out most favorably for them; they also gerrymander the geographic bounds from which the group is drawn, so that a suburban employer accused of hiring too few blacks may find its numbers compared with those of the whole metropolitan area, while one in the inner city may find the comparison pool drawn only from within city limits. Nothing deliberate or invidious need be shown, and proof of nondiscriminatory intent is irrelevant. Virtually all neutral hiring practices show disparate impact: educational requirements show it against blacks, height requirements against women, and so forth. As a result, all are suspect.

• *Validate* means that the employer must be willing to offer affirmative, more or less scientific studies to back up its decision to use such a selection method. Such studies, if done from scratch, can cost hundreds of thousands or even millions of dollars. The EEOC maintains fabulously stringent guidelines for validation, which the courts only sometimes accept (being at other times more lenient toward employers). Even when courts approve a method as adequately validated in one case, they seldom set out a green light for other employers: plaintiffs can go back to challenge the same method again when it is used by the next employer, and not infrequently they get it struck down.

• Business necessity, more than the other terms, has varied in stringency with changes in the mood of the Supreme Court and lower courts. Fans of adverse-impact law, in line with the usual meaning of *necessity,* think courts should make it virtually impossible for employers to validate procedures unless they are necessary for them to stay in business. Only a minority of courts have taken that view; the Supreme Court wavered for years, then in *Wards Cove* v. *Atonio* (1989) moved toward a markedly more permissive view in which employers would have to show only the general rationality of their selection methods. In 1991 Congress reversed *Wards Cove* and restored the earlier (but far from coherent) state of the law.

EEOC and court interpretations have turned the disparate-impact theory into a thing of magnificence, a regulatory Eighth Wonder of the World, endowed with a seemingly endless array of oubliettes, hidden vaults, and sunless dungeons. Virtually every set procedure an employer might choose to make part of its hiring process is suspect. Does it recruit only by advertising, or never by advertising? Either practice might have disparate impact on one group or another. The chill on minimum education or experience requirements has helped scare many employers out of asking for diplomas and transcripts, even though many courts have in the event upheld such standards. New York City has found that the best predictor of police recruits' performance—of the questions it is still permitted to ask—is their record in previous jobs, but groups suing the city charge that "favor[ing] candidates who have been able to hold a single job for several years" perpetuates "white, middle-class values."

Having grown out of discrimination law, disparate-impact doctrine is still mostly discussed on the basis of its implications for minority interests. But it has far wider effects, which are felt in countless situations where minority status as such could not be the issue—that is, where neither of the candidates vying for a position is white or male, or where both are. Thus minimum height requirements for security guard or firefighter positions are subject to disparate-impact challenge because of their adverse impact on Asians and females; the law, however, equally forbids the use of the criterion to decide between two Scottish-American males of markedly different height. In fact, it is quite erroneous to imagine that the disparate-impact theory somehow applies only when employers are suspected of somehow wanting to exclude a group by proxy. Flight attendants with surplus poundage won millions by arguing that airline weight requirements had disparate impact on women, who find it harder to keep their weight down. But whatever can be said for or against weight rules, we may be sure that airlines did not devise such rules as a way of reserving flight attendant jobs for men; women held the great majority of attendant jobs, and indeed male applicants were winning in other courts after alleging the airlines had consciously favored women.

In so-called pattern-and-practice cases, the EEOC can identify a practice with disparate impact and then demand "back pay" for the entire class that went underrepresented in the employer's workforce, even though this may constitute a group ten or fifty times more numerous than the actual number of positions for which the employer was hiring. In the 1980s, Chicago utility Commonwealth Edison hired females for 11 percent of its meter-reading jobs. The commission said this was not enough, but the company would have had to turn away large numbers of women in any event, because it got an estimated 100 applications for each position. So the EEOC simply negotiated a settlement dividing $3 million equally among all 3,000 women who applied ($1,000 for each), on the apparent theory that when all have won, all must have prizes. (This case refutes clearly enough the widely held notion that the function of "back pay" is somehow not to punish the employer but to make everyone whole.) In another well-known case, the commission demanded that the Daniel Lamp Company place $10,000 worth of ads to find black applicants against whom it might have discriminated, and pay a further $123,000 as supposed back pay to those who might step forward as a result—a sum apparently arrived at before any look at the situations of the not-yet-unidentified claimants. The actual complainant received back wages of $340.

———

Cataloguing the EEOC's novel applications of disparate-impact law would take a book in itself. Among the most remarkable is its crusade against word-of-mouth hiring, which it considers legally suspect since it tends to perpetuate the (invariably out of balance) demographic makeup of a company's current workforce.

For most managers, avoiding grapevine influences on hiring would be somewhat like avoiding breathing. Especially in immigrant communities, nothing is more common than for particular businesses to draw heavily from one ethnic group—Pakistani, Dominican, Irish, or whatever. Taxi fleets in Washington, D.C., have thus been organized along a wide variety of ethnic lines, with dispatchers for at least one fleet announcing destinations in Amharic. Yet the EEOC regularly files complaints against employers that fill positions by word of mouth, using the doctrine to extract surprisingly large settlements from surprisingly small companies (as with the $2 million it got from an obscure candy maker named World's Finest Chocolate). It also routinely goes after companies whose use of grapevines attracts lots of minority employees, but not the right *mix* of them. Thus its very active Chicago regional office filed cases against a small machine shop with too many Hispanics and too few blacks, and another against a janitorial service whose work force was predominantly Korean.

The Korean-janitor case brought the agency a certain amount of adverse publicity, not that anyone seemed to care much in Washington. Prominent Seventh Circuit judge Richard Posner stingingly rebuked the commission for its "sorry parade of witnesses," including one who claimed to have responded to a *Chicago Sun-Times* ad even though the company had never advertised there. Though completely vindicated, the company closed down after running up $200,000 in legal costs during the eight-year fight. "After 32 years in the United States, my dream is shattered," former president Andrew Hwang told *Crain's Chicago Business*. "My business is totally gone." Hwang was now looking for work as an employee of others. "We won the battle and lost the war," said his attorney, Cary Kabumoto. "If you're a small company, you may as well roll over."

Another noteworthy EEOC crusade has been against employers' right to consider applicants' police records, which is yet another practice with adverse impact on minorities.

Several early court cases gave the agency the opening it was seeking. In one, a federal court ruled that a defense contractor had unlawfully taken into account the fact that a job applicant had been arrested fourteen times—those arrests being presumably just an innocent guy's streak of really bad luck. That was followed by an Eighth Circuit case striking down across-the-board employer policies against hiring applicants with criminal convictions (as opposed to arrests). The court's apparent rationale was that some convictions are "little" and not really worth considering; of course, it wasn't prepared to trust employers to decide for themselves which those were.

EEOC doctrine leans heavily on the notion that employers must ignore all past convictions that are not "job-related," a circular term of art. Thus in its view employers should often have to ignore even quite serious crimes unless they are both recent and closely related to a job's subject matter. It ruled against a company that did not want to rehire a crane operator who was released after serving six years for first-degree murder; a portrait photographic studio that wanted to turn away a convicted forger (because even though his offense was job-related, it was six years old); and against a company reluctant to hire a convicted shoplifter as a dock worker (because even though the crime was job-related, the items taken *weren't very valuable*). "Generalized concerns about customer or co-worker loss of confidence, absenteeism in the event of future arrests, or minor losses from pilfering are not sufficient to rise to the level of necessity," approvingly remarks the author of a leading treatise.

The agency has also declared unlawful any general employer policy of firing workers caught lying on their applications, even when the questions to which the applicants were responding were otherwise legitimate—a position that goes beyond even that of the Massachusetts court in Martin K.'s "right to lie" case. It explains that firing liars has an adverse impact on ex-cons because they, more than others, feel a need to falsify their work record (in order to conceal stretches of imprisonment).

The EEOC does not always win these cases. It lost one in 1989 where it had demanded that a trucking company hire felons to handle "high risk" freight such as computers and pharmaceuticals; federal judge Jose Gonzalez tartly observed that if applicants "do not wish to be discriminated against because they have been convicted of theft then they should stop stealing."

In the law schools, though, the main worry appears to be that current doctrines against criminal-record bias don't go far enough. The *Fordham Law Review*'s commentator thinks worried employers are just being foolish: "There is little evidence that employees with records are poor workers or safety risks." No "tendency is apparent" for ex-offenders to abuse drink or drugs at any greater rate than the general public, agrees the most widely cited academic account, in the *Catholic University Law Review*. Despite years of EEOC efforts, the author laments, "persons without criminal records have an advantage" on the

job market. To curb this problem, employers approached by an applicant with even a very recent and job-related conviction "should have
to demonstrate . . . that the applicant [still] has the propensity to engage in that criminal conduct." How they or anyone could succeed in
doing so is left unclear. Naturally, the author also advocates construing "job-related" narrowly: thus a company whose inventory includes
valuable industrial materials should not be permitted to turn away a
convicted embezzler, since "stealing such items is very different in
form from embezzlement," while a factory should not be allowed to
say no to a violence-oriented sociopath concededly unsuitable for customer service, "since working with things rather than people is the
major part of the job."

In general, as such passages suggest, the law review commentary on
employment law tends to be almost comically remote from employer
concerns. A widely noted *Harvard Law Review* comment proposes that
employers be made to "reevaluate their commitment" to "the standard
face-to-face interview" because this "prejudicial" process permits "illegitimate appearance evaluations" of the disabled, elderly, or just
plain homely (looks-ism being pervasive in the business world). Solu-
tions might include "restructuring the hiring process to eliminate or
reduce information about applicants' appearance" by using so-called
Chinese walls to keep interviewers from passing data on physical
appearance to final decision-makers, "expanded use of telephone interviews," and—the Harvard author is not offering this as a parody—
interviews held behind screens.

———

Hiring law exemplifies the new employment law's aim of controlling
the psychological intangibles of work. The interview process, even
more than most of life in the business world, is rife with verbal fencing, byplay of personality and undisclosed agendas, even as everyone
stays on best behavior. "Small talk" and general chat can cut the tension and also give "a picture of the person," as Irene Larsen (the manager of an agency that referred domestic workers to homeowners) told
Robert Hamburger in his oral history of domestic work, *A Stranger in
the House.* "I can tell very well," Larsen said, "if I ask, 'How old were

the children?', and she says, 'Oh, I don't remember how old they were'—she doesn't like children. If you like children, you're going to remember how old those children were."

Studies have confirmed the commonsense idea that first encounters, even when they prove the prelude to productive relationships, often pose a rough spot for those who differ from the majority in some way. Thus when able-bodied persons in one study met disabled newcomers, they showed more rigidly controlled behavior than when meeting others, gestured less, and "expressed opinions that were less representative of their actual beliefs." Another study found black visitors treated with "verbal overfriendliness, coupled with vocal and behavioral cues of affective retreat."

It is far from clear that the introduction of legal compulsion has helped to reduce the awkwardness of first encounters. When it comes to the visible human differences associated with major disabilities, many interviewers have been tempted to try breaking through the unease by openly acknowledging differences in either a joshing or serious way. Now they know better. "It has put a damper on the dialogue," said quadriplegic attorney Kathi Pugh. "They know they can't ask about your disability, so the subject is never brought up and they assume the worst."

We're said to live in the Information Age, but when it comes to hiring, our law much prefers ignorance: the less employers know about those they propose to employ, the better. The accident- or embezzlement-prone have to work somewhere, after all. Sure, more people may get hired for jobs they won't do well, but as one enthusiastic commentator sums it up, workers deserve the right "to fail *on the job*" (emphasis added).

Do workers as a group benefit? Getting hired is a competitive sport, and if the law gives one contestant a leg up it must artificially hobble someone else; if no disfavor may be shown to felons, then no favor may be shown to those who have faced similar temptations but always stayed clean. The legal chill on references chokes off more helpful, positive references from past employers than backbiting, negative ones. The game of waiting for applicants to volunteer information that can't be asked for directly gives an edge to those with outgoing personalities and those who know what is expected; the shy lose out, as do those who unknowingly ramble on about the wrong topics. Some win the right to lie, but others who refuse to gild their résumés miss their chance to shine. And the honestly hired but mismatched new worker is hardly better off if, after failing on the job, he must be eased out to face the whole strained process again from a weaker position.

Many rules bar employers from probing for information that would count in a candidate's favor. It's considered too risky to inquire into unpaid community and family responsibilities, for example, though these are often important strengths for homemakers trying to re-enter the workforce. New York, trying to assist adherents of controversial political causes, forbids inquiry into applicants' participation in any community groups not narrowly focused on career or business matters—even though most employers probably count such involvement as a plus most of the time. With "diversity" in business vogue, unusual personal backgrounds might be expected to be in demand, but employers aren't supposed to ask about them.

As liability-chary employers look for ways to reduce the pesky human element, one natural development has been a steady growth of interest in interview software. A 3M division markets LPA SelectPro, which offers more than 225 questions to help make a "structured, consistent interview." Another maker of employee-selection software, reports Suzanne Oliver in *Forbes*, "is always searching for new indicators that aren't yet forbidden by the courts" and puts in questions about cigarette smoking, favorite games, and television habits.

————

Common sense, for years now hermetically excluded from the law of hiring, would start by recognizing that people thrown together in a room will talk, with no clear line to separate chat that is job-related from that which is not; that grapevines are inevitable and largely a good thing; that the filling of jobs is a rushed, highly imperfect process torn between fear of making a bad pick and the need to act before good candidates go elsewhere or unperformed work piles up to the crisis stage. It would demolish and give a decent burial to the disparate-impact doctrine, and aim to recreate the law of job references circa 1957 if not earlier. Instead we have devised a hiring law as punitive, contradictory, and hard to comply with as wit could readily manage—all the better, it would seem, to teach employers that they should conduct as little of this antisocial activity as possible.

Chapter 2

TENURE TRACK

Veronica Stone's new job at the Mission Bay Mortgage Company hadn't worked out, and she wasn't happy about it. At the interview, she understood manager Richard Wood to have said she'd be let go only if her work proved unsatisfactory. Yet when she got the sack just two weeks later, she was told it was because business had slowed down.

So she sued in Nevada state court. She didn't charge discrimination, harassment, or things of that sort. Instead, she said the company had broken a *promise* not to fire her without good cause—a legally binding promise; in fact, a contract.

Mission Bay objected. It pointed to the line accompanying her signature on its job application: "I understand and agree that my employment is for no definite period and may, regardless of the date of payment of my wages and salary, be terminated at any time, without any previous notice." In addition, manager Wood had told her in so many words that her first weeks would be a probationary period. Nothing he said at the interview had been intended to create, or had accidentally amounted to, some sort of pledge to go on employing her indefinitely. On top of that, the centuries-old rule known as the Statute of Frauds requires that long-term commitments be in writing if they're to be legally binding. Specifically, the Nevada version of the statute declares void "Every [oral or otherwise unwritten] agreement . . . not to be performed within 1 year from the making thereof."

But a state appeals court decided her suit could go forward, accepting her characterization of the disclaimer in the application as being "for informational purposes only." It observed that calling her a "probationary" employee wouldn't logically rule out having pledged to keep her permanently on certain conditions. As for the Statute of Frauds, the court joined other courts that had creatively reinterpreted that rule out of existence as it applied to employment cases. After all (these courts had ruled), a promise of job tenure wouldn't have to last for more than a year; the employee might drop dead, or the company do the same by going out of business. Mission Bay itself had given the court the opening it needed—hadn't it said Veronica was a probationary employee? If so, the court concluded on a note of somewhat circular triumph, "the contract *could have been* terminated within one year."

––––––––

Under the principle of "employment at will" that prevailed through most of American history, both employers and employees were free to terminate a working relationship with each other at any time unless they'd agreed beforehand on some set longer duration, such as a year's hiring. The idea had long roots, and it was viewed as a simple corollary of the freedom Americans were accustomed to enjoy (north of the Mason-Dixon line, at least). Back in England, Adam Smith had called restrictions on the terms of employment "a manifest encroachment upon the just liberty both of the workman, and of those who might be disposed to employ him. As it hinders the one from working at what he thinks proper, so it hinders the others from employing whom they think proper."

A classic statement came in an 1892 Oliver Wendell Holmes opinion. The town of New Bedford, Massachusetts, had dismissed a policeman for politicking in violation of a local ordinance; he went to court, pleading free speech. "The petitioner may have a constitutional right to talk politics, but he has no constitutional right to be a policeman," Holmes wrote. "There are few employments for hire in which the servant does not agree to suspend his constitutional rights of free speech, as well as of idleness, by the implied terms of his contract. The servant cannot complain, as he takes the employment on the terms which are offered him."

Indeed, the courts saw the constitutional protection as running the other way: employment at will was part of the liberty guaranteed by the Bill of Rights. As the Supreme Court put it in the 1908 case of *Adair* v. *United States,* "it is not within the functions of government— at least in the absence of contract between the parties—to compel any person in the course of his business and against his will to accept or retain the personal services of another." Thus the courts repeatedly struck down laws that sought to force employers to hire or retain on their payroll employees who'd made themselves unwelcome by supporting unions. Such laws, the Court said in 1915, infringe on "freedom of choice," a "fundamental and vital" right. "The employee's liberty of making contracts does not include a liberty to procure employment from an unwilling employer. . . . Nor may the employer be foreclosed by legislation from exercising the same freedom of choice that is accorded to the employee."

In 1937, by a 5-to-4 vote, the Court abandoned constitutional protection of free choice in employment—not because it had been convinced otherwise, but in submission to a show of sheer force. President Franklin Roosevelt, irate at seeing his New Deal programs struck down, had threatened to pack the Court by getting Congress to increase the number of justices so he could appoint enough to tip its balance. The Court majority then agreed to reverse itself, in the famous "switch in time that saved nine." Congress and state lawmakers proceeded to enact various measures sought by unions and other reformers that infringed on the employment-at-will principle, such as a ban on discriminating against union supporters. Still, these laws remained exceptional incursions on the general rule: most employers were still free to deal with whom they wanted, as workers were free to choose whom to work for.

———

Of the various harsh consequences of a modern open economy, few have seemed harsher than the risk of being without a job. Most liberal reformers have seen the insecurity of employment as among the most troubling problems of capitalism; the historic Left saw it as *the* basic problem from which others flow. In the long run, to be sure, many look back on losing a particular job as a blessing in disguise, one that cuts them loose from dead-end work or forces them to confront weaknesses or seek new skills. As Churchill remarked on losing his elected job, though, if this is a blessing it is very effectively disguised indeed: not the least of the burden, both psychologically and financially, consisting in not knowing how long a spell of joblessness will last.

Reformers have long sought to soften the blow in ways that did not actually do away with the premises of an open and voluntary economy. Probably the most central such attempt was the development of unemployment compensation, introduced widely in this country in the first decades of this century.

Compared with many government social programs, unemployment compensation looks like a success: certainly it arouses little controversy given its size and economic importance, though lawmakers sometimes trim back benefit levels when they get so high as to hurt business or discourage jobless workers from leaving the rolls. Much of this success must be credited to the modesty of its goals, which carried forward a tradition of mutual aid among earlier fraternal societies and trade unions. The unemployment program aimed not at utopian transformation of the workplace but at modest cost-spreading; hence it is frequently referred to as unemployment "insurance." Benefits were limited, running out after a set term such as twenty-six weeks—a period long enough for most job-seekers to find work. Part of the rationale behind this limit was to give workers a definite incentive to find a new job by the time benefits ran out; there was also a feeling that at some point long-term unemployment must stop being a previous employer's responsibility and become someone else's.

Payroll levies would fall not solely on businesses that laid off workers (which would have amounted to something like a mandatory severance policy) but would be spread more thinly over employers in general (though "experience rating" might tilt the burden toward industries with more frequent layoffs). Again, this reflected a balance of incentives: heaping the entire cost of relieving a distressed worker onto whichever company had most recently tried to employ him might discourage many job offers in the first place. Finally, benefits were scaled but with a ceiling, so that workers who had been earning more would get higher benefits (and their employers pay higher premiums on their behalf), but only up to a point. The scaled coverage again represented a sort of insurance principle, while the ceiling reflected the widely held view that a compulsory program shouldn't seek to guarantee the $250,000 executive the same share of his lost salary as it did the $25,000 clerk. (Put differently, the executive was seen as having more responsibility to build up savings during good times.)

Thus matters stood until the 1960s, when some entirely different ideas on what to do about the insecurity of employment began to be heard from the nation's law schools.

One of the most influential articles appeared in 1967 between the sedate, powder-blue covers of the *Columbia Law Review*. Its author was Professor Lawrence Blades of the University of Kansas, who was later to become dean of the University of Iowa Law School.

Blades pointed out the harsh consequences of being fired from a job, consequences that were often severe even after the palliating effect of unemployment compensation. The law had long accepted that an employer could impose this fate on an individual worker for any cause—good, bad, or none—but things didn't have to work that way. Much of the American workforce, in fact, already enjoyed protection against firing without good cause. Nearly all union contracts in this country include clauses by which management agrees not to dismiss or discipline workers without good cause and to set up a process by which the union can take such actions to arbitration; such provisions commonly head a union's list of negotiating demands, in part because it wants to keep management from using firings to pick off key union sympathizers. Civil service rules provide government employees (another big sector of the American workforce) with similar security. Finally, some European countries had begun to extend these principles to private workers, whether union or nonunion, by establishing official tribunals in which workers could challenge dismissals.

It was time, Blades said, for American workers generally to enjoy such across-the-board protection: every employer should be barred from dismissing workers without good cause. What was truly novel, though, was his proposed method of instituting this new right. Workers who believed they'd been fired without good cause should simply be given the right to *sue*—to take their employer to court, just as if it were a driver who had collided with them at an intersection.

This was a daring idea. The existing models of dismissal review all involved setting up some sort of counter-institution with professional expertise: unions with shop stewards, civil service commissions with permanent staffs, or European government tribunals with investigative officers. In this case, the equivalent would have to be a privately hired lawyer and a judge or jury with no particular familiarity with the workplace in question.

The notion perfectly suited the emerging spirit of the times. By the mid-1960s the law schools were beginning a love affair with the lawsuit; ever-wider social benefits were to be had if only private lawyers and litigants could be turned loose on society with the broadest possible powers to sue. Earlier generations had tried to discourage litigation except as a last resort, seeing it as phenomenally expensive and time-consuming; brutal and divisive; harmful to privacy, reputation, and peace of mind; susceptible to abuse and sharp practice; and dangerous to the innocent on either side. Almost any way of handling a social problem was worth a look if it could avoid this slow-motion train wreck.

Now these views began to seem passé. "We don't sue enough," said peripatetic Harvard professor Alan Dershowitz, summing up the new wisdom. "Suing is good for America." One could hardly open a law review without finding proposals for new rights to sue, any more than one could find a food magazine without recipes. Entrepreneurial, profit-seeking law became the rage: another well-known academic wrote of the "professional responsibility to chase ambulances." The answer to almost every social problem—and firings for bad cause were no different—was to sue earlier and more often for higher damages, always making sure some "deep pocket" was on hand to absorb the deterrent lesson. The whole process recalled the *New Yorker* cartoon caption where an official behind a desk is barking orders: "And see that you place the blame where it will do the most good."

Of course, a few nostalgics still saw employment as a voluntary and freely entered arrangement on both sides, but Blades dismissed that view as a holdover from days of "rustic simplicity." In those bygone days, a worker who fell out with one employer might move on to another, but now employees had few choices about where to take their skills. Given the "ever-increasing concentration of economic power in the hands of fewer employers," the "great majority" of employees already fall "easy prey to the employer's overreaching demands." This trend toward concentration was "irreversible," Blades wrote, and as it proceeded employees "will become even more easily oppressed by their employers."

The prediction that fewer and fewer employers were going to be doing more and more of the hiring turned out to be a singularly bad bit of market forecasting. The share of jobs in the overall economy provided by the nation's largest firms was to peak and then begin a decline that picked up speed in the 1990s as "outsourcing" spun more jobs off into smaller businesses and entities; inevitably, labor critics saw this new trend away from the concentrated hiring market as further deepening workers' oppression.

Blades conceded there might be a few practical problems in letting every fired worker sue. Cases would often hinge not on hard evidence but on recollections of long-ago conversations and incidents, and the extensive testimony needed to weigh claims would hardly be ideally reliable, since the witnesses on each side would not be objective. Moreover, plausible points were apt to appear on both sides: a great many workers can demonstrate some degree of arbitrary or insensitive treatment, but "the employer in most cases can counter with equally credible evidence of inefficiency, neglect or insubordination." That left a very real prospect, Blades conceded, of close calls and "vexatious lawsuits." Thoughtful judges, however, could undoubtedly work to minimize such problems; right now, the important thing was for them to summon the boldness to move forward. After all, lawmakers had showed little interest in abolishing the old rule of employment at will and replacing it with some new scheme of litigation. In a logical leap that wonderfully typified the new mood in legal academia, Blades argued that this very lack of legislative interest made it all the more urgent for courts to step into the breach and invent such a right on their own.

Blades's pioneering article was followed by dozens of others in the law reviews. Employment at will, commentators soon agreed, was lacking in fairness; it was oppressive, making workers feel they had to keep their heads down and not rock the boat; it even fell short as to economic efficiency, because how could anyone achieve his full productive potential unless he felt confident of fair treatment? One might have expected some defense from some quarter of legal academia of a practice that would hitherto have seemed central to the way America did business. But aside from a maverick or two, such as Richard Epstein of the University of Chicago, hardly a discouraging word was to be heard. By the 1980s, writes Harvard's Paul Weiler, the case against employment at will was "well on the way to becoming the conventional wisdom" and "now seems virtually self-evident to many sophisticated commentators."

———

As he later testified, Charles Toussaint felt he could go on working for Michigan Blue Cross and Blue Shield "as long as I did my job." In fact, he'd asked about job security at the interview, and the supervisor had told him "I wouldn't have to look for another job because he knew of no one ever being discharged."

But that happy state of affairs was not to last. Blue Cross let Toussaint go anyway, for bad cause, in his view. And aside from his recollection of the supervisor's comments, he even had something in writing—of a sort. Blue Cross put out a handbook for its employees that contained the following sentence: "It is the policy of the company to treat employees leaving Blue Cross in a fair and consistent manner and to release employees for just cause only." This clause, his lawyer argued, should be viewed as legally binding. A jury agreed, found that Blue Cross hadn't lived up to this promise, and awarded Toussaint $73,000.

Blue Cross appealed. It argued that the language of employee handbooks was meant, to borrow Veronica Stone's phrase, for informational purposes; a half-dozen old contract doctrines stood in the way of reading them as legally binding promises, and courts had never in fact read them as such. What the jury had done was quite unprecedented.

As they say about things unprecedented, though, there's always a first time. The Michigan Supreme Court's 1980 opinion upholding Toussaint's award touched off gasps of delight around legal academia and gasps of bewilderment around the personnel offices of America. Wielding novel legal arguments like a miracle Ginsu knife, the court in short order reduced the half-dozen old contract doctrines to cole slaw. "Mutuality" was unneeded: Toussaint could hold Blue Cross to a future obligation of indefinite length even though he'd made no reciprocal commitment to stay with the company. "Reliance" was also unneeded: he could invoke the handbook language without showing it had influenced his decision to join the company or any other decision of his (in fact, the book was given to him after he'd already accepted the job). Additional or special "consideration," which courts sometimes look for before they agree to enforce an unusual promise, was unneeded as well: he needn't show he'd given up anything special to explain why the company might make him a special promise of tenure. All that mattered was his claim of a "legitimate expectation" of tenure under all the circumstances.

Aware it was breaking new ground, the court went on and on for pages, and many of its pronouncements boded ill for future employers. It said jurors didn't have to content themselves with examining whether an employer acted reasonably or in good faith; instead, they could in effect substitute their own judgment about whether there was adequate cause for firing. And in a dictum with many implications for the future, it warned that an employer could expect to rely on disciplinary rules only if it had consistently enforced such rules in the past.

Other courts around the country soon followed the Michigan court's lead. By 1990 a survey found courts in at least thirty-eight states, along with federal appeals courts in at least nineteen cases, had cited *Toussaint* v. *Blue Cross & Blue Shield of Michigan* with approval. Thousands of new lawsuits followed.

————

Having been drawn up mostly by personnel managers who didn't imagine they were drafting legal commitments, the existing handbooks were full of fuzzy language setting out grand aspirations of fair treatment. As such, they gave plaintiff's lawyers a lot to seize on. If a manual seemed to promise regular evaluations or written warnings for poor performance, then it was plainly improper to fire even the worst performer until the company had performed its share of the bargain. Exxon's manual encouraged employees to enter drug or alcohol rehab without fear of having "future opportunities jeopardized," which led to a $750,000 hit after the Valdez disaster when the company tried to transfer an oil tanker's chief engineer with a drinking history to a less safety-sensitive slot at no cut in pay.

Lawyers also began combing company correspondence for phrases helpful to their clients. Polite language in a welcome letter expressing the hope that a new employee would "stay and grow" proved enough to get to trial in a 1982 federal case. Many companies got in trouble describing employees who'd passed a temporary or probationary stage as "permanent." A written job offer proposing a salary of so much the first year and so much the second could be read as a promise that employment would last at least two years, warned attorney Eleanor Acheson, later a Clinton administration official.

"Look for words like 'career,' 'pension,' 'security,' 'opportunity,' 'family'. . . treat it as an oral contract for purposes of your complaint," said plaintiff's lawyer Cliff Palefsky in a bar association speech reprinted in the 1983 *Michigan Bar Journal*. Classified ads, headhunter listings, and even motivational slogans can be turned to account, he said. An implied contract can be based on a comment "in the margins of a memo patting you on the back for a job well done," advises attorney Lewin G. Joel III in *Every Employee's Guide to the Law* (1993).

Recollected oral representations were wide open for legal prospecting as well. On the same day as *Toussaint,* the Michigan high court handed down a decision in a companion case where it found an implied promise of tenure in the phrase, alleged to have fallen from a supervisor's lips, "if you are doing your job, you can be assured that you will not be discharged." (One can imagine the snappish exchange: "Are you going to fire me?" "Not if you do your job. Now get to work.")

In many ways the admission of verbal comments was far more ominous for employers than the handbook ruling in *Toussaint,* because while a company can burn its old handbook in a ritual ceremony at midnight, it has no way of knowing what comments its long-departed managers may have made. Stray comments by supervisors were the favorite, but remarks by other employees ("No one ever gets fired around here") could also help prove reasonable expectation. Even past remarks by the worker himself could help establish his reasonable tenure-expectation if managers hadn't piped up to contradict him, despite the danger this would seem to pose of giving workers reason to make such remarks tactically. A Massachusetts federal court held a new employee's expressed wish that this be his "last job" to support the inference of a contract.

As in Veronica Stone's case, many courts jettisoned the old Statute of Frauds to admit previously excluded oral promises. Others got the job done by a stretch on the idea of "special consideration." Some old cases had recognized that peculiar circumstances might justify an offer of lifetime employment, as when an employer offered to take care of a worker hurt on the job if he agreed not to sue, or when a proprietor had sold or given his business on the understanding he could go on running it until he retired. In both cases an employee's willingness to give up something of distinctive value might have explained why the employer had agreed to a promise few would otherwise make voluntarily. Now courts in New York and other states ruled that far less drastic sacrifices could support a promise of lifelong pay: an employee might have offered special consideration by moving to a different town to take a job, even if his suit demanded not his moving expenses but years of future pay. Quitting an old job could be special consideration enough, too.

––––––––

The handbook cases were inevitably a transitional matter. Once the *Toussaint* shock had sunk in, companies moved to cut dangerous language from their handbooks and employee communications of all kinds, running such literature past their own lawyers or buying off-the-shelf boilerplate materials vetted by someone else's attorneys. Most big firms began announcing their right to fire at will in job applications or handbooks, as Mission Bay vainly tried to do. Verbal slips could never be wholly policed, but companies could train supervisors in how to keep their lips zipped at interviews.

Plaintiff's lawyers tried to make the best of the deteriorating situation by arguing that when a company had issued successive handbooks it was bound by the least favorable language it had used anywhere along the line, but this was plainly a delaying action. The fiction of implied consent—an attractive one to courts because they could spin it out of familiar, safe-seeming legal stuff—was too easy for employers to escape. So the search began for cords they couldn't untie.

Different theories showed promise. Even if a company had grounds enough to fire an employee, its insensitive manner of doing so might constitute *intentional infliction of emotional distress*. If it hadn't come clean about its intentions or motives, it ran afoul of a newly minted *duty of good faith and fair dealing*. An influential California Supreme Court case pushed this duty further, construing it to require that "like cases be treated alike" at any given workplace—which meant an employer was in trouble if it departed from its usual "book" of procedures, and maybe also if it failed to maintain such a book.

Some courts imposed damages for firings that ran afoul of *public policy*, as when a worker claimed to have been sent packing for refusing to violate a government regulation. The intriguing hypothetical of a long-haul trucker dismissed for refusing to exceed the speed limit apparently never ripened into a reported case; perhaps no truckers were sufficiently intent on obeying the law.

Not all courts required that the public policy in question take the form of an actual law. Several salespeople dismissed by a Vermont car dealership sued under state law charging age discrimination, even though the state hadn't banned that form of discrimination until a year after the firings. No matter, said the state's high court: the public policy involved was grand enough to cast a shadow backward in time. Borrowing the language of a 1916 Ohio case, it declared that public policy—which Vermont employers would henceforth have to heed—consisted of "the community common sense and common conscience" that "is sometimes expressed under the title of social and industrial justice." Dissenting justice Louis Peck didn't find it altogether fair that "defendants went to bed knowing that they had fully complied with the law . . . only to wake up the next morning to learn that as they slept" their actions had become unlawful.

When the Michigan judges soon expressed second thoughts about their handiwork, leadership passed on to California, whose courts adopted all the main theories early even though their own legislators appeared to have written employment at will into state law (the relevant section provides that an employment with no specified time span is terminable "at the will of either party, on notice to the other"). In 1990 a California court announced that a jury could infer an implied promise of lifetime tenure "from all of the circumstances surrounding the employment," including such presumed smoking guns as raises, promotions, and "lack of criticism of the employee's work." A San Diego manager got $3.5 million even though his written employment contract specified that Sun Life of Canada could terminate him without cause at thirty days' notice.

The likeliest way to prove grounds for firing was to document a worker's misconduct, but doing so invited a suit for *defamation,* an old legal category whose application to the workplace now broadened spectacularly. Courts have found that workplace defamation "may be oral, written, or in the form of action," an *Employee Relations Law Journal* account observes; even reasonably based allegations of serious misconduct—indeed, even allegations that turn out to be true—can lead to "extreme jeopardy before a jury" if they can be construed as malicious or as casting the employee in a so-called false light. Plaintiff's lawyers were quick to jump on the new trend by adding defamation counts to their complaints. "Spread the word," said founder Paul Tobias of the National Employment Lawyers Association. "Every wrongful discharge must be looked at as a defamation case."

Confronting the worker with evidence of misconduct also risked a suit under creative new interpretations of the old legal concept of *false imprisonment:* courts began ruling that an employer could be sued for this offense if it permitted the "appearance of confinement." According to another *Employee Relations Law Journal* survey, even if the worker is in no way restrained from leaving an interview, such an appearance can be satisfied if he reasonably believes that "leaving would appear to confirm the allegations of impropriety" and damage his reputation. "The burden to prove reasonableness of the confinement—including its duration and manner—is not on the plaintiff but on the employer," it adds.

Many other legal claims arose from the time, manner, or style of a firing or the investigation that led up to it. Since dismissing an employee within earshot of others invited charges of defamation, false imprisonment, and emotional distress, some companies began using off-site locations to break the news, a trend stopped in its tracks after a jury voted $8 million against a drug company that chose a diner as the venue for firing a veteran salesman.

Though courts like California's were in the vanguard, the legal ferment was a nationwide affair, affecting every state to some degree. One survey found the number of state courts accepting implied-contract theories rose from six at the beginning of the 1980s to twenty-seven by the end, while those adopting public policy exceptions rose from seven to at least thirty-one. *Wrongful discharge,* hardly a legal category at all before 1980, had become a thriving specialty, with specialized lawyers hanging out their shingles in every big city and tens of thousands of cases pressing forward at every level. By the early 1990s a survey published in the *San Francisco Recorder* found million-dollar employment verdicts in the Golden State running at a rate of one a month, with median verdicts standing at $500,000. Employers were settling the great majority of cases, terrified of letting them get to trial.

———

By the glacial standards of the common law, it had been a revolution of breathtaking speed. No court had quite managed to abolish employment at will, but its surface was now riddled with so many pitfalls for unwary employers that it was coming to resemble a sieve more than a floor. As late as 1975, a leading legal reference text could state that "few legal principles would seem to be better settled than the broad generality that an employment for an indefinite term . . . may be terminated at any time by either party for any reason or no reason at all." By 1985, though, few legal principles appeared to be less well settled.

Sorting out the resulting cases was clearly going to be a big and continuing job for the courts. As of the late 1980s private nonunion employees numbered something like 72 million, of whom an estimated 1 to 2 million a year were being fired on an individualized basis (most of the theorists were more hesitant about inviting courts to second-guess group layoffs motivated by business slowdowns and similar factors). Experts differed on how many of these individualized firings are for bad cause, and any such assessment obviously depends crucially on one's view as to which causes are bad, but common estimates run at perhaps 10 percent, or 100,000 to 200,000—not counting some additional number of cases that could be contested even though courts would eventually find the cause to have been adequate.

Among the most influential groups to enter the lists against employment at will was the venerable American Civil Liberties Union, which had steadily been redefining the cause of civil liberties into new areas. The ACLU now launched an entire project devoted to "workplace rights," with the primary goal of overthrowing employment at will. Director Lewis Maltby called the doctrine an "embarrassing relic"; the "fundamental" premise of any replacement, he asserted, should be a "requirement that all employees be fired only for cause. This is more than an exception to the rule of employment at will—it abolishes it and substitutes a new rule, that employees have a right to keep their job unless their performance or workplace conduct is deficient."

To implement this new right, employers would be expected to set up elaborate internal "due process" mechanisms to hold adversary-style hearings before dismissing workers. Some companies already had instituted similar-sounding procedures on a voluntary basis, providing informal grievance procedures and "open door" policies that let dissatisfied employees go up the line to higher bosses. But these models were "not an example of due process," in the view of David Ewing of the Harvard Business School, because they did not partake of the sort of formal, adversarial rights-orientation of a court process; this failure made them unacceptable "even if the employee gets her way."

Most proposals instead favored the use of outside arbitrators, such as those used to resolve contested grievances in unionized workplaces. Indeed, many commentators suggested simply piggybacking on the existing record of union arbitration to fill in the blanks as to what was meant by good cause in firings. "Over time," wrote the ACLU's Maltby, "many thousands of arbitration decisions have created a 'common law' of just cause that provides reasonable consistency and predictability."

Plaintiff's lawyer Cliff Palefsky may have been optimistic—or simply premature—in his 1983 bar association speech. Employment at will is "dead," he proclaimed—"maybe not completely dead in your jurisdiction's common law, but dead in the big picture."

Chapter 3

ALL PROTECTED NOW

By the time Anheuser-Busch fired him, Finley Muldrew had become a prodigy of absenteeism. He ran up 101 unexcused absences in calendar 1977, 114 in 1978, and 32 through the first five months of 1979, the point at which the brewing company's patience finally ran out.

Aggrieved, he sued Anheuser for discriminating against him on the grounds of his race. (He was black.) A search of company records did not at first seem to offer much help for his cause: over the relevant period, the company had fired eleven white employees for absenteeism but only one black—Muldrew himself. Still, his lawyers found one way to slice the statistics that seemed better than nothing. A white employee named Resinger showed an absenteeism record that made it almost into Muldrew's league, chalking up 142 unexcused absences in the years 1977 and 1978 compared with Muldrew's 215. Yet when the company fired Muldrew it didn't fire Resinger at the same time (though it did fire him the next year). And it had suspended Resinger only twice, as opposed to Muldrew's four times—a suspension rate of once every 71 absences, compared with Muldrew's once-every-54.

This "smoking gun" was good enough for a St. Louis jury, which agreed that the company had not treated Muldrew as well as it might have had he been white. It awarded him reinstatement with full seniority rights and $125,000, a sum that included more than $50,000 for emotional distress (he'd testified that after losing his job he "began experiencing marital problems, and he felt that his children respected him less"). The court also ordered Anheuser to pay Muldrew's attorneys' fees, as is standard practice in bias cases. The Eighth Circuit federal court of appeals approved the award over a dissent, conceding that the company's defense was "plausible" but citing the deference owed a jury as finder of fact.

———

For two generations the continued expansion of employment discrimination law has been one of the great themes of American public life. Such cases now comprise a major part of the federal courts' workload: job bias suits filed there rose by 2,166 percent between 1970 and 1989, a period in which filings in other cases were rising by 125 percent. Complaints to the Equal Employment Opportunity Commission, which tend to prefigure trends in lawsuit filings by a couple of years, jumped from 64,000 to 95,000 between 1991 and 1994, fueled by such new enactments as the Americans with Disabilities Act, the Civil Rights Restoration Act of 1991 (which increased the monetary rewards for suing), and a boom in harassment complaints. The standard legal reference, United States Code Annotated, spends 1,100 pages recounting the standard one-sentence descriptions of the holdings of employment discrimination cases—compared with, for example, 1,030 pages for 200 years' worth of cases dealing with the free-speech guarantee of the First Amendment. A large volume of litigation is also filed in state courts, under state and local laws with provisions that are often more liberal than their federal equivalents.

Employment discrimination law has generated a stupendous volume of academic and popular commentary, which mostly divides into two broad camps. The vastly larger camp enthusiastically endorses virtually every application of the 1964 Civil Rights Act and the many add-ons that came afterward in areas like age and handicap, often urging the law's extension into more new areas. The other declares itself in favor of the "core," "basic," or "garden-variety" kind of discrimination law but deplores what it sees as an overlay of goals and quotas, group rights, and equality of results—all of which are said to be a far cry from the equality of opportunity lawmakers had in mind when they passed the 1964 act.

Most critics see a great contrast between the two main branches of discrimination law, the laws of *disparate treatment* and *disparate impact*. Disparate-treatment law (the main body of core or basic discrimination law) is portrayed as straightforward, fair, and balanced; concerned with the furthering of "merit" and economically rational hiring decisions; legally menacing to employers only if they have engaged in knowing discrimination; and faithful to the original scheme of the 1964 act. In contrast, disparate-impact law (which allows challenges to employment practices that lead to imbalances in overall hiring statistics) is portrayed as forcing employers to show that their decisions were not at fault, thus reversing the normal presumption of innocence; as menacing employers with liability even if they have never engaged in conscious bias; as encouraging them to hire protected-group workers not on merit but merely in order to stay out of legal trouble; as turning formerly neutral law into a simple engine of minority advancement; and, finally, as the product of judicial activism that has pushed the law into areas undreamt of by the original 1964 lawmakers.

This critique is heard often enough, but it suffers from a flaw. The seemingly uncontroversial disparate-treatment law—which was, in fact, the kind Finley Muldrew was suing under—displays all the same vices as the more often criticized disparate-impact branch. It, too, sets up employers for a fall even if they've never harbored conscious bias; gives them strong incentive to depart from merit hiring; abounds in tricks and traps for the benefit of the cagey lawyer and complainant; tilts wildly toward protected groups at the expense of traditional ideas of legal neutrality; and is the product of relentless judicial activism unforeseen by the 1964 drafters.

The 1964 Civil Rights Act was at first billed as being a very minor abridgment of most employers' freedom to hire and fire as they wished: if they hadn't maintained a color bar, they might not notice any big change. As for employers that did maintain such a bar, more numerous in the South than elsewhere, one might have expected the course of legal action against them to follow much the same history as that of the 1964 law's "public accommodations" sections, the ones applicable to restaurants, theaters and similar gathering places: an initial flurry of legal action, followed by subsidence to a relatively low level of litigation as establishments yielded to the realization that the law indeed applied to them.

But that has not at all been the pattern of job bias litigation. Unlike litigation over public accommodations, it has mounted year by year. It is endemic in North and South alike, in every major industry, in those considered highly progressive and in those where backward attitudes are suspected. Nor would it seem easy to attribute the ongoing surge in litigation to any growing willingness among employers to break the law: as the volume and stakes of litigation have mounted, compliance efforts have if anything become more frantic.

When the 1964 Civil Rights Act was debated, many moderates of both parties who accepted the general idea of a ban on private discrimination were nonetheless alarmed at the thought that the law might lead to extensive litigation by workers against their employers. To reassure them, a carefully balanced political compromise interposed an agency between the potentially litigious parties.

This basic device is familiar from other federal laws. Workers who believe their employer is unlawfully refusing to let them unionize head not to court but to the National Labor Relations Board; those who believe their employers to be violating federal safety standards file complaints with the Occupational Safety and Health Administration; and so forth. Occasionally these agencies wind up suing employers later—for instance, when there is a dispute about the scope of the law—but the great majority of cases never see court. There is, in legal jargon, no "private right of action" to bypass the agency's vital screening and conciliation function.

The new Equal Employment Opportunity Commission set up to administer the employment portions of the 1964 law was entrusted with screening responsibilities similar to those of traditional agencies. Individual workers who felt discriminated against had to file complaints with the EEOC and submit to a lengthy "conciliation" process in which the commission staff would try to resolve the problem. If it failed, workers might eventually be allowed to sue on their own behalf, but a number of provisions in the law discouraged any idea that such resort would mean easy money. Federal judges, not juries, would hear cases. They could order a worker hired or promoted, but the more lucrative remedy of cash damages—supposedly meant to represent money the complainant would have earned if hired earlier—was left strictly to their discretion, and in any case limited to two years' worth. Crucially, the law flatly disallowed the open-ended, guess-work-based damage categories that can turn lawsuits into lottery tickets: punitive damages, damages for emotional distress, and the like. In a departure from standard American practice, which denied an award of attorney's fees to prevailing parties, the law also gave judges discretion to make such an award to the "prevailing party," whichever side that might be. This wrinkle suggested a real downside potential to bringing a weak case.

———

In an extraordinary binge of judicial activism over the decade that followed, however, the U.S. Supreme Court knocked down one of these obstacles after another, with the consistent effect of turning bias claims from objects of conciliation into objects of high-stakes litigation.

In the 1975 case of *Albemarle* v. *Moody*, the Court ruled that though the language of Title VII, the relevant section of the Civil Rights Act, had provided that courts "may" grant so-called back pay where appropriate, it really obliged them to do so. Judges had sometimes declined to hand out big awards in cases where equities were mixed—

for example, when an employer had not intended to discriminate, where it had relied on a precedent that was later overturned, where a complainant's own conduct had been less than admirable, or where a big award might hurt innocent third parties (such as students who attended a public university, or users and employees of an ambulance service that might be driven out of business, to cite the circumstances of two actual cases). *Albemarle* declared an end to such misgivings: full back pay would henceforth be an entitlement.

In equally daring maneuvers, the Court managed to turn the discretionary awarding of attorney's fees either way into a mandatory award in favor of complainants. One decision established that notwithstanding the statutory language about judicial discretion in both directions, prevailing plaintiffs almost always should get fees; a second ruling provided that prevailing defendants almost never should.

The Court's most amazing creative flight allowed racial plaintiffs to obtain emotional and punitive damages, jury trials, and more than two years' worth of back pay, all of which had been denied them as part of the 1964 legislative compromise. It plucked this new right from the air by reinterpreting a Reconstruction-era law known as the Civil Rights Act of 1866, which had languished in obscurity on the books ever since accomplishing its purpose more than a century earlier. Congress had passed the law to undo the "civil disabilities" some southern states had placed on free blacks, depriving them of the legal capacity to own property, enter binding contracts, serve as witnesses in court, and so forth. Section 1981 of the 1866 law declares that all persons

> shall have the same right, in every State and Territory, to make and enforce contracts, to sue, to be parties, give evidence, and to the full and equal benefits of all laws and proceedings for the security of persons and property as is enjoyed by white citizens, and shall be subject to like punishment, pains, penalties, taxes, licenses, and exactions of every kind, and to no other.

In what can most charitably be described as one of its worst interpretational goofs ever (and less charitably as a scandalous intellectual fraud on the public), the Supreme Court now proclaimed an entirely new reading of this language. By guaranteeing blacks a right "to make and enforce contracts," it declared, Section 1981 really gave them an entirely separate right to compel other citizens to enter contracts with them whether or not these others cared to—by means of a right to sue anyone who engaged in contracting of any sort (presumably right down to the sale of lemonade from a front-yard stand) but declined to offer them the same terms as he had offered an arguably similarly situated white. In short, Congress had really passed a modern Civil Rights Act a full century before 1964, and one conveniently free of the tiresome list of exceptions and limitations to be found in the actual 1964 legislation. Seldom in Court history has there been as daring an end run around congressional intent, around the plain meaning of language, and around law itself.

The newly reinterpreted Section 1981 was of great and immediate value to complainants. Punitive and emotional damages, the right of trial before a jury as opposed to a judge, and quantities of back pay exceeding two years had all been specifically excluded under the 1964 compromise; now they were all available. Before long every racial employment suit was routinely throwing in a Section 1981 claim, which could be cashed in as a lucrative component of an eventual settlement.

Still further victories lay ahead in the campaign to boost damages. A 1974 appeals court case called *Johnson* v. *Goodyear,* though little ballyhooed outside legal circles, was to become greatly influential. A federal court had struck down the big tire company's former practice of requiring a high school diploma and the passage of an aptitude test for advancement to many positions at its Houston synthetic-rubber plant. (Such rules had "disparate impact" on black workers, who were less likely to possess the diplomas or do well on the tests.) Now the question arose whether, besides scrapping the rules, Goodyear should have to write a huge retroactive "back pay" check on the assumption that it would long ago have promoted the plant's black workers to the disputed positions—and, if so, which workers should get how much.

Lawyers for the black workers argued that their clients should get a maximum check, premised on the assumption that all would have applied for promotions at the earliest possible dates and held the better jobs ever since. Goodyear protested that some of the workers had never shown an interest in applying for promotions, while others might not have performed adequately in the new jobs or might not have put up with the jobs' less attractive features, which included more demanding schedules. At this late date, of course, any testimony on such issues would inevitably be self-serving. The court agreed that recreating a hypothetical past would be an "exacting and wearisome" task that might lead down the road of "pure conjecture," so it simplified matters by laying down a sweeping new principle: "any doubts about entitlement to backpay should be resolved against the employer." Not only would Goodyear bear the burden of disproving any worker's claim, but it would have to do so by "clear and convincing" evidence.

This ruling was cited hundreds of times in later years in regard to pretty much the entire range of discrimination claims. It came to stand for a clear principle—when in doubt, award more money.

———

Other mileage was gained by way of the legal concept of a *prima facie* case, a needed preliminary showing that, in the Court's words, "raises an inference of discrimination . . . we presume these acts, if otherwise unexplained, are more likely than not based on the consideration of impermissible factors." If a complainant establishes such a case, the employer must rebut it or lose without further ado. The key Court formula, announced in the 1973 *McDonnell-Douglas* v. *Green* decision, provides that a job applicant can establish a prima facie case by demonstrating

> (i) that he belongs to a racial minority; (ii) that he applied and was qualified for a job for which the employer was seeking applicants; (iii) that, despite his qualifications, he was rejected; and (iv) that, after his rejection, the position remained open and the employer continued to seek applicants from persons of complainant's qualifications.

This curious definition ensures that a steady supply of employers will be found to have triggered an "inference of discrimination" even while harboring no invidious motives at all. Most, after all, do not accept the first minimally qualified applicant of any group who shows up. It's common to turn away the first dozen who apply—whites or blacks, men or women—simply because only a few of those who are qualified on paper kindle true enthusiasm, and in fewer cases still does the enthusiasm survive a round of interviews. Yet the employer who rejects a minority applicant this way must be prepared to face the business end of a prima facie case in court.

In court, moreover, the employer will not be the final arbiter of whether any particular applicant counts as qualified. Others will get to do that, under standards that may bear no relation to any sane businessperson's evaluation of the issue. "[A]nyone who could read was qualified for the job," said an EEOC official after the agency settled for $3 million its complaint against Chicago's Commonwealth Edison over hiring of meter readers. Courts have also ruled that a complainant can establish a prima facie case even though the candidate eventually hired was a member of the same protected minority group as he, and indisputably better qualified; and even though the manager who did the hiring was a member of the same protected group as both.

In effect, the prima facie standard forces the employer to mount an affirmative defense of its hiring decision. It will lose at once if it merely denies having acted from improper motives, points to a good general record of hiring members of the protected group, and invites the court to compare its impressions of the interview to the complainant's and decide which is more credible. It must offer tangible reasons, and according to leading commentators those reasons must be both "clear and reasonably specific" and "legitimate": "arbitrary, idiosyncratic reasons are not 'legitimate.'" Whole categories of explanation are held in suspicion as overly subjective. Thus, according to one leading treatise, interview notes with such reactions to an applicant as "poor personality," "bad attitude," or "showed no interest" are insufficient defense, since they do not give the complainant a target to shoot at. An employer must be prepared to offer a definite reason why it has disappointed the minority hopeful, and a court may not choose to accept bad "chemistry" as an adequate reason—no matter how often it is the actual reason candidates of any race get screened out.

A remarkably wide range of qualities are considered too subjective to stand up in court. Thus commentator Alan Koral cautions that interviewers should not "generalize (from a middle-class context) about subjective attributes like 'personality,' 'attitude,' 'grooming,' 'motivation' and the like," none of which a court may accept. Other traits courts have found overly subjective in challenges to employee evaluations, as compiled by another pair of commentators, include temperament, habits, demeanor, bearing, manner, maturity, drive, leadership ability, personal appearance, stability, cooperativeness, dependability, adaptability, industry, work habits, attitude toward detail, and interest in the job. One wonders what is left.

――――――

The only debate about discrimination law, it appears, is how rapidly to extend it to more protected groups. To race, religion, sex, and national origin have already been added age, disability (a category said to cover 43 million persons, a sixth of the population), lack of citizenship, credit status, Vietnam-era veteran status, and many more. Within a single group, such as disability, are included not only the deaf, blind and paraplegic but those disabled by alcoholism, drug addiction and mental illness as well as such "invisible" and often controllable conditions as diabetes, epilepsy and heart disease. Protected groups at state and local levels include smokers, welfare recipients, people of differing sexual orientation, those who rent (rather than own) their homes or cars, people of "Appalachian heritage," and so forth. The District of Columbia bans bias based on "matriculation, political affiliation, [or] family responsibilities."

An endless series of analogies to the black condition couple the cars on this modern freedom train, and even groups that were never abducted or enslaved are considered to partake of the moral authority descending from the abolitionists. "Ageism is as odious as racism or sexism," proclaimed Rep. Claude Pepper, the Florida Democrat and chief sponsor of the Age Discrimination in Employment Act Amendments of 1978. "[D]iscrimination against families with children is every bit as bad, as pernicious, as race discrimination," crowed attorney John Relman after winning $2.4 million for a Maryland woman from a landlord who had tried to run a quiet-adults building. Local authorities had pursued a variety of policies on the question of whether it was okay for tenants in public housing to keep dogs and cats, but friends of Fido soon found they could get Congress to join their cause by redefining it as one of "discrimination against pets," thus lifting it quite out of the practical realm of worries about barking and dander.

Employment discrimination law soon emerged as a vital pivot of identity politics, a litmus test for whether society was for or against a newly visible group. Opposition to the idea of extending bias law to Vietnam vets or gays or legal aliens was a sure sign that someone harbored hostility toward that group. Speeding up even as it took on more freight, the freedom train came to symbolize a whole project of transforming social attitudes, in the workplace and off. "Now able-bodied people won't look down on us as individuals," a paraplegic told the *Chicago Tribune* when the ADA passed. "It created a much better self-image," agreed Bruce Blower, the disability services director in Suffolk County, New York. "The ADA will emphasize to people with disabilities . . . 'Hey, you are in fact a person and with the passage of this bill you have the same rights as any other American citizen.' It's an empowering kind of thing."

Nowhere does the moral authority of employment discrimination law stand higher than in the law schools, the American Bar Association, and other sectors of the legal establishment. It's seen as perhaps the purest and most idealistic manifestation of modern law, one of the few things government gets right; in retrospect, the failure of so many earlier generations to think of putting such laws on the books can only reflect badly on their moral character. The tens of thousands of pages on the subject that annually choke the law reviews and the storerooms of the treatise publishers are almost unanimously devoted to the idea that employment discrimination law is vital to the well-being of protected groups and the wider society alike, and should be expanded further without delay in many directions.

New groups are continually roped into coverage by the simple expedient of reinterpreting existing law, as opposed to passing new legislation. Thus in the 1970s federal officials smoothly redefined disability bias to include bias based on alcohol and drug addiction, a classification carried forward in the later ADA. Discrimination based on accent is nowhere prohibited as such in federal law, but courts and the EEOC have swept it in under the existing heading of national-origin discrimination. A long series of attempts to cover obesity under one heading or another finally succeeded in the early 1990s when federal courts and regulators announced that it was a protected—though unenumerated—handicap category under the ADA.

Obesity cases raise one of the hot current questions in bias law: namely, the coverage of so-called voluntary conditions. In the EEOC's view a handicap is a handicap, and it doesn't matter whether it may have arisen from voluntary choices or might be reversible by a complainant's own efforts. The California Supreme Court, it is true, took a seemingly more cautious position when it sent back the case of 305-pound Toni Linda Cassista, who sued after being turned down for a retail clerk job (in a health food collective, as it happened). The court ruled that lawyers would have to argue before a jury whether her condition was the result of involuntary metabolism, in which case she could win, or controllable overeating, in which case the store would win—what was dubbed the medically versus morally fat issue. Aside from the extraordinary indignity to which California law would make itself party by such proceedings, the whole approach was highly unpromising as a way of obtaining any actual answer to the question: given the lack of either a professional or social consensus on the relative importance of metabolism and will, it's hard to see what would be gained by calling in twelve people off the street and putting it to a vote.

Protection for voluntary conditions would clear the way for a more general ban on bias on the basis of personal appearance, a position that is much favored in the law reviews and has had some success in courts. Santa Cruz, California, enacted a municipal ordinance banning personal-appearance discrimination following agitation by the local Body Image Task Force. (Twenty-two-year-old Cooper Hazen had lost his job as a psychiatric aide after showing up with a wooden post in his pierced tongue, to add to his multicolored hair, earrings, shoulder tattoo, and nose ring: "Thith ith wha gah me thierd," he told a reporter.) A Vermont ski resort was ordered to face a lawsuit after asking a chambermaid to put in her dentures when customers were around: "Employees will be expected to have teeth and to wear them daily to work," its ill-fated memo had read.

Even the ban on religious discrimination has led to surprising results. A federal court found the Salvation Army liable after one of its battered-women's shelters fired a counselor who'd admitted using the office copier to duplicate a list of rituals relating to her own religion, which turned out to be witchcraft ("Satanic-Wiccan.") "If you could see it, you would agree it was horrible," said a lawyer for the group. "It talked about sexual things, around the fire, lots of things that are contrary to Salvation Army policies." The judge ordered further proceedings to consider the woman's demand for $1.25 million in damages.

Perhaps logically, cases are also beginning to appear that extend protection of belief beyond the realm of religion as such. "There's no question Bob's interest in UFOs was a determining factor in his not getting the promotion," said a lawyer for Robert Dean, who settled his failure-to-promote suit against an Arizona sheriff's office for more than $100,000 as well as the sought-after promotion; the complaint had also charged age bias. The lawyer said his client had wrongly been depicted as a "kook." According to a news account, Dean "considers himself a professional researcher of UFOs" and said he had held a "cosmic top-secret clearance" while in the military. "Any day now, the lid is going to be blown off this whole UFO thing."

A regular theme of the new bias law was the impropriety of letting employers offer any kind of cost or inconvenience factor to justify discriminatory practices. "Economic considerations" cannot form the basis of exceptions to bias law because "precisely those considerations were among the targets of the Act," a court explained when it forced United Air Lines to invest princely sums to hire and train aviators in their late fifties, even though a federal rule required commercial pilots to retire at the age of sixty. Another federal court ruled against the idea of taking age into account in handing out apprenticeships. The bigger the fortune society sinks into the cause of assisting a worker, the more sincerely it shows it wants to help him (at some employer's private expense, admittedly, but aren't those the breaks?).

An important corollary is that it will normally be improper for employers to defend discriminatory actions by citing the wishes, views, or preferences of either customers or co-workers. The standard example offered is that of racial bias in the old South, where businesses used to say they discriminated against blacks because their white customers and employees wanted them to. As other protected groups were added to the list, it was easy to replicate the analysis, if more tenuously each time. The key precedent came in an early case called *Diaz* v. *Pan Am:* the late airline had tried to defend its preference for female flight attendants by offering customer surveys showing that both male and female passengers felt more comfortable being fussed over by women. A federal court dismissed its argument, declaring in sweeping language (which would be much cited later) that employment decisions may be based only on the "essence" of an employer's business, which in an airline's case was the simple movement of passengers from Point A to Point B, and not mere considerations of "a pleasant environment" or "cosmetic effect."

Few air passengers were likely to care deeply one way or the other, but the precedent was soon in use to exclude customer wishes as a factor even on knottier questions of sexual modesty. Nursing homes and similar institutions were swatted down when they tried to arrange for female residents' intimate functions to be seen to by women, while lawyers easily overcame the claims of male modesty to get female sports reporters into pro male locker rooms (though the reverse didn't seem to happen). The EEOC was unmoved when more than ten thousand members of the Women's Workout World health club chain signed petitions protesting its efforts to force the chain to hire male attendants.

Consulting the preferences of co-workers was no more legitimate. This circumstance proved important as the law expanded to cover mental and emotional deficits, since co-workers are often the ones who bear the brunt of a problem worker's shortcomings—shouldering the heavier workload when he is incapable or absent, risking injury if he gets near the heavy machinery, and experiencing his behavioral and personality disabilities on the front lines. In negotiating with a disabled applicant, "never say the accommodation would be 'bad for morale,'" warns a University of Wisconsin ADA expert.

The nature of enforceable legal rights as rights, after all, is that the heavens are expected to fall in their defense. Thus ADA supporters pushed for a definition of the law's "undue hardship" exception that would oblige an employer to accommodate disabled applicants even if it would lose money on the hiring, or even if the cost of the accommodation would plunge it from profit to loss overall. The law, they said, should concede undue hardship only at the point where a business was left with no choice but to close down operations, presumably after exhausting its cash reserves and lines of credit. Amazed business representatives dubbed the provision the "bankruptcy out."

———

As the laws tilted toward complainants, the monetary rewards for suing were multiplied, and the culture lent its enthusiastic support, litigation soon became the natural-seeming course for a worker who felt discriminated against. Plaintiffs' lawyers got involved in more cases from an early stage, increasingly reaching out to potential clients through advertising and more direct approaches. EEOC conciliation was soon reduced to a paperwork turnstile; the key was to get the agency to sign off and issue a "right-to-sue letter," so the real action could begin. The maximum monetary settlement, as opposed to reinstatement, became the normal objective.

As job bias litigation became a thriving legal specialty, the docket began to shift from hiring to firing suits. This might seem strange on the surface, since one would expect bigotry to manifest itself more in refusals to hire people than in the self-defeating practice of hiring them only to turn around and fire them. But the trend is unmistakable. Until the early 1970s, hiring and firing complaints to the EEOC ran at around equal numbers. As hiring claims remained flat, though, firing claims boomed to the point that by 1984 dismissal complaints ran at six times the number of hiring complaints. "My office sees ten discharge suits for every hiring suit," a Los Angeles defense lawyer told *Forbes*. Claims under new categories follow a similar pattern:

though ADA advocates had dwelt heavily on the hiring issue, for example, fewer than one-sixth of actual claims under the law relate to that stage, while more than half arise from firings.

What was happening? Surely a large part of the answer is that being fired is still by far the most common reason workers cast about for a reason to sue, and protected-group status (whether grounded on age, sex, race, or handicap) has increasingly served such workers as "something to hang their hat on" to get into court. Now, as always, the termination process is full of arbitrary and oafish bosses, backstabbing office politics, and perceived unfairness of every kind. Discrimination law offers a remedy provided a worker agrees to see a link between his ill treatment and his protected-group status.

There is no need to speculate about whether the law gets used in this fashion: lawyers' own literature confirms that it routinely does. "Every decision discharging a woman is a potential source of litigation and is subject to strict scrutiny as to its fairness," observes one leading manual. Any protected-group members who feel their jobs are at risk should "call a lawyer immediately," advises a lawyer quoted in *New York*'s cover story on firing law. Shouldn't they hold back unless they think the layoff or firing might have been motivated by their minority status? Apparently not: *"Whether or not a firing is in fact discriminatory,* members of [these] groups will have increased leverage in a severance negotiation" (emphasis added). ACLU attorney E. Richard Larson advises in his how-to-sue manual that "you always should assert your rights under as many of the laws as are available." If you're an older black woman and feel less well treated than others on the job, "the chances are that you in fact *are* the victim of sex, age, and race discrimination [emphasis in original]. There is no need to try to figure out which form of discrimination has been practiced against you, and there is no reason to give your employer the benefit of any doubt. Instead, assume the worst."

In short, discrimination law provides a way for protected-group members—now a substantial majority in the American workforce—to obtain a valuable free-ranging right to sue for damages over workplace maltreatment whether or not it is obviously linked to their status. If a worker can get to a jury at all, many have noted, the overall perceived equities of his situation will often count for more than the particular question of whether bias as such was the cause. Professor Judith Mc-Morrow of Boston College, writing of age-bias cases, says a jury is likely to look more at the broad question of "whether the employer treated the employee fairly" than at "the narrow question of whether any unfairness was based on . . . discrimination."

The final, perhaps inevitable step will be for discrimination law to fill in the chinks to cover those last few still-unprotected demographic groups (such as those half-dozen straight white men under forty). During the ADA debate, some supporters proposed banning discrimination by reason of "any physical or mental characteristic" of an employee—which would seem a promising way to do the trick, since traits that lack a physical dimension are generally mental. And voices here and there are beginning to propose "universal" discrimination coverage, with the phrase "discrimination based on _____" permanently left blank as regards any qualities not "job related."

It seemed perfect. Everyone at long last would be protected. Or was "protected" the right word?

Chapter 4

FEAR OF FLIRTING

The Orange Unified School District, sprawling over a stretch of suburban southern California, had been going through a tough period of internal wrangling and budget fights. Then came a sudden, headline-blaring scandal. The district had hired a consultant to carry out an "audit" of its practices on the issue of sexual harassment—an "environmental scan," as the consultant, Mary Jo McGrath, called it. Shockingly, the scan had found harassment running rampant at the district's highest echelons. Two officials were charged, deputy superintendent Richard Donoghue and chief fiscal officer Joyce Capelle. Assorted charges against Donoghue included off-color remarks and inappropriate touching. The charge against Capelle raised an eyebrow or two: she was accused of "tolerating sexual banter."

The district headquarters was an administrative center unlikely to have impressionable kids around. Still, both officials were immediately placed on "home assignment"—put more plainly, forbidden to come to the office—while interviews went forward with what would eventually number forty co-workers. McGrath explained, apparently with no irony intended, that excluding the two would encourage others to "speak more freely."

Capelle defended herself in a talk with a *Los Angeles Times* columnist. Yes, she said, she'd heard others tell "dirty stories, and dirty jokes" at the office. While she didn't tell such jokes herself, she also didn't "feel responsible for people who are at least my peers, if not my superiors, organizationally." In fact, until the recent panic, she'd never heard anyone complain about such jokes at all. Which left her wondering: "If I'm going to be publicly vilified and have my professional career ruined over something as widespread as bantering in the workplace or, let's say, an off-color birthday card, then where does that leave everybody else?"

In commenting on an unrelated case during the affair, *Times* reporters interviewed experts who agreed that recent legal trends had indeed called into question the legality of permitting sexual banter in the workplace. Said attorney Judith Kurtz of Equal Rights Advocates, "Don't look at what has been tolerated in the past."

Sexual harassment is "not complicated to define," write Ellen Bravo and Ellen Cassedy in the *9 to 5 Guide to Combating Sexual Harassment;* they proceed to describe it as things that "bother" a co-worker. It may consist of "almost anything the employee finds offensive," adds one expert quoted in the *New York Times;* "things that make people uncomfortable," chimes in another by way of clarification.

The best known of these uncomfortable-making things is smut, loosely defined to include not only *Playboy* but racy greeting cards, tacky photocopier humor ("Highway Signs You Should Know"), come-hither calendars, ribald cartoons, and tawdry computer screen savers. Proposed EEOC guidelines have called for banning "circulation" of offending materials anywhere "on the employer's premises," including inside closed desks and lockers. In one of the most celebrated cases, involving a shipyard in Jacksonville, Florida, a federal court ordered the employer to prohibit workers from bringing in any "reading material" deemed "sexually suggestive," apparently including novels. The time had come, the court said, for "cleansing the workplace of impediments to the equality of women."

The cleansing must apply to talk as well as printed matter. An advisory panel to the U.S. Commission on Civil Rights says harassment may include "annoying or distracting comments" that "may appear to the bystander to be humorous or insignificant." Those include condescending endearments, as in a successful lawsuit at a Virginia Volkswagen dealership arising from the use of "sweetheart," "hon," and "Fahrvergnügen girl." Gossip, social exclusion, and "shunning" or "silent treatment" of individual workers can all run afoul of the law as well.

All these forms of communication may need cleansing whether or not they were *intended* to offend. The Chicago Board of Education's policy specifies that "sexual jokes [and] language" and the display of "suggestive objects, pictures, magazines or cartoons" will generally constitute harassment "whether intentional or not." "The fact that he didn't intend for her to overhear the remark is no defense," said an EEOC official after a veteran writer at the *Boston Globe* got caught using a vulgar synonym for "henpecked" during guy talk at a water cooler. A complainant, the New Jersey Supreme Court has ruled, "need not personally have been the target of each *or any* instance of offensive or harassing conduct" (emphasis added).

Also capable of triggering a legal complaint are remarks, however chastely worded, that can be interpreted as showing hostility toward women generally or their competence in any line of work, or toward a particular co-worker's individual competence or job performance if she construes the criticism as showing "gender animosity." Federal guidelines in other civil rights contexts have cited "negative stereotyping" as a prohibited practice; a federal court sent a Minnesota suit to trial based in part on generic comments by male miners that women didn't belong in the pits. "Blatantly sexist" computer messages led to a crackdown at the Los Angeles Police Department.

It only aggravates matters when the perpetrators in these cases imagine that the comments are somehow humorous. A Pennsylvania employer lost after a reference to a female associate as a "broad." "Dr. Gonzalez' dismissal of these anti-female remarks as mere 'jest' may demonstrate his insensitivity to them," declared another federal court. "Belittling comments about a person's ability to perform, on the basis of that person's sex, are not funny."

The authors of the *9 to 5 Guide* advise potential complainants to "trust your instincts" about what constitutes harassment. Men wondering how to behave, however, would be very ill-advised to trust *their* instincts: one Bay Area attorney says that in more than half the investigations his firm carries out, men didn't realize their conduct constituted sexual harassment. "Excessive male handwringing over what is and is not acceptable behavior" comes in for short shrift in William Petrocelli and Barbara Kate Repa's *Sexual Harassment on the Job,* a self-help volume in the Nolo Press series. Men should understand that for a woman to express seeming approval when she really is upset by male behavior may just be part of her "coping strategy." Among the ways a woman "shows that the behavior is unwelcome," Claudia Withers of the Women's Legal Defense Fund told the *New York Times,* is "in some cases, by not responding." "Who decides what behavior is offensive in the workplace?" write Bravo and Cassedy. "The recipient does." "Our basic rule of thumb is what we call a 'gut-check,'" says Petrocelli. "If you feel like you've been sexually harassed then you have been."

––––––

The legal regulation of sex is nothing new, and employment law carried on a certain share of it during the many centuries it spent as a branch of the law of domestic relations. As late as 1895 a legal treatise could describe employers of apprentices and underage servants as morally bound to "exert a good influence" on their "mental and spiritual well-being," which included an obligation "to see that they attend public worship, and in general, to take due care of their morals." In England, where custom and law bound many servants to yearly hirings, courts could release them with full pay if Master or Young Master had made an attempt on their virtue. Various other laws prohibited sex outside marriage (whether or not it was within an employment relationship), as well as such offenses as unwelcome solicitation to indecent acts and the public use of obscene or blasphemous language. More often than not these laws regarded women as needing special protection not extended to men; thus laws in many American states prohibited the public use of obscene language in the presence of women.

The steady rise of legal parity between men and women in this century cast doubt on many of the old protections; in 1972, for example, the Supreme Court threw into question the continued constitutionality of the old obscenity-in-the-presence-of-women laws. In principle the Court could have imposed symmetry either way—perhaps prohibiting bad language in men's presence, too—but in practice it was likely that women would have to endure more roughness rather than men less. The law had placed them in a middle ground somewhere between men's fully adult status and the cosseted status of children; thus, while child labor laws barred children from nearly all occupations, parallel women's-labor laws placed only a relative few occupations off limits to women, preventing them from tending bar or working unusually long hours. Infantilizing men as a class held little appeal: who but Prohibitionists wanted to prohibit men as well as women from tending bar? But fuller access for women to the job market could mean new responsibilities as well as opportunities, which might also mean developing the thicker skin men had been expected to wear all along against indignities—including the same responsibility to walk out of bad job situations.

But given the new premise that the law should forbid firings for bad cause, it was almost certain that it would sooner or later curb resort to one of the most vividly bad causes for firing—namely, resistance to pressure for sex by the boss. As it happened, however, legislators had not chosen to pass laws specifically or recognizably aimed at this abuse. Some courts tried to apply existing laws of other sorts to cover the gap. Thus in 1984 the Eighth Circuit proposed construing an offer of job benefits in exchange for sex as an offer of prostitution, a stratagem that might succeed in rendering unlawful much of the male behavior in question, but which also suggested that entirely consensual affairs might be subject to legal attack as harlotry when they led to job advancement. It also implied that women in such affairs might be as legally culpable as men, a message that was not exactly what most feminists had in mind.

Had lawmakers been forced to confront explicitly the issue of whether and how to regulate sex in the workplace, there is no telling what balance they might have struck. They might have brought some nuance and complexity to the questions of what to do about unsubstantiated allegations, of how to keep accused persons' careers from being ruined without proof, and of how to handle the mess left by voluntary romantic affairs that go sour. Or, given their record in laws like the Americans with Disabilities Act, it is possible that they would have passed something as extreme and ill-considered as anything the courts could devise.

We may never know. As it happened, fully in the new spirit of the times, the courts jumped in and began regulating sex in the workplace by themselves without any legislative go-ahead. The rules they contrived would be advanced by way of high-stakes individual damages suits (as usual) not against the specific mashers, wolves, and joke-tellers but against their employers, the ones with the bank accounts (again, as usual). Courts would proclaim retroactively that the existing ban on sex discrimination had always included a ban on traveling-salesman-and-farmer's-daughter jokes; we just didn't realize it until now. And thus in almost every respect they picked up and ran with the general analysis laid out by Catharine MacKinnon, the well-known feminist professor now at the University of Michigan Law School.

Few contemporary figures can boast as much direct influence on American law as the Savonarola of Ann Arbor. Aside from virtually inventing sexual harassment doctrine in the form that judges were to accept and install as federal law, the busy MacKinnon also emerged as a leading commentator on free speech, and the first such leading commentator in a long while whose work was aimed at justifying tough new restrictions on speech. (Harvard Law School invited her to lecture on civil liberty, which was somewhat like inviting Frank Perdue to lecture on chickens' rights.)

The first brilliant step, which actually had been accomplished before MacKinnon stepped to the plate, was the hijacking of the word *harassment* itself. That word derived from the verb *to harass*, defined as follows in the 1948 *American College Dictionary:*

1. To trouble by repeated attacks, incursions, etc., as in war or hostilities; harry; raid. 2. To disturb persistently; torment, as with troubles, cares, etc.

Everyday usage suggested that harassment was *intended to annoy:* playing loud music that keeps the neighbors awake is merely disturbing the peace if your aim is to dance, and rises to harassment only if you're playing it in order to keep them awake. It was likely to *single out its targets* in some way: maliciously waking up the whole neighborhood is a dubious case of harassment, while aiming the noise at one house is a classic example. It was *intrusive or line-crossing:* though it might convey hostility very effectively to cut someone socially or return a contemptuous reply to their inquiry, harassment requires something more, such as hang-up calls to their residence. (In much this way we describe our submarines, but not our trade embargo, as harassing a rival nation's shipping, even if the embargo hurts them more than the subs.) Finally, the word suggested *one-sided* and *persistent* conduct against someone who is at least momentarily passive: a sniper may harass, but the gunfight at the O.K. Corral would not seem to qualify, nor would a single sucker-punch.

Before long, harassment theorists had succeeded at getting the term applied to behavior that differed from the old usage on all five points: things like overheard jokes, shouting matches, dirty looks, and "shunning." As a semantic coup, it paralleled the success of disabled activists at redefining all the routine ways in which the world catered to majority tastes (such as printing menus in English but not Braille) as discrimination. If staircases and narrow aisles could be defined as barriers and exclusion, then swear words certainly could, too; more of us feel unwelcome around the latter than the former.

The progress of the new ideas was by no means unobstructed—many courts turned down such claims at first—but with firm support in elite law circles they soon carried the day. By the time the U.S. Supreme Court accepted the invention of sexual harassment law it was pretty much a fait accompli, and the Court's decisions mostly ratified lower courts' adoption of the new scheme.

A few observers noted striking contrasts between the emerging new regime the Court was endorsing on manifestations of sex at work and its earlier pronouncements regarding manifestations of sex in the public square. Decades of First Amendment precedents had provided extensive protection for a great deal of speech that upset and disturbed its listeners—indeed, speech meant for that purpose. Thus the Court had decreed the right of protesters to wear T-shirts with highly offensive mottoes into courtrooms where the eyes of bailiffs and stenographers might keep involuntarily falling on them for weeks on end. Freedom, the Court seemed to be saying, may require a high degree of willingness among the rest of us to avert our eyes and ears.

Now all that changed. And to make things odder yet, most of the cartoons and off-color language that courts now allowed to form the basis of harassment suits fell miles short of the ruling standard for obscenity; in fact, they often fell short of the standards prevailing on radio and television and thus beamable to eight-year-old children everywhere. (Every so often the coarse stuff routinely allowed in the one realm would slop over and sully the purity expected of the other, with legal consequences: someone would sue for harassment, for example, because co-workers had tuned the office radio or TV to dirty programs.) The Court's earlier obscenity jurisprudence, in addition, had leaned heavily on the notion of community standards—a recognition that things that would shock in Cincinnati may go over in Las Vegas. The workplace would seem to cry out for a similar concept, ranging as it does from hymnbook societies and bridal registries to strip clubs and auto body shops; how could one standard on sexual discussion work everywhere? But the Court recognized no such doctrine when it came to harassment law.

———

Cases where men threatened job reprisals if women did not go out with them soon emerged as only a tiny sliver of all cases—a pretext, as it were, for the introduction of the rest of harassment law. Harassment charges filed with the EEOC doubled between 1989 and 1993, from 5,600 to 11,900. Of this number only an estimated 5 percent involved any quid pro quo, either threats of harm if the offender is turned down or offers of benefits if he is accepted. The remainder are charges of *hostile work environment*.

The term itself was a brilliant coinage. Once guilt was transferred to the environment as such, ordinary office practices or wall postings that long predated a complainant's arrival—and thus couldn't possibly have been aimed at her—could now be banned. Employers thus routinely will lose cases where the men in a previously all-male workplace keep using off-color language even though there are now ladies present. As Wayne State law professor Kingsley Browne has put it, "The real claim in many harassment cases is that the work atmosphere did *not* change in response to the addition of women (or minorities) to the environment" (emphasis added).

A related new phrase, popular in the law reviews, was *sexualized environment,* which (although it sounds like a description more appropriate to a Dali landscape) made clear that even implicit hostility was not required. Risqué goings-on were soon being challenged in all sorts of configurations: men sued over other men's girlie magazine stashes, while women sued over other women's raunchy bachelorette parties or gag-gift showers. Sometimes male and female complainants said they'd been injured by the very same behavior, thus allowing the law to lift off balloon-like from its original premise that the problem with bawdry in the workplace was that it somehow intrinsically discriminated against women as a class. A Florida federal court found harassment of women in a cartoon poking fun at lone male sexuality, with nary a female in sight. Workers have also sued over *not* being included in sex talk, as when male employees of the largely female Jenny Craig diet company complained, per a *New York Times* account, of being "excluded from office chitchat about pregnancy and menstrual periods."

Hostile-environment law has yet more in common with its contemporaneous development, handicap accommodation law. Both attempt to force the workplace to adapt to its most fragile and sensitive participants. Under handicap law, as we shall see, those with frail lungs can apply for dusty jobs and then demand that they be made dust-free. Similarly, under harassment law those with frail ears can go into commodities pits or locker rooms and demand that they stop sounding like those places. In both cases, the fact that others have chosen to "fit in" sets no precedent; previous deaf employees' willingness to use low-cost means of accommodation doesn't mean the new one has to get along without a sign translator, and likewise previous women's willingness to join in an atmosphere of coarse ribbing doesn't mean the next has to find the jokes funny. ADA guidebooks stress that the safest course is to ask each disabled worker what he'd like done—who knows the needs of the disabled better than they themselves?—and harassment guidebooks similarly tend to propose letting the pace at work be driven by whoever is most thin-skinned about doubtful speech. In both cases, it's considered not merely legitimate but a praiseworthy form of pioneering for a sensitive person to secure a job at exactly the "wrong" kind of workplace (that is, where the likely disruption is greatest) and then demand it be cleaned up.

––––––

Unlike firing cases, many harassment claims involve little visible financial injury to the complainant. Under yesterday's ideas of suitable damage awards, such cases might not have been worth pursuing in court except maybe for the principle of the thing. But soon courts here, as they increasingly were doing in other areas of the law, began awarding the equivalent of stand-alone damages for sheer insult, couched in categories like "punitive damages" and "emotional distress" that invited juries to pick any number that appealed to them. The New Jersey Supreme Court ruled that a plaintiff who shows a hostile environment can sue for cash with no need to prove any "more tangible or serious" injury, such as loss of income. In her much-publicized case, complainant Rena Weeks had jumped to a better job shortly after her two-week stint at the law firm of Baker & McKenzie, severely limiting her economic damages; the jury awarded her $7 million anyway, although the total was reduced by the judge to $3.7 million. A jury in Jefferson City, Missouri, soon topped that by voting $50 million to forty-seven-year-old Peggy Kimzey, who was offended by comments by co-workers at the Wal-Mart in nearby Warsaw. She conceded she'd used some pretty raw language herself, and she didn't claim anyone was trying to put the moves on her, though once a supervisor had tried to give her a kiss.

Cases without even that much touching hit the million-dollar mark, too. A Long Beach policewoman was voted $1.7 million after co-workers hazed her over her broken-off relationship with a supervisor. Chevron agreed to pay \$2.2 million to four women in a case revolving around unwanted e-mail and smut sent anonymously in interoffice envelopes; one of the cited pieces of evidence was an e-mail list of "25 Reasons Why Beer Is Better Than Women."

Men suing over women's misbehavior also did well, notwithstanding Mary McCarthy's catty comment that the male defending his virtue is always a comic figure. A jury awarded \$1 million to Sabino Gutierrez on his claim that boss Maria Martinez had pressured him for sexual favors; the case arose, almost too perfectly, at a California company that made hot tubs.

Although sex was what made the headlines, speech on racial, religious, or other protected-group topics was far from safe. Racial harassment was a common charge, reflecting the wide incidence of both serious animosity and jokes. Religious harassment, growing fast as a complaint category, might include both scoffing at belief by those of little faith and proselytizing carried on by persons of strong religious conviction. In the latter case, regulators have described unwelcome suggestions that someone read scripture or mend sinful ways as religious "advances," which would seem to hint that harboring designs on someone's soul may be legally analogous to coveting his or her body. A court upheld an Oregon regulation providing that "religious advances constitute discrimination when the employer's motivation for making those advances is that the employee's religious beliefs are different from the employer's." Handicap-based harassment claims are on the rise as well. A Michigan woman sued after co-workers at the bank where she was employed made disparaging remarks about her weight.

———

Wall and desk postings were a constant source of trouble. In one widely reported case, supervisors at the University of Nebraska ordered a grad student to remove a five-by-seven-inch bikini shot from his desk, though the pictured woman was his wife; the public library in Ridgedale, Minnesota, made a cataloguer take down from his cubicle a *New Yorker* cartoon in which fully clothed male characters comment on the Lorena Bobbitt case using an anatomical term by then familiar from a thousand newspaper stories: "to see the offending word in the caption," one report noted, "a person has to put his or her nose right up close." New York's highest court came within one vote of a statewide ban on ethnic-joke gifts in a case involving "Polish" coffee mugs with handles on the inside, despite a dissenting judge's assertion of every ethnic group's "fundamental right" to be free from "ridicule." A desk plaque reading "Even male chauvinist pigs need love" drew judicial ire in a federal appeals case.

Art exhibits became a common target, too. A WPA-era mural in Vermont depicted scantily clad Indians greeting fully clothed European settlers, one of whom wore a crucifix—thus scoring a race-gender-religion insensitivity triple-header. Some employers responded to complaints by covering up displays in whole or part; thus an Illinois town temporarily hung a bedsheet over its post office mural, while officials in Menlo Park, California, covered strategic portions of an exhibit of woodcuts with Post-it Notes, termed "the fig leaves of the '90s."

Advertising could also create a hostile environment, experts warned. The EEOC filed a complaint against a machinery manufacturer whose ads personified its Japanese competition by way of accurately depicted samurai and sumo wrestlers; the agency said the pictures could create a hostile environment for employees who happened to be of Japanese descent, though none seemed to have complained. Lawyers for female employees at the Stroh brewery cited its television ads featuring a pulchritudinous "Swedish bikini team," though the ads got away without recorded complaints from Swedish-Americans.

———

Court and EEOC interpretations have brought enormous rigor to the practical application of these rules. Companies that have never bothered with an ethics policy or safety policy must maintain a "harassment policy," and it's not enough just to post guidelines on a wall and get back to work. "As has always been [company] policy," read a Texas company's memo, "there is to be no Sexual Harassment or Innuendos as a condition of employment, promotion or hire. This applies to all Company Employees." This memo was not good enough, said a federal court, because the company had not made sure its policy came to the notice of all employees and laid out a formal complaint process.

A state-of-the-art policy will apparently follow a rule of resolving doubts in the direction of suppressing more employee speech. The *9 to 5 Guide* emphasizes that management should make sure to crack down on sexist joke-telling whether or not any women are around to hear the jokes, and it should not tolerate joking about the harassment policy itself. (Example: "Hey, you brushed against my arm. I'm filing a sexual harassment charge.") "The formal structures won't be effective if employees undercut them by acting disrespectfully," the book says.

Ease of complaint is another desideratum. "To maximize options for the complainant, the policy must allow for several different channels," explains the *9 to 5 Guide*. All complaints must lead to investigations; failure in this regard can endanger an employer's legal interests even if the neglected complaints were unfounded.

Once a complaint is made, speed is of the essence in launching an investigation. Two attorneys from New York's Weil, Gotshal and Manges firm say it's desirable to get a company's internal probe under way by the next day, if not the same day. Many companies give harassment investigations an emergency priority, jumping them ahead of other employee misconduct probes, not to mention ongoing business crises of every other sort. DuPont provides a beeper to each of the four harassment specialists assigned to its hotline. Yet immediate all-out investigation can actually be counterproductive if a longer period of surreptitious observation would be more likely to catch a wrongdoer unaware.

Harassment investigations are unusually complicated affairs because both the accuser and the accused often wind up suing or considering suit (against the company, of course; it seems to be almost unheard of to sue the individual accuser). The accused supervisor or worker sues for wrongful discharge, constructive or otherwise, or for defamation: the employer has spread the accuser's story or somehow signaled that it believes it. It is not always easy to conduct an investigation without the appearance of doing either of these things.

Companies should use two investigators so that "if either the victim or perpetrator sues the company, the two investigators can corroborate each other's testimony at trial," advises attorney James J. Oh, writing in the *Employee Relations Law Journal*. "To prevent leaks and reduce the risk of a defamation lawsuit, the investigators should try to type everything themselves during the investigation and avoid using support staff to type, copy, file, or deliver documents relating to the investigation."

Many employers feel it advisable to separate the parties from each other after a complaint, and the safer course is to impose the entire burden of any such adjustment on the accused. In a 1992 Veterans Administration case the agency placed the accused man on midnight shift but also altered the woman's schedule so the two would not run into each other. A federal court later found that the charges arose from a romantic relationship gone sour—it rejected the woman's claim that the two had never been involved—but the Ninth Circuit still ruled in her favor on her contention that the VA should have arranged the changes so as not to inconvenience her in any way.

Of course, complaints that prove erroneous must not be subjected to any sort of penalty or even reprimand, since this would hint at discouragement and retaliation; when it comes to eliciting complaints, quantity is job one. Interest is growing in anonymous denunciation methods in which the accused would not be entitled to learn the identity of an accuser. Cornell's Arts College has instituted a so-called lock-box system in which denunciations of faculty members are kept under seal to be brought out at some later day; faculty have no right even to know what is being said about them until perhaps years later, when the box is opened and the target expected to rebut its contents.

If an employer does determine that what has taken place counts as harassment, the Ninth Circuit has ruled that its action "must be of a disciplinary nature" and must lead to penalties "sufficient . . . to assure a workplace free from sexual harassment." One court found demotion sufficient in a case of a one-time bestowal of unwanted hugs and kisses. A federal court ordered the corrections department of Suffolk County, New York, to impose "prompt and severe discipline" to enforce "an absolute prohibition on racial 'joking'" and "the use of racial, ethnic or religious slurs and humor." A frequent theme is the need to discipline employees at the first offense; some courts have hit employers with punitive damages for not doing this. "[S]ome form of discipline," as opposed to a simple instruction to cease, is necessary on a first offense, agree the Weil, Gotshal attorneys: "However, counseling coupled with a reprimand and warning that repeated behavior may result in dismissal *may* be sufficient for a first offense for such harassment as sexually oriented jokes" (emphasis added).

The quality of mercy is apt to get a bit strained. After one harassment incident, a Texas food company reprimanded the offender, adopted a companywide policy and complaint procedure, and trained all employees; two years elapsed before the miscreant was caught in a second offense, at which point it fired him. It lost the subsequent lawsuit on the grounds it should have fired him the first time.

In the widely noted Jacksonville case, the shipyard already had a harassment policy that included a hotline for informants and a promise of immediate action against offenders, but the court said this fell short. It ordered the company to make dismissal automatic not only for any purposeful touching interpreted as sexual, but also for any threat of such—which would apply to, say, a gesture threatening to spank. It ordered automatic suspension of any employee found to have resisted the new policy by committing retaliation, defined as "providing inaccurate work information to, or refusing to cooperate or discuss work-related matters with any employee." And it appointed the National Organization for Women Legal Defense and Education Fund to monitor the worksite "even in the absence of specific complaints" and advise and consent in the naming of harassment inspectors, whose phone numbers would be posted at the workplace and who would be guaranteed "reasonable access . . . to inspect for compliance." NOW legal director Deborah Ellis hailed the order: "I don't think there are that many places that are different from Jacksonville Shipyards."

———

Like handicap accommodation law, harassment law lends itself to the roving compliance tour in which a consciousness-raised complainant, or in-house compliance officer anticipating the wishes of such a complainant, roams the corridors pronouncing, "This has to go—that does, too."

Faced with something objectionable, Bravo and Cassedy suggest objecting in "any tone that feels right to you." (Sample wording: "If you touch me/talk to me that way one more time, I'll report you so fast you won't know what hit you.) Petrocelli and Repa's Nolo Press book notes that the aggrieved employee can take "a series of escalating steps." For example, "If you were made uncomfortable because of jokes, pin-ups or cartoons posted at work, confiscate them—or at least make copies." If an "anti-woman joke makes the rounds of the office," try to look for a linkage to specific (compensable) harm, such as by finding among the chain of joke-repeaters a manager who recommends promotions. A table suited for copy-and-clip use explains the ground rules as follows:

What a Lawyer Wants to Hear

- Fairly serious harassment . . .

- Personal injuries—the more serious, the better . . .

- A solvent defendant.

A network of hotlines and harassment trainers (often paid for by the taxpayer, United Way, and the like through rape crisis centers and other institutions) has sprung up to counsel workers; it often maintains close ties with the employment plaintiff's bar. In a *New York Times* interview, harassment trainer Lorna Brown Flynn advises workers to keep secret notes, surface with a witness when you stage a confrontation with the offender, and bring a witness again when you demand your personnel files. "If a company suggests in-house counseling to resolve the problem, forget it," she offers. "Usually, that's intended to get you to drop the complaint."

———

Harassment law has paradoxically protected many workers who themselves have posed a menace to workplace decorum—for example, by taking part in a bawdy atmosphere with all evident enthusiasm before they apparently thought better of it. Thus one federal court sympathetically noted that a plaintiff's own use of profanity "could be part of [her] efforts to fit into the environment at hand." The result, commentator Kingsley Browne has observed, can be to give complainants the right to dish out foul language or prankery for a long time, then quit while they're ahead by invoking their rights against co-workers who are riled against them.

————

Discrimination law covers all the "terms, conditions, or privileges of employment," which a federal appeals court noted in an early case is "an expansive concept" in that "employees' psychological as well as economic fringes are statutorily entitled to protection."

Those psychological fringes emerged as the core of many harassment complaints, as in a 1993 federal case turning on the issue of disability harassment at a Maryland industrial firm. Sales assistant Marie D., who had contracted multiple sclerosis, sued after a long deterioration in relations with her supervisor, Ned Bumgarner. According to her suit, he had "perpetuated and enhanced myths" about Marie and her condition, "fostered an atmosphere of resentment and pity among plaintiff's co-workers, blamed plaintiff for office staffing problems and errors that she did not make, threatened to remove her special computer equipment, hovered over her excessively while at work, and denigrated her abilities both in private and in front of fellow employees." One especially hurtful moment came when he told her she was only performing at a 50 percent level. She felt he had "mimicked and ridiculed her speech and her gait, two traits that her MS had affected." Once he had made loud steps behind her in a corridor and then laughed, even though she was upset. Then there was the Doughnut Incident:

> A meeting was ongoing to which someone had brought doughnuts. D. had taken a chocolate one, placed it on the table, and went to the restroom. Bumgarner came in and, not knowing that D. had pre-selected that doughnut, picked it up and ate it. When she returned, she asked Bumgar-

ner if he had eaten the doughnut, and he said yes. She could not believe it, and no more chocolate doughnuts were left. D. acknowledged that once Bumgarner learned that she had selected that doughnut, he apologized to her.

Federal judge John Hargrove, despite hints of impatience, nonetheless ruled in Marie's favor, sending the harassment claims to trial and rejecting the company's request to throw them out as insubstantial. It was just too hard to gauge the psychological overtones from a distance; maybe the complainant was misinterpreting the steps in the corridor and the alleged mimicry, and overreacting to the excessive criticism and lack of knowledge about MS. Or maybe she was right in her interpretation, and her workplace was one of constant schoolyard cruelty. It was hard to know without letting the lawyers and witnesses go at it in a full-dress trial—if one could be sure even then.

———

Before long, complaints began to be heard: the workplace didn't seem as friendly as it used to be.

Many employers have expressed interest in banning dating, not just between supervisors and subordinates but between all employees. Even when they do not, staffers often get the message. "For myself, it's an unwritten law," said twenty-seven-year-old Price Waterhouse clerk Alex McLaren. "I would never date anyone in the office." Backers of harassment law generally deny that this is what they intended: when asked about voluntary requests for dates, NOW Legal Defense and Education Fund lawyer Alison Wethersfield allows as how "he could ask once, carefully."

New York sanitation workers said that after their four-hour mandatory sensitivity training, they'd concluded "the only way to stay out of trouble was to avoid the women." At the Los Angeles Police Department, deeply harrowed by harassment investigations, many male and female patrol partners are reported to exchange barely a word with each other during a shift. In the corporate world some men now avoid being alone in an elevator with a female co-worker, the same way gun-shy teachers and camp counselors now avoid one-on-one situations with children. When mixed workplace conversations take a social or personal turn, others go into what a *Boston Globe* writer calls "machine mode." Not surprisingly, many women begin to feel shut out: with fewer chances to join in informal lunches, business travel, weekend socializing, and general camaraderie, they may find it hard to do their jobs as well or rise as far as the men.

Of course, one possible response is to propose yet another round of legal compulsion by rattling legal sabers over the very acts of failure-to-mentor and withholding of good fellowship. "If the only reason a woman is not being asked out to dinner is because she's a woman, that's discrimination," declares consultant Freada Klein.

———

The Orange Unified School District probe lasted nineteen months, during which time Donoghue was forced out of his job and Capelle was allowed to resume work but demoted. (By this time the charges against her had been redefined as "immoral conduct, intimidation, and creation of a hostile working environment.") Finally, in a 160-page report, a hearing officer completely exonerated both Capelle and Donoghue. The hearing officer concluded that personal rivals of the two within the district had trumped up the charges; some of these rivals had carried on in the same way as regarded banter or its toleration, but hadn't been charged. (The district's officer in charge of sexual harassment prevention had been among those who engaged in the same supposed sins.) At the end of it all, the district wound up writing Donoghue a check for $160,000. The investigation and hearings had cost it an added $350,000 to 400,000; McGrath, the outside harassment expert, had billed $150,000 for two and a half months of work.

For Capelle and Donoghue, one of the old feminist slogans might have begun to take on a whole new significance. Maybe it wasn't about sex; it was about power.

Part II

THE AGE OF ACCOMMODATION

Chapter 5

MISTAKEN IDENTITY

When Congress took up the proposed Americans with Disabilities Act in 1990, disabled persons were not doing well in the American workplace. Most were not employed at all, drawing government checks instead; those with jobs earned an average of 30 to 40 percent less than their able-bodied counterparts.

Most discussion of the ADA accepted the premise that the main reason for this situation had little to do with the intrinsic limitations of being disabled—that is, of having to compete on the job market while lacking (for example) the ability to see, hear, or walk. Instead the problem was said to be a combination of employer discrimination and the lack of accessibility for the handicapped at all levels of society. Employers "simply do not want to hire or accommodate physically disabled workers," declared the National Council on Disability's Sandra Swift Parrino, which is why the latter are "forced to accept welfare." The shortage of disabled persons in high-level jobs, agreed law professor and ADA drafter Robert Burgdorf, Jr., "appears to be largely the result of discrimination." After all, surveys had found most working-age disabled said they'd like to work, and experts agreed there

85

were plenty of jobs they could do well, yet most were out of the labor force. What more evidence could we need that the fault lay with those doing the hiring?

Hence, it was argued, the need for strong new laws like the ADA, imposing tough penalties for discrimination and requiring employers to offer "reasonable accommodation." Laws mandating access would "pay for themselves," Frank Bowe, author of the popular tracts *Disabling America* and *Rehabilitating America,* had written. "Spending money on independence will save much more on dependence. . . . This is a problem we can 'solve by throwing money at it.'" The press had found this line of argument irresistible: it seemed hardheaded rather than sentimental. *USA Today's* account cited expert views that "not only will [the disabled] pay taxes, they'll give up an annual $60 billion in government disability benefits." "Enabling millions of disabled people to work will more than repay the cost of making such accommodation," predicted a *Boston Globe* editorial that found the new ADA's "only flaw" to be its lack of even broader coverage. The editorial writers for the *New York Times* considered such arguments "crucial," while *Business Week* hailed the law as "long overdue" and said it came "just in time to meet the needs of an economy that faces looming labor shortages."

A couple of years later, when numbers began to emerge about how the disabled were faring in the post-ADA workplace, many of these commentators must have been shaken. Barriers had at last come down; businesses and towns were spending tens of billions to make facilities accessible; and job bias was now the target of tough penalties and a mounting volume of lawsuits. Finally, disabled persons had their long-sought chance to work—but they weren't working. In fact, the number of disabled participating in the workforce had fallen from 34 percent of men in 1991 to just over 30 percent two years later. ADA advocates got to work and rushed out numbers the next year indicating that the number of "seriously disabled persons" with jobs had actually gone up a couple of percentage points. Yet payouts in the federal disability program were sharply up, not down, from $27 billion in 1991 to $37 billion in 1994.

No one should have been surprised. The history of other discrimination laws and the past course of disabled employment both made it predictable that the law would miss the mark in moving the disabled to jobs from idleness. Far from being any rational step toward integrating this group into the productive economy, ADA was a venture into freelance social reconstruction inspired by the kind of overwrought identity politics that ran wild in the 1970s and 1980s. Indeed, its failure to ameliorate the employment situation of the disabled raises many questions about the limits of that brand of politics.

———

The history of identity politics, like the history of discrimination law, has been built on a continuing series of analogies to the condition of blacks, each less convincing than the last. One contributing factor, no doubt, has been the legacy of the historic Left, which has led reformers to presume that the nexus of subjugation for any oppressed group will be the employment relationship. Why would one group oppress another—why would enmity and misunderstanding arise between different subsets of the human family in the first place—if not to allow the extraction of surplus value from others' labor?

In the case of blacks, this view had a certain plausibility. Their forebears had been brought to this country specifically to carry on hard labor, and the word *exploitation* sums up their fate under slavery. As late as the 1950s, blacks were still doing far more than their share of society's most toilsome and least esteemed work; in the South, where most of them still lived, Jim Crow employment laws aimed at holding their wages down by, for example, forbidding the activities of labor agents recruiting for work in northern factories.

It was quite a stretch to compare women's situation with that of blacks. For educated women (the ones who began raising consciousness in big cities in the 1960s), much of the perceived unfairness in existing social mores lay in their being considered too delicate for challenging jobs, rather than being driven too hard in them. Then, too, the changes in sex roles that were under way had all sorts of dimensions and were being advanced or resisted on many fronts; employers' choices as such were not obviously among the most important factors deciding whether more women would pursue careers.

The notion of group exploitation began to break down completely when it came to the elderly. Older workers as individuals run into distinctive and vexing problems in the labor market, but there is not a particle of evidence that they have been subjugated as a class. By the conventional indices—the kind regularly used to measure blacks' or women's progress in the workplace—they might even have to count as an oppressor rather than oppressed class. They are paid more than younger workers, and their rates of joblessness are lower. They carry on less grinding physical work and more high-level managerial work; in the latter capacity, as CEOs and senior executives, they set personnel policies for most big employers. Of course older workers also display higher productivity, but labor economists have found evidence that the pay advantages of age tend to be even greater than such factors would account for.

Each of the groups above had been covered by strong new antidiscrimination laws, but the results (if, indeed, they *were* results) differed from one case to the next. Women had been surging into paid employment in large numbers before bias law covered them, and they continued to do so afterward, just as they did in many advanced democracies that made less ado about such laws. Black males, after coming under protection, experienced a calamitous drop in labor force participation. Older males had shown a decline in labor force participation before the advent of age bias law, and that trend continued afterward. The most that could be said of these laws was that they showed no clear or consistent effect on the rate at which a group would be employed.

————

Disability differed from earlier protected statuses in at least two rather dramatic ways, both of which the campaign for the Americans with Disabilities Act managed to duck. First, there was vast uncertainty as to who counted as a member of the group. Disputes over who qualified as disabled already supported a thriving sector of the legal profession in Social Security and workers' compensation law, and in nearly

all these disputes people were battling to get *into* the supposedly oppressed category by securing the "disabled" label for themselves.

Second, the most obvious form of workplace discrimination affecting the disabled was that in their favor. Explicit hire-the-handicapped
campaigns had been standard for decades in government and big companies alike. ADA advocates spoke of the hostile attitudes that were
still sometimes encountered, and at hearings they produced a few witnesses who had been grossly insulted at job interviews, but hardly
anyone claimed such barbarities were typical. Instead, sponsors such
as Rep. Steny Hoyer (a Democrat from Maryland) cited the kind of
"unconscious, unthinking discrimination" so deeply ingrained that
hiring managers could not always hope to recognize it in themselves.
As a theory, this was unanswerable—who can convincingly deny unconscious bias? But it failed to explain why all the open and institu-
tionalized favoritism should have failed in its purpose. If even a
quarter of potential employers are willing to give you an explicit preference, it's hard to blame your joblessness on subtle and unconscious
bias at some undetermined number of others: the good guys dispense
a wide range of jobs, and no one is forcing you to deal with the obtuse.

In a casual libel against the past, ADA advocates commonly left the
impression that earlier generations in America (and other Western industrial nations) had been content to leave the handicapped to idleness, often in institutions—the favored verb was "to rot"—while we
alone had been enlightened enough to think of finding them work.
The truth was closer to the reverse. Work has been the norm for disabled persons over the centuries, just as it has been for everyone else
outside hereditary elites; idleness was the relatively recent and unusual development. Traditional societies commonly set disabled persons to work in one capacity or another rather than countenance the
evils of beggary. Later, the rise of industrialism saw much more systematic efforts to arrange jobs to suit the group's special needs, from a
mix of motives that included the self-interested (periodic labor shortages and the chance to obtain the services of the frail for lower wages
than those of the hearty) as well as the humanitarian.

Modern government, too, has been trying to place the disabled in
jobs for a long time, impelled in part by a sense of responsibility for

the plight of war veterans. In 1920, a time when Washington's involvement in most social welfare issues was slight, Congress began supporting state "vocational rehabilitation" programs aimed at putting the disabled to work; like hire-the-handicapped campaigns, these programs aided not only veterans but also civilians disabled by birth, illness, or accident. Among the functions of voc-rehab agencies are to cajole employers to hire disabled workers; to keep tabs on suitable job openings; to consult on (and sometimes pay for) needed accommodations; and to train disabled persons for the kinds of jobs expected to be available in local labor markets. Save for the element of coercion of unwilling employers, the general game plan would seem a lot like that of the Americans with Disabilities Act of 1990.

For decades, voc-rehab pegged along as an uncontroversial and apparently successful part of the welfare state. In the late 1970s, though, successful placements fell by more than a third. In fact, a more systemic problem soon became evident: disabled persons' participation in the labor force had begun a rapid decline. For disabled men, it fell from 64 percent in the early 1970s to 54 percent by the mid-1980s; disabled women also lost ground compared with women generally. Those who remained employed were retreating from full- to part-time work—by 1988, only 23 percent of disabled men worked full-time, compared with 30 percent only seven years earlier. During roughly the same period the earnings gap between disabled and able-bodied workers widened from 23 to 30 percent for men and from 30 to 38 percent for women. In short, by the time ADA came along, a clear and dismaying trend had been in progress for years: the disabled were moving out of the labor force

Technological developments made this decline even more baffling. Over this very period the rise of computers and similar technologies had been hailed as a triumph over bodily limitation, the greatest leveler of physical capacities in all history. Voice activation, talking screens, miniaturization of everything, and the widespread replacement of physical with keyboard controls were bringing a much wider range of desirable jobs within reach of disabled persons.

The only way oppression theory could explain these reverses was by positing that societal persecution of the disabled had become much more intense since the early 1970s, but no one could believe anything of the sort. A whole series of very powerful new laws over these years had brought "accessibility" to such areas as public transit and elementary and higher education; these laws, like the later ADA, had been (erroneously) advertised as sure to "pay for themselves" by increasing the employment rates of the disabled. One of the new federal laws—Section 504, which applied to government contractors and local governments—had required most larger employers to practice affirmative action toward the disabled, refrain from discrimination against them, and accommodate their special needs. Meanwhile, a vocal disabled movement had met with great success in raising consciousness about its issues over this period.

Before this period of unprecedented ferment and progress in disability rights, most disabled men held down full-time jobs. Afterward, unaccountably, most sat idle. The explanation requires a look at the third "great unmentionable" of the ADA debate, well known around the capital but consistently ducked: the federal Social Security disability program.

In the early 1970s Congress devised and grafted on to the existing Social Security program a massive new income-support program for the disabled, replacing what had been a patchwork of state and federal benefits. The new law greatly boosted the benefits available and made it much easier to obtain a disability determination. Outlays on the new program soon began mounting, from $2.8 billion in 1970 to $7.7 billion in 1975, $15 billion in 1980 and $24 billion in 1990. The number of pre-retirement-age persons legally defined as disabled tripled in sixteen years, as if the country had been through a major war, though public health surveys revealed no decline in the underlying well-being of the population.

The problem, of course, is that disability is far from an objective medical matter. Over the sixteen years, an industry had proliferated of lawyers who knew how to steer cases through the Social Security hearing process and friendly doctors willing to provide a disability diagnosis in doubtful cases. By the 1990s the program had begun to welcome substantial numbers of persons whose disabilities had arisen from alcoholism and drug abuse, along with many children and young adults diagnosed with emotional disorders. The general rule was that once you got on the adult disability program you could stay on it for life, a rule confirmed after Congress slapped down an ill-fated scheme by the Reagan administration to make existing recipients prove they were still disabled.

The Social Security program's expansion had greatly steepened the "welfare trap" by which recipients find themselves not much better off financially (and often worse off) if they take a job than if they stay home. The "traditional" disabled population, most of whom had formerly held jobs, now found itself faced with this disincentive to employment, as did the many borderline disabled who had sought a designation precisely because they wanted a source of income other than work. Indeed, this welfare trap was deeper than that of the much-discussed (and smaller) Aid to Families with Dependent Children program, simply because it was much more generous. In other programs whose clients were caught in a disincentive trap, surveys in which they expressed an abstract desire to work had proven of little value in predicting whether they'd actually take available jobs. Nor had program officials had much success getting recipients to work by tinkering to make the schedules of available jobs more convenient, to match the prospect's skills and preferences more closely, and so forth. Yet the promises for the ADA followed this same format: offer a wider choice of more closely tailored jobs, and welfare dependency will end.

———

Meanwhile, a movement had sprung up to convince disabled persons that the system was to blame for their increasing estrangement from society.

Handicapped persons in America are victims, it was said, of an "oppression" that "bears striking resemblances to that practiced against ethnic minorities" and also has a lot in common with the "systematic oppression" of such groups as "women, gay people and the elderly in present-day America." To end this state of affairs, the time had passed for appealing to the goodwill of the able-bodied; what was needed instead was an effort to "compel" them to come across with better treatment, using "every weapon in the political arsenal."

All of these quotes are from John Gliedman and William Roth's acclaimed 1980 volume *The Unexpected Minority: Handicapped Children in America*. No tract of an obscure Berkeley sectlet, this book issued forth from one of the mainstays of the Washington liberal-reform establishment, the Children's Defense Fund, headed by future presidential adviser and honorary-degree champ Marian Wright Edelman; serving as research assistant on the book, in a footnote of historical interest, was fund associate and future First Lady Hillary Rodham Clinton. The volume was then issued as a report of the excruciatingly respectable Carnegie Council on Children; though book, fund, and council all invoked children in their names, all had a relevant agenda that extended very much to the world of grown-ups.

The authors of *The Unexpected Minority* have little patience with the traditional view that Nature has dealt the blind or deaf person a bad hand. Instead, they argue, the evils of disability should be seen as society's fault for not redesigning itself to cater to them. Were it not for this omission, disabled people would be just as affluent and successful, or almost so, as their intact brethren. That is why (in a jujitsu reappropriation of everyday terms) the absence of a handrail should really be seen as a "barrier," and the failure to hire a sign translator as "exclusion." Senator Lowell Weicker of Connecticut, who popularized the new ideas in the political arena, summed it all up: the chief reason for disabled people's woes in life is "not what God wrought but what man imposed by custom and law."

Imbibing deeply of the academic spirit of their times, Gliedman and Roth go yet another step, saying we should see the whole concept of disability as socially constructed, a matter of definitions and baseline assumptions. There's really nothing intrinsically better, it would seem, in sightedness as opposed to blindness; we've just accorded the one a privileged position by our unwillingness to provide Braille and audio labeling everywhere. Scarcely have the authors advanced this novel thesis than they have to begin backtracking; they concede, for example, that Nature has left the profoundly retarded in such plight that no imaginable bending over backward by the rest of society could bring about an equality of outcome.

But the point is to liberate what they view as the other 90 percent of the disabled. Naturally, if things are to change, this group will have to stop collaborating in their own victimization. Of particular concern, as later advocates pointed out, fewer than half agree in polls that they are "a minority group in the same sense as are blacks and Hispanics." Many disabled persons are also loath to impose on others, put up with great inconvenience rather than do so, and even are content to hold what Gliedman and Roth curdlingly describe as "honorable but humble" jobs, a phrase they invoke in the inevitable context of house slaves in the days of *Uncle Tom's Cabin.*

The disabled-movement literature that emerged in the 1970s and 1980s follows similar identity-politics themes with relentless single-mindedness. Typical was Harlan Lane's highly praised, Foucault-quoting history of education for the deaf, *The Mask of Benevolence,* whose title says it all ("there are no good and bad members of the oppressing class—only those who accept their reality as oppressors and a few who do not.") The views of the able-bodied majority, pronounces a *University of Pennsylvania Law Review* author, are "pervaded by ignorance, misunderstanding" and of course "fear of the unknown or the different." A report issued by the U.S. Senate was quite severe on the failings of the lawmakers' constituents, finding that "the American people" are "insensitive to the difficulties [facing] individuals with handicaps."

Though generalizing a blue streak about the able-bodied population, disability activists tended to bristle at generalizations running in the opposite direction, even the ostensibly sympathetic or favorable kind, which fail "to recognize them as fully human." Off limits, according to the National Easter Seals Society, are such terms as *wheelchair-bound, suffers from, disease* (should be *condition*), *victim, unfortunate, invalid,* and such individual characterizations as *sensitive, bitter, full of self-pity, courageous, brave,* or *inspirational.*

This matter of sympathy emerged as a particular sticking point. Oppressed minorities are supposed to be persecuted, but the disabled were being love-bombed. In one survey 92 percent of those polled said they felt admiration when they met a severely disabled person. Workplace studies had found a "halo effect" in which supervisors initially overrate the quality of a handicapped person's work. The federal disability program drew far less public antagonism than welfare for the able-bodied, though it was costlier and growing faster. Hire-the-handicapped preferences were considered just fine by most of those who viewed race and gender preferences with alarm. These cloyingly favorable sentiments had their downside—it might do a disabled person no good to spare him frank criticism, for example—but still on balance would seem to betoken the kind of reservoir of goodwill other minority groups could only envy.

Oppression theorists saw the favorable attitudes as yet another mode of victimization. The inspirational view of the disabled, writes Joseph Shapiro in *No Pity: People with Disabilities Forging a New Civil Rights Movement,* is "widely viewed as oppressive." Any "atmosphere of sympathy," said the *University of Pennsylvania Law Review* author, is only "alleged" and "apparent," and indeed a problem that "must be overcome" if equality is to be gained.

History, art, and literature all got packed into the grinder of Cultural Studies, the fashionable new academic discipline, to emerge as tidy links of oppression. The honor roll of revered cultural figures missing a faculty or two—blind Milton and Homer, deaf Beethoven, and so on—hardly proved anything because the disabled status of these greats was seldom considered important in discussions of their work, thus rendering disability "invisible." Granted, it was hard to deny that the century's most popular and powerful democratic leader, President Franklin Delano Roosevelt, had been a wheelchair user, and had even reached eminence in the very country that cultural theorists generally saw as the arch-source of discrimination and stereotyping. Some proposed the only way FDR could have been so popular was for the general public to have been unaware of his physical condition, a theory undercut when old-timers piped up to say they remembered the contrary.

As for fictional portrayals, mocking or scary depictions of disability turned up most frequently in the literature of the nursery—the land of

Captain Hook, Rumpelstiltskin, and the rest. Analysts predictably concluded that exposure to such portraits had been to blame for instilling backward views in children, rather than reflecting their already observable fascination with surface differences. The media would be expected to do better in future: "We feel Porky Pig is always shown as a victim," said Ira Zimmerman of the National Stuttering Project.

Social construction arguments became all the rage. Edward D. Berkowitz, in the Twentieth Century Fund report *Disabled Policy: America's Programs for the Handicapped,* toys with the idea that only convention leads us all to communicate by means of voice as opposed to hand signals, anyway—a view that might seem to slight the problem of getting the attention of someone in the next room when our arms are full of packages, and would seem to raise the question of why our ancestors went to the evolutionary trouble of developing vocal cords in the first place. Shapiro's *No Pity,* a leading popular account of the disabled movement, reports that many deaf activists view their condition not as "regrettable" but as "an identity to be adopted with pride." Some vow to oppose future surgical procedures that might restore hearing to deaf infants—even should they turn out to work perfectly—on the ground that they would lead to "genocide" of a cultural minority.

Which again raised the question: what exactly *was* the disabled identity? Deaf persons who have had the condition since childhood can stake the best claim of any disabled group to culturally separate status, having formed communities based on the shared use of American Sign Language (ASL). But those who lose their hearing late in life have little in common with this culture, typically showing scant interest in learning ASL or giving up their existing social patterns. And the larger group of persons who merely grow hard of hearing have yet other needs. Each might prefer a different form of assistance at, say, a public seminar: sign translation for one, subtitles for another, and amplified earphones for the third.

Any semblance of "disabled nation" unity fell entirely to pieces when other disabling conditions were added to the comparison. Many persons with permanent, stable disabilities get annoyed (and not unreasonably) at the outside world's habit of "medicalizing" their condition, or expecting every paraplegic to pursue a vain struggle to walk rather than get on with life. Soon, however, it was announced that all the conditions requiring the greatest medical intervention and personal effort to fight—cancer, heart disease, contagious diseases such as tuberculosis—counted as disabilities, too. So did alcoholism and drug abuse (even if they'd been conquered and the person had been sober for years), as well as mental disorders.

Presumably aware of the political benefits to be had by claiming a large constituency, ADA campaigners settled on 43 million as the number of disabled persons in America, a number they wrote into the law. In fact, the three traditional disabled groups that had been the focus of government policy numbered less than 3 million: an estimated 1.7 million deaf, 720,000 wheelchair users, and 400,000 blind persons. But it is easy to make these numbers grow by including persons with less remarkable departures from the norm: 21 million people are said to have trouble hearing, tens of millions find it harder to get around than they used to, and 8 million have vision problems that fall short of blindness, not to mention all the eyeglass wearers. The count of those with mental problems can be kept low by stopping at those with classically defined disorders such as psychosis and severe retardation, or boosted to pretty much any desired level by including attention or learning disabilities, substance dependencies, neuroses, and anxieties.

"The definition of disability," observes John Kiernan of the International Center for the Disabled, "depends on where you're coming from and what you want the numbers to do for you." To reach the 43 million figure, advocates simply counted everyone over the age of sixty-five as disabled. They also roped in sufferers from health conditions like diabetes, cancer, epilepsy, and HIV infection even if those conditions caused no current debilitation, were controllable or indeed curable by medication, and were "invisible" to job interviewers or other suspect classes. In short, they could just as well have picked a figure of 4 million or 143 million. If invisible and asymptomatic conditions are to be counted as disabling, it's hard to see why not to go all the way and include millions more people who have these same medically serious conditions but don't know it themselves yet.

THE AGE OF ACCOMMODATION

Wheelchair sit-ins soon emerged as the perfect way of educating politicians about these issues. Catnip to the camera crews, these protests figured in a long series of movement victories over the years: blocking commuter traffic on the Golden Gate Bridge, occupying the federal building in San Francisco (a monthlong media extravaganza complete with catering, courtesy of Black Panthers who whipped up meals from food donated by local Safeways), and a midnight descent on the home of the secretary of the Department of Health, Education, and Welfare in the Carter administration, Joseph Califano (whose memoirs say he'd previously "welcomed" the prospect of protests, since "nothing is likelier to evoke sympathy than the poignancy of a demonstration by the handicapped"). Thanks perhaps to the oppressive climate of sympathy, these assaults never seemed to bring down any serious legal backlash; after a particularly disruptive series of actions that closed down parts of the U.S. Capitol, a Washington judge stepped down from the bench to congratulate demonstrators, shake their hands, and fine them a mere ten dollars.

Remarkably, many of the early demonstrations protesting ostensible government indifference were actually orchestrated from within the government itself. "Several staff members of both OCR [HEW's Office of Civil Rights] and congressional committees were involved in planning for the sit-ins," reports sociologist Richard Scotch in his fascinating history of early disabled-rights law, *From Good Will to Civil Rights*. Also keeping things rolling were such HEW grantees as the American Coalition of Citizens with Disabilities, which helped organize takeovers of HEW's own offices.

The usual "how a law is made" chart depicts an aroused public airing its grievances, after which the authorities respond with appropriate lawmaking. In this case, though, the laws actually emerged before the grievances. Accounts of the period agree that in 1973, when Congress enacted the first major federal initiative on the subject (known as Section 504), it was under no grass-roots pressure from any organized disabled-rights movement or any other source. Purely on their own initiative, congressional and executive-branch staffers had drafted a rider to a pending bill providing in vague but promising language that no "otherwise qualified" handicapped person

> shall, solely by reason of his handicap, be excluded from participation in, be denied the benefits of, or be subjected to discrimination under any program or activity receiving Federal assistance.

Once this clause was on the books, these staffers began calling existing disability-service groups, which were mostly organized around single conditions such as blindness, with the word: Did you know there's this new law you can use to demand that local governments, universities, and hospitals help out your constituents? Facing the legal hassle of a complaint, targets were often willing to offer big concessions. At this point the established groups began hiring lawyers and Washington representatives and going political; within a few years, the disabled movement was proceeding full blast.

Many completely new rights groups sprang up as well, aided by foundation and federal grants, while law schools and the American Bar Association helped with litigation strike forces. Congress funded multimillion-dollar programs to train handicapped persons and their families "how to fight for services," as one supporter put it. A network of more than one hundred federally supported "independent living centers" sprouted around the country, based on a model pioneered by a group of Berkeley students in the 1960s, dispensing know-how and consciousness-raising advice to constituents, including advice on how to get maximum benefit checks as well as push for more accessibility.

A panel appointed by none other than Ronald Reagan was the first to propose a general law toughening Section 504 further and applying it to private parties rather than just the government and contractors. Reagan's successor, George Bush, tirelessly supported the idea and often cited the resulting Americans with Disabilities Act among his chief domestic achievements—a somewhat ironic circumstance, since his staff wound up delegating much of the bill's drafting and negotiating to the Washington office of the American Civil Liberties Union, an organization Bush had flayed in a defining and crowd-pleasing moment of his winning campaign. Early in his presidency Bush had signaled his commitment to the issue by naming as EEOC chairman not the customary black or woman but Evan Kemp, Jr., the paraplegic former head of a Ralph Nader–funded litigation group called the Disability Rights Center. Sen. Robert Dole, also disabled, was another powerful voice in favor, as were handicapped family members of legislators and other influential persons.

Soon after the ADA's passage, analysts from the National Association of Manufacturers described it as potentially the most expensive business mandate in history. Yet criticism from organized enterprise was "surprisingly muted," as Joseph Shapiro, a friend of the law, describes it; few well-known companies were willing to go on the record against the idea or even fight behind the scenes, though some opposition was felt from the National Federation of Independent Business and other small-business groups. Few in Congress would take the lead either, especially after disabled activists seized the office of Pennsylvania Republican Rep. Bud Shuster, who'd introduced an amendment to soften a couple of its more extreme provisions. (This act of intimidation was treated with the usual impunity, the activists escaping any serious later punishment.)

Everyone else was busy congratulating each other on the bipartisan consensus. Future House Speaker Newt Gingrich joined Senate conservatives Orrin Hatch, Strom Thurmond, and Phil Gramm and virtually all liberal Democrats to support what the *New York Times* was later to call this "unabashed venture into social engineering." Even some of its few vocal critics found themselves pulled by a resistless attraction into the yes column. Republican Sen. Ted Armstrong of Colorado called it a "legislative Rorschach test, an inkblot whose meaning and significance will be determined through years of costly litigation," adding that "it will engender wave upon wave of court rulings that will extend the bill far beyond its intended purposes"—then voted for it anyway. Only 6 of 100 senators voted no; the House tally was a scarcely less lopsided 377 to 28. "Congress so seldom does anything wonderful that we should pause and salute it on those rare occasions," wrote the *Washington Post*'s Mary McGrory.

Backers likened the bill to a twentieth-century Emancipation Proclamation, a second Bill of Rights, and a fresh Declaration of Independence, while President Bush himself compared its passage to the fall of the Berlin Wall. The bill's Senate floor manager, Democrat Tom Harkin of Iowa, said it "will change the way we live forever." On July 26, 1990, Bush signed the measure into law before an estimated crowd of two thousand disabled advocates from around the country (the largest bill-signing ceremony ever, according to the publicity). Those present agree that the atmosphere was electric, charged with a heady sense of power. Over whom, exactly, this power was to be wielded would become clear only later, after the gathering had dispersed.

Chapter 6

THE AGE OF ACCOMMODATION

When it was passed, backers of the Americans with Disabilities Act insisted its burdens would fall quite lightly on regulated parties. Yes, employers, retail shops, and local governments might face $50,000 fines for first violations—or even higher sums in private lawsuits—if they failed to accommodate disabled persons' special needs, but the law required only "reasonable" accommodation and exempted businesses that would suffer "undue hardship." So how onerous could it be, really?

Besides, most requested accommodations weren't that expensive. Two widely cited studies had found that the great majority of adjustments cost employers less than $500, and half cost nothing at all. "There is nothing in this bill that should be terribly threatening to anyone," said an activist quoted in the *St. Louis Post-Dispatch*. Much of the press had pursued this line of what might be called aggressive reassurance. *Business Week* dismissed cost concerns as "highly exaggerated." "Businesses should not fear large monetary lawsuits under the act," opined a *Seattle Times* editorial.

Even after reports began to surface of extreme-sounding claims being made under the new law, supporters put forward a united front. Although "some journalistic naysayers have charged that the law imposes unreasonable burdens," wrote Clinton administration attorney general Janet Reno and her Bush administration predecessor Richard Thornburgh in a jointly signed piece, the truth is that it "encourages low-cost ways to solve a problem." Walter J. Kendall III, a law professor at John Marshall Law School, denied claims that the law was vague, calling it "clear" and "a narrowly crafted recognition of both economic realities and common sense." Reno and Thornburgh echo the last point, saying that the law "merely codifies common sense."

As often happens in Washington, officials' public pronouncements were curiously at odds with their underlings' actions. For all the talk of common sense and reasonableness, ADA supporters had pushed tirelessly behind the scenes in the law's drafting and later enforcement for a cost-no-object approach that recognized no economic or budgetary constraint on what might be demanded of the law's targets. Despite the occasional necessary short-term compromise, they had achieved considerable success in getting this principle established. And the Justice Departments of Richard Thornburgh and Janet Reno had very much been at the forefront of the efforts to keep the check blank.

———

The point of the ADA had been to expand and elaborate greatly on the earlier law known as Section 504 of the Rehabilitation Act of 1973.

Section 504 never quite became a household word, but it was well known in Washington as the law that stopped a thousand buses, the bane of town halls across America, one of the costliest mandates in federal history. It had required government programs and contractors to make their facilities accessible to wheelchair users and other handicapped persons; hospitals, universities, and museums had all laid out fortunes to comply, sometimes electing to tear down grand old buildings that were too expensive to "retrofit." Local government in particular had been undone by the law's application to public transit: poor rural counties faced numbing price tags to acquire wheelchair buses even if no one living on a route used or planned to use the special features, while older cities spent hundreds of millions drilling elevator shafts into cramped subway stations. Study after study showed it would often be cheaper to offer disabled residents door-to-door paratransit with vans and attendants, but advocates had rejected this approach, which they said recalled the old South's "separate but equal" practices.

One might expect a law with such convulsive effects to have been the subject of exhaustive debate, but Section 504 perfectly exemplified the use of legislation to extend federal power when no one is looking. "It would not be an overstatement," notes one account, "to say that Section 504 was enacted into law with no public comment or debate." Staffers drafted the provision giving "otherwise qualified" handicapped persons a new right to equal use of federally aided programs, and members could see no objection. Committee reports on what eventually became the Rehabilitation Act of 1973 said nothing about how the clause might work, why it might be needed, or how much it might cost. Nor did members discuss the provision on the floor of either house of Congress; and President Nixon did not mention the clause when he signed the eventual bill, after having vetoed an earlier version for unrelated reasons. Years later the measure's sponsor, Ohio Democratic Rep. Charles Vanik, admitted that he "could not even have imagined" that it would trigger billions in mandated spending on wheelchair transit.

The section's ambitious language was obviously destined to raise knotty issues of implementation for Nixon's appointees, but the staffers on Capitol Hill, then at the height of its Watergate-era war with the executive branch, didn't seem to worry. "I'll tell you the frame of mind we all had," Senate majority staffer Nik Edes told sociologist Richard Scotch, who obtained many unusually frank interviews in writing his history of Section 504:

We were angry at the Nixon administration. . . . It was an important thread running through everything that was done at those times. It was: I'll get those sons of bitches, they don't want to show any positive inclination toward doing things at all, then we're going to really stick it to them.

And in the process, help people. I mean I don't think that those are necessarily incompatible goals.

The prevailing view, Scotch says, was that if the law proved hard to
implement, "so much the better"—the hated Nixonites would wind
up looking "inept, illiberal, and willing to subvert laws passed by
Congress."

A key moment came when the Office of Civil Rights within what
was then the Department of Health, Education, and Welfare carried
out a power play within the government to grab control of the right to
enforce the new provision. OCR was famed for its adversarial stance
toward those it regulated: it had won glory staring down state governments in the South in the days of "massive resistance" and brought the
same intransigence and sureness of moral ground to later showdowns
with school systems, nonprofit institutions, and local governments in
the North. Its staff members soon set out to expand their authority to
enforce the new clause, and one maneuver became an immediate classic in the political science literature. Finding that the law contained
no provision granting it or any agency authority to issue regulations
on handicap accessibility, an omission that might leave the agency's
position shaky in court, members of the OCR sat down with staffers
on the congressional side and concocted a *retroactive* "legislative history" for the law—fully a year after it was passed—declaring that
though Congress had said not a word about the matter, it had really
intended all along for OCR to have authority to put out rules.

The agency staff also turned its attention to resolving doubtful
questions of statutory scope in favor of broader coverage. Section 504
contained at least two potentially limiting phrases: it applied only
when disabled persons were excluded "solely" because of their disability, and only if they were "otherwise qualified" for admission to
the program. A crabbed reading of those clauses might have restricted
the law to make it prohibit only, say, invidious or irrational refusals to
serve handicapped persons. The OCR staff soon disposed of that notion—positive accessibility measures would be called for, and plenty
of them.

For local governments and other regulated parties, the only question was how far those positive steps would have to go. Accommodations for the handicapped, like gifts in the Neiman-Marcus catalogue, start at inexpensive price points and eventually escalate to the show-off or stunt level. A museum might help out deaf visitors by handing them a standard brochure annotating its exhibits; or it might engage a sign-language interpreter to come in once a week, asking patrons who wanted such service to come by then; or it might hire two or three full-time interpreters working shifts so that every casual drop-in can be assured of such services on the spot. Which should it be?

No one really knew, but answers emanating from OCR were likely to be expensive. The agency was wedded to the notion that accommodation was a right, and hence brooked no economic constraints— a view that soon became dogma throughout the disability-rights community. Thus the agency proclaimed with apparent pride that its formula defining discriminatory failure to provide access "does not take into account the cost or difficulty of eliminating" such a condition. Scotch writes that disregard of costs was "a major tenet of faith" within the agency; the cost of compliance "was officially a 'nonissue,' one whose consideration was felt to be illegitimate by most of the OCR staff, including the key decision-makers." Leading staffer Martin Gerry said his nominal boss, Ford administration HEW secretary David Mathews, "really just didn't get the idea that these were rights and that you weren't really talking about nice things to do for Easter Seal children." "In our office the party line was that it doesn't cost anything, and I don't know what the hell we think it costs to even build a ramp," staffer Sally Foley told Scotch. "We constantly say that it doesn't cost anything. We constantly say the costs are exaggerated, exaggerated by the nasties out there who don't want the handicapped to have access."

Another point the OCR staff managed to establish during this period proved crucial in setting the eventual scope of the ADA later on: alcoholics and drug users should be legally protected as disabled, just like people missing their sight or legs. The idea reportedly drew consternation when it reached the desks of then-Secretary of Health, Education, and Welfare Patricia Harris and President Jimmy Carter, but even though they were nominally in charge, it was too late to turn back. Staff attorneys had already established the rule as part of the agency's practice, and the precedent was considered set.

In the years that followed, disability-rights advocates succeeded in pushing through a number of other important new laws, most partaking of what the British prime minister Lord Salisbury called "the Draconic character which usually marks philanthropic legislation." One such law armed the parents of disabled children with rights to demand individualized learning plans and a variety of other services from public schools; "special education" soon began putting a desperate strain on school budgets nationwide, while classroom disruption spread as children with emotional, behavioral, and other time-demanding deficits exercised their right to "mainstreaming" at the expense of other students and teachers. Another federal law required many subsidized housing projects for the elderly to admit the disabled of all ages; youngsters whose "disabilities" consisted of alcohol and drug addiction moved in and went on cat-among-the-pigeons crime sprees among the luckless elders.

———

The new ADA was meant to go far beyond Section 504. It would apply to the whole country instead of just the government and its contractors. It would also include tough rules on employment (such provisions in the earlier law having been only sporadically enforced), along with a raft of other provisions.

Though organized business declined to resist the bill in principle, it did put up a fight trying to put some limiting definitions on the relevant concepts so that businesses might have some idea whether they had achieved compliance. What constituted "reasonable accommodation," and when did it reach the point of "undue hardship" for those obliged to accommodate?

ADA advocates were taking a hard line on both issues. On the undue-hardship point, they were pushing the so-called bankruptcy out, which would accord a business an exemption only if the cost of accommodation would otherwise force it to shut down. Of course, an argument could be put up at any point prior to that as to whether the business was genuinely on the brink or just bluffing—a discussion the firm could end only by closing down to show it was in earnest, much as certain accused witches were once considered to prove their innocence only by showing the grace to drown.

As for "reasonable accommodation," ADA drafters were extremely anxious *not* to adopt a well-established definition of that term available in federal law: the one used in religious discrimination cases. Employees with religious convictions occasionally sued when bosses refused to let them take their Sabbath day off work or wear head coverings required by their faith. The Supreme Court had interpreted religious bias law as prohibiting these refusals to accommodate only if they were arbitrary and unrelated to business concerns, and it deemed to be arbitrary only those refusals where the expense, inconvenience, or disruption factor to the employer appeared quite small—*de minimis,* as the phrase goes. In short, employers would have to make accommodations that would involve very little cost, but would be free to set their own policies beyond that.

Whatever the Court's stated legal grounds in these religious-accommodation cases, it's not all that hard to guess at its implicit social reasoning. As in its speech and establishment cases, the justices were concerned about preserving official neutrality between different faiths as well as between belief and unbelief. If the law gave believers the right to demand expensive accommodations that inconvenienced or drew the envy of other workers, it would risk stirring up enmities and turning religion into a source of contention in the workplace; it might also cause some to advertise belief on a tactical basis to obtain benefits, like the soldier in the Philip Roth story "Defender of the Faith." But this sort of neutrality was the last thing disabled advocates wanted: their official pronouncements repeatedly emphasized that they did not want the religious bias standard carried over to the ADA, and it wasn't.

There was another stopping point that was likewise ignored. Some of the more moderate state laws had limited the accommodation mandate by imposing a cap, either of a stated sum (an employer might not have to spend more than $5,000 accommodating any single worker) or of a percentage figure (so that an employer might not have to spend more than 10 percent of a worker's annual salary, or, say, 10 percent of the revenue if a sale were at issue).

ADA advocates had the votes to defeat all such attempted limits, and they used them, making clear that they would not accept any ceiling. They did yield to a sort of compromise on undue-hardship language that provided factors for a court to consider—the size of an affected facility or branch, and the size of its parent enterprise if any— but resolved nothing; some disability advocates continued to proffer the bankruptcy-out idea as a suitable interpretation.

———

Meanwhile, ADA activists faced the delicate task of spreading the impression among the general public that the law's new demands would not amount to anything terribly expensive or inconvenient.

They constantly cited two surveys from the 1980s showing (or so they said) that the costs of accommodation were low; one had been compiled by a federally aided hotline that advises employers on how best to meet accommodation requests. As noted earlier, the surveys had found that the great majority of recommended accommodations cost employers less than $500, and half cost nothing at all. But this in fact proved very little. To begin with, the numbers shed no light on the aggregate cost of accommodations nor even the average cost per worker, only suggesting that many of the accommodations were cheap. Counting lots of trivial adjustments can readily result in such a finding even if the aggregate bordens of accommodation are high; it is like trying to guess the overall value of a store's inventory by noting all the inexpensive goods on display, without factoring in the jewelry counter. In the 1982 survey, individual accommodations apparently reached into the tens of thousands of dollars, with 2 percent exceeding $20,000.

In addition, both surveys counted only a portion (and probably not the largest one) of what most economists would regard as the real cost of accommodations. In particular, they concentrated on out-of-pocket expenses: if an employer used in-house labor to build ramps, for example, only the cost of materials might show up. Rearranging other employees' schedules around a colleague's absences, an oft-sought accommodation, is free only in the sense that it doesn't involve writing a check. And in many cases the main cost of an adjustment—but a severe one—is managerial time and attention, which of course is expended more copiously in adversarial situations or cases with high legal risk.

Which brings up the most basic problem of all with the cheap-accommodation surveys—namely, that they were entirely circular. Employers had been conducting accommodations either voluntarily or, if they were covered by Section 504, under a good bit less legal pressure than ADA was expected to impose. The whole point of the new law was to give employees leverage to make the kinds of demands that would not previously have gotten as far as a hotline call.

If taken seriously, the surveys finding that most accommodations were cheap should have made a powerful argument against cost-no-object absolutism. They suggested that a law requiring only lower-cost accommodations would secure most of the benefits being promised for ADA, such as bringing disabled persons into jobs. Why not try going that far, and see how things worked before proceeding further? Of course, supporters weren't giving the time of day to such arguments.

———

The most familiar form of accommodation was the use of ramps, elevators, and floor-plan redesigns to assist wheelchair users, which alone would have kept employers busy, especially when applied to factory floors and other intensively designed spaces where small changes can have big productivity implications. Carolyn Lochhead's report in the *San Francisco Chronicle* found hospitals planned to spend $20 billion over ten years meeting ADA requirements, on top of earlier expenditures for Section 504, while hotels expected the costs to run $15,000 a room (a cost more thinkable for a downtown Hyatt than for a converted bed-and-breakfast on a side street). The construction industry didn't mind, especially since the economics of accessibility tended to tilt the balance toward tearing down old buildings and starting anew; many historic-preservation buffs were less pleased, though they generally held their tongues.

Bathroom and closet redesign and enlargement, allowance for turning radiuses at corners, and widening of passageways—standards for federal buildings had required hallways wide enough that two wheelchairs could pass each other—required not merely rearrangement of space but sacrifice of other uses, as in elderly housing where residents' other living space had to be squeezed to make way for the new standard bathrooms even if no one used a wheelchair. In company auditoriums as in movie theaters, ADA advocates demanded that wheelchairs be able to reach seats in all parts rather than be "concentrated near the main aisles and exits," even though this meant ripping out more regular seating and adding to evacuation worries. Wide-aisle mandates also hastened the market trend toward warehouse "superstores" and away from earlier bookstore or hardware-store formats whose need to fit into a small Main Street lot was apt to require cramp and clutter.

For all the talk of reasonableness, legally reliable exceptions and dispensations were few. Willingness to escort a handicapped visitor was considered no substitute for unattended accessibility; locations such as bowling alleys, ski lift platforms, and department-store display windows had to be converted because you could never tell when a wheelchair user might want to accompany someone else there.

Other physically disabled groups have seen fewer victories. Those affected by dwarfism (who are far less well organized than the wheelchair users) have been given much less accommodation, perhaps because retailers resist the idea of not being allowed to stock goods on high shelves. Some manufacturers are reportedly arranging for goods to be shipped in smaller packages for the aid of enfeebled warehouse personnel, so as to avoid more expensive customized power-lifting equipment. A perennial problem is the implicit conflict of needs between different handicapped groups: the curb cuts and clear gangways favored by wheelchair users are often less than ideal for the blind or for Alzheimer's patients, for whom a few physical barriers can be a good idea.

Interior design and signage falls under a great many peremptory dictates—Martha Stewart with a badge. To help those with failing vision and the confused, one ADA writer recommends all employers

THE AGE OF ACCOMMODATION

move to a generic Scandinavian-children's-bedroom look: functional color contrasts, no dark or single-color schemes, and certainly no "busy or changing patterns (especially on floors/carpeting)." Lighting must be bright enough to serve some ("minimum of 300 lumens in public areas") yet mellow enough for others ("eliminate harsh fluorescent colors/tints, cover bare bulbs, [and] relocate lamps away from eye level"; there may be a "nightclub" exception). Signs and informational postings in this homogenized, same-in-Kauai-as-Presque-Isle world should "avoid hard-to-read scripts" and "unusual fonts" and feature large type on everything, advises contributor John C. DeWitt in the Milbank Memorial Fund's 1991 *The Americans with Disabilities Act: From Policy to Practice*—a volume that, like most disabled-rights literature, itself curiously appears to be available only in regular-sized type.

Discussions of accommodative office equipment have focused on such computer-age marvels as voice recognition, talking screens, and eye-movement-driven hardware, as well as home offices and laptop computers. Given the lack of any clear guidance tying the quantum of expense incurred to the productive output of a given job, advocates have inevitably begun to demand that such items be provided not just for high-level scientific and executive posts but for routine clerical positions—every man a Stephen Hawking. Workers with attention-deficit disorder may require "memory aids, such as personal assistant devices, alarm clocks, stick-on notes and cue cards," notes a *Wall Street Journal* contributor, as well as such helps to concentration as "color-coding task files." Also needed may be "buddy systems" where workers keep each other on task, and written as well as oral instructions; of course, "all of these accommodations must be at the employer's expense."

The federal courts have generally emerged as somewhat less friendly toward cutting-edge ADA claims than advocates had hoped, and they have turned back a number of claims based on such handicaps as allergies. Thus a judge disallowed a claim by a Philadelphia letter sorter whose sensitivity to paper mites in her view required the Postal Service to furnish her with a paper-free environment. Those who believe themselves ultrasensitive to widely used chemicals and toiletries have had only scattered success at getting employers to rid the workplace of fumes from cleaning supplies, new carpets, error-correction fluid, and co-workers' after-shave and shampoo scents. "Our basic premise is that we who are disabled because of our chemical sensitivity need to have access, just like people in wheelchairs need to have access," explains Julia Kendall of the anti-perfume Citizens for a Toxic-Free Marin.

The issue that brought cost most prominently to the fore was demands for sign-language interpretation for the deaf. In its first enforcement action under the new law, the Bush administration went after the Becker CPA Review, which offers cram courses for aspiring accountants; the company had offered transcripts of its lectures and visual aids but had turned down a deaf applicant's request for a full-time sign translator on the grounds that it would cost several times as much as the tuition he'd be paying. Rather than fight the Justice Department, Becker folded and agreed to pay substantial damages as well as change its policy; a second applicant soon demanded two interpreters, relieving each other in spells lest they contract carpal-tunnel syndrome. In filing the action, the Bush administration threw the federal government's weight behind a principle with wide implications—namely, that the law may demand accommodations even if they wipe out not only the net profit a business might have hoped for from its dealings with a handicapped person, but many times the gross revenues. Economics writer Susan Lee reports that Texas ophthalmologist Roy Levit spends somewhere around $3,000 a year hiring obligatory signers at $50 an hour for deaf patients; total Medicaid reimbursement for an office visit is $8. (Dr. Levit was lucky in another respect, however; his office chairs already had adjustable arms, so he didn't have to spend thousands removing and reattaching them for the sake of extremely obese patients, as some doctors had.)

If businesses could be forced to hire signers at a cost many times higher than would render the transaction uneconomic for them, it was hard to see why employers should not be made to pay for accommodations costing far more than the salary of the disputed job. And sure enough, ADA-based demands are emerging for personal attendants: readers for the blind, page-turners and document signers for

THE AGE OF ACCOMMODATION

the handless, "job coaches" for the retarded, mobility attendants for the paralyzed, and so on. "Personal assistance services are the new, top-of-the-line issue for the disability-rights movement," writes Joseph Shapiro in *No Pity*. As with the voice-activated screens, expense is no object. "Most disabled people are beginning to believe they have a right to technology," says one advocate. "It is no longer a luxury."

Employers, rubbing their eyes in disbelief, have dubbed it "two for one" hiring: the EEOC has already announced that they may have to furnish page-turners and job coaches, and its guidelines have declined to spell out where if anywhere the process will stop. EEOC chairman Evan Kemp, the *New York Times* reported, "said the rules were left vague on the subject of personal attendants on the job to allow for the expansion of interpretations in the future." "Whether or not a personal assistant would be required for toileting and eating is going to have to be determined on a case by case basis," declared ADA drafter Chris Bell. "We didn't rule it out. . . . . It may be in some circumstances that will be required."

Employers' biggest accommodation challenge may arise less from the gravely disabled, who are relatively few in number and often far from keen on forcing their services on reluctant hirers, than from the general working population—people who manifest or announce less profound disabilities after they've already been at a job for a while.

Only 8 percent of employment complaints under the law have come from wheelchair users, and a mere 3 percent from the deaf or blind, bringing the total for these traditional disabilities to 14 percent, or one in six claims. The larger categories are the less visible or measurable impairments: 19 percent cite back problems, 12 percent neurological woes, and 12 percent emotional/psychological ailments, with substantial overlaps and gray areas between all three categories.

Without ever debating it as such, Congress seems to have devised a general federal law allowing workers to challenge uncomfortable working conditions—factories that are too hot or cold or drafty, schedules that are too demanding, jobs that involve too much heavy lifting or noise, exposure to bad weather, and so forth—provided the worker interprets the discomfort as an aggravation of an existing disability. That is often not a hard jump to make, since most of the population older than forty knows firsthand some of the ills to which flesh is heir: lower back discomfort, tendinitis, and a wide range of symptoms from insomnia to jumpiness that can be categorized as mental or neurological in origin. Since arthritis sufferers often experience "morning stiffness," employers should expect to allow them to show up late on their bad days, one ADA expert proposes.

Lawyers already get involved heavily in workers' compensation claims where the extent of disability is hard to document, and ADA has allowed them to play a case both ways. After his lawyers and hired doctors said he'd never work again, a Texas jury voted Santa Fe Railway worker Timothy McNeill $305,000 for his on-the-job back injury. Eight days later he demanded his old job back at the point of an ADA suit, though an incensed judge threw out the action when he learned of its timing. Railroad attorney Douglas Poole calls it "as common as dirt" for supposedly disabled workers to demand their jobs back once their disability verdict is in hand: "Now they try for a third bite at the apple by suing under the ADA."

Asthma is a reasonably well-defined and objective disorder, but it led to problematic results in the 1988 Section 504 case of *Ackerman* v. *Western Electric*. Western Electric's telephone cable installing operations called for a lot of work in confined and dusty spaces that was typically assigned to junior installers. This work might seem a peculiarly unsuitable career choice for an asthmatic person, but one applied anyway and sued for the right to skip the grungier jobs and proceed directly to the more desirable "low-dust" assignments. Federal judge William Schwarzer ruled that the unpleasant tasks were not an "essential" part of the job description—they could be assigned to her co-workers, after all.

Disabled applicants have come into wider conflict with co-workers over the question of "light-duty" posts. ADA doctrine appears to hold that though employers can't be forced to design new light-duty positions from scratch for disabled applicants, they must offer them any such positions that have already been created. Traditional practice in many demanding or dangerous lines of work, however, has been to create such positions only for veterans who have either been injured in the line of duty or, at a minimum, spent years facing down front-line dangers. Now, to the intense annoyance of unions and rank-and-filers alike, disabled applicants from off the street may have legal grounds to lay claim to such jobs from day one.

Applicants are also entitled to keep their disabilities secret until they get a job offer, at which point they can unveil their accommodation demands and send the employer scurrying to pull together experts for an impromptu combination of diagnostic consultation, rehabilitation-prospects seminar, and workplace-redesign brainstorming session. If the employer disagrees over whether the condition counts as a disability or whether accommodation is feasible on the worker's terms, it must then affirmatively withdraw its job offer, a step akin to painting a red bull's-eye on its chest with "SUE ME" written underneath.

If a worker wishes, he can continue to keep his disability secret from co-workers and supervisors, who are then merely apprised of what demands they must not make of him, what special perks he's entitled to, and what sorts of excuses they must accept from him. A federal agency director tells of arriving on the job and being handed a list of protected-group staffers, of whom she deduced some (because they were white males below the age of forty with no other evident qualification) were probably disabled. On asking whether this was true and what their disabilities might be, she was told that to disclose this information to her would violate their privacy; the important point was that they were protected.

Unionized companies face further problems if they yield to or even agree to discuss accommodation requests, because federal labor law prohibits bypassing the bargaining unit to cut special deals with individual workers. When an accommodation need emerges during a job interview, some think the best answer is for the employer to halt the interview and call in a shop steward—though the interviewer may not be entitled to tell the steward what the disability is, and though everyone agrees that the tension at a job interview escalates massively if more than two persons are present. Aware of the inconsistency, a federal task force tried to draft regulations coordinating ADA with labor law but gave up when neither responsible agency would budge; most authorities seem to expect the disabled advocates eventually to defeat the labor advocates on the issue.

––––––––

If the disabled can demand high-tech gear, training, or job redesign, the question arises: why shouldn't everyone be allowed to demand those things—especially if they'd make the difference between losing and holding on to a job? Many other aging workers would like large print, comfortable seating, and lower noise levels at work; why make them go through the rigmarole of proving they're disabled? A seriously debilitated person is apparently entitled to demand automatic lifting equipment to obtain a warehouse job; why should someone merely at the low end of normal range be denied the same job for lack of the same equipment? The answer can hardly be that it would be costly or disruptive in the one case, since we stop our ears to such considerations in the other. Nor can it be that good alternative jobs are available for the complainant in the one case, since employers are not permitted to raise such a defense in the other.

In fact, other areas of the new employment law are beginning to push employers in the direction of accommodating other sorts of workers. Thus businesses have downsized heavy tools, replaced equipment tote-belts with rolling carts, and mechanized formerly physical tasks in order to meet demands that they hire women. The Pentagon, the same goal in mind, has reportedly downgraded military police revolvers from .45 caliber to .38s (which are less effective, but more easily controlled) and has held back from upgrading from the 5.56-millimeter M-16 to the heavier NATO standard of 7.65 mm.

The Family and Medical Leave Act is another accommodation law that is used by many of the same workers who levy ADA demands; they may invoke either law to make the employer schedule around their doctor visits, for example. Academics have proposed extending the accommodation model to workers whose native language is not English. A much-cited 1991 *Yale Law Journal* article notes that we make employers accommodate "absence of speech" in the form of muteness, so why not make them accommodate "difference of speech"? Among the adjustments would be forcing employers to hire supervisors familiar with the languages their workers wish to speak in, and banning the practice of preferring workers with readily understood accents. If supervisors feel they aren't communicating adequately with workers, explains the Yale author, they might try "using sign language," written instructions, and "pictographs."

————

For years, the new employment law purportedly aimed at requiring employers to treat workers neutrally and impartially on their merits, all alike; even affirmative action was shaped in accord with this sort of officially declared goal. But now discrimination is quietly being redefined as the *failure* to treat each employee differently. Nondiscrimination really requires the most subtle and pervasive discrimination, or so the theory goes; treat all employees alike, and you've broken the law.

The implications are far-reaching. Under the new principle, complainants will be entitled to demand that the workplace be reshaped and sculpted to fit their needs, preferences, and sensibilities, which might be quite different from (and indeed at odds with) those of their co-workers. From the premise that workers own their jobs, it was an easy jump to the idea that they also owned the environment that went with the jobs and had the right to shape that environment to their pleasure—from its architectural and decorative to its climate-control and scheduling elements. And perhaps, as employees and co-workers began to discover, its human elements as well.

Chapter 7

ACCOMMODATING DEMONS

In October 1993 Northwest Airlines announced it had agreed to re-hire Norman Lyle Prouse, a former captain who'd completed an alcohol rehabilitation program. Experts quoted in the press praised the airline's decision, saying it reflected a modern trend of encouraging drinkers to enter treatment by letting them pick up their careers where they left off. The ADA also protected alcoholics who entered rehab, and though Northwest might have tried to take shelter under an exception, it was plainly bowing to the law's spirit. The head of the pilots' union at the airline also expressed satisfaction ("It's a very positive message"), but there was one discordant note: a company spokesman "acknowledged that some Northwest employees might be bitter" about the rehiring.

Their feelings could be traced to the morning of March 8, 1990, at Hector International Airport in Fargo, North Dakota. Someone had phoned the local Federal Aviation Administration office with a tip to check out the crew on tomorrow's 6:30 A.M. Flight 650 to Minneapolis. FAA inspector Verl Addison met the crew of three at the gate and didn't like their bloodshot eyes and the smell of liquor on their breath.

He suspected they'd broken the agency's "bottle-to-throttle" rule: no drinking within eight hours of takeoff. (Northwest had an even stricter in-house twelve-hour rule.) Also, Captain Prouse had a bad-looking gash on his forehead.

When Addison confronted the crew, one of them offered to take a blood-alcohol test, while Prouse simply went ahead with preparations for the flight. Addison, who wrongly thought he lacked authority to stop them, went to call his superiors in Chicago. After a brief wait, Prouse shoved back the Boeing 727 and took it down the runway, with fifty-eight passengers aboard. The plane lifted off into what developed into a difficult weather situation of sleet and rain.

Despite the bad weather the flight landed without incident in Minneapolis, where FAA officials were there to greet it. An investigation began. The crew admitted they'd had some drinks the night before in Fargo's Speak Easy lounge, where the tipster had seen them. How long had they stayed? In sworn statements, Prouse at first told investigators he'd left the bar by 8 or 8:30 P.M., and the others said they'd left earlier.

Then the results of blood tests came back. FAA rules prohibit flight crew members from operating planes at a blood level any higher than .04 percent alcohol; Minnesota law defined drunk driving at .10. The tests showed Prouse with an alcohol level of .13 percent, roughly that of a man who's downed eight drinks, and the other two crew members at .06 and .08. And these samples had been taken at 9:30 A.M., three hours after the plane had taken off. All three men were placed under arrest for flying under the influence.

It was an unprecedented black eye for Northwest, or any major airline in this country. A single drunken flyer was disgrace enough, but never had a whole crew been caught going off to get sloshed knowing they'd have to fly in the morning. For weeks comedians aimed gibes at the airline's "designated pilot" program, or the Northwest skipper who couldn't land until the ground stopped circling. Smart-aleck passengers offered drinks would ask for "whatever the captain's having."

When investigators reviewed the Speak Easy's receipts and talked with its servers, they found a story quite at odds with the sworn statements. In fact Prouse hadn't left the previous night until 11:30, by which time he'd tossed back somewhere between fifteen and nineteen rum and Diet Cokes. The gash in his forehead came near the end of the bout, when he fell off his chair to the ground ("a hell of a crack . . . I really hit my head big time," he said later). The other two left in mid-evening after sharing six or seven pitchers of beer. Asked about the inconsistencies, Prouse later testified he'd been distracted while giving the sworn statement. "I saw the end of my career ahead of me."

Entering rehab at once, the pilot expressed profuse regret, as he continues to do ("I am responsible for it, and I accept the responsibility. Period."). This did not keep him, however, from efforts to beat the criminal rap. Asked about his fall at the trial, he suggested the chairs were unsteady in the first place. *Aviation Week* dismissed as "ludicrous" his defense that as a seasoned alcoholic he'd built up a tolerance and thus could handle a high blood level, and as "equally lame" the crew's defense that after all they'd landed the plane without incident; the test of safety in the air is whether you're ready for the unexpected, as recalled in the old line about flying consisting of hours of boredom punctuated by moments of terror. When the crew appealed, Judge Frank Magill of the Eighth Circuit wrote that the case was "not even close" and that their lawyers' efforts to exclude the blood tests had sought to "twist the language" of irrelevant laws in a way "completely without merit." All three were sent to prison.

In the old days, such a case would have set off a shuffle on the pecking order of pilothood: some lucky stiff who'd been flying for years on a regional airline might get a crack at one of Northwest's coveted and highly paid pilot slots, a charter pilot might step up to a regional, and a crop duster or flyer of beach ad banners would get the hoped-for chance to fly charters. Perhaps the ex-offender would not actually have to make amends over a lifetime to live down his past, like Lord Jim; his experience in the majors would give him a big leg up. But the top-of-the-heap glamour of a leading airline would be a far-off goal.

In the 1990s, though, no such moral re-apprenticeship is called for. When Prouse emerged from prison after more than a year, the airline agreed to rehire him. And though at his trial he'd said he had no hope of ever flying again, his views apparently changed. Initially the airline assigned him to work as a ground trainer, but lawyer Peter Wold felt flying passengers again would be therapeutic for his client: "This whole thing will come full circle when Lyle is back flying again and the people on the airplane know exactly who is flying the plane. His recovery will be validated at that point." It didn't take long; in July 1995, Northwest quietly confirmed that Prouse had returned to passenger service.

———

"Certain classes of disability, including drug abuse, alcoholism and mental illness, have frequently been misunderstood and viewed in a negative light," laments the author of a 1989 academic history of handicap-rights law. Now all that's changed. As moderns we take care to avoid the fear, moralism, and other negative views that used to grip earlier generations when they contemplated the demons of human nature. And so the disabled-rights movement has found it easy to include mental as well as physical frailty in its crusade. "A professional with a mental disability is legally no different than a blue-collar worker with a serious back injury," declares ADA drafter Christopher Bell. Why should trouble controlling impulses be seen as different from trouble carrying packages? Why should inability to maintain sobriety or a rational flow of thought be seen as different from inability to reach a high shelf?

The havoc wrought by alcoholism and mental illness in the workplace has never been in doubt. "[E]rrors in judgment, aggressive behavior, insubordinate behavior, inability to get along with coworkers, absenteeism, [or] a quick temper" may "constitute notice to an employer that an employee has a mental disability," notes attorney Margaret Hart Edwards in the *Employee Relations Law Journal.* EEOC guidelines say disabilities which employers may have to accommodate include deficits in "thinking, concentrating, and interacting with other people." Many abusers are relatively good at maintaining job performance for long periods—at best a mixed blessing, since it can result in a higher level of damage when they finally do spin out, especially if they've gotten into habits of concealment. Unlike the problems of simple incompetence or bad character (which typically either are there or are not), alcoholic misconduct and serious mental disturbance tend to come and go, with plenty of ambiguous behavior: spectacular flameouts followed by evidently sincere vows to reform, more backsliding, and imaginative rationalization through second, third, and fourth chances. This festering, interminable quality was well suited to the ministrations of the new employment law.

Public-sector managers have long found the handling of addicted and disturbed employees a headache under civil service rules, one that began to worsen in the 1970s as HEW's Office of Civil Rights began interpreting the Rehabilitation Act of Section 504 fame to require substantial additional accommodation of such employees. The result was a remarkable series of cases in the courts and before the federal government's in-house Merit Systems Protection Board.

The MSPB got things rolling with a ruling ordering the General Services Administration to reinstate an alcoholic guard found sleeping on the job. It ruled that to "afford reasonable accommodation to an employee who is handicapped by alcoholism," an agency would have to offer him therapy with sick leave, and until it had done so it could not discipline him for related misconduct. Moreover, the offer had to be a rather formal one: GSA had told the guard at an earlier disciplinary hearing that help was available if he wanted it, but the board found this not pointed enough. Such a formal offer must be made "before [rather than simultaneously with] initiating any disciplinary action for continuing performance or misconduct problems related to his alcoholism."

The next turn of the screw came in the 1984 case of *Whitlock* v. *Donovan*. Judge Gerhard Gesell of the federal court in Washington ruled that not only must employees be given a chance at rehab, but one chance will hardly be enough: after all, "relapse is predictable in treatment of alcoholics." So, frequently, is an uncooperative attitude, as appeared in another case a few years later where a federal employee came to the workplace "in an intoxicated and belligerent condition. He created a disruption and was placed in lock-up for four days." He entered a recovery program that terminated him under the heading "rehabilitation failure," citing his "lack of commitment to the treatment process and poor attendance record." The Fourth Circuit ordered him reinstated, noting that "the disease of alcoholism requires that there be a continuum of treatment and that the alcoholic be permitted some opportunity for failure."

A 1985 case added the final horse to the merry-go-round. Once a worker agreed to enter rehab, the agency would have to wipe the slate clean of offenses committed during his wet period, since "reasonable accommodation of an alcoholic employee requires forgiveness of his past alcohol-induced misconduct." Given the right to relapse, this might have to happen again and again. The "legislative perception of alcoholism as a disease," in the court's view, meant that "behavioral problems [should be seen] as a part of the symptomatology rather than the product of volitional acts of dissipation."

———

In a cliché come to life, the employer that has most often been taken to court by employees with serious mental illness is the U.S. Postal Service.

Few American employers go as far as the Postal Service to provide workers with due process rights. If such procedures made for a satisfied workforce, you'd expect post offices to be veritable hives of contentment. Instead, disgruntled-worker-slays-five-wounds-eight-is-shot-by-police headlines have become to the Service what Nobel prizes used to be to the old Bell Labs. After enough such incidents—including the 1986 killing of fourteen at a post office in Edmond, Oklahoma, and shooting sprees by Michigan and California employees on the same day in 1993—the tendency was enshrined in slang: someone who snapped violently had "gone postal."

Charlotte F., who suffered from paranoid schizophrenia, worked for ten years at the post office in a Cincinnati suburb. During that time she repeatedly displayed what a judge later called a "belligerent attitude towards her coworkers and also towards the public," but "was never at any time disciplined or reprimanded for such attitudes." Off the job she was arrested for assault, disorderly conduct, and passing bad checks. During her last four years of work she repeatedly went off her medication, taking 464 days of unpaid leave (which included involuntary hospitalizations).

In early 1976 she showed up at the office of Ohio governor James Rhodes carrying a concealed weapon, got in a fight with guards, and had to be subdued and hospitalized. The Postal Service's response was firm: it made her promise to stay on her medication in the future. Later the same year she again was physically subdued trying to force her way into Rhodes's office. The American Postal Workers Union again negotiated her reinstatement.

Like many who grow frustrated trying to get things done on the state level, Charlotte F. then raised her sights to Washington. In 1979 she tried to force her way into the White House, assaulting a Secret Service agent and winding up in St. Elizabeth's, the federal hospital. That did it. The Postal Service finally discharged her—only three months after the White House incident, an eyeblink in the world of postal tenure. But thanks to the new Rehabilitation Act, she had even more rights, which she used to tie up the Postal Service for a few years by pursuing a losing lawsuit to completion in federal court. Troubled persons, it seems, sometimes are better at maintaining litigation than at maintaining other things in their lives.

Postal unions, incidentally, have their own explanation for the rash of violence. They contend the cause is stress and frustration brought on by autocratic management practices, and that the solution is to institute more due process and job security for their members.

———

ADA supporters were not keen to get into a big public debate about alcohol, drug, and mental illness coverage, or to draw attention to the track record of the issue at federal agency employers. For the most part, they preferred to dwell on safe themes such as the undeniably high costs such disorders impose in the workplace (which, in the case of mental disorders, one federal agency declared with a great show of precision to be $57 billion a year) without confronting the question of whether the law would raise or lower those costs.

At the same time, advocates made a concession or two suggesting that private employers might not have to go quite as far in accommodating these disorders as the federal government had been obliged to. They put in language, for example, seemingly assuring employers that they could hold alcoholics and drug abusers to the same standards as nonusers. There should be "no fear," said Maryland Democratic Rep. Steny Hoyer, "that we are imposing on an employer . . . someone who is abusing alcohol . . . that impacts on [his] performance." They also agreed to disclaim legal protection for proven *current* users of illegal drugs, while strengthening it for those who presented themselves as past users only.

Some weeks before the House ADA vote, a worker with a long record of threats and irrational behavior massacred eight colleagues and wounded twelve at the Standard Gravure printing plant in Louisville before killing himself; according to published reports, he'd previously invoked handicap law to win reinstatement. A few ADA critics cited the incident as the kind of thing worth worrying about, but indignant mental health advocates suggested that to raise such questions was to tar all persons with psychiatric illness as being like the Louisville killer. This logic was apparently considered unanswerable, and the issue went nowhere in the press.

Advocates did make one shrewd concession by agreeing to exclude a named list of conditions such as pyromania, kleptomania, compulsive gambling, and various conditions related to sexual behavior and gender identity. This ensured opponents could not take advantage of a couple of talk-show-fodder cases that had already come up under state law, like that of the transsexual engineer who sued Boeing when it ordered him not to use the women's restroom or wear highly feminine apparel at work until after his surgery. (That case featured several reversals until the aircraft company finally won in the Washington Supreme Court.)

Though everyone claimed to have moved away from moralistic views of mental health, the listed conditions excluded from coverage in fact had nothing in common except being sensational and unsympathetic. In no way did the selection reflect any reasoned judgment of which conditions are involuntary or hard to accommodate in the workplace; most employers surely would find it easier to work with the occasional bisexual employee (excluded) than the occasional paranoid schizophrenic (covered). The result was a meaningless, arbitrary patchwork of exceptions: an irrational urge to destroy the property of one's employer is legally protected under the ADA unless one insists on inflicting the damage by fire, which would bring it under the named exception for pyromania.

———

Despite advocates' hopes of avoiding tabloid controversy over the ADA's mental and substance-abuse coverage, such a case occurred anyway in Hamden, Connecticut, not long after the law went into effect.

Picked up twice by the police for drunk driving, school superintendent David Shaw had pleaded guilty and got off with a fine and license suspension. When it became clear the press would report embarrassing details of the second arrest—he'd been picked up leaving an adult bookstore, dressed in what appeared in a police photo to be women's clothing—he proceeded to flee the state "without his Prozac," as the *Hartford Courant* put it, and made himself unreachable for about two weeks in April, in the thick of the school year.

Local television went wild covering the women's clothing angle, but it would be wrong to think of Hamden (a New Haven suburb, and a rather liberal community by most national standards) as some calloused town without pity. As mayor Lillian Clayman pointed out, many townspeople initially felt sympathetic toward Shaw but changed their minds on seeing how he behaved on his return. "He walked off the job and left us high and dry," said board chairman DeWitt Jones. "Then he came back with a gunslinging lawyer to browbeat us."

It worked, too. Attorney Hugh Keefe, who'd previously gotten the town's police chief reinstated in a suit that cost the town an estimated $600,000 to defend, said he told the board, "You can have it one of two ways: I will work with you in effecting a smooth transition of David back to his job as superintendent of schools, or I will sue you." The resulting charges included a claim of alcoholism as disability (his client had, of course, entered rehab by this point), as well as the usual charm bracelet of employment-suit etceteras: breach of contract, defamation, interference with contractual rights, intentional infliction of emotional distress, civil rights violations, and violation of federal Education Department regulations. The suit demanded punitive damages. Two months later Hamden officials settled, for a reported

$240,000. The town's attorney said that "termination would have been difficult because of the ADA."

———

The handling of suspected tipplers on staff soon emerged as one of the trickier ADA areas. One newsletter advises employers to see a lawyer before taking "any adverse employment action against suspected alcoholic employees"; to publish a policy, as on sexual harassment; to train employees how to recognize alcoholism (one early case having hit a big company with punitive damages for failing to do so); and to allow the employee a full measure of paid and unpaid leave under both the ADA and the Family and Medical Leave Act. On the giving of time off, the indicated course is to emulate the Ontario arbitrators who ordered the city of Toronto to give Emmerson Phillips sick pay, rather than making him take a vacation day, after a hangover kept him out of work one Monday. ("It's not just a day's pay," he told the *Toronto Star.* "It's the principle. . . . I was sick and they should have believed my story that I was sick.") One court applying Section 504 proposed that if an employer would have allowed a worker a set number of leave days to recover from a heart attack, it should give him exactly the same number for an alcoholic binge.

Especially vexing for the employer was the question of when, whether, and how to confront a suspected abuser. Courts had already ruled that the federal government as an employer had a positive duty to confront. Thus a court awarded $150,000 to Clarence Ferguson, saying the National Marine Fisheries Service should have called him on the carpet about his pint-of-gin-a-day habit. Ferguson missed 389 days of work between 1980 and 1983, but the agency said it had never been entirely sure what his problem was: co-workers testified that he hadn't smelled of booze, slurred words, or been caught sneaking drinks.

Of course, if employers do lead glazed-looking workers into the personnel office and pull out a Breathalyzer, they set themselves up for suits over privacy invasion, defamation, and similar outrages. In a 1988 case an employer confronted a worker who'd been performing poorly and whose wife had expressed concern about his drinking, only to be hit with $100,000 punitive damages when it turned out his problem was depression rather than booze.

Thus it seems necessary for firms to address problems without identifying them, hinting heavily and getting their meaning across through the use of significant pauses, like a fine stage actor. Managers should "not even . . . mention drinking, let alone diagnose alcoholism," warns *Business Week*. The goal, says the McNair law firm's South Carolina employment newsletter, is to "help the employee unilaterally realize his problem" and yet "if possible, confine any alcohol-related discussions to the employee's job performance." The Merit Systems Protection Board, in reinstating the snoozing guard, tied itself in verbal knots trying to explain how this could be done. A supervisor "need not confront him with the . . . belief that the employee has a drinking problem," yet "must make the employee aware in general terms that the supervisor suspects the employee has a problem affecting his performance or conduct, and that the supervisor recommends that the employee participate in a particular rehabilitation or counseling program which is available to him." Perhaps the answer is to propose he enter an arduous detox program just as a lark or as a valuable life experience, and not because he has anything to be detoxified from.

ADA practice was happy to borrow selectively from the tenets of the recovery/rehabilitation movement, which, resembling an industry and a religion by turns, had transformed popular American attitudes toward abuse and addiction. Many versions of rehab favor what they see as less punitive employer policies meant to coax drinkers out of denial by showing them they have less to lose by admitting their problem. Such employer policies are not without ambiguity as regards their effect on long-term intemperance, since while encouraging those in trouble to grab for the life preserver they may also reduce the disincentive to drift into trouble in the first place. (Northwest had implemented one such understanding policy well before its crew in Fargo took off on Flight 650.) Still, lawmakers were happy to seize on this idea and give it binding force.

At the same time, the logic of the Americans with Disabilities Act at times runs counter to some other ideas popular in the movement.

Some views of recovery assign a key role to a climactic confrontation scene in which not just one but a whole cross-section of people from the target's life tell him in no uncertain terms that he has to change; diplomatic, one-on-one approaches are not thought to achieve the same impact. But the needed degree of verbal aggression and bluntness can easily land an employer in a defamation/emotional distress suit, and cooperating in any way beforehand with the worker's family is fraught with legal dangers ranging from defamation to intrusion into private or off-job concerns. It is much safer for supervisors to conduct a work-only confrontation in measured if not timid tones, and to make sure not a word gets to the family about it.

Much rehab wisdom holds that the most effective jolt in getting an addict to go straight is to threaten his job; the new law tends to postpone that threat and deprive the employer of control over its timing. Many also suspect that clients who enter rehab strategically—as a condition of a suspended sentence, for example—do less well than highly motivated volunteers convinced that their lives, marriages or jobs are truly at risk. Rehab entered on the advice of one's employment lawyer may count as being more like the former than the latter.

Notwithstanding the reassurances of some in Congress, it soon became clear that the ADA was indeed going to require employers to forgive a good deal of alcohol-related misconduct so long as employees were willing to enter rehab. A Dallas jury socked the Coca-Cola company with a $7.1 million verdict (although damage limits ensure that the eventual payout will be less) for firing an executive who entered rehab three days after what the company called "violent and threatening behavior" at a party with working colleagues.

Courts and many others show great faith in the idea of rehabilitation, yet its success rates are painfully modest. Even the most widely admired programs have high relapse rates, and most first-timers appear to backslide no matter which program they enter. What happens then? The employer wins the right to begin the laborious process of documentation again and negotiate the same legal shoals over the timing and content of the next confrontation. A *Berkeley Journal of Employment and Labor Law* article predicts that despite the seemingly limiting clauses in ADA about the right to hold alcoholics to prevailing work standards, "judges may adopt the *Whitlock* analysis"—with its right to relapse—as consistent with the law's "spirit."

———

One of the first widely reported cases on ADA coverage of mental disorders arose at GTE, the giant telecommunications company. Admirers of America's litigation system disapprove of the telling of "horror stories" about its workings, but presumably they wouldn't count the case of *Joe H.* v. *GTE* as being such a story. After all, the good guys did win eventually.

The case arose at a Tampa subsidiary, where a rash of sneak thievery from purses and desks had been traced to Joe H., a $47,000-a-year team leader. A police detective led him away in handcuffs; Joe later admitted stealing thousands of dollars from fellow workers.

For whatever reason, the company didn't see fit to fire Joe on the spot. But he'd left his briefcase behind, and the next day a colleague opened it. The loaded handgun inside was the last straw. Whatever GTE's views on theft, it had a firm policy against firearms on the premises.

Then Joe's lawyer called. My client has made some mistakes, he said, but he's been suffering from a mental disability brought about by a chemical imbalance in his brain. The ADA requires "reasonable accommodation" of such infirmities, which should mean giving him another chance to behave himself on proper medication.

If GTE thought this case was frivolous and sure to be thrown out of court, it was in for a shock. "When poor judgment is a symptom of a mental or psychological disorder, it is defined as an impairment that would qualify as a disability under the ADA," ruled federal judge Elizabeth Kovachevich. Rejecting GTE's summary judgment motion, she sent the suit to trial, with language strongly hinting Joe would win there. But his luck did not hold: at trial a different judge presided, and he chose to award GTE a directed verdict (which meant Joe would lose even if the court accepted his account completely). Still, the second ruling in no way wiped off the books the legal message of the first:

workers in Joe's position are entitled to get past summary judgment, and their employers have to take their chances on trial. In practice, suits that can get that far usually command very respectable settlement offers.

A few bits of limiting verbiage in the ADA and its implementing regulations had been offered as reassurance to nervous employers, but Joe H.'s case revealed how insubstantial these limits were. For example, a company can supposedly dismiss a worker who poses a "direct threat" to others. Judge Kovachevich gave this clause a narrow reading, saying GTE could invoke it only after assembling the "best available objective evidence" about both worker and job, including the "most current" medical opinion from a parade of "doctors, rehabilitation counselors, or physical therapists" as the case might be. It would have to show that the risk was definitely a major one, couldn't be reduced by any other means, and so forth—the kind of advance impact analysis you might expect of someone planning to dam Yellowstone. GTE hadn't done anything like that. Likewise, the EEOC had seemed to concede that the ADA did not automatically cover anger or insubordination as long as they were within "'normal' range." But since bringing a loaded gun to a quiet suburban office was hardly normal, Joe was covered on that score. The result was to reward extreme and bizarre behavior: an outburst at a supervisor would be subject to ordinary discipline if the circumstances were so provoking that anyone might have done the same thing, but the law would kick in to provide protection if it had been entirely unprovoked and irrational.

———

Among the early results of the Americans with Disabilities Act were successful suits to keep medical and other licensing boards from asking applicants about their alcohol, drug, and mental health histories. A high share of misconduct by doctors is linked to substance abuse and mental illness, but a federal court ruled that even if physicians conceded they'd had problems of this sort, the New Jersey Board of Medical Examiners had no right to pursue the matter at license renewal time. Many such boards use disclosure of past problems not as an automatic bar to practice but as a way to make sure an applicant is offered extra help, explain an otherwise inexplicable pattern of complaints or violations, and aid in catching recurrences early.

When the *Wall Street Journal* reported that some state bar screening panels were continuing to inquire about bar applicants' mental health, fearing that lawyers would miss clients' court dates or squander trust funds, executive director Peter Ross of the National Foundation for Depressive Illness reacted angrily in a letter, saying "stupid, bigoted" questions of this sort displayed the panels' "ignorance and bias." "Someone suffering from a properly treated so-called mental illness," he added, "is no less likely to be a good and responsible attorney than someone who is being properly treated for diabetes, heart disease, or myriad other medical problems." Leaving aside the curious use of *so-called* by a spokesman for a group that presumably believes mental illness to be a genuine phenomenon, this line of argument would seem to assume that proper treatment of a lawyer's mental illness either (1) has a 100 percent success rate, or (2) when it falls short of success, has consequences no more serious for his clients than the failure of his therapy for other conditions. Yet while a lawyer fighting a losing battle against diabetes or heart disease may be in the worst kind of trouble on a personal level, most of his clients would probably consider their legal interests in considerably more danger if they learned that he was fighting a losing battle against paranoia or mania.

The view that to be under treatment for a mental illness is functionally equivalent to not having it at all runs perfectly parallel to the assumption that by entering rehab, an alcoholic is miraculously rendered no more hazardous an employee than the lifelong teetotaler at the next desk. Indeed, a job or accommodation demand in the mental health case will commonly be premised on a worker's promise to stay on medication, just as the drug or alcohol user will promise to stay *off* his inverse kind of medication.

Many patients, of course, do get excellent results on therapy, and some are restored to lifelong good health. In other cases, for ill-understood reasons, mental maladies lift on their own and go away permanently even without therapy. And it is tempting to regard as success stories the ADA's role in helping some patients who have done well on therapy; it has protected, for example, a manic-depressive man with a good record on lithium against an employer that did not want to hire him as a crane operator given the machinery's unusual destructive potential. Unfortunately, it is impossible to know which patients will achieve permanent recovery and which will relapse. Just as drug and alcohol rehab participants suffer a high relapse rate, so are mental patients known as the arch-example of pharmaceutical "noncompliance," going off their medication at a high rate—the vagrant urges arising from a not-perfectly-controlled illness often contributing to the suddenly insistent impulse to stop taking the drug.

Detailed psychiatric evaluations can be highly useful in predicting which patients will do well on therapy and which will not. Unfortunately, the usual tangle of legal liabilities—privacy, exclusion of off-job information, and the reluctance of ex-employers and others with relevant information to risk defamation liability by supplying it—discourages companies from pursuing such inquiries. The alternative, presumably, is to accept a note from the employee's doctor.

———

Few laws have done as much as the Americans with Disabilities Act to make a note from your doctor something you can take to the bank. Much ADA discussion has proceeded as if mental and emotional disorders were as easily and objectively diagnosed as chicken pox. For some "classic" mental illnesses there is indeed a fair consensus regarding diagnosis and treatment, but the bounds of many others are almost entirely a function of line-drawing by psychiatric professionals. "If you look at [the diagnostic manual]," Yale professor Jay Katz has conceded, "you can classify all of us under one rubric or another of mental disorder."

Over fifteen years, the number of listed maladies in the American Psychiatric Association's *Diagnostic and Statistical Manual of Mental Disorders* has risen from 106 to more than 300. In its pages, we all can recognize possibly symptomatic troubles of our own: insomnia or sensitivity to criticism, anxiety or lack of appetite, giddiness or glumness, jealousy or torpor. Code 315.2, "Disorder of Written Expression," covers those whose grammar falls short. Code 313.81, "Oppositional Defiant Disorder," describes children who give adults a hard time. Depending on where the line is drawn, estimates of the annual prevalence of mental disorder range up to 25 percent and beyond.

Personality disorders listed in the manual come in ten varieties, two short of a horoscope. They include Avoidant Personality Disorder ("social inhibition, feelings of inadequacy, and hypersensitivity to negative evaluation"), Histrionic Personality Disorder ("excessive emotionality and attention-seeking"), Narcissistic Personality Disorder ("a pattern of grandiosity, need for admiration, and lack of empathy"), and Antisocial Personality Disorder ("disregard for, and violation of the rights of others"). Inconsistent display of bits of various patterns may signal Borderline Personality Disorder ("instability in interpersonal relationships, self-image and affects, and marked impulsivity"). The tenth, a floater, is "Personality Disorder Not Otherwise Specified." As a guide to talk therapy, or a way of categorizing what can go wrong when personality quirks turn into something worse, this approach may have its uses. As law to be enforced against resistant parties, it's a formula for perennial uncertainty as to who is covered and how—and for endless shootouts between costly hired-gun experts.

Prominent among the newer afflictions is attention-deficit disorder (ADD) and its offshoot, attention-deficit/hyperactivity disorder (ADHD). *Wall Street Journal* contributor Gary Eisler makes it sound easy for an employer to recognize ADD sufferers. Such workers

> get into power struggles, which they seem to prefer to negotiation; they have bad judgment, shoot from the hip, act impulsively. They become irritable, especially when interrupted or forced to make changes. They procrastinate. Their desks are a mess; they can't find things in the files. You can have what you think is a conversation with them and five minutes later you realize they haven't heard a word you said. They forget people's names. They don't like to go through established channels or respect set procedure. They start projects with a flourish and get bored or overwhelmed before they finish. They are always in a daze, getting distracted from one thing to another.

ADD began as a diagnosis in children, where a respectable body of opinion thinks it may constitute a distinctive condition; only recently has it been suggested that adults may also suffer from it. Even among children, no laboratory tests are generally accepted as diagnostic for the condition, and no one agrees as to at what point it shades from being a mere personality type into an actual disorder. Similarly, there is no consensus as to what it signifies that many children appear to achieve more and give their families less trouble when they are given such drugs as Ritalin and Prozac.

Adult ADD, despite its shaky status in scientific circles, is off and running as a legal workplace excuse. In 1994 the federally funded Job Accommodation Network found ADD calls rising to one or two a day, from one or two a week just a year earlier. A salesman fired because he couldn't follow verbal directions invoked ADD and won a settlement, while Steve Howe, banned from baseball for life because of cocaine violations, beat the rap in arbitration by blaming ADHD. The range of accommodations for ADD workers includes such perks as private offices, more personal contact with supervisors, and longer work deadlines. Eisler adds, "It may be in the company's best interest to accommodate if ADD is only suspected."

———

Mental disorders come in great variety. The Seventh Circuit ordered the Environmental Protection Agency to accommodate a worker whose numerous psychiatric problems included narcolepsy, the tendency to fall asleep at inappropriate times. The agency, it said, should be willing to tolerate an "occasional nap." Other accounts confirm that some employers have begun to accommodate narcoleptic employees by setting aside nap space for them. Narcolepsy and obesity were the protected categories in a jury award of $610,000 under Michigan discrimination law against a suburban Detroit hospital; the prevailing plaintiff (rather unnervingly) worked as a surgeon.

Momentously, employers "may be required . . . to reduce stress as a reasonable accommodation," as the *Employee Relations Law Journal* puts it, citing a 1991 case where a retarded and emotionally disabled Veterans Administration staffer experienced "difficulties with interpersonal relationships, extreme sensitivity to derogatory comments and criticism, anxiety, and emotional outbursts":

The court held that the employee was entitled to reasonable accommodation in the form of sensitivity training of coworkers which included training in appropriate remarks and jokes to make in the workplace to workers with disabilities. The court additionally required the employee's supervisor to use care in discipline to avoid direct criticism or undue stress.

Stress-accommodation cases have gone both ways. The Sixth Circuit ruled against a Tennessee Valley Authority employee whose doctor's note described him as "a very depressed man whose self esteem is very fragile. . . . If there is the slightest hint of rejection or criticism, he becomes extremely anxious and depressed." (The court declined to order the agency to spare him "the slightest hint of rejection or criticism.") On the other hand, Pacific Gas & Electric lost a $1.1 million award after an arbitrator ruled it should have agreed to reduce the work hours of a depressed attorney and make other adjustments. The man's lawyer had demanded not only a guaranteed satisfactory work review for his client but also a change of boss: "A person with an illness like that may respond better in a supportive environment than working for someone who has a critical style."

The Postal Service has remained in the forefront of mental health case law under the ADA. It did win a case against a Massachusetts custodian with "explosive personality disorder" who was in the habit of throwing furniture and screaming obscenities and admitted to having homicidal thoughts about his supervisor. But it lost the case of a postal worker in Portland, Maine, whose belligerence and volatility were attributed to "post-traumatic stress disorder." "The Postal Service could have fired Lussier for his irascibility alone," a judge concluded, but in this case the supervisor had acted from fear that the man's mental condition might lead him to violence—and that was an improperly discriminatory motive.

Of course, not all such claims succeed. Depression did not keep a Florida judge from being kicked off the bench after being caught shoplifting. A Maine professor lost after blaming his pattern of sexual harassment on a "handicap of sexual addiction," and a Boston University professor fared little better when he attributed multiple charges of the same offense to mood-altering prescription drugs that "loosened his inhibitions." A Northwestern University professor was considered unlikely to prevail in blaming "severe depression and procrastination behavior" for his action in pocketing $33,000 worth of his mother's Social Security checks for five years after she died.

———

"In retrospect," columnist John Leo has written, "the 1980s seem to have ushered in a golden age of exoneration." Following the famed "Twinkie defense," which secured a reduced sentence for a San Francisco political assassin, baseball great Pete Rose blamed his woes on compulsive gambling, while American University president Richard Berendzen's penchant for placing obscene phone calls turned out to be a case of uncontrollable impulse disorder. Although ousted United Way chief William Aramony did not succeed in blaming brain shrinkage "common in older men" for having diverted charitable funds to pay for his girlfriend's New York City apartment, a Maryland weightlifter did escape jail time on burglary and arson charges by citing "organic personality syndrome" brought on by use of anabolic steroids. Caffeine dependence—that is, coffee jitters—turned up as a criminal defense, while tax nonpayment was successfully blamed on alcoholism and the agreeably circular "failure-to-file syndrome." A judge released former FBI agent and convicted Soviet spy Richard Miller after nine years of a twenty-year sentence, citing his weight gain and depressed mood. After a soured love affair led New York chief judge Sol Wachtler into extortion and threatened kidnapping, psychologist John Money said a "law-and-order treatment" of Wachtler's problem was "the equivalent of making it a crime to have epileptic spells." A Boston judge let off a man who viciously and unprovokedly beat up the city police commissioner's chauffeur, on the grounds he hadn't taken his lithium for two months. The commissioner was described as "a little upset": "If someone gets drunk and commits a crime, they get convicted," said a spokesman. "This guy goes off his medication and does not get convicted?"

It seemed unlikely that the workplace could resist what the wider society was accepting. Yet in one case—which stands virtually alone—public outcry led to reversal of a decision to reinstate. In 1991 the official Massachusetts Commission Against Discrimination ruled against the South Shore town of Duxbury for improperly refusing to rehire firefighter David Freeman after his treatment for depression. It ordered the town to reinstate Freeman, accommodate his ongoing emotional difficulties by rearranging his job duties, and hand over back pay and other damages eventually totaling $500,000.

Carol Zoroya learned about the ruling on the radio. The news took her back to the early hours of May 13, 1984, after she'd told Freeman she wanted a divorce. That night she awoke to find him standing over her, a club in his hand. His attack fractured her skull in six places, broke her nose and other bones, and left her permanently deaf in one ear. She moved out, but Freeman continued to stalk and harass her for months. After her complaints the town dismissed him from his public safety position, perhaps reasoning that local women might not see him as a suitable rescuer in an emergency at their homes.

Freeman beat the criminal rap on a plea of temporary insanity (Zoroya had moved out of state and was not present) and was sent to the state mental hospital. Its curative powers were commendable, because after staying only a month or two he was declared fit to reenter society—and to demand his old job back, under the state's handicap-rights law. Because he wanted to be relieved of emergency medical treatment duties, he also added an accommodation claim, citing what his lawyer said were continuing flareups of his condition.

It was an easy win. The town hadn't proved Freeman was physically incapable of performing his duties, nor that some specific and direct harm would be sure to result from letting him back, nor that it couldn't meet his accommodation request. The commission awarded him the works: back pay, "front pay" for lost future work, bonuses, longevity pay, and holiday pay, along with $20,000 in emotional-distress damages based on the town's having resisted his claim in the first place. The commission generously allows 12 percent interest to accrue on such claims (compared with a national inflation rate around 3 percent), a practice that helped bring the total as of 1993 to around a half-million dollars. The town of Duxbury, whose annual budget runs around $27 million, prepared to cut services to cover the award.

Handicap-rights litigators seemed to find the case nothing special.

THE AGE OF ACCOMMODATION

"Perceiving someone to be crazy and treating him in an adverse manner is against the law," said MCAD regional director Jerrold Levinsky. The award was "run of the mill," said attorney Jane Alper of the Disability Law Center, which represented Freeman. "Mental illness frightens a lot of people."

Had Carol Zoroya not been listening to the radio that day, Freeman's award might indeed have passed routinely into the archives. But Zoroya talked to the press, who found her story compelling: she had moved twenty-three times and held thirty or forty different jobs since the beating. "It was bad enough that I never saw him go to jail," she told the *Boston Globe*. "But to have him basically paid for what he did to me. . . . How do you live with that?" Following a press outcry, MCAD reversed itself and denied Freeman's award. It was the only time it had reversed one of its decisions in its forty-seven-year history.

Chapter 8

SURPRISE FAREWELLS

Sometime around the late 1970s, a new phenomenon began to pop up in the American workplace. An employer would quite abruptly announce it was offering long-time employees a deal: if they left its payroll at once, they'd get a special benefit package that included enriched or accelerated pension benefits, "bridge" health insurance, a lump sum payable up front, or some combination of these. Since older workers with long service were prime targets, many of these offers were initially labeled "early retirement," a description that changed to "early out" or "accelerated departure" after it was observed that workers in their early fifties, forties, and even thirties were getting bought out as well.

Within a few years the idea was cropping up everywhere. During the 1980s something like four-fifths of the nation's largest firms announced early-out plans, and the pace continued strong into the 1990s. State and federal governments joined in: one Postal Service offer yielded 46,000 retirements, the Pentagon used buyouts to shed civilian staff as the cold war wound down, and the Clinton administration's "reinventing government" scheme leaned heavily on the idea in hopes of trimming other overstaffed agencies. The University of California at Berkeley used buyouts to cut its faculty by more than a quarter over three years. New offers multiplied when the economy entered a recession, but continued at a surprising clip even when it returned to apparent prosperity.

The point of the offers, everyone agreed, was to let employers cut payroll without resort to involuntary layoffs. Described that way, the idea sounded appealing enough, since benefits in the plans were often generous. One survey found an average lump sum payment of $38,000, and the value of deals as a whole can exceed a year's pay when pension enrichments and other goodies are added. General Motors, for example, threw in a $10,000 voucher toward the purchase of a new car.

On closer inspection, however, the offers had some less attractive features. To begin with, employers typically announced them as a surprise, kept under close wraps beforehand. Like a blue-light special at K-Mart ("Attention, shoppers!"), they had a preset expiration date, usually affording workers only a few weeks before the "window" would snap shut. Bad luck or rushed decision-making could thus cost plenty: retire a little too early or too late, and you'd kick yourself for a long time. The plans were also precisely targeted, sometimes segmented by departments, job titles, and years of service or simply listing the names of eligible individual workers. Either way, some who'd have liked to receive offers didn't get them, while others saw their naming as an unsubtle signal that their services were no longer necessary. "Some people complain because they were included, and others because they weren't," says Boston College law professor Judith McMorrow.

Almost always, the offers were framed with an elaborate show of voluntariness: no one was being required to accept them, and management made no recommendations to who should or shouldn't do so. Still, there were often unpleasant hints or outright announcements that the voluntary plan was just an initial step; phase two might include involuntary cuts on less attractive terms. Details about that phase would follow after the window closed.

The new plans had other off-putting overtones as well. Some old-timers sensed the opposite of a welcome mat: it almost seemed that the longer you'd been around, the more eager the company was to show you the door. Other evidence pointed in the same direction. Thus the *Wall Street Journal* reported that firms had quietly but steadily done away with "longevity awards," the gifts and recognition ceremonies by which they used to honor workers who'd reached twenty or twenty-five years of service. Workers quoted in the report saw the trend as one more sign that community was a thing of the past, the modern world having reduced everything to the cash nexus. "This is the age of the free market," said one.

But actually this isn't the age of the free market—not in this department, at least. Since 1967 the handling of older workers has come under a complex and ever more stringent body of *age discrimination* law. This law was supposed to educate employers about the hidden talents of older workers on their payrolls, but the lesson has curiously not sunk in; indeed, they seem to have rushed off in the opposite direction, making veteran workers feel less a part of the enterprise than before. The story of the Age Discrimination in Employment Act is a story of the workings of the law of unintended consequences.

―――――

The campaign to extend oppression theory to older persons always did tempt the gods of absurdity. Far from being denied the vote or civic responsibilities, the old have long voted in great numbers and dominated public office. The great majority of legal distinctions based on age, from Social Security eligibility down to discount bus tickets, work to the benefit of the supposedly persecuted group. For reasons of this sort the Supreme Court has flatly declined to treat age as a "suspect class" needing, as the formula goes, "extraordinary protection from the majoritarian process." In polls, elderly persons themselves have expressed little inclination toward the view that they are an oppressed minority group.

What about employment? When they choose to participate in the labor force, older workers do very well as a group—with low jobless rates, high earnings, heavy overrepresentation in sought-after managerial posts, and so forth. "It is as if the vast majority of persons who established employment policies and who made employment decisions were black, federal legislation mandated huge transfer payments from whites to blacks, and blacks occupied most high political offices in the nation," writes Richard Posner in his book on aging. "It would be mad in those circumstances to think the nation needed a law that would protect blacks from discrimination in employment."

Like those in all other age groups, of course, older workers encounter distinctive problems arising from their stage in life; while opening many new options, the advance of years inevitably limits others. Some lines of work are oriented toward youth: chasing that fickle market is often seen as central to much of the advertising, fashion, and entertainment businesses. Pyramidal corporate hierarchies can also pose a problem: if competition for promotion is a defining force in a company's culture and there are fewer jobs at each level up, then either some of those passed over for advancement will have to depart or else the whole organization will age in place.

Among the perennial problems of older workers is the difficulty in finding a comparable new job when displaced from a good former one: their stock of experience, a key factor in high pay levels, may relate too closely to the particular company or industry they leave behind. Employers may in addition worry that the older hire will retire soon after large sums have been invested to bring him on board; obsolescence of skills is also a natural concern, since from both the worker's and the employer's point of view there is less incentive to spend time and energy learning new skills that may get only a few years' use. Many hirers also hesitate to place younger supervisors in charge of older deputies, a sentiment that obviously works strongly in favor of the mature as a group (as would be clear if the same reluctance were seen in other demographic combinations) but can redound to the detriment of oldsters who happen to want the lower-level jobs.

Some commentators have sniffed oppression in the much-deplored practice of "stereotyping"—widely defined as the forming of generalizations about members of a protected group, whatever the accuracy of those generalizations. Thus managers are said to preconceive of older persons as more set in their ways than youngsters, less up on the latest fashions, less likely to enjoy long hours or boisterous atmospheres, and so forth, with the result that such managers fail to take elders seriously when they apply for certain jobs. Since obviously some individuals are exceptions to the rule, the argument goes, aren't they—isn't everyone—oppressed by these preconceptions?

Reformers ask much of human nature when they demand that preconceptions based on age be done away with. Indeed, the impulse to generalize about people based on their age is so strong that even ageism buffs probably never manage to resist it for long except as a stunt, the way one might avoid using words containing the letter *t*. All of us rely constantly on age to "place" someone's likely attitudes, interests, and behavior; this is one reason we have grown to expect unfamiliar personages to be introduced in casual conversations and news stories with some signal as to whether they're nineteen or seventy-four years old.

Given older workers' sharply higher pay and responsibility levels when they land new jobs, the most salient kind of preconceptions about them would seem to be the positive kind: employers expect them to be more reliable and trustworthy than the average twenty-five-year-old, show better judgment, and so forth. (The whole concept of "experience," central to so many hiring choices, depends on similar generalizations.) In fact, older workers who file employment-law suits on other grounds not infrequently consider it damning that they *haven't* gotten a better shake than younger counterparts. A federal court inferred probable bias from its observation that a chemist's "age and experience were not given proper consideration" in setting her salary. A Fifth Circuit 1991 case hinged on a worker's claim that it amounted to constructive discharge to see his pay cut and be told to report to a youngster seventeen years his junior. Yet the favorable generalizations too have their exceptions: not every older worker is as wise or self-controlled as every twenty-year-old.

In the Age Discrimination in Employment Act of 1967, the U.S. Congress reacted to this age-old complex of economic and human problems and considerations with its usual subtlety. Summoning all the moral dudgeon it could find for miles around, it flatly banned as dis-

criminatory a vast array of actions, decisions, comments, and preconceptions concerning older workers as a class or any single such
worker, including a great many that are baldly logical. It bestowed on
the new class of victims broad rights to sue for generously defined
damages. It cut through the involved tangle of (usually) more or (occasionally) less favorable treatment of older persons by the simple expedient of making the ADEA "one-way": seniors could sue over
alleged preference shown to the young, but not vice versa. (The same
one-way principle turned up later in the Americans with Disabilities
Act.) In this respect it gave its highly affluent target group a better deal
than racial minorities, since it assured employers who continued to favor the former that they would not have to worry even theoretically
about reverse-discrimination charges.

How to delimit the new protected class? With majestic arbitrari-
ness, Congress decreed that it would consist of all those who'd passed
their fortieth birthday—suggesting, in the manner of friends teasing
about "the big one," that the one-day passage from thirty-nine to that
age marks a leap to a new station in life (akin to changing one's race
or sex, one might even think from the analogy). The broad definition
invited further skepticism about Congress's premise, since even advocates who worried about the special problems of displaced sixty-one-
year-olds seldom contended that the oppressed class extended all the
way down to those forty-two years of age.

At first the law allowed differential treatment of workers older than
sixty-five, thereby leaving intact the custom long found in many large
organizations of requiring employees to step down at that age. The
usual name for this practice was *mandatory retirement,* a misleading
term in more than one way since the worker displaced might (and often did) take a job elsewhere—often quite a good job—rather than actually retire. According to at least one survey, the practice actually
covered fewer than half the jobs in the economy; nonexistent over
much of the small business sector, it was most firmly entrenched
among high-level jobs at hierarchical enterprises such as corpora-

tions, universities, and nonprofits, very much including many of the most admired and progressive of these organizations.

Ironically, given what was to come, many labor reformers of the past had not only welcomed mandatory retirement policies but had campaigned to lower the threshold retirement ages; this has been a goal of the German labor movement, for example. "Family wage" ideas that were influential in Europe sought to reserve the most desirable jobs for family breadwinners by curbing competition from real or potential pensioners; similar notions have probably contributed to the American policy, favored by some labor advocates, of docking the Social Security benefits of older persons to discourage them from earning too much in paid work.

Another instructive example is Japan, a country famously run by old men. Large Japanese companies are said to expect the salaryman who does not make it into top management by age fifty-five or sixty to move over to contractor/consultant status, which means a likelihood of being cut from the rolls at the next business downturn. Yet employment rates for older Japanese men are reported to be notably high, not low; when eased out of the "rat race," many migrate to more psychologically rewarding work. At the same time, Japanese firms typically reward age and long service quite richly, with a steep rise in the earnings curve as a worker gets into middle age. In his book *Japan as Number One,* Ezra Vogel links the two practices: "Since retirement age is normally in the late fifties, salary increments can go up fairly rapidly without a company's worrying about having very high-paid elderly employees for many years."

Views in this country, of course, soon diverged sharply: once automatic retirement began to be conceived as a form of age discrimination, its days were numbered. In 1978 Congress raised the legal threshold to the age of seventy, and agitation soon was heard to do away with the ceiling entirely. The "retirement decision should be an individual option," said a Senate report, declaring that employees deserve "freedom of choice . . . in deciding when to retire." To achieve that commendable objective, of course, freedom of choice on the employer's part would just have to be done away with.

The unanimity, in retrospect, was what was most astonishing. In 1987 the House voted by a margin of 394 to 0 to lift the age limit entirely and abolish automatic retirement, and the measure was scarcely more controversial in the Senate. With no real idea what the consequences might be, lawmakers simply decreed the peremptory overthrow of a practice deeply ingrained in important parts of the economy. Not one libertarian could be found to stick up for voluntary relations and freedom of contract; not one traditionalist could be found to ask lawmakers to try figuring out what purpose a major custom served and why it had evolved before declaring it illegal; no labor advocates cared to press the family-wage issue; and the reputedly all-powerful business lobby put up no fight at all. The only pocket of resistance came from university administrators, who were associated in no one's mind with laissez-faire thinking; they saw problems down the road if tenured faculty could stay indefinitely. Lawmakers responded by allowing them a seven-year exemption, which duly expired in 1994. Public safety employees were also exempted temporarily, and the very top level of corporate management permanently (the prospect of CEOs hanging on forever being seen as somehow less than appetizing).

The moral high ground—surely the most underrated piece of real estate in Washington—had as usual made all the difference. To vote down the bill, said grievances-of-the-aging impresario Rep. Claude Pepper (a Democrat from Florida), would be to deny older workers "something to get up for . . . the impetus to carry on." California governor Jerry Brown, signing into law his state's version of the idea, called it "a necessity for collective survival." Of course more mundane factors also entered into legislators' calculations, including the prospect of help with their own budgeting—if workers could be induced to stay on the job longer, there might be fewer people taking out of Social Security and Medicare and more paying in. The real message, though, was simply that ruling opinion had thoroughly ceased to believe in employment at will. Employers had no business asking decent people to leave their payroll without good cause, and reaching a sixty-fifth birthday wasn't a good enough cause.

Having declared unlawful the views and practices of prior generations as a way of showing its respect for age, Congress then moved on to other issues, leaving managers to see what would happen next.

———

Among brands of identity politics the struggle against "ageism" has remained distinctly a poor cousin, arousing little mass enthusiasm. You might therefore guess that age bias law would have remained an obscure annex to the main edifice of job bias law. But in fact it's among the busiest categories of litigation. Race and sex complaints may get far more ink, but age complaints increasingly get more of the action. Age claims at combined federal and state levels hit 31,000 in 1992, up 30 percent in two years; plaintiff's lawyer Leonard Flamm has described it as a "deluge of cases."

One factor that helps encourage both lawyers and claimants is that age suits net considerably higher verdicts than other bias categories, often coming in twice as high as race. A Cincinnati jury ordered the accounting firm of Ernst & Young to pay $3.7 million to a forty-six-year-old partner it had let go. McDonnell Douglas paid $20 million to settle an age-based class action suit, while IDS Financial Services agreed to fork over $35 million to settle charges of bias against thirty-two division managers over forty. Employers, a *Employee Relations Law Journal* commentator agrees, see age cases as "the most dangerous type of discrimination case to take to trial."

Why do age complainants do so well? One reason is that they come across favorably on a personal level—accomplished, well-spoken, and accustomed to command. Richard Larson (in *Sue Your Boss*) encouragingly adds that "many juries are composed primarily of older persons," but even younger jurors reportedly lean toward more mature plaintiffs. Congress also provided a right to jury trial for age complainants from an early stage.

The underlying economics helps as well. Age plaintiffs start out earning more than other plaintiffs, being farther along in their careers and often holding positions as managers and executives; thus their platform for back-pay calculations is higher, and they are more likely to stake claims for lucrative options and the like. Unlike other bias laws, the ADEA provides for the doubling in many (apparently most) cases of ordinary back-pay damages; this is supposed to be in lieu of punitive damages, although lawyers ask for such damages anyway by invoking other liability theories.

Crucially, too, age complainants are less likely to succumb to one of the great temptations of the employment-law plaintiff—namely, stopping the all-important lost-pay clock by accepting another job before trial. The spread of strategic employment litigation has been dampened by the unwillingness of most workers to put up with un- or underemployment for the requisite years of delay to trial. Even worse, once they accept decent new jobs, these employees become good bets to settle their old complaints. (As lawyers put it, these clients lack "staying power"). In contrast, some workers who sue in their sixties begin drawing Social Security and a pension and enter into what looks a great deal like retirement, complete with hobbies, travel, and even a move to a sunnier clime—while assuring the court that their idleness is quite involuntary and that they would have happily continued on the job had they not been forced out. With the banning of automatic retirement, there is no natural terminus at all to the period of lost pay. New York management attorney Allen Fagin says it is now "typical" for age plaintiffs to allege that they would have "worked till they drop."

————

Employers find it easy to trigger age claims without meaning to. Courts have been willing to presume age to be the prima facie motivation for a firing, for example, if the worker hired as a replacement is as little as five years younger than the one let go. But in the natural course of events all employers tend to replace departing employees with younger picks, simply because people age on the job: if the typical manager comes in at age forty-seven and leaves at age fifty-three, an ordinary replacement decision may trigger an inference of age motivation even though the average age of the workforce has remained stable over the period. (By contrast, women fired from traditionally female jobs may find themselves in relatively weak legal positions because their employers are likely to have replaced them with other women.)

Verbal slips with age implications are common as well; supervisors who would never think of racial or religious wisecracking don't always realize that recycled Jack Benny jokes can be just as dangerous. "Your get-up-and-go has got up and gone," said one supervisor; the older employee to whom he addressed the lame jest didn't sue, but another did and won. Kodak lost a million-dollar verdict after a manager opined that a salesman was "not keeping up with the times." One court refused to interpret as a smoking gun a manager's remark that he and the complainant were not on the same wavelength, declining to accord the "posited youthful quality to the word 'wavelength.'" On the other hand, any reference to "deadwood" is considered grounds enough to pull out the checkbook, while "new blood" helped get a plaintiff to a jury in an Eleventh Circuit case. Management lawyers went into conniptions when the Second Circuit ruled in 1991 that "overqualified" might really be a code word for too old. "Journalism tends to be a young person's game. It's not something where people tend to grow old gracefully," said Fox News president Van Gordon Sauter in a printed interview; the words were thrown back at his company in a suit. Lawyers warned that memos expressing a preference for "dynamic" or "aggressive" employees could set a company up for a fall.

The EEOC, as usual, went even further. It embraced the remarkable view that employers violate age law when they consciously prefer workers they can hire for lower salaries, since after all such workers are likely to be younger. Though the Supreme Court (after dodging the issue for years) has now cast doubt on that interpretation of the law, lawyers continue to cash checks on its strength. In 1993 a jury socked a telecommunications firm with a $7 million award after it ousted two executives "to replace them with younger, lower-cost employees." Plaintiff's lawyer Flamm points out that the current state of the law lets him go after the "ordinary businessman" who "wants to save a buck."

As usual in bias law, while concern for workers trying to get hired had played a central role in fueling the legislation, once the law was in place the main action shifted to suits challenging firings. In fact, age bias law, though full of uses in contesting dismissals, turned out remarkably weak in some ways on the hiring side. One reason was that no one had the stomach to enforce hiring quotas or their more respectable cousin, statistical methods of proving discrimination. Even the EEOC didn't pretend that each age bracket would naturally contribute its exact share of lifeguards, bicycle messengers, and MTV announcers, the way it liked to believe women would hold 51 percent of jobs as meat cutters and hardware sellers if not for discrimination. The courts did apply numerical scrutiny, however, to layoffs and other downsizing methods. This policy led directly to the widespread corporate practice known as "age-balancing the RIF" (reduction in force)—as when, according to later court documents, a downsizing scheme at the oil company Amoco

> called for sales personnel in each region to be divided into four categories: women, racial minorities, persons over forty, and white males under forty. . . . White males [under forty] were not "protected." Women, racial minorities, and employees between forty and sixty-five years of age were to "retain their proportionate share of the jobs."

A consequence of the insistence on sheltering the old from disparate treatment in layoffs was to stymie some employer policies that might otherwise have seemed attractive on humane and egalitarian grounds. For instance, the city of Altoona, in accord with a Pennsylvania law, tried to lay off workers who qualified for full pension before those who hadn't yet reached eligibility. Not a bad policy at all, you might think, but a court declared it age discrimination, striking down the operation of the state law and ordering the city to cough up back pay. Likewise, the Borden company tried to soften the blow of a plant closing by offering special severance payouts to workers who didn't qualify for pensions. It lost, too, on the grounds that it was unlawful for the younger workers to get any benefit at all that the old weren't getting, though no one disputed that the pensions remained much more valuable than the severance. The lesson for companies was that they should redivide their severance pots to give even more to the workers who were already in the best shape—or skip severance entirely, which remained an entirely legal option.

Old age, as is notorious, sneaks up on you. Knowing he wouldn't necessarily recognize on his own when he was slipping, Oliver Wendell Holmes famously asked his Supreme Court colleagues to let him know when the time came. (They deputized one of their number to tell him, and he bowed out gracefully.) Even if we never reach what Thomas Jefferson (again referring to judges) called the "imbecilities of dotage" there come subtler dullings of our physical or mental edge; we may notice these deficits only when we need our full capacities in an emergency, or we may never recognize them at all.

The followers of Claude Pepper never actually denied that reaction time, memory, physical endurance, and many other qualities decline with the passing years. They found it damning, however, that the customary age for automatic retirement had been set at a point at which even most employers agreed most workers were still performing adequately or better. The only answer, given the insistence on abolishing discrimination of any form, was for employers to carry out case-by-case determinations of when any given individual's decline had reached a point of incompetence or public hazard.

The forces of caring-and-compassion thus appeared in an unusual light, calling for a great new binge of personalized firing. And it got worse. When universities complained about having to retain indefinitely professors whose best years were far behind them, Pepper replied that they "ought to weed out incompetents when incompetence is recognized rather than waiting for mandatory retirement to force them out at 65 or 70." But that would mean pushing many out at the point of most economic vulnerability during those danger years in the late fifties and early sixties when Social Security is not yet available but starting a new career may seem a poor option. Paradoxically, mandatory retirement had actually worked to the benefit of many underperforming workers approaching the close of their careers: employers could keep them on for the last few years at relatively low financial risk, knowing they'd be gone as of a date certain.

The wider problem in the case-by-case prescription was the prospect of an unending succession of differences of opinion leading to litigation and its threat, not all workplaces being as pleasantly collegial as Holmes's Supreme Court. What turned out to save most employers from this danger was most workers' strong preference for retirement over work (shaped, admittedly, in substantial part by Social Security and tax incentives). This preference for the retired state appeared to be growing: fewer men in their sixties were choosing to stay in the labor force, though they were healthier than ever. (Among women, the trend was somewhat masked by the general surge of women into paid work.)

The trend toward earlier retirement, however, was by no means uniform. Workers in blue-collar and routine white-collar employment showed every sign of being glad to bail out at earlier ages. On the other hand, managers and professionals in well-paid, challenging, and prestigious jobs often prefer to stay at work; the monetary, social, and psychological rewards are all greater. And as it happened, the old mandatory retirement rules were most likely to affect exactly those sorts of jobs.

Elite university professorships were a prime example. When Congress raised the automatic retirement age to seventy, only a small fraction of workers in general reaching sixty-five chose to stay on for the five extra years, but more than three-quarters of Yale faculty and five-sixths of Harvard Medical School faculty did so. Life as a senior professor at a prestigious university—or sometimes as a high-ranking foundation, media, arts, or scientific executive—is simply more attractive than retirement. When the law's exception for tenured professors expired in 1994, a further profound shift began in the age distribution of faculty at top institutions. A study by law professor Richard Epstein and mathematician Saunders MacLane of the University of Chicago found that once an institution reached "steady state" one in four professors would be over age sixty-five with half of that number over seventy. The decade or two of aging-in-place in the meantime would bring about a severe drought of new openings: bad news, MacLane warned, for his own discipline of mathematics, in which the youngest scholars often carry out key breakthroughs. Several noted academics and college administrators quoted in the *New York Times* were sharply critical of the trend. Harvard biologist and faculty dean Jeremy Knowles pointed out that yesterday's scientific knowledge quickly becomes obsolete. "The new law clogs the arteries," said seventy-eight-year-old historian Oscar Handlin, who had published five books since his retirement. "It won't allow young people to move in."

Small wonder that universities have been in the forefront of the crafting of aggressive and expensive buyout schemes. Dealing with economists is the worst, explains one executive, because they are so good at calculating just how much they can take you for. Stanford's plan, according to *Scientific American*, is "designed so that those valued *least* by their departments get the most when they leave" (emphasis added).

———

Buyouts as an institution are full of similar quirks and irrationalities that make sense only as a reaction to the legal environment, starting with the ambush-like surprise and the unnatural tension of the short decision deadline. (Polaroid's retirement director described that firm's experience as "pandemonium.") Some plans devised at great expense fall flat. Others flush out many more workers than expected: DuPont saw more than 11,000 workers take an offer meant to attract 5,000, while IBM had to budget $2 billion more than expected after one rush to the exits. New York City's teacher buyouts drove out many math and science educators, who were already in short supply. Buyouts left the troubled Chicago post office so shorthanded that management had to give up imposing suspensions for repeat employee misconduct.

Sometimes, to everyone's chagrin, employers have to start rehiring for key positions, as happened after buyouts at Lockheed and the University of Southern California. The New York state government found itself filling 4,000 vacancies after a 1984 offer. Even when the right general number of employees leave, the resulting vacancy patterns can be lumpy and unplanned. One answer is to rehire these same former employees as consultants: after all, who knows more about doing their job?

A small army of lawyers, accountants, and actuaries huddle around the clock to devise the details of buyout offers, whose standardized and impersonal format well reflects the new law's emphasis on arm's-length treatment of employees and insistence on copiously documented due process. Consultant William Miner at the Wyatt Company, a leading designer of early-out plans, says avoiding liability associated with other methods of staff-cutting is "one of the primary considerations in almost any window that I see." The voluntariness of the departure provides the basic protection, but many companies take no chances and ask the worker to sign a waiver: thus an American Express employee signed a form promising to forgive the company of any claims "from the beginning of the world up to and including the date of this Agreement and Release." Miner also confirms that the dollar amounts offered various classes of employee in the plans are often linked to the expected settlement value of legal actions they might bring: "We're actuaries, and we can figure out the percentages as well as anyone."

Liability fears add a special cruel twist to workers' uncertainty. In case after case, they yearn for the answer to one question: what are my prospects if I stay? But the new law strongly discourages employers from giving them an answer, however candid or accurate it might be. Courts have construed a company's hint that a particular worker would do well to accept the offer as "steering" and tantamount to constructive discharge. "Almost anything you say might be deemed to be coercive," notes management lawyer Fagin. As a result, standard employer practice is to order supervisors to keep completely silent on this question, often going so far as to withhold even routine employee evaluations lest they be seen as trying to send a message. The result is that more workers commit needless mistakes in both directions: they stay when in fact they are destined to be targeted by the next downsizing, or they jump into an uncertain future when the company would have preferred them to stay.

A Senate report has noted that buyouts are becoming "a permanent fixture" of the American economy in good and bad times alike. Yet as they become ever more normal and expected as a way to depart corporate jobs, their distortive effects worsen. Companies may offer periodic buyouts even if their overall employment levels are basically stable (helping fuel unwarranted panics); dramatic one-shot cuts will do the job of a decade's attrition and retirement under the old regime. Economist Finis Welch of Texas A & M University sees signs that the offers are beginning to be "built into employee expectations." Voluntary retirement not only comes to a near-halt during the rumor period that precedes an offer, but also begins to fall off at other points in the cycle.

Indeed, there are signs of mounting resentment among those who for one reason or another have to retire "for free." Thirty-four-year Pfizer veteran Jim Mullins took ordinary retirement after quizzing a plant manager about pending buyouts and being told nothing was "under serious consideration." Six weeks after his departure the company announced a buyout that could have given him an extra $39,000. He sued, and a court ruled he could go to trial with his claim that he'd been misled.

————

The experiment with age-bias law is still very much in progress; some of the first wave of workers entrenched by the law are still aging in place, and behavior can be expected to adjust as new generations grow up accustomed to ground rules under which, as Paul Wallich and Elizabeth Corcoran put it in *Scientific American*, "all retirement is 'early.'"

Yet it is not too soon to observe that no rational worker asked to design a fringe benefit would have come up with the buyout format. Its perpetual uncertainty does away with a chief virtue of the old regime—namely, the scope it gave both sides to plan their affairs well in advance. The company could project future attrition and thus payroll, while the worker could arrange everything from mortgages to children's educations with a definite retirement date in mind. Buyouts pull out many workers far earlier than they had expected to go, while leading others to delay retiring year after year in search of an offer that will never come.

Buyouts also distribute cash windfalls whimsically (or unfairly, to be blunt) among equally deserving employees. Those who work at very small companies will often simply get fired rather than bought out, while a few lucky staffers at large firms pocket a year's lump-sum salary and then find a new job within weeks, or bounce around collecting multiple buyouts. Buyouts bestow nothing at all on the median janitor or part-time telemarketer, and riches on many of society's most affluent professionals. Yet even among such professionals at large firms, many go away empty-handed because personal necessity requires them to leave when no buyout is available; some of these will be among the hard cases, not yet at pensionable age but without skills in high demand. Money rains down gratuitously on those who neither need nor demand it, while if the employer attempts to redirect the funds to ensure a modest competence for all it defeats the objective of regaining control over its payroll.

When it gave birth to age-bias law, Congress promised with a great flourish that it would bolster the position of workers late in their careers, put in their own hands the timing of the retirement decision, and bring their persons and talents new respect from employers. The opposite has happened on every front. Older workers now have less effective choice than ever over the timing of their departure; they are treated with less consideration and respect than before; and increasingly, for safety's sake, employers are flushing them out even earlier than either party desires. The moral: when the government tells you it is abolishing rain, run out and buy an umbrella.

Part III

THE EXCUSE FACTORY

Chapter 9

THE EXCUSE FACTORY

When Connecticut school officials examined the results of the state's ninth annual basic-skills exam, they noticed a cluster of unusual scores from New Haven's Hill Central Elementary School. A closer look confirmed their fears: the questionable scores had come from a single classroom, and the answers showed nearly identical phrasing, spelling, and punctuation. Even worse, this was no cynical high-school crew, but a class of fourth-graders.

Nor, investigators soon found, had this been a case where children passed around a blue book while the teacher wasn't looking. Teacher Debra Liburd had actually written out answers on the blackboard and helped students with the test in other ways. An official called it "the most egregious example of cheating we have seen" in the test's history.

But tenure rules make it almost impossible to fire a teacher. The most the local school board thought it could give Liburd was a one-year suspension—and it couldn't make even that stick.

When Liburd's grievance over the suspension went to arbitration, the arbitrator conceded that her "unethical and dishonest" behavior constituted a "betrayal" of the standards of her profession and her students' real interests alike. Still, he said, things had to be kept in perspective. What with crime in the streets, child abuse, and the rest of "the violent world of the 1990s," mere connivance at cheating did not appear so "horrific." So he knocked the suspension down to thirty days.

Officials and local parents alike reacted with outrage. State official Lorraine Aronson was "stunned" at the arbitrator's not-as-bad-as-if-she'd-knifed-someone rationale: "If our standard . . . is that anything short of a felony can be explained away, our schools are doomed." New Haven school board chairman Patricia McCann-Vissepo commented that "people don't accept the consequences for their behavior because there aren't any."

But as teacher tenure cases go, this one was not so unusual. A Chicago fourth-grade teacher bungled her job so badly that all twenty-two students in her class had to repeat the material over the summer: "These children have suffered," said principal Dyanne Dandridge-Alexander, "because they have a totally inept teacher that no one has been able to fire." New York City was paying full salary to a principal charged with stealing $10,000 in school funds, a teacher who'd sheltered a runaway student in his apartment, a gym teacher charged with having sex with a student in the weight room, and, most remarkably, a special-ed administrator convicted of selling cocaine from his office and serving out a prison term upstate. In short, the Connecticut official had actually underrated the problem. Even a felony *could* be explained away.

When the law-school theorists came up with their new tenure-through-litigation idea, they consciously modeled it on the examples of union grievance arbitration and civil service protection, both of which require management to show that firings and other adverse action were based on adequate grounds. Both systems also guarantee a heaping measure of due process along the way, such as a right to hearings, representation, and written charges. Obviously workplaces with these protections were fairer and more rational than those without; why not force private nonunion employers to catch up?

In retrospect, unionized workplaces and government-agency employers might have seemed a curious choice of model for the future. Unions by the 1960s had begun a long decline as an institution, their public esteem and share of private employment falling each year. Civil service systems were continuing to grow as regarded numbers of workers covered, given the steadily climbing rolls of public employment, but the idea could hardly be called a fighting faith any more. Increasingly, civil service rules were seen as a special-interest obstacle to sound public governance. Curiously or not, the one place the two institutions showed a great deal of dynamism and growth was where they intersected: unions were offsetting their steady decline among private workers by signing up government employees in droves.

Both union grievance arbitration and civil service procedure have generated a large record of published cases and literature, obscure to the general public but well worth a closer look. (On arbitration, the discussion below owes a great deal to *Just Cause: The Seven Tests*, a 1985 book by Adolph Koven and Susan L. Smith.) Generalizations can be perilous, since these institutions behave differently from one state and workplace to the next: what civil service panels let pass in Idaho they may resist in Rhode Island, and the "law of the shop" at an oil refinery may differ a lot from that at a community college. Yet in both cases the process has turned out to have its own logic, which has given great force in practice to curbs on management that might have looked modest on paper. Debra Liburd's victory turns out to be no fluke.

———

A list of remarkable tenure cases among unionized public employees could be extended to almost any length. What follows are a few in recent years from the state of Connecticut alone:

• The principal of a Waterbury high school collected his $88,000 salary at home while contesting his dismissal over charges that he'd harassed four school officials and a family with children attending his school by ordering expensive C.O.D. packages and reams of junk mail to be sent to their homes. "I feel I've been, you might say, overpunished," he said.

- A ferry worker who admitted to stealing toll money agreed to a thirty-day suspension, gradual restitution (at his convenience) of the sums taken, and a transfer to a job where he wouldn't be handling cash. "It's very important to apply discipline that you believe will stand the test of the grievance process," said an official.

- Some police cases: (1) The town of South Windsor got nicked for three years' worth of back pay after arbitrators ruled it had been too severe in dismissing an officer for various misdeeds, which included tipping off a drug dealer about an investigation. (2) A state trooper was reinstated after getting a ticket fixed for his business partner on the grounds that he hadn't fixed the ticket himself, but had merely asked a colleague to do so. (3) An East Hartford police dispatcher, given community service and probation after she admitted bilking the city out of $2,800 by filing false time cards, was reinstated with $11,000 back pay when arbitrators conceded that her misconduct was "extremely serious" but held the town should have contented itself with a sixty-day suspension.

- A Ridgefield teacher won back pay after a court ruled that, though the school had succeeded in proving her incompetence in two of the three subjects she taught, it had not done so in the third subject and thus should have kept her on to teach that.

- Two guards at the state veteran's home had to get a drunken resident upstairs; rather than carry him, they stuffed him into a laundry dumbwaiter and tried to hoist him up. The man's ankle was broken when it got caught between floors, an injury that the state medical examiner found contributed to his death from heart failure a few weeks later. The two were convicted of first-degree reckless endangerment and given probation, then were reinstated in their jobs after arbitrators noted that they hadn't hurt the man on purpose.

- The state eventually dropped criminal embezzlement and forgery charges against a bookkeeper at a state orphanage when auditors could make no sense at all of his record entries. After a long paid leave, he went back to work for the state.

Behind such cases is the "fundamental" assumption of modern labor arbitration, as a leading commentator describes it: the "employee owns the job."

Many consequences flow from this assumption. One is simply that the employer gets assigned the burden of proof in a dispute, which can make the difference by itself. Writer Mickey Kaus quotes an attorney who relates a classic story, told by both sides, about a worker caught taking a snooze:

> The only reliable means of sustaining guilt beyond a reasonable doubt is to lift the grievant from the chair in which he has been snoring and bounce him off the floor until he opens his eyes, blinks in confusion, and angrily inquires, "What's the big idea of waking me up in the middle of a shift?" Otherwise the grievant may successfully claim that he was deep in meditation concerning the problems of the job.

Reasonable suspicion is not enough, even when the offense involved is grave. Thus a worker who'd accompanied a friend to a phone booth where the friend called in a bomb threat to the company won reinstatement with full back pay, since management hadn't proved his direct guilt.

Even if misconduct is shown, the famous arbitration principle of *progressive discipline* holds that except in the most lurid cases, management may not proceed to dismissal until it has run through all sorts of lesser penalties so as to give the wrongdoer ample chance to mend his ways. Thus a Philadelphia transit worker who'd committed an indecent and unwelcome act toward a passenger was reinstated on the grounds the company could have reassigned him to a job with limited public contact. Employers are expected to work closely with a misbehaving worker to overcome his problem—giving him warnings and notices, steering him away from temptations to break the rules, and of course offering him second, third, and fourth chances to stop the offending behavior. A worker shown to have been drinking on the job was reinstated with full back pay because the company merely documented his behavior when it might have intervened and confronted him earlier with opportunities to shape up. Koven and Smith report that what they call the more hard-line arbitrators tend to uphold dismissals only if they are convinced not only that the employer has tried all lesser steps, but that all steps will be futile if tried again.

Also important is the principle of *condonation:* if employers learn about misbehavior but fail to punish it promptly and consistently, they may lose the right to do so later. The Lockheed company delayed in cracking down on drinking and pot-smoking in its parking lot, for example, and lost a ruling because by the time it acted workers "looked upon the lots as sanctuaries for this relaxation." The arbitrator in this case was not impressed with the company's explanation that it had held back for fear of disturbing an ongoing criminal investigation. The accepted method by which a company can move against previously unpoliced misbehavior is by loudly announcing beforehand that it is about to start doing so, thus giving the foxes a sporting chance to scatter before the hounds catch their scent.

Grievants can mount a challenge to company rules themselves under an all-purpose standard of *reasonableness*—which, as Koven and Smith put it, is "determined not by management's standards alone but by standards acceptable to the labor relations community." Thus the Social Security Administration could not prohibit its workers from bringing TV sets into the office, because the sets had some legitimate uses (during lunch hours and the like). Similarly, a Wisconsin cemetery could not bar its employees from wearing tank tops, because the labor relations community apparently didn't agree that grieving families deserved dignified surroundings for their visits.

A far-reaching principle is that nearly all off-the-job misconduct must be ignored. Even extremely serious misconduct—resulting in a felony conviction, for example—may not justify dismissal if it occurred on a worker's own time. An employer's mere wish not to employ lawbreakers, its fear of harm to morale and company reputation, carry little if any weight. Even sworn law enforcement officers, who might be considered less than trustworthy to uphold the law by day if they casually break it by night, have won many such arbitrations. As a result, a series of cases (which have given unease to feminists and others) have restored to the beat cops who've knocked around their wives, girlfriends, or complete strangers during off hours. Nor do fears about reckless behavior carry over readily: an Oklahoma man who pleaded no contest to felony manslaughter charges after a drinking-and-boating fatality won reinstatement even though his particular municipal job—a driver for the fire department—might seem peculiarly unsuitable for someone with his record.

———

Modern labor arbitration in many unionized workplaces affords a striking degree of protection to the worker with a drinking problem. To begin with, the emphasis on making management prove an affirmative case can make it tough to prove impairment on the job: reports of erratic behavior may be subjective, few companies want to keep Breathalyzers on hand, finding liquor in a desk does not prove the worker drank any of it, and so forth. Many indicators that frequently signal a problem, such as a cluster of DWI arrests, will commonly take place off the job and thus be excluded from management's consideration. "This was completely unrelated to his job," said a lawyer for a veteran Northwest pilot picked up on the road (not before a flight) with a blood alcohol level of .33; a judge said it was amazing he could walk at all.

Even if proved, alcohol-related misconduct (like other kinds) must be met with a willingness to work with the employee and offer second chances. Summarizing his colleagues' view, one arbitrator observes that before a company may fire a worker for such misconduct it must have encouraged him to seek treatment; if he agrees, only "fail[ure] to make substantial progress over a considerable period of time" could justify termination. A study of workers reinstated by arbitrators after alcohol abuse found that only a quarter of them improved their performance after reinstatement.

Excuses based on mental disturbance can also be quite liberal. A 1982 *Arbitration Journal* article describes the more "compassionate" arbitrators as recognizing that some employees "are so afflicted or troubled as not to be deemed responsible for their actions." Thus a

Sara Lee worker was reinstated after insubordination, threats, and "vulgar and abusive language"; the arbitrator ruled he was "helpless to prevent what he did while mentally ill." Another arbitrator was swayed by the hope of the worker's psychiatrist that a return to the job might itself be therapeutic for his client. Companies are frequently ordered to forgive menacing behavior after the worker promises to go on medication. As in the drug and alcohol case, the literature concedes that workers who make no progress under treatment shouldn't expect to stay on indefinitely; management will be allowed to let them go "at some point." Nevertheless, that point can recede into the horizon. Arbitrators "seem inclined to give an employee another chance if there is some hope of recovery," observed a *Michigan Bar Journal* case roundup. An Amoco worker was reinstated despite violent threats against management in hopes that treatment for his paranoia would be successful, while a National Steel worker was ordered rehired despite testimony that his period of remission from schizophrenia would likely be short.

Complicating further the task of proving that a troubled worker is too unstable to stay on the job, arbitrators have tended to limit the ability of employers to request psychiatric evaluations. In one case an employee had previously been suspended for roughhousing with a jackknife in the company cafeteria, was arrested off the job for driving under the influence of drugs (and admitted to a mental hospital for observation), and then was fired when he came to work under what a foreman considered the visible influence of something. An arbitrator reinstated him with back pay, ruling that the company had no grounds to require him to submit to further psychiatric evaluation before he could return to work. After years of emotional outbursts a telephone operator went "out of control," yelling and screaming at her supervisor, and took sick leave; the company lost a back pay award because it had insisted on a psychiatric evaluation before letting her return.

———

Even an employer confident in the substance of its case faces a long series of hurdles if it proceeds to arbitration. Procedural lapses are fatal: one company lost because, after sending a seized substance to an outside lab (which confirmed it to be hashish), it did not produce the lab technicians themselves so the worker or his representative could cross-examine them. Another company dismissed a worker, known for his temper, who admitted to an off-hours quarrel at a tavern, after which he'd returned with a gun and shot the bartender. It lost in arbitration on the purely procedural grounds that though he hadn't in fact offered extenuating circumstances, it had denied him a hearing at which he *might* have offered such circumstances.

Arbitrators commonly will consider only the stated grounds that the company offered at the time of a firing, and not equally valid or better reasons that it may have discovered since then. This practice parallels the requirement that prosecutors match their proof to their charges, but it is far more demanding than the standard by which we allow fortunes to be taken away from defendants in civil litigation (where complainants generally can get into court on one charge and switch to a more promising one later). One arbitrator carried this principle to a logical extreme by ordering back pay in a case where the company had charged the fired worker only with obstructing its investigation into a theft; it lost because it hadn't sustained the obstruction charge to the arbitrator's satisfaction, though in the meantime the worker had been tried and convicted in a regular court of the theft itself.

Some arbitrators forbid companies from proving even the stated grounds of firing by way of any evidence that was not in their hands at the time. Thus in a 1981 California case the East Bay transit system had fired a bus driver for using faked sick leave to moonlight at a second job; records obtained from the driver's other employer fully confirmed the wrongdoing, but the transit system lost because it hadn't had those records in its possession when it acted.

————

The obvious parallel for all these copious doses of due process is criminal law: wisely, society insists on highly elaborate procedural protections when government seeks to charge a citizen with punishable crimes. The terminology of labor relations helps establish the analogy by characterizing any employer reaction to a perceived dereliction as a "punishment," "penalty," or "discipline." As for actual firing, it commonly gets described (in what one maverick arbitrator called a triumph of analogy over common sense) as "industrial capital punishment," on the apparent view that persons who leave a job on bad terms have no hope of finding another. Koven and Smith quote the old saw about how it's better for ten guilty men to go free than for one innocent to be punished. The maxim is precious when a defendant stands accused of murder or high treason; why shouldn't it fit for an accusation that someone is goofing off on the job?

The arbitration literature abounds with half-digested analogies of this sort. It is as if refusal to engage in further dealings with someone—a fate we all inflict on many a small businessperson over minor dissatisfactions—were somehow akin to sending in sheriffs to arrest him and throw him in jail; as if ceasing to write checks to someone were equivalent to chopping off his head.

Many commentators are at pains to deny that arbitration rules consciously imitate the rules for criminal prosecution, yet the parallels are striking. Criminal prosecution is rightly expected to follow a rule that offenses be preannounced with specificity, and ambiguities construed in favor of legality; such rules also turn up in arbitration, where the case for them is far less compelling. An aviation company worker reported for duty with 0.14 percent alcohol on his breath—the state drunk-driving limit was 0.10—but won full back pay and reinstatement because the company, unlike the state lawmakers, hadn't spelled out how much intoxication was acceptable. Another won because company rules provided only that a misbehaving worker "may" (rather than "will") be fired. A third won because the union contract gave management the right to fire on a first offense of insubordination, but—a triumph worthy of a Gilbert and Sullivan hero—his was a *second* offense.

Arbitration in recent decades has even developed parallels to the revolution in criminal procedure launched by the Supreme Court during the tenure of Chief Justice Earl Warren. There's a right-to-representation series of cases, typified by a ruling holding it an unfair practice for an employer to interrogate an employee without the presence of a union shop steward although the employee had asked for one. (Some arbitrators hold that an employee need not cooperate with a company investigation at all.) The expanded insanity defenses have resulted in the forced return of workers after acts committed in fits of violent rage. And miscreants can win despite damning evidence by arguing that they were "provoked into adverse behavior," or that supervisors or investigators "tricked, coerced, or misled" them into harmful admissions. Koven and Smith agree that the result is often one of "reinstating an employee even though his misconduct was established."

Actually, the due process levels demanded of employers are often *more* stringent than those prosecutors have to observe. One employer lost because its managers saw a worker misbehaving but had not used an available camera to snap a photo of the incident, thus violating a putative moral obligation to secure the best evidence. Others lose on the ground that their case against a worker has been accumulated by watching him with unnatural care so as to "build a record"; no such doctrine binds prosecutors. Prosecutors are generally entitled to use newly developed evidence that was not in their hands at the time of indictment, and to press charges against conduct that has gone unprosecuted in the past without fearing a defense of "condonation"; nor are they expected to work closely with crime-prone individuals to dissuade them beforehand from making the big mistake.

Of course, grievant/workers don't always win; in fact, they often lose, or they get only a split decision (in which the arbitrator upholds a suspension of lesser length than the company had wanted). Even some firings are upheld. For instance, the Silas Mason Co. was allowed to dismiss a mentally unstable employee on a showing that all available jobs at the company involved handling high explosives. St. Raphael's Hospital in New Haven, Connecticut, was permitted to say good-bye to a worker who'd screamed obscenities and death threats at his supervisor for an hour before being taken away by security. A relevant factor was that he'd had the bad judgment to stage his outburst in the hospital wing that housed recovering cardiac patients. (The union cited his illiteracy as an extenuating factor; it also noted that although the worker "did not deny making any of the statements . . . when he has an incident with that kind of rage, he blacks out.") Not many unions exercise as much clout in the process as the New York newspaper drivers' union described in Richard Vigilante's book *Strike:* "If you couldn't get a guy back to work in a few days, even after he slugged a foreman, you just weren't doing something right," union chief Jerry Cronin recalled.

Still, even facing a relatively impartial arbitrator or civil service board and a union that would like to be reasonable, employers must weigh whether they're willing to go through the expense and complication of the process. Civil service systems often require multiple levels of formal review; dismissing a Chicago park worker for incompetence, for example, requires eighty-four steps. By the 1970s Boston's scheme had evolved to the point where public employees could contest firings before four different panels—and since none had authority over the others, any of the four might overturn a firing and award back pay. The employee did not have to petition all simultaneously, but could wait until one had ruled before moving on to the next.

A New York survey found that ousting a teacher cost the average school board just short of $200,000; New Jersey boasts that it has streamlined the process, but it still takes a year and $100,000. In Michigan, a relatively extreme state, a *Detroit Free Press* investigation found ousting a teacher took an average of seven years; one case lasted sixteen years, fourteen of them spent in court. Saying good-bye to a middle school teacher cost the town of Dansville $135,000 in legal fees even though it prevailed at every level of appeal. It has not tried to shed any teachers since then, the principal explains: "One in a lifetime is enough."

The process also burns managers' time. School board hearings in an effort to eject an East Lansing counselor went on for fifty nights. Coworkers, parents and children, higher-ups, and assorted bystanders may all be asked to testify again and again, and if some move out of town or give up on the process, everything may go back to square one. "If you miss a step in any way, shape or form, you've blown a whole year's work," Detroit elementary principal Eileen Rodak told the *Free Press.*

Firing a worker or putting him on long-term suspension carries a painful fiscal risk: if the arbitrator knocks the penalty down to a short-term suspension, the employer may owe a huge slug of back pay with nothing to show for it. In the troubled police department in Washington, D.C., more than one hundred suspended officers a year were winning reinstatement with back pay by the early 1990s. Leaving workers in place, however, can pose its own dangers to morale and operational success. Police chief Perry Anderson of Cambridge, Massachusetts, told the *Boston Globe* that "even the most egregious abusers of department policies" can take advantage of an "endless maze of review. . . . It may go on forever with them still working."

Some employers resort to paid leave, "home assignment," or transfers: the *Detroit Free Press* found that administrators shifted unwanted educators from school to school in what was called "the dance of the lemons." Other managers resort to war-of-attrition penalties, imposing many short suspensions they hope will not be worth the worker's time to contest. Of course, there's also the age-old technique of making people's lives miserable in the dozens of small ways no grievance process can catch—a skill perfected, whether for defense or offense or both, by numerous public-sector managers.

The other popular alternative is to bribe problem employees to leave. After a nine-year battle, Detroit coughed up $225,000 to buy out a teacher described as her supervisor as having an elementary student's command of the English language, and whose assignments contained grammatical errors and misspellings. (Her subject, painfully enough, was high school English.) The *Free Press* found that even teachers headed for jail managed to get buyouts: suburban Farmington paid $19,000 to obtain a resignation in a case of criminal sexual conduct with a female student to which the teacher later pleaded guilty and served a year in jail. In Minnesota, a professor at the state university's Duluth campus who pleaded guilty to possession of child pornography got a $75,000 settlement.

Most of these cases occur in systems where the announced standards for firing do not seem outlandish; the employer is supposed to have the right to fire for "good cause," to pursue reasonable management prerogatives, and so on. The practice is very different, suggesting that as such systems evolve, distinctions between good and bad cause may not form a stable equilibrium or stopping point. A 1976 survey by future Harvard law professor Gerald Frug found that though the letter of civil service law appeared to permit dismissals of incompetent employees, the onerousness of the procedures had led public employers to a routine policy of retaining such employees.

———

What about the new employment law? Would "good cause" be interpreted, as many leading advocates of the new law wanted, to follow the precedents of arbitration and civil service procedure? A lot depended on which court you landed in. As of the mid-1990s, most judges—especially those at the federal level—were less inclined to second-guess firings than the median arbitrator or civil service panel; many of them even threw out on summary judgment some kinds of case that the worker might have won at arbitration. But others sent the cases on to juries, who can in many cases pretty much do whatever they feel like. This tendency can lead to results like those in the widely remarked 1990 federal case of *Sanders* v. *Parker Drilling*.

If you go by the management manuals on how to be a good corporate citizen, the Parker Drilling company did just about everything right. Like other operators of offshore Alaskan oil rigs, it knew it had a problem with employee drug use. Searches with sniffing dogs had turned up huge stashes; since living spaces on the rigs were communal, though, the company could do no more than confiscate what it found. Along with most safety authorities, Parker also believed strong steps were appropriate to prevent use on the job: between the thrashing machinery, temperatures of thirty degrees below zero, a rotating and mud-slickened floor, and oil ready to blow, Arctic rigs pose extraordinary risks both to the environment and to the life and limb of workers. So the company consistently enforced a policy against any impairment on site, firing even high-ranking employees who'd been seen drinking or whose breath had smelled of liquor even once. But it declined to institute urine testing—though it could have legally defended such a step—because it didn't want to invade its employees' privacy and dignity; aside from that, the latter spent long stretches of their own time away from the rigs on R & R, and Parker didn't presume to control what they did there.

When two supervisors reported they'd personally seen three workers smoking pot on the rigs, the company asked them to put it in writing and launched an immediate probe, which it entrusted to a team of managers unacquainted with any of the workers. The investigators interviewed a former roommate of the trio who said, "I told those guys this was going to get them ... that is why I moved out of that room. . . . I told those guys this was going to happen to them."

Parker still managed to lose the workers' wrongful-firing claim, to the tune of $360,000. A Ninth Circuit panel led by Judge Stephen Reinhardt did not deny that the company's investigation (which concluded that the three workers had indeed been smoking pot on the job) had been carried out in good faith. But it said Parker had the burden of retrying the charges to the jury, inevitably recalling a criminal trial in which it had to prove the workers guilty rather than vice versa. It would be permitted to cite only evidence actually in hand at the time of the firing; that meant, for example, that it couldn't introduce the co-worker's later testimony clarifying his above statement by confirming that he'd personally seen the defendants smoking the pot. And the case gave Judge Reinhardt a chance to declare—though other federal courts have been slow to take up his suggestion—that courts should interpret the new wrongful-firing law to provide workers with rights akin to those found in union arbitration.

———

Arbitration and civil service practice did not emerge full-blown but developed their remarkable qualities over years in which grievants (and, of course, management) pressed the logic of earlier cases into new areas. The new employment law changes year by year, too—at a breathtaking clip, in fact—and few employers care to predict where its evolution will take it five years hence in the minds of a judge or jury. The massive advice and compliance literature for managers on how to cope with the new employment law is therefore full of self-protective advice: generate an elaborate paper trail and conduct an exhaustive investigation before trying to fire a worker; set formal procedures on dismissals and stick to them unswervingly, no matter what the commonsense reasons for departing from them; base decisions only on evidence you can later document in some objective way; expect to bear the burden of proof, no matter what the law may say; and fire only after proceeding through a long series of warnings, deadlines, and opportunities to shape up.

No one ever passed a bill in Congress or any state legislature providing for such an outcome. Yet it's beginning to happen. There is a "greater sense" in the private sector now that "some workers have a property right to their job," Brookings economist Gary Burtless has commented. "It's not the civil service or Europe yet, but it might look that way to some employers."

Chapter 10

DROPPING THE STRETCHER

When lawyers sued to challenge the civil service exams for its fire department, the city of Houston could see the handwriting on the wall: other cities had sought to defend such exams in court and lost. So it settled by agreeing to drop any and all exam questions on which minorities scored poorly compared with whites. Other cities had made similar concessions as regarded the issue of which past questions they would reuse on future exams, but Houston went further and agreed to purge questions *retroactively,* changing scores for applicants who'd already taken the test.

The city thus identified and removed more than two dozen questions from the exam for fire department driver, which 308 of 815 applicants had originally passed. That allowed thirteen applicants who'd failed the original test to pass—but it also caused thirty-two applicants who'd passed before to fail. Many were furious. "It's simply not fair to the ones who studied for six months and who made a good grade to turn around and tell them they have now failed the test," said one. Another agreed: "You have to buy all the books and spend months studying. It's a real strain on your family."

The recalculation helped some minority hopefuls, but it turned out to hurt others. According to the *Houston Chronicle,* the applicants who had previously failed but now passed included four blacks, four Hispanics, and five whites. The thirty-two who now failed included twenty-two whites and also six blacks, three Hispanics, and an Asian. When all the factors were taken into account, dozens of applicants had been pushed up, down, on, or off the list; the net minority gain amounted to a grand total of one position.

During the 1970s and 1980s, federal authorities came very near to banning the use of standardized employment tests. Had history taken an only slightly different course, they might have tried to make them mandatory.

By the nature of things, all hiring criteria fall on a continuum between objective and subjective: "We hired the ones with the best college grade point averages" is closer to the former end, while "We went on our gut feeling of who we could work with" is near the latter.

Because of the special conditions of public hiring—specifically, the need to prevent favoritism and corruption—the nineteenth-century civil service movement had championed objective, numerical, and on-the-table methods of filling vacancies, as exemplified by the idea of competitive examination. Private industry began large-scale testing in this century for a different set of reasons. Experiments by the U.S. Air Force had shown that well-designed tests were often better at predicting who would succeed at a wide range of tasks than experience, declared interest, interview ratings, or school grades; of course, predictions derived by combining information from all these sources were more accurate than those from any subset alone.

After World War II, a new generation of employment tests were hailed as one of the first broadly useful applications of the emerging discipline of psychology. Testing had already been recognized as a good way to measure capacities such as physical strength, knowledge of specialized subject matter, and command of grammar and spelling. Now it took on new roles, such as matching applicants to tasks they would enjoy. Industrial engineers had found that tests could reduce injury rates by identifying not only physical aptitudes (such as hand-eye coordination) but also personality profiles that correlated with accident avoidance. Tests for such qualities as psychological stability, skill in interpersonal dealings, and even honesty showed substantial predictive power in real-life job situations.

Testing proponents emphasized that the question was not whether tests were perfectly predictive, but whether they could add usefully to the highly imperfect sources of information employers would rely on otherwise. Managers had always "sized up" whether applicants looked strong or skillful, how they behaved at the interview, and what happened when they were given a sample assignment. Each of these methods, though, admitted some degree of luck and reliance on possibly deceptive appearances. Testing could add a systematic and objective dimension. It was particularly good at finding hidden strengths among those who may not have made a good first impression. Its great advantage—ironically, in light of its later legal fate—was in minimizing the effect of what was known as interviewer bias.

Quite apart from its practical advantages, many observers admired testing because of what they saw as its moral dimension: it could make the distribution of life's chances more fair, assisting obscure talents and lessening the role of "who you know," of personal and family connections. Japan is so notoriously gaga for testing at all levels that it televises college entrance exams, while in countries like Britain computer systems aimed at the small business market sometimes come with bundled applicant-testing software.

As civil service employers knew, competitive examination was a particularly good way of demonstrating that decisions were not being made on the basis of supervisors' biases. Coincidentally, the 1964 Civil Rights Act was pushing private as well as public employers toward objective, on-the-record methods that courts could be sure were not masks for animus. The act even included specific language authorizing and protecting employers' use of professionally developed tests. And after the 1964 act passed, the use of tests indeed surged.

Then came the doctrine of disparate impact. Every meaningful test displays adverse impact on one or another protected group—and the more neutrally one tries to devise a test, the surer it is to do so. Tests soon became the EEOC's number one target. The specific language in the 1964 act authorizing testing, like so many such limiting phrases in civil rights law, was soon dismissed as so much meaningless verbiage, a mere scrap of paper. The EEOC decreed that all tests would have to be "validated," and its principles for validation embodied a one-two punch that few useful tests could survive.

———

The first punch consisted of a rule that for a test to be valid, its passing score would have to be set at a level of mediocrity or worse. The EEOC's famous Uniform Guidelines on Employee Selection Procedures provide that employers must not set score cutoffs any higher than they find consistent with "acceptable" job performance. New York City set a cutoff for its police exam that was lenient enough to pass twenty times as many candidates as there were available slots, but lost when a court ruled it should have been set yet lower. The commission's practical application of the rule has been even worse: it has argued that an employer should not use a cutoff unless it is prepared to prove that no applicant who fell below it *could* have done an adequate job—much as if teachers were obliged to set passing grades low enough to be absolutely sure any student who fails is ignorant of the material, and has not just had a bad test day.

The other punch consisted of requiring employers, once they had lowered the passing mark to a level consistent with mediocrity, to grade the results on a pass-fail basis. Most employers naturally wanted to give those with perfect scores preference over those who had barely squeaked by. Now the EEOC insisted the only issue was whether job seekers were "qualified"; if they were, they should all be considered equally eligible, and an employer had no business inflicting more "adverse impact" by seeking out the better qualified.

Some courts let the EEOC, and private litigators who were challenging tests, get away with a remarkably lame argument along these lines. They had framed the issues as whether cities had validated the practice of letting hiring decisions hinge on one-point score differences. Had they proved scientifically that everyone who scored 70 would outperform everyone who got 69? Of course they hadn't, and so (the commission argued) acting on such distinctions was clearly not a validated practice. And since any ranking scheme allowed some one-point gaps to make a difference, none was valid . . . which meant cities couldn't count thirty-point differences, either. It was like announcing that since no one can infallibly distinguish one-degree differences in temperature, there's no harm in locking someone outside on a cold day.

By 1983 the leading treatise on employment discrimination law was calling test validation "exceedingly difficult, if not impossible." The Fifth Circuit declared it improper to test clerk-typists for grammar, spelling and punctuation. The Ninth Circuit vetoed the testing of Los Angeles police recruits for agility, though subduing suspects by force is part of the job. "When courts have applied the EEOC Guidelines in detail," a leading textbook explains, "the tests have generally failed to survive."

Because not all courts were willing to defer to the EEOC guidelines, testing was kept fitfully alive. But even aside from the issue of whether they deferred to the guidelines, many courts applied what a *Harvard Law Review* commentator praises as "extreme factual skepticism" toward employers' factual justifications for their use of tests. The 1986 case of *Brunet* v. *Columbus* shows the process at work.

———

Strength disparities between the sexes have been found at all places and times where adult bodily strength has been measured in the human race, deriving from the same sorts of physiological differences that allow ornithologists to pronounce with confidence that the rooster of a certain species is larger than the hen. In Chicago's 1985 fire department exam, the highest-ranking woman placed at number 1,200 of 7,500 applicants; in a New York exam, the top female contender came in at number 4,652 of 21,000, and the next appeared after a further drop of about two thousand names. As physical education teachers know, upper-body strength shows an especially wide gap: in this category (important for tasks such as lifting hoses and smashing down doors), the fittest one-fifth of women roughly match the strength of the least fit one-fifth of males.

In short, adverse impact by gender runs rampant in strength tests—

and, as a result, virtually every big city in the country has been taken to court over the use of such tests for fire, police, or sanitation workers. The ACLU launched a whole project on the issue; its director publicly compared firefighter strength tests to the literacy tests by which states in the old South prevented blacks from voting, definitely a hot-button comparison for a civil rights activist.

Like other cities, Columbus, Ohio, had found that male applicants tended to accomplish simulated fire-scene tasks much more quickly than female applicants. For instance, when garbed in bulky protective gear the average male took 66 seconds to get up a six-flight staircase and back, while the average woman took 102 seconds. Men required 11 seconds to hoist sixty-five pounds of equipment to the equivalent of a third-floor window, while women needed 27 seconds; and men achieved 58 standard maneuvers with a pike pole (a tool used to rip down walls and ceilings during fires), while women managed 39.

The highlight of the Columbus test sequence was a dummy rescue, in which applicants had to carry a 125-pound sandbag along a twisting course. Counting time penalties assessed for knocking over poles or for dragging the dummy instead of carrying it, men took an average of roughly 19.5 seconds to get the dummy through, women 38.

To validate its test Columbus had hired the respected local Battelle Research Institute, knowing that the slightest hitch might lead to an order of back pay and attorneys' fees for rejected applicants. By using a selection formula that assigned a lot of weight to nonphysical qualifications, it also managed to hire two women among 126 openings, joining four who had entered in previous classes. That didn't save it from being sued by lawyers for rejected applicant Ann Brunet.

Federal judge Joseph Kinneary conceded that the test had been a "reasonable approximation of the actual tasks" required at a fire scene. "Firefighters must frequently climb stairs," he allowed, "though it appears that in tall buildings they use elevators when possible."

Then the extreme factual skepticism set in. Criticizing the stairway climb, Judge Kinneary was impressed by the plaintiffs' argument that the task of getting fire equipment up stairwells is commonly done in relays—though it was unclear why applicants slower at getting one load up six flights would not also be slower at getting six loads up one

flight. He observed that shorter applicants (who were disproportion-
ately female) had more trouble using the simulated pike pole, again
without commenting on the likelihood that for similar reasons they
might find ripping out real-life ceilings a greater challenge. And he
said the city should have considered using costly joint-articulated
dummies instead of sandbags for the rescue exercise, noting that "the
shape of the bag makes it awkward to carry, depriving individuals of
the opportunity to use lifting techniques and leverage"—with nary a
word on why the chance to use such techniques would not have improved men's as well as women's scores.

The plaintiffs had also pounced on the city's failure to test applicants
for agility or endurance, thus defying the idea—which the judge pronounced to be sound law—that a good test should in principle "reflect
all or nearly all the important aspects of the job" (although the alternative toward which the city was being pushed was to measure fewer
such aspects). In fact, the city had tested for agility in previous exams
and found that women scored poorly (averaging 36 compared to 50 for
the males); courts had also struck down agility tests in other cities. As
for endurance as distinct from strength, cities have excellent reason
not to test the limits of recruits' capacity along that dimension; it may
take hours to push them to the verge of collapse, and recruits whose
limits are miscalculated may suffer heart or kidney failure and die.

Further setbacks were in store for the city. The plaintiffs had argued
that in smoky rooms, firefighters sometimes find it safer to drag rather
than carry bodies to safety. Why, then, assess a penalty on recruits who
chose to drag the bags in the dummy rescue? Judge Kinneary accepted
this objection as well, implying that the city should be content with
firefighters who could practice at least one rescue technique rather
than preferring those who could practice both—and leaving Columbus residents to hope that the hazard in any room where they lay in
need of rescue was smoke rather than broken glass or burning fluid on
the floor.

The city's worst sin had been preferring the candidates who'd shown
outstanding strength to those who'd barely made the pass. Judge Kinneary, overstating the case only slightly, said earlier courts had been
"unanimous" in rejecting ranking and requiring a pass-fail approach.

Closely related to the city's improper interest in outstanding performance was its insistence on timing the test results. The plaintiffs objected to the use of timing, and Kinneary agreed. He found it telling that, as he paraphrased their arguments, "Firefighters infrequently run up stairs, both for safety reasons and to marshal their energy to perform when they arrive at the fire." In other words, they run up stairs only *sometimes,* and often take care to save their energy because they'll need it even more for what they find at the top of the stairs. From this he concluded that any applicant who made it up the steps at all should get equal ranking with everyone else who did. Summing up, the court found that "sometimes firefighters work all-out, and sometimes they pace themselves; it depends on the task at hand." The case for putting out blazes quickly was merely "anecdotal"—the ultimate dismissal. "Anecdotal evidence regarding the speed at which firefighters must work is not sufficient to justify a timed, competitive examination."

No greater triumph of factual skepticism could readily be imagined. The anecdotal feeling in society that fires ought to be put out quickly is so strong that traffic cops inquire of speeders, "Where's the fire?"; that parking in front of hydrants is against the law even if you leave your phone number on the dashboard so you can be asked to move it; and that homeowners whose kitchens catch fire notify the authorities by way of frantic 911 calls rather than registered mail. They want the flames put out right away, because they've heard anecdotally that fires left undoused tend to burn more things.

But the favored position among courts came to be one of high-minded agnosticism about exactly what it took to fight fires, a tone that was adopted in many press accounts as well. City hall officials defending tests "say speed is critical" in fighting fires, reported the *New York Times.* In the best tradition of unbiased, we-take-no-sides journalism, it added, "Opponents argue that it is not."

———

Not all women were happy about the assumptions the courts were making. "You have to ask yourself, if it was your child or your mother, who do you want to go and get her down the ladder?" asked Lauren Howard, for years the only woman on the Chicago fire department. "Do you want somebody big, incredibly strong, [and] extremely fast, or someone who is average?"

That kind of thinking cut little ice with the courts, or with the activists and legal academics urging them on. Under pressure, Los Angeles and many other cities abandoned timed physical tests. Many courts struck down hose-lifting and dummy-rescue simulations, and cities often watered down what remained to the point of meaninglessness: San Francisco, which had formerly asked fire department recruits to lift a 150-pound sack up a flight of stairs, agreed to let them drag a 40-pounder across a smooth floor.

Police fared no better. In 1986 the New York Police Department agreed to drop its pre-employment physical for recruits, under threat of lawsuits. Within a few years more than one in five city cops was considered out of shape; some hires, according to an exposé in *New York* magazine, had fallen in "the almost inconceivably unfit first percentile," that is, "worse than 99 percent of others their age and gender." "It is scary," said a spokesman. A training tape showed recent recruits unable to lumber over a five-foot wall in a simulated chase. The number of police injuries had risen 15 percent between 1987 and 1993, and disability payouts were soaring. On the other coast, politicos were pressing Los Angeles to tear down its six-foot wall for police recruits, lending new meaning to the concept of "lowering barriers for women."

Cops without the physical ability to catch or subdue suspects by force, of course, might have to resort to using their guns—assuming they could land a hit, that is. Some New York City officers were found to lack the hand strength to pull the trigger of their standard-issue revolvers. And after lawyers argued women and minorities might lack the familiarity with firearms allegedly typical of white male recruits, Pittsburgh agreed to give more tries to those who failed a silhouette-target test, thereby establishing bad aim as another legally protected category.

Standards for city garbagemen have met much the same fate. Those in New York City used to have to show their stuff by doing things like scaling an eight-foot wall and holding a 60-pound container in the air for a full minute. After the usual siege of the city's physical test, applicants were allowed to drag an empty sanitation basket to and from a truck, rather than carry a full one. Nearly everyone passed the test (a figure of 98 percent was reported one year), and the city used a lottery to choose among those who did. It was considering saving money by simply doing away with the test, as other cities had done.

Unions in the uniformed services have often protested the lowering of standards and have even intervened in court cases, only to be rebuffed—as a federal judge did rather rudely to New York's sanitation union when it tried to block such a move. "You can't have 95 percent of the people getting 100 percent and have it mean anything," said Edward Ostrowski, president of the Uniformed Sanitationmen's Association. "Over a period of time this is going to take its toll. You're going to have people getting hurt on the job because they physically can't handle it." Presumably, this says nothing of the reaction of other crew members when a newcomer asks if he can be the one to carry the empties, the way he did on the test.

———

Itself recalling the collapse in stages of a house afire, the crumbling of one set of standards tended to bring down others. As physical standards were undercut, civil service employers had to assign proportionally more weight to pencil-and-paper testing—but that increased those tests' adverse impact on black candidates, and thus the legal pressure for them to be diluted or abandoned as well.

According to an account in the *New Republic,* this kind of effect led to the step-by-step demolition of the venerable Foreign Service exam. To help black applicants, the service first tossed out its credit for foreign language attainments, however relevant such skills and interests might be to its mission of preparing diplomats. Since this was very bad news for female applicants, who had excelled in that category, the service compensated by upping the weight it assigned to English-language skills, another area where women did well—only to find it had hurt the black men again. Women still seemed to need more help, though, so it "began to recycle questions on which women did better than men," according to a State Department report.

One other solution was downgrade test areas on which both women and blacks did poorly, such as history and politics. (The first questions dropped from the federal civil service exam when it headed downhill were on arithmetic and algebra.) Eventually a federal court required the department to "pass applicants only according to their English Expression scores" for the 1985 through 1987 exams, thus seeming to vindicate philistines who felt success as a diplomat required no more than the ability to speak well. Like many other employers, the department then tried "norming" the scores—that is, awarding extra points to members of protected groups on the theory that it should really measure their relative performance within their group. In 1991 Congress banned norming as well, without specifying any means by which testing could lawfully go forward.

Other attempts to find acceptable halfway testing measures have foundered as well. New York City paid a consultant $400,000 to devise a new firefighting test that gave applicants partial credit if their second or third choice on an answer was right, in hopes of reducing "test anxiety." Court rulings had "crippled" Gotham's efforts to recruit the most qualified applicants, explained city personnel director Juan Ortiz. "The city is whipsawed between different judges and different legal proceedings." Another official, in charge of preparing New York's written police exam, publicly observed that a functional illiterate might pass it. Washington, D.C., was hiring everyone who passed its police exam, though Congress had rebuffed Mayor Marion Barry's proposal to hire by lottery. By the time Washington's written exam for firefighters had made it through the legal process, its passing grade was set at a "score one could expect to receive if one answered the questions randomly," a federal appeals court acidly noted. "Dart-throwing methods of test answering sufficed."

————

Plaintiffs attacked tests on a number of other grounds as well. In one landmark ruling the California courts found it improperly invasive of privacy for a discount store to give security guard applicants an off-the-shelf test designed to gauge their psychological stability, though such a quality might seem useful in employees who may use physical force for which their employers are legally liable.

One early result of the passage of the Americans with Disabilities Act was a surge in demands for accommodation in testing, including professional licensing and qualification exams. A New York woman won the right to take the state bar exam over four days rather than two, and in a separate room to cut down on distractions, so as to accommodate her dyslexia and attention-deficit disorder (ADD). (The inevitable question was whether judges would also agree to extend her deadlines for filing legal papers once she started practice as an attorney.) A federal appeals court ruled that a Virginia woman could sue for the right to take the National Teachers Examination with no time limit to accommodate her learning disability; she'd failed the test eight times, even though officials had allowed her more time than other test-takers and provided her with a printed transcript of the test's oral portions. Demands for additional time, the right to bring notes, and similar accommodations soon far outnumbered ADA-based demands for things like Braille or audio translations.

The development was predictable enough, since disability-education law had been transforming the climate of testing at the school level for years. Accommodation demands by students taking the Scholastic Aptitude Test rose from 16,000 in 1989 to 27,000 five years later, with the great majority requesting extra time. Colleges are likewise being hit with extensive demands to excuse these students from required courses and allow them to bring notes to tests or take extra time; they can seek cash damages if universities deny the requests. The number of younger persons diagnosed with ADD, learning disability, dyslexia, or math disability has swollen by hundreds of thousands in a relatively few years, and cynics expect the number to keep rising given the range of legally driven special educational benefits obtainable with such designations. An entire new "disabled generation" may be growing up, learning to explicate its problems in medical terms and to take advantage of favorable entitlements; as its demands for legal accommodation move up the age cohort, they are likely to hit the workplace in force.

Another remarkable EEOC guideline prescribes that a standardized test given to any applicant should be given to all: if it has not been given in the usual case, it must not be given in a doubtful case where it would appear useful. For example, if a docker has never bothered with strength tests because no one less than highly fit has ever tried to apply for a stevedore's job before, it will be in trouble if it wants to test the mettle of a scrawny-looking newcomer. Likewise, an employer that wants to retain the right to test any applicants for English proficiency may be well advised to make the most obviously fluent applicants sit through such tests as well.

For years, asked what tests it might consider acceptable, the EEOC cited typing tests given to secretarial applicants. By the late 1980s, however, federal agencies are reported to have stopped testing the typing of their own secretarial applicants. Economist Robert Adams has written that when his institution, the University of California at Santa Cruz, put out word that such tests were no longer permitted, faculty began resorting to subterfuges such as looking to see whether an application form itself contained any typed errors and watching to see how long it took the prospect to fill it out.

———

Despite the casual assumptions of many test critics, efforts to prove that tests are unfairly biased against protected groups have fallen flat. Tests do not underpredict the performance of blacks on the job, for example, and given the history of testing around the world it is hard to imagine that racial animus, as opposed to perceived practical usefulness, could be responsible for its popularity over so long a period in so many different countries.

By the 1980s, most private employers in this country had simply given up on testing because of the legal difficulties. Since then its use has crept back at the edges, in part because of a couple of Supreme Court decisions upholding particular test uses as legitimate. Many lower courts have continued to go their own way, however, regularly striking down tests. One of the high court's opinions had upheld a teacher competence exam; that did not prevent an Alabama federal court from stymieing the state's efforts to run such exams, ordering reinstatement with back pay for a teacher who had flunked one such test twice and another three times.

As for the ideological opponents of testing, few have budged. When Congress took up the proposed Civil Rights Restoration Act of 1991, the bill's advocates brought to Washington as their star witness Columbus plaintiff (and by now firefighter) Ann Brunet, who warned that if the high court's recent *Wards Cove* decision were not overturned future women in her position might not win their lawsuits. Press coverage was uncritical, nor did senators care to contradict Ms. Brunet, and lawmakers proceeded to overturn *Wards Cove* as requested.

The irony is that for all the tumult in court, the actual number of women firefighters seems to have remained quite small. After two decades of feminist legal activism, a couple of gung-ho cities have gotten their total up to 5 or 10 percent, but the nationwide percentage is more like 1 percent. Few women either apply in the first place or persist once they learn of the job requirements; others wash out in training or on the job, or go on disability. And even many male veterans who dislike affirmative action in the firehouse acknowledge that a certain number of less powerful physiques can be mixed into a working team, in part by careful assignment of job tasks (a lesson that is familiar to armies facing wartime personnel shortages).

What may be most corrosive about the courts' crusade against strength tests is that it keeps services from upholding standards among *men:* if they can drag the forty-pound dummy, they're in. The damage done by the decline in fitness among the 90 percent or more of the force that remains male may in fact be worse than the problems of accepting more female recruits as such. As Houston found in its experiment with score-changing, the trashing of tests is something like a low-accuracy bombing raid—it inflicts all sorts of collateral damage in areas that weren't its seeming target at all.

———

For employers, the lesson was simple enough. No method of hiring—subjective, objective, or anything in between—could satisfy opponents or avert lawsuits. Nothing short of a standardized test would meet the law's demands for objectivity and impersonality, but any standardized test could be tortured and stretched until it gave up the ghost on the rack of "validation" (if not in one court, then next year in another). Much like the *Camelot* tenor wondering in song at which season it might be even thinkable to leave Guinevere, and ruling out each in turn, the courts had begun to suggest that there never was a legally safe occasion for preferring one applicant to another. Plaintiff's lawyer Darien McWhirter, noting the paradox, points out its implication: "Perhaps flipping a coin should be the only legal method of employee selection."

Chapter 11

THE NEW MEANING OF COMPETENCE

The scandals that hit big-city police forces in the 1980s and early 1990s were among the worst in living memory. New York's "Dirty Thirty" 30th Precinct blowup set back years of strenuous anti-corruption efforts. At one point, 10 percent of the Miami force stood accused of major felonies. By 1993 more than a hundred officers in Washington, D.C.—once considered to have one of the nation's best police departments—had been charged with major felonies ranging up to kidnapping and murder, and the FBI had set up a special unit to enforce the law among its own hometown cops. A remarkable number of D.C. police were themselves said to be dealing drugs, and theft of department property, cash, and other valuables was rampant: close to three thousand seized guns had disappeared from the city's inventory, and office typewriters in some precincts had to be chained down to protect them from the staff.

Bad hiring was blamed for many of the problems. The D.C. force, like many elsewhere, "routinely" hired officers with misdemeanor records; it was legally prohibited from considering even murders committed while an applicant was a juvenile. "If you bypass someone for a minor criminal offense, that person can challenge you and get a re-straining order, tying up the whole list," explained city manager Robert Healy of Cambridge, Massachusetts; the town's police com-missioner had made headlines by threatening to resign after city hall leaned on him to hire eight recruits whose rap sheets sported such charges as assault and battery, breaking and entering, drunk driving, and receiving stolen property, as well as bad references from previous jobs. Some cities wound up taking on recruits who had worked for drug gangs in their civilian days. New York City waved through appli-cants who lived in notorious drug buildings and had relatives high up in the drug trade. A Brooklyn detective later charged with defrauding a widow of $75,000 had two arrests for armed robbery before joining New York's finest.

Competence was in short supply as well. D.C. cops at one point were wrecking a squad car a day, and the city had trouble with out-right illiteracy among recruits. A *Washington Post* probe found the city was losing millions in traffic fines because four of ten summonses were filled in incorrectly. Courts were dismissing about a third of mur-der indictments, often because the police paperwork did not stand up or had been misunderstood by prosecutors; once upon a time, the Dis-trict of Columbia had closed 100 percent of its homicide cases.

"Hire them now, we'll fire them later," Washington's police chief re-portedly vowed at the time as he let in bad apples. That vow turned out to be a hollow one: a maze of grievance challenges and restrictive employment laws made it impossible to fire even many egregious of-fenders later.

———

For a while, advocates of the new employment law presented them-selves as the true friends of merit in the workplace. Most of the new laws on their face seemed only to rule out employment decisions based on improper factors such as bias, spite, personality conflicts, and the like. During the debate over the 1964 Civil Rights Act, Sena-tor Hubert Humphrey foresaw a new emphasis on "qualifications" in hiring, wrenching employers away from their presumed preoccupa-tion with other matters, with the result that the law would "not only help business, but also improve the total national economy." "National prosperity will be increased," ran another congressional prediction during the 1964 debates, because "the country is not making satisfactory use of its manpower." We were not only going to keep on permitting merit hiring; we were going to require it. So what was the problem?

The rapid rise of reverse preference and affirmative action inevitably changed the tone. By 1968 the University of Minnesota had adopted a pioneering "policy commitment" that included a not-exactly-inspiring promise to "hire and promote disadvantaged persons wherever there is a reasonable possibility of competent performance." An EEOC consent decree provided for an "affirmative action override" allowing AT&T to "promote a 'basically qualified' person rather than the 'best qualified' or 'most senior'" employee. ABC-TV's "20/20" assembled cases from federal hiring: Federal Aviation Administration guidelines provide that "the merit promotion process . . . need not be utilized if it will not promote your diversity goals"; "in the future," a Defense Department memo specifies, "special permission will be required for the promotion of all white men without disabilities." The U.S. Forest Service achieved a formulation that was hard to improve on: "only unqualified applicants will be considered."

Not surprisingly, policies of this sort have come under attack almost from their inception. Even if reverse preference and affirmative action disappeared tomorrow, however, the new employment law would continue to prevent employers from filling jobs with the most competent workers. Prevailing EEOC doctrines would still divide workers into "qualified" and "unqualified" universes and forbid preference for the highly qualified over the minimally qualified. Most ways by which employers measure or document merit at either the hiring or the firing stage would still be under a legal cloud. A dozen laws would still make it risky to fire or discipline rebellious underperformers.

As the law has found itself ever more at war with traditional ideas of what it means to do a good job, our legal culture, led by the law schools, has come to the rescue by proposing to rethink those ideas. Aren't skill, merit, and competence really socially constructed and relative sorts of concepts, maybe even subjective or unknowable? Thus is theory bent to conform to practice.

In the early years of the new law, the courts tended to go easy on second-guessing employer decisions where the consequences of getting
the answers wrong seemed ominous. Thus, while freely ordering employers to revamp hiring practices in supposedly routine clerical or
industrial jobs, early judges showed more reluctance to interfere with
decisions on the filling of such "high-level" jobs as executives, physicians, pilots, or college administrators. They also trod carefully in
cases where safety seemed at stake. In a series of decisions that
cheered employers, the Supreme Court allowed New York City to turn
away recovering heroin users from transit jobs, allowed states some
leeway to say no to prospective prison guards of slight build, and declined to help out a would-be student nurse who was deaf (a more
challenging distraction than merely being off reading a magazine
when patients tried to summon her).

But both categories of exception came under sustained attack in the
law reviews. An influential *Harvard Law Review* article assailed the
high-level-job exception, while a *Texas Law Review* treatment similarly blasted the court for its "inexplicable deference to employer decisions that involve public safety." Wasn't it all the more demeaning to
be turned away from a job because it was considered "too important"?

The critics were quite right in one sense: there *is* a continuum between high-level and safety-related jobs and the ordinary kind. In almost any job the difference between an outstanding and a wretched
jobholder can count as a serious matter for the world's welfare, as suddenly becomes clear in an emergency; and few jobs are truly free of
safety implications, least of all those that strike outsiders as routine.
The logical conclusion might be that incompetence should no more
be legally protected in supposedly routine jobs than in the elite or perilous kind. But the law reviews concluded the opposite, and the Court
seems to have found it hard to ignore them. The justices began to look
at high-level cases such as those reviewing the granting of law or ac-
countancy partnerships in much the same manner as the rest. And on
the safety issue they reversed field with a disability-rights decision
known as *Arline*, rebuking a Florida school district for its fear that a

tubercular teacher might go off the medication which kept her from being contagious in the classroom. Henceforth, the Court said, employers wishing to invoke safety reasons for personnel decisions would have to prove "substantial" risk, and the Court's disapproving tone made clear that such claims would be less welcome than in the past. The "inexplicable deference" that was so offensive to the *Texas Law Review* authors had been withdrawn.

Though they have seldom reached the high court, safety cases have been the subject of a whole jurisprudence of their own. One line of cases has established the principle that employers must not screen out workers from jobs on the grounds that they are likely to injure themselves; the most commonly occurring pattern was that of the applicant who had previously complained of back problems and was now invoking disabled-rights law to procure a heavy-lifting job despite a possible renewed risk. Courts ruled that even showing a material risk would do the employer no good, dismissing out of hand the concern that employers could be left footing heavy disability payments when the worker reactivated the old injury.

The passage of the Americans with Disabilities Act was a decisive victory for those who thought a little risk helps spice things up. Barbara Lee writes in the UC Berkeley employment-law journal that the ADA "will make it very difficult for employers to make a successful safety defense in any but the most extreme cases." ADA advocates have repeatedly stressed that an employer cannot win merely by showing an "elevated risk" of injury to customers or co-workers; it must also prove that the risk is "substantial," "direct," and not to be mitigated by any possible accommodation. In doing so, it must not rely on general rules, but consider every detail of each new case afresh.

This counts as one of the riper ironies of the new employment law. In other situations when business gets sued, the standard line of attack is that no price is too high to pay for even the smallest reduction in a risk of injury. Knowingly going forward with a business practice that involves a marginally higher risk—say, by holding take-out coffee at too high a temperature—is the moral equivalent of deliberately dumping scalding water in the lap of a named person: you may have been taking only a one-in-a-million chance, but sell a hundred million cups of coffee and someone's number is bound to come up. And so our legal system regularly hands out punitive damages for just the kind of decision that it here forces on hirers—and here the odds of injury will often be a lot worse. Of course, many of the same activist organizations and litigation groups that have helped create the punitive-damage culture applaud the employment-law rules that forbid employers to consider elevated levels of risk.

Were we to insist on the same safety logic in employment that our law enforces in other business decisions, we would probably require employers to engage in extensive employee screening. Indeed, federal regulations still do that in a few areas where the safety implications are too obvious to duck: age limits for airline pilots, required psychological screening for nuclear plant operators, criminal record checks for bankers and day-care operators, security checks for airport personnel, and so forth. Federal law requires that bank officers be dismissible at will even if both the bank and the officer would prefer to provide for a longer relationship by contract: "It is essential that a bank be able to remove immediately any employee suspected of dishonesty or carelessness," notes a commentator. Yet a trivial difference in classification between two jobs of similar function may result in a complete reversal of what is legally permissible. If a financial-sector job strongly resembles a bank officership but does not fall under the National Bank Act, for instance, the employer may not be able to capture the safety benefits of employment at will, even if the worker explicitly consents to such an arrangement at the time of hiring.

The ADA poses a wide range of safety concerns, some of the more vivid of which relate to communicable disease. Most public discussion has focused on HIV (the virus that causes AIDS), which appears virtually impossible for workers to transmit to others in the course of ordinary work. A better ground for worry may be hepatitis B, a highly serious virus—it strikes 300,000 and kills 7,000 a year—that is thought to be at least a hundred times more easily passed by bodily fluids than is HIV. A UCLA heart surgeon apparently spread hepatitis B to eighteen patients in the early 1990s; the working theory is that the virus passed through holes in his gloves. Higher-ups had known about his condition: "The hospital's decision to allow the surgeon to keep on operating even after he was found to be infected," it was tersely explained, was "in compliance with federal regulations." That case is likely to be only the first. "Seen through the lens of the ADA, public health regulation may be regarded as discrimination against people with disabilities," as prominent disabled-rights advocate Laurence Gostin has put it.

Bowing to safety concerns, Congress in its 1986 amendments to the Age Discrimination in Employment Act temporarily exempted police and fire officers from its ban on automatic retirement. At the end of 1993 it allowed this provision to expire, thus giving superannuated public safety officers a right to stay indefinitely unless their employers could prove them unfit; Senator Howard Metzenbaum, an Ohio Democrat, had blocked a move to extend the exemption. Federal officials defended the phaseout but conceded that older workers showed not only a decline in strength and stamina but also a higher risk of incapacitation in emergencies. Trying to put the best spin on these results, the federal study offered the reassuring thought that not many of the extra heart attacks would occur during really critical rescue moments—and roughly half the time enough other officers would be present to get the job done, so that needless death or injury to third parties would occur only 135 times a year. Rank-and-file organizations (as well as the AFL-CIO) had endorsed a continuation of automatic retirement, to no avail. "I know of no issue which has broader or more passionate support among our membership," said Frederick Nesbitt of the 200,000-member International Association of Fire Fighters; protected workers' "inability to perform [their] duties" will be "certain to result in the injury or death of innocent people."

Tenure also prevents removal of many who have already shown themselves accident-prone. By the time one New York City bus driver struck and killed a Manhattan pedestrian he had been in forty accidents, according to a *New York Post* investigation; a second driver had been in forty-two mishaps before getting into a fatal accident with a bicyclist. A third, with eighty-two accidents on his record, had yo-yoed through the all-day training seminar twenty-five times; the toughest discipline he'd been given was a one-day suspension. A fourth was still behind the wheel despite 103 at-fault collisions over

THE NEW MEANING OF COMPETENCE

twenty-two years; between the sixty-eighth and sixty-ninth collisions, he was given a safe-driving award. The *Post* reported that "virtually every" TA attempt to discipline drivers gets appealed, and arbitrators routinely reverse the discipline. The driver involved in the bicyclist fatality had lied about his driving record to the state department of motor vehicles; his drivers' license had been revoked twice and suspended twice, and state investigators had recommended several years before that he be pulled off the road. But even after the fatality he was put back on the road, where he was involved in two more accidents. State investigators found a fifteen-accident veteran fully to blame after he struck and killed a twelve-year-old with his bus; he served eight days of a twenty-day suspension and was then put back at the wheel, where he injured an elderly man. Asked about the incidents, a union spokesman called for more intensive training efforts and blamed overwork, saying there was "too much stress out there."

After an American Eagle flight crashed near Raleigh, North Carolina, in December 1994, killing thirteen people, a probe by the National Transportation Safety Board found that the pilot (whose error had caused the crash) had nearly been dismissed from his previous job because of poor performance; American Eagle didn't know this, because it hadn't asked. Such ignorance was par for the course these days, according to the safety board; the *New York Times* quoted investigators as saying that "few airlines will tell another about a former employee's performance, for fear of being sued by the applicant if the information is used to deny the person a job." The board had identified four crashes (with seventy-two fatalities) in which pilot error had been preceded by the failure of the reference process to disclose a poor job history. "It is extremely important that liability issues not drive transportation safety," said NTSB chairman James E. Hall.

The *Detroit Free Press* found similar patterns in an investigation of teachers charged with sexual misconduct with students: threatened with litigation, many school districts had agreed to keep silent as well as pay substantial sums to secure their resignation. Thus Roseville agreed to pay $50,000 to a teacher charged with sexually approaching a student, seal his files, and provide neutral references. He soon got a job at a parochial high school and was promptly accused by another student of forcing sex. Convicted of criminal sexual conduct, he managed to land a job at yet a third area school, where he took his students on a field trip to the courtroom where he'd been tried. Asked why they hadn't checked his references, archdiocese officials said doing so would have been a waste of time given the reference climate.

The law-school crusade against rap-sheet inquiries has combined with the gutting of references to make life safer for many persons who make life less safe for others. Two-thirds of crimes at fast-food restaurants are committed by current or former employees, according to an executive with the Hardee's chain. One survey found that within a single year, guards employed by leading security firms committed 261 serious crimes, including 38 murders and 29 assaults. Lax screening was blamed: in one case an employee who shot and killed a teenager at a dance he was supposed to be guarding had been fired from two earlier security jobs and was a suspect in twelve drive-by shootings. Employee theft and fraud, which drives more than a few small firms out of business, is reported to cost $120 billion a year; according to company recruiters, lying in resumes and interviews (also viewed indulgently by the new regime) has become epidemic, with the youngest applicants showing by far the worst habits.

Nor are high-level jobs any longer an exception. The Central Intelligence Agency is "a culture where personnel problems tend to be passed along rather than dealt with," commented former director R. James Woolsey after Aldrich Ames was revealed as a Soviet spy; according to a *New York Times* investigation, Ames had a reputation as deadwood, a malcontent, and a drunk, but a slew of unfavorable assessments from his stint in Mexico City weren't forwarded to the Soviet division when the agency transferred him there as counterspy chief.

Competence and accountability problems beset the public service in cumulatively debilitating ways. In 1989 a commission headed by former Fed chairman Paul Volcker found federal employment in a "quiet crisis." "I've talked with hundreds of line managers and administrators from practically every federal agency," Pat Ingraham, a government professor who took part in the Clinton administration's "reinventing government" effort, told the *Washington Monthly*. "And what I hear is the quality of new hires is just getting worse and worse." A federal commission headed by Paul Volcker found a "widespread sense that the overall quality of federal entry-level employees is declining" and the *Washington Post* reported that the legally straitjacketed hiring process was "almost universally blamed." For eight years a court suspended the use of the federal government's PACE exam for executive and professional federal employees, with results that former Office of Personnel Management director Constance Horner called "nightmarish."

Most new employment-law ideas, with accommodation of alcohol and drug abuse being a typical example, strike first and hardest in public employment. Such was also the case with the lifting of automatic retirement: "Many government offices are saddled with employees in their seventies who can't really cut the mustard," the *Washington Monthly* found in 1990. The assault on standardized testing struck public employers with special force because civil service rules, meant to take away scope for favoritism, had required them to rely much more heavily on such tests than did most private employers. Legally inflicted delays in the hiring process are harmful in themselves because they encourage the best candidates to accept other offers: at the New York Police Department, which has at times put applicants through a three-year wait, former personnel chief Michael Julian has said that "the people you get are the people who are unemployable elsewhere."

The trappings of tenure discourage even modest efforts by public managers to get a grip. Since a common feature of public employment is that low supervisor ratings may themselves be contested as an adverse action, nearly all workers tend to get the middle rating of "satisfactory," and reductions in force must proceed without taking note of relative competence. In the Washington, D.C. school system, considered one of the nation's more troubled, only one-half of 1 percent of teachers were recently getting a rating below satisfactory, a figure the *Washington Post* called "ridiculously low." Involuntary transfers are also often viewed as adverse action, with the result that problem employees get "kicked upstairs" to jobs they will accept voluntarily. A Brooklyn teacher reassigned to administrative work for striking a student was sent back to the classroom and promptly struck another student, an action a panel later concluded had been taken on purpose so as to return to the more desirable job.

———

In their 1981 volume *Teachers and the Law,* Louis Fischer, David Schimmel, and Cynthia Kelly dispute the notion that it is virtually impossible to get a poorly performing teacher out of the classroom. As evidence they offer five real-life cases in which districts were upheld in ousting educators for incompetence. Of the five teachers in their cases, two were mentally ill, one having been twice hospitalized for paranoid schizophrenia. The other three showed severe deficits in communication: one mangled grammar and punctuation, another "mispronounced words" and lacked other verbal and technical skills, and the fifth, a principal, had grown too deaf to understand ordinary conversation.

Since then, the Americans with Disabilities Act has made the authors' examples obsolete; it would give all five of the teachers a shot at contesting their removal. One of the milestones marked by disabled-rights law lay in this revising of the definition of competence itself. An "employer who performs the traditional 'can the person do the job' analysis," explains Barbara Lee in the *Berkeley Journal of Employment and Labor Law,* "generally will have violated the ADA." An employer must not insist on the capacity to handle any particular task unless it is demonstrably "essential" to the job. Some ADA advocates had claimed that employers would not have to redesign jobs around the limitations of particular handicapped applicants, and EEOC guidelines officially endorse "the same performance standards and requirements that employers expect of persons who are not disabled." But despite such "soothing language," writes Lee, in practice "employers should prepare for a substantial amount of second-guessing about essential functions and . . . production standards."

Indeed, it's hard to think of a type of shortcoming in a worker that might not be a potential manifestation of some disability. Trouble handling numbers could signal a math disability; a short temper may stem from an emotional disability; failure to make it through training could result from a learning disability; and so forth. And even deficits arising from causes other than disabilities increasingly must be ignored, accommodated, or both. Those who fall short in English proficiency because English is not native to them, for example, have been brought under legal protection by the simple expedient of stretching the bans on national-origin and alien-status bias. The Justice Department's immigrant-rights division has placed ads in newspapers and in the New York subways warning hirers that the "ability to speak fluent English" must not "affect your decision about hiring a prospective employee." Alan Koral's compliance manual warns the employer not to demand more English proficiency than it can prove is necessary for its business. "Sometimes only a very rudimentary vocabulary—'stop,' 'don't,' 'look out,' etc.—is all that is needed to perform a job."

From the perspective of the customer who is left shouting at the uncomprehending taxi driver or hospital orderly, an inability to communicate clearly in English might appear to raise a simple issue of competence or perhaps safety. But the *Diaz* v. *Pan Am* line of cases, establishing the illegitimacy of customer preference as a criterion in hiring, encourages courts to ignore such feelings. It is "necessary to reject customer preference arguments," agrees professor Mari Matsuda in a widely cited *Yale Law Journal* article calling for stronger legal enforcement of the emergent legal doctrine against accent discrimination. If customers fail to understand an accent, Matsuda suggests, it might be their own fault for having "lived a monocultural life." Their complaints may indeed arise from "a need to judge and control others," perhaps because they "fear change." Matsuda concedes that requiring employers to hire heavily accented speakers for customer-service jobs "will admittedly impose some hardship on businesses that rely heavily on pleasing customer whims"—an impressive formulation, reducing as it does to a mere "whim" humans' desire to communicate with each other easily in transacting their affairs. A 1991 *Harvard Law Review* article by Stanford professor Mark Kelman chimes in with a suggestion that "difficulty in understanding those with less common accents is socially contingent, and that customers will ultimately adjust to the accented speaker if our civil rights law insists that accented speakers be allowed to hold positions in which they regularly communicate with the public." The reference to "the accented speaker" sidesteps the complicating fact that not one but hundreds of different accents are at issue, and that comprehension problems may be worst between pairs of speakers with different strong accents. Attorney Alan Koral warns employers that in choosing between native-born applicants they must not favor those whose "manner of speaking" more closely "reflects the norms of the Caucasian community." And California has passed a pioneering law requiring employers to accommodate illiteracy among their workers.

Bilingual education policy has already set the precedent, requiring schools to find qualified math teachers fluent in Amharic, Urdu, and Laotian. After the schools in Westfield, Massachusetts, assigned an instructor with a heavy Spanish accent to teach a first- and second-grade class, four hundred parents signed a petition asking that instructors be proficient in "the accepted and standard use of pronunciation." The state's attorney general promptly handed down an opinion that any consideration of teachers' accents was illegal, while the National Education Association rushed through an annual-meeting resolution declaring its opposition to any disparate treatment on the basis of "pronunciation"—a far cry from the days when pedagogues were thought to be sticklers for correctness on that very subject.

The Americans with Disabilities Act has the potential to force the rethinking and watering down of every imaginable standard of competence, whether of mind, body, or character. "In the past," a Chevron manager told the *New York Times* after the ADA passed, "in the manufacturing and producing segment of the company, there has been more of a standard that a person is either 100 percent qualified or not. . . . That will have to be very carefully reconsidered."

The law reviews have been abuzz with proposals to push these ideas further. In the *Texas Law Review,* Thomas McGarity and Elinor Schroeder argue that rather than letting employers go on finding excuses to prefer physically stronger candidates for heavy-lifting jobs, the law should consider requiring them "to reduce lifting requirements for all employees." Abolish heavy lifting by law—why hadn't anyone thought of that before?

Mark Kelman's widely cited eighty-nine-page 1991 *Harvard Law Review* article refers casually to the "illegitimacy of mainstream judgments of merit." Many people, Kelman concedes, may imagine that "an individual merits a particular benefit as long as he actually possesses the specified qualifications for the benefit," but that is to take "a completely static and formal view of merit." A properly "contingent view of personhood and merit" would recognize that qualifications for a job relate more "to meeting ever-shifting social needs." What this means in practice is that even if "by hypothesis" certain workers are better able to perform some jobs, it is "not obvious" that they are in any way "entitled" to them. "More politically progressive commentators," among whom there is little doubt the author is included, deny "the legitimacy of allowing private employers to distribute [jobs or income] in accord with either current or potential productivity."

Another leading *Harvard Law Review* article, by Elizabeth Bartholet, laid out the case against courts' deference (which was already diminishing rapidly) toward employers' decisions in filling "high-level" jobs. Bartholet traces such deference to "The Meritocratic Myth," which she proceeds to dispel by observing that any notion of what it means to be a good doctor, school principal, or company executive is "necessarily value-laden" and requires "often essentially political choices." That means there is no reason to go on conferring the more desirable jobs on what another writer, whom she quotes with evident approval, describes as "people who can get good ratings, especially from big shots." The author herself must be presumed well situated to opine on the subject, having nabbed one of the great brass rings the legal profession provides to those who get good ratings from big shots—namely, tenure at Harvard Law School.

The affirmative action debate has yielded many similar pronouncements. "Music is music," said Michigan state senator David Holmes, asked about his successful withholding of $1 million-plus in state aid to strong-arm the Detroit Symphony into hiring black instrumentalists without competitive auditions. "Do-re-me-fa-so-la-ti-do. I learned that in school." Syndicated feminist writer Ellen Goodman voiced frustration at "the whole peculiar matter of 'qualifications' . . . there is something insidious about the 'qualification issue.'" *New York Times* editorialist Brent Staples scoffs at "'pure merit,' whatever that might be," agreeing that "the world works more on insiderism and inherited privilege."

Even the presumably hardheaded business community is full of diversity experts who now assure executives that competence is really a situational, subjective, and culturally contingent concept, as Heather Mac Donald reported in the *New Republic*. "'Qualifications' is a code word in the business world with very negative connotations," says one; another adds, "The weight placed on math, science and engineering credentials may be considerably biased." "We haven't started to ask what are expendable requirements, such as the two-page memo or a certain writing style," says the vice president for education and training at a big West Coast bank. Alan Koral's compliance guide says that to "do your part toward supporting the company's affirmative action commitment," interviewers should be "prepared to question traditional concepts of 'qualifications'" by suspending objections to "persons whose writing skills (e.g., in application forms) are unconventional or simply poor."

An axiom, they say, is a premise so fundamental that even people who attempt to deny it behave as if they believed in its truth. And so it happens that each institution to lead the assault on the "meritocratic myth" recruits fresh talent for itself by ruthlessly competitive means. Top law schools expect world-beating board scores and wrinkle their noses at transcripts organized along the pass-fail lines that their professors prescribe for the hiring of firefighters. Bar associations administer famously demanding exams to determine who will get a chance to practice, then set them loose to undermine everyone else's standards. Law-culture pundits deplore the mediocrity of this or that Supreme Court pick, while judges dole out clerkships to the brightest students. All may affect for public consumption a nihilist view of

THE NEW MEANING OF COMPETENCE

competence and accomplishment: "no one can really tell what such things mean," "they're all culturally relative," and so forth. And all may back it up by plugging their fingers firmly in their ears as the evidence mounts that bad things begin to happen in the wider society when competence ceases to count. But do they manage to fool even themselves?

Part IV

KID GLOVES AND
BRASS KNUCKLES

Chapter 12

KID GLOVES AND
BRASS KNUCKLES

In any list of the most successful employment lawsuits, a high place would have to be accorded to *Rajender* v. *University of Minnesota*. Filed on behalf of women faculty, the case led to sweeping court orders designed to advance women's interests at every level of the giant institution—orders almost as ambitious in their way as the classic 1970s court orders mandating cross-district school busing or taking over state prison systems. From the standpoint of many fans of the new employment and discrimination law, *Rajender* reads as a sterling example of what courts can do.

Like many big lawsuits, this one grew from small beginnings. Minnesota had a reputation as being generally friendly to women's advancement and specifically a pioneer of affirmative action among universities, but the chemistry department, like some others in the hard sciences, lagged behind in female representation. One newcomer to the department, Shyamala Rajender, had noticed that certain male post-doctoral students lunched regularly at the faculty table, but no one suggested she or other women join the table. So one day a few of them just sat down uninvited. An awkward silence descended, and

211

the men soon drifted away. Rajender felt the incident confirmed her suspicions that the department's senior professors had a problem with women; she filed a bias complaint that eventually matured into an actual lawsuit.

Coming to federal court, her lawyers soon ran into good fortune: they drew as a judge Miles Lord, a former state attorney general renowned for his populist views and the comet-like trail of controversy he left behind wherever he went. "It evens out the sides," Judge Lord once declared, "if I look out at the litigants and I ask are they rich and powerful, or are they poor and oppressed?" Opinion on his merits could not be more sharply divided: he made it onto *American Lawyer*'s list of the country's worst judges, only to be named the best federal district judge the next year by the Association of Trial Lawyers of America. The parent Eighth Circuit had sternly rebuked him for what it saw as his partiality toward discrimination complainants. When he retired from the bench, he set up practice as a personal injury lawyer, complete with full-page ad in the Minneapolis yellow pages.

As the case inched forward Rajender's lawyers added wide-ranging charges that women were treated unequally throughout the giant university, not just in her corner of it. Discouragingly, however, the complainant received "no support" from her women colleagues, to quote a *New York Times* report. One of her lawyers pleaded to "at least put some warm bodies in the courtroom so that when the judge looks up, there are a few women out there who are interested in the case." Early in the affair her lawyers offered to settle the claim for $35,000, but the university turned them down.

For the university, it was one of those Indians-selling-Manhattan decisions. In a series of sweeping rulings, Judge Lord certified the case as a class action; upheld the claims of sex bias; appointed three "special masters" with wide-ranging authority to intervene in every school policy and personnel decision over the next ten years to ensure the most favorable shake for women; and tagged the university with $2 million in fees payable to Rajender's lawyers.

Over the decade that followed there was no question that the number of women at all levels of the university rose impressively. Of course the same thing was happening at institutions of higher learning nationwide, including those that hadn't been sued; the biggest single factor was surely that female talent had surged into the profession.

Results were hard to measure, but the effects on the university's governance were not. When the institution's presidency fell vacant and trustees selected Kenneth Keller to fill the post, *Rajender* plaintiffs went to court to demand his ouster on the grounds qualified women had not been given enough consideration; their motions held his appointment in suspense for six months before the court finally let it go forward. The case "has had an enormously polarizing effect on the university," report George LaNoue and Barbara Lee. "It's a disaster for higher education," said Sheldon Steinbach of the American Council on Education, calling it "part of the pattern of the erosion of the peer review process."

Faculty women themselves were of two minds. Professor Charlotte Striebel was glad the suit had opened the university's internal processes to scrutiny: "When I want data I talk to my attorney and my attorney talks to their attorney and their attorney talks to the people with the data." Physics professor Phyllis Freier, who had waited twenty years to get tenure, was less pleased. "Filing official complaints really dirties your relationships with people," she said. "The university is one of the most important institutions in the state. I hate to see anything bad and wasteful happen to it."

What about Rajender herself? She did get a six-figure cash settlement, but she didn't get the academic career she'd hoped for; instead, she left the university to become a patent lawyer. "I am sure the case is having an enormous impact in higher education," she later said, "but from my personal point of view it was a terrible price to pay. I will carry the scars of battle for the rest of my life." One of her attorneys, Ellen Dresselhuis, declared that she intended never to take another academic discrimination case because they were too hard on the clients. Backing up her distaste with the most sincere gesture known to lawyerdom, she declined to put in for any share of the court-awarded fees.

———

Employment law began, of all things, as a branch of domestic-relations law. That was in the days when most hirings included room and board, and many employees were underage servants and apprentices. With modern times came an expectation that workers would pursue domestic lives apart from their employers, fending for themselves as independent adults rather than wards. Thus by the end of the nineteenth century the law of master and servant had gradually pried itself loose from domestic relations to fuse, like a prehistoric land mass, with the vast new continent of contract law—symbolizing the movement, so celebrated by Henry Maine, from the unchosen relations of status to the voluntary relations of contract.

Over the past couple of decades, something quite different has been happening. Harvard professor Mary Ann Glendon sums up the change by saying that America has increasingly reversed its legal treatment of employment and matrimony. Thirty years ago we used to require people to show a judge good cause before they could get out of a marriage, while employment was left to the continuing will of the parties. Now we prefer a fresh start instead of an attempt to force parties to sup at the same unhappily matched table—if that table is located in a home. If it is in an office suite, they may have to stick it out forever.

It's not surprising that employment disputes resemble domestic disputes; the two bodies of law attempt to govern the two essentially intimate realms that divide the waking hours between them. Daily interactions spreading over years can be sifted for evidence of cruelty or neglect, as whole circles of associates choose sides. Say what you will about the evils of lawsuits over traffic accidents or trademark infringement, those lawsuits have at least one redeeming feature—they're probably waged against strangers who've never been important in your life, and who'll go back to being strangers when the fighting is over. The people whose lawyers are saying terrible things about you, jerking you around with their tactics, and generally ruining your day never really knew you, which helps explain how they could behave that way and go on facing themselves. Your experience with them may not have to intrude psychologically into your "real" life. But there's little hope of such dispassion or distance with workplace or family litigation.

———

As in divorce, many of the most brutal cases come when the warring parties insist on living under the same roof. The issue often arises where a worker has filed a suit over harassment or failure to promote but continues to come in to the office every day.

In the natural course of events, employers want to get rid of such an employee; even if managers do not directly exercise this option, they will often be tempted to "fire" him or her by subtler means. Inevitably the law developed methods to curb this sort of thing, including prominently a doctrine known as *constructive discharge.* Both federal labor law and state unemployment compensation law had come to accept the basic idea that not every resignation from a job is truly voluntary: quitting may be but a formality if your boss has moved a stone planter into your parking space and emptied the contents of your desk into a large trash bag in the lobby. On the same time, neither system was eager to encourage claims by workers who'd quit in less than extreme circumstances. So they set a relatively high hurdle. In a 1964 case, for example, the National Labor Relations Board ruled that an employee could claim constructive discharge only if his employer had "deliberately" made working conditions "intolerable."

This definition was not nearly liberal enough for those who were shaping the new employment law. Commentators and courts soon came up with a much nicer formula: a jury could find that an employer had committed constructive discharge if it knew a worker was under great stress but didn't move to fix things. Overly demanding work schedules, ranting and yelling by the boss, and lack of expected staff support all might count toward a finding. After an argument with a worker, a supervisor saw her pack her bags and called after her, "You're not being fired"; constructive discharge was found nonetheless. A company might get socked even though it had pleaded in all earnestness for an unhappy worker to stay.

Next to go was with the requirement that the employer even know that the worker was under stress; the important thing was that it *should* have known. If it could have learned of its employee's unhappiness by paying a modicum of attention, then it had "constructive knowledge" that constructive discharge was going on—fiction atop fiction. Before long companies were getting hit with suits from former employees who'd quit apparently on good terms and then shown up at the door months later, lawyer in tow.

As courts jettisoned the requirement of deliberateness, they also relaxed the measure of what was considered intolerable. Courts began ruling that denying complainants raises and promotions might help support a finding of constructive discharge. The D.C. Circuit court of appeals found the "predictable humiliation and loss of prestige" of getting only one promotion, where more had been expected, was tantamount to firing in a case where the employer was also charged with ignoring the worker's requests for transfer and slighting his educational opportunities. If breaking someone's momentum on the fast track would predictably cause him to depart, the employer would have to budget for back pay just as if it had physically thrown him into the streets. Some employers thus faced a predicament: if they granted a promotion a court might conclude they'd implicitly promised tenure by signaling their satisfaction with the employee, but if they denied it they might have given him a push toward constructive discharge.

In constructive discharge cases, as in outright firings, insensitive management attitudes were apt to enrage juries. A California jury voted $8 million, including $4 million for emotional distress, to an executive in the pressure-cooker business of commercial construction who was first fired and then rehired on the spot when the boss decided he was needed for a project after all; the last straw had been the company's failure to give him an expected raise and Christmas bonus, at which point he checked into a psychiatric hospital.

Countless other management practices came under scrutiny as contributing to constructive discharge: saddling a salesperson with an inferior territory; requiring an employee to work under a manager with whom she'd had personality clashes; transferring an employee to another outlet in a drugstore chain; or failing to offer desired transfers to others. *Harvard Business Review* editor David Ewing has written of a case where a jury found constructive discharge in a worker's being forced to sit next to someone who smoked foul-smelling cigars.

———

Far broader is the requirement, a vital and intrinsic part of the new law, that employers not commit *retaliation*.

Rebecca F. worked as a records clerk at an AT&T Long Lines office in Washington, D.C. Dissatisfied at the company's failure to promote her more rapidly, she filed a complaint with the EEOC, saying the company had discriminated against her because she was black. Her relations with her supervisors went downhill from there, and a year and a half later the company dismissed her.

A federal court exonerated AT&T completely of the race bias charge: "It is clear from the evidence that plaintiff was never an exemplary employee during her tenure at AT&T and that she frequently violated the rules relating to her employment." Both black and white supervisors had repeatedly rebuked her for frequent lateness and absenteeism and for spending too much time on personal phone calls; there was no reason to think a white employee would have been treated differently. Nor was there evidence to support her contention that a rule preventing more than two employees from taking lunch breaks at the same time was meant to keep her from socializing with white co-workers. The court concluded flatly that Rebecca F. "was not discriminated against because of her race."

But there was more to the case. After she'd filed her complaint, managers had huddled in meetings and put out word "to keep your eyes and ears open, if you saw anything that looked significant to write it down, and bring it to the attention of the proper persons." They began to keep detailed records of her lateness and excessive telephone use, and to call both to her attention as they occurred. This faultfinding and "constant surveillance" did not extend to other employees, as one co-worker noted in an oddly poignant bit of testimony:

> Well I noticed several people and in particular myself—I wasn't too punctual—and other employees were not reprimanded as much or more—I know I should have been reprimanded more.

In short, the court concluded, the managers "set out to build and document a case against her for the sole use of defending against the EEOC complaint." This effort had been successful, of course, since it amply documented in the court's own view the company's adequate grounds for refusing to promote and eventually dismissing her. Still, that didn't change the fact that she'd been subjected to "special conditions of employment not applied to similarly situated employees"— and thus improper "retaliation" for having filed the complaint. The court ordered her reinstated with full back pay and attorney's fees.

The requirement that employers avoid any retaliation against complainants like Rebecca F. is among the most logical and inevitable, yet also impractical—and even utopian—demands of the new law. It's logical because otherwise most workplace lawsuits would doubtless soon turn into firing lawsuits: even if the company didn't actually usher the worker out the door, managers (and, in many cases, co-workers) would be likely to ostracize him effectively enough to get the message across. At any rate, most of the new employment laws have included anti-retaliation provisions; where legislators omit to do so, courts sometimes invent such provisions on their own authority, bringing the total to at least thirty statutes in connection with which such rules are applied.

At the same time, the idea is utopian because managers are human: in deciding who deserves the next promotion, they can't step outside themselves and forget that one of the candidates has been calling them terrible names in court and in the papers. They might refrain from making his life miserable. They might even, leaning against their own inclinations, give him more than his due so he'll have no ground for complaint. But it's unlikely they'll succeed in paying no attention to the matter at all.

The ban on retaliation applies to a range of actions and policies as broad as the workplace itself. Obviously, letting someone's status as a complainant influence his pay, title, bonuses, or promotion path will count. Taking away valued job responsibilities might count as retaliation, and so might adding new responsibilities that the complainant finds unwelcome. The same is true of consideration for the timing of vacations, the doling out of corner offices, or access to travel and entertainment opportunities the employee had been getting or that are given to other employees of an arguably comparable level. Negative performance evaluations are among the employer actions most often challenged as retaliation.

Indeed, courts broadly construe retaliation to consist of any downward modification in a complainant's working conditions, or any denial of a benefit that others get. Quite a few complaints cite disputes over allocation of parking spaces in the company lot; one cited the removal of a comfortable upholstered chair. An employer can trigger legally robust retaliation charges by withdrawing an amenity it hadn't been obliged to furnish in the first place (and perhaps had not been furnishing to any other employee).

The chances for retaliation, whether actual or claimed, do not end when a complaining worker leaves a company. Bad references given afterward are a favorite target for retaliation charges. Management manuals warn against even the bare act of telling a caller that a former employee ever filed complaints, nor would it be safe to respond to inquiries with anything resembling the line "I'm afraid we can't comment on his time here—we're still in litigation with him."

Courts have ruled that retaliation need not be deliberately intended as such; inadvertent or negligent actions by the company can count, too. Nor need it be ordered from on high by the brass, since ostracism by co-workers is frequently claimed as retaliation absent any allegation that managers have encouraged it. One accepted method for proving retaliation is simply to show that working conditions deteriorated within some interval after a complaint, perhaps six months or a year. Such a pattern, courts have ruled, can "justify an inference of retaliatory motive," thus leaving the employer to prove that it is not guilty. Sometimes retaliation is charged even though there is no sign that the particular officer in charge of dispensing a benefit (who may work at a distant site) even knew the worker in question had filed a complaint; courts in such cases have been willing to assume "constructive knowledge" of complaints.

Clearly, retaliation law offers a lot to argue about. Like everything else, the business world is in constant flux: departments move out of old offices and into new ones, the alternation of slack and busy times plays havoc with vacation schedules, and unexpected departures require fast reshuffling of job duties. What should be done to the legally protected worker in these cases? Standing pat is impossible, and each new shuffle will give him different cards than he held before: he can't stay in the old building, but any office assigned him in the new will have some better and some worse features. If managers are so inclined, they'll find ways to deal him the office in the sub-basement by the boiler, the equivalent of the restaurant seat by the kitchen door (which, as the maitre d' likes to point out, makes sure you'll get your food piping hot). If the worker is so inclined, he'll find fault with everything short of the corner office with the best view. And in practice, if both sides are feeling combative, the issue will be handed over to lawyers for negotiation—and added to the retaliation counts in the complaint if it doesn't get resolved to the worker's satisfaction.

Retaliation doctrine can offer a worker certain undeniable benefits. It protects his pay, perks, and working conditions (broadly defined); it makes managers think twice if they'd been considering firing or demoting him; and it gives him negotiating muscle in future shakeups. Some employees find these benefits attractive. And to get them, all they need to do is commence a public legal conflict with their employer.

Street-smart workers and their lawyers are not exactly unaware of this possibility, any more than veteran tenants in some cities are unaware of the leverage to be gained over their landlord by getting the city to write him up on a code violation. "Employees do 'go public' to try to immunize their behavior," agrees Robert Dwoskin in *Rights of the Public Employee*. As a "practical matter," notes attorney Lewin Joel, filing a safety complaint "can actually add to your job security." Knowing that new retaliation charges can seem less plausible if they are based on stale complaints, some freshen the mix by adding new charges every six months or a year. The *Washington Monthly* tells of a laggard federal employee who, after transferring to a new agency from one where he'd made himself unwelcome, promptly filed a grievance against his new supervisor to set up a retaliation claim should he need one.

Employment lawyers now add retaliation counts as a completely routine matter, the equivalent of a keyboard macro. Sometimes they wind up either dwarfing the original grounds of the litigation or (as in Rebecca F.'s case) standing alone after the original claim falls. Such counts can massively increase the cost-infliction factor by providing the legal basis for broader use of such offensive maneuvers as depositions of company officials. As "whistleblowing" authority Stephen Kohn has put it, retaliation charges can turn an initially simple claim into "highly adversarial, complex, and costly litigation."

Closely linked as they are to showings of perceived hostility in the workplace, retaliation charges have considerable overlap with such popular claims as harassment and defamation. A single exchange of sharp words with a supervisor might result in four counts: harassment, because the words spoken signal hostility to the worker based on minority status; defamation, because they unfairly malign his professional competence; infliction of emotional distress, because they were meant to wound; and retaliation, because they're fueled in part by malice at his having previously insisted on his rights.

Because it's so easy to fall back on one or another of these theories, many managers find it advisable to avoid direct confrontation with the litigious employee. Cleveland lawyer Mary E. Reid, writing in the *Wall Street Journal* "Manager's Journal" column, warns that "criticizing an employee's job performance" could prove defamatory because it might suggest "incompetence or inability to perform" or "insubordination or disruption of workplace harmony." Just "to be safe," Reid writes with no irony apparently intended, "employers should avoid expressing—and discourage others from expressing—negative opinions of co-workers in the workplace."

———

While employers are pondering this sort of advice, self-help manuals, particularly those written by practicing lawyers, are encouraging the disgruntled worker to engage in almost comically adversarial tactics.

Some suggest that workers demand written job descriptions and formal performance reviews even if their company doesn't normally follow either practice, and demand to inspect the contents of their personnel files as often as every few months. This not only serves an admonitory function, letting human-resources types know they're being watched, but also provides a chance to demand that unfavorable material be removed from and favorable material inserted into the files. (A few courts have ruled that critical internal assessments can defame an employee just by sitting in his file under lock and key, though most require that they be shown to someone before a legal claim emerges.)

"If you receive verbal praise, write a note of thanks to create a record of it," suggest Ellen Bravo and Ellen Cassedy in *The 9 to 5 Guide*. If your company revises its handbook, advises Darien McWhirter, "[w]e suggest employees who like the old handbook send a letter to the employer by certified mail, return receipt requested, stating that they do not accept the new handbook." Of course, nearly all of these writers advise lining up legal help well in advance. As McWhirter says: "*Talk to an attorney early*. . . . Many employees could avoid throwing their cases away if they would talk to an attorney *before* doing something stupid, like resigning or admitting guilt" (emphasis in original).

Near-obsessive documentation is a big theme of the self-help literature. One adviser suggests creating a file every time you take any new job and saving in it every scrap of paper the company ever gives you. "The one with the biggest pile of paper wins," writes attorney Lewin G. Joel III in *Every Employee's Guide to the Law* (1993). If you hear such things as "wisecracks about your age," Joel comments, keeping a file of them is "your chance to get even"; you should take notes on supervisors' remarks "even at a chance meeting at a ballgame or nightclub." "Employers often let down their legal guard while making morale-building speeches," he offers. "Don't wait until you get home from work. As soon as you are alone and have a chance to write them down, do it. Go to the rest room if you have to. Remember to bring a pencil."

Other documentation techniques have proved popular among aggrieved employees as well: many swipe confidential papers from the office, and a remarkable number go so far as to smuggle in tape recorders or wear concealed wires, a practice that does not seem to have received much attention from privacy advocates. Many judges have let workers introduce the contents of such tapes as evidence even when they were gathered in violation of state law. San Francisco employment lawyer Mark Rudy told the *Wall Street Journal* that about one in five of his clients inform him they've secretly taped conversations. For years, manager Irwin Heller wore a wire when speaking with superiors at the big paper company Champion International; when the company learned of the taping, it fired him. The Second Circuit approved Heller's jury verdict over the firing, which eventually netted him a reported $300,000. Dissenting judge Ellsworth van Graafeiland proposed that his brethren might have taken a less relaxed attitude had their own clerks brought in a hidden mike to tape their deliberations, and he thought it unfortunate that "every disgruntled employee in the Second Circuit henceforth will feel free to report to work with a tape recorder hidden on his person."

Preventing civil war in the workplace was not always simple. After a bitterly fought employment case against New York's Suffolk County, a federal court decreed that lawyers for both sides "shall direct their respective clients to forgo any gloating or recriminations over this litigation"—as if it were that easy. Other courts didn't seem much to mind the upset. "Disharmony and friction" in the workplace are "healthy but natural," observed the California Supreme Court (in a curious use of the conjunction *but*). "Almost every form of opposition to an unlawful employment practice is in some sense 'disloyal,'" noted the Ninth Circuit in 1983. "Can you bite the hand that feeds you and insist on staying for future banquets?" an arbitrator once asked. Most authorities seemed to think the answer was yes.

————

In practice, most private nonunion workers who sue their employers do end up leaving the workplace; this may be proof that they're retaliated against, or simply a sign that the ordeal of civility eventually gets to be too much for both sides. Universities, with their custom of tenure, are sometimes an exception. "Nothing has changed, but I avoid them [colleagues and administration] at all costs," said a professor who won her suit.

A similar issue arises when fired workers prevail in their suits, and courts have to decide whether to order them reinstated. It is noteworthy that in the occasional situations where the fact pattern is reversed—in other words, the employer is suing to enforce a commitment of continued labor that the worker now regrets—courts will generally not order the worker to participate in the relationship. One of the reasons, a *Cornell Law Quarterly* writer observed in 1921, is that they are unwilling to enforce a "relation which has become intolerable to one of the parties." Another commentator describes courts as reluctant "to compel the continuance of a personal association after disputes have arisen and confidence and loyalty are gone." An exception is made in the case of a few "star" talents, such as athletes and opera singers, but even for them the employer's usual remedy is to enjoin them from selling their unusual skills elsewhere.

Return to work after a suit is often unattractive for both sides, as the Second Circuit recognized in a leading case where it found animosity "so intense that reinstatement was impossible." (Union Carbide's former chief labor counsel had filed an employment suit against the company—rather as if the former commandant of a fort had showed up one day under the Jolly Roger to lay siege as head of a pirate armada.) The court decided that rather than order the odious reunion, it would devise a substitute remedy, a remedy that presented employers with a new and different headache: front pay.

Back pay, of course, was the now-accepted notion of making an employer fork over all the earnings, bonuses, vacation pay, overtime and so forth that a fired worker might have earned to date had he stayed on the job. (Needless to say, it does not require the performance of "back work.") *Front pay* added the further idea of reimbursement for earnings some distance into the future: the complainant was still unemployed, after all, and who knew how long it would take till he found his next job? For a while most courts resisted the front-pay idea as overly speculative; perhaps they also suspected that it might add to the worker's already very strong incentive as litigant to avoid finding a new job before trial. But eventually their resistance was broken down by the near-unanimity of commentators, and front pay became a rich new entitlement. By counting front as well as back pay, a San Francisco jury managed to include a total of fifteen years' lost pay in the $1.1 million award it voted fired life insurance manager James Ryan.

Cynical lawyers for employers were already familiar with the miracle-recovery syndrome, in which a complainant who purportedly had been unable to find work during the long run-up to trial found it quickly once the case was over. The advent of front pay added a whole new layer: after paying out three or four years' worth of front pay (on top of back pay) to reflect a jury's belief that the claimant's future was bleak, the defendant might land a perfectly nice job within weeks of cashing the check. A few employers asked courts to reopen the damages question in such cases, but most lost, given the finality principle that when a lawsuit's over it should be over.

———

The great majority of employment lawsuits, as with those of other kinds, are settled short of trial; the most expensive and hard-fought stage is usually that of "discovery," where attorneys employ compulsory process to extract information from their adversaries. An attorney should demand "every document, note or memo that in any way deals with the performance (or lack of performance) of your client," as well as massive data on personnel policies and the like, advises prominent plaintiff's attorney Cliff Palefsky. "Ask the person to state every single reason for termination, every single problem with performance, every alleged warning or conversation, with the terminated employee." The results can bewilder targets. "They felt that we had nothing better to do than sit [in a deposition] for an entire eight-hour day," said a Koch Poultry Co. manager after his firm's run-in with the Equal Employment Opportunity Commission.

After an employee at Diners Club's Denver credit card facility complained of the company's failure to promote her, the EEOC demanded the names of all employees promoted over the past eight years, all managers who had ruled on promotions, and everyone who had so much as recommended that anyone be promoted—though no one else had complained on the subject. Since the company had kept no records of recommendations, the commission demanded that it re-create the entire eight-year history by way of one-on-one interviews—a project that would require two full-time staffers and still wouldn't unearth much of the needed data, since more than four-fifths of the managers who had been with the company a decade earlier had departed. By this point the original complainant had settled her case; the commission was simply surging forward on its own momentum.

Document demands in cases initiated by single employees often cost hundreds of thousands of dollars. "It was devastating," said the president of one small company about subpoenas for decades' worth of personnel records in an age bias complaint (filed even though the average age of his employees was over fifty). In the EEOC's famous failed twelve-year lawsuit against Sears, Roebuck, the retailer spent an estimated $20 million and at one point employed 250 full-time work-ers merely to respond to document demands. The legal literature is virtually unanimous that plaintiffs should be given maximum discov-ery power, with doubts about relevance resolved against employer-defendants. Anyone who resists is handed over to the secular arm. In 1981 a federal judge ordered the jailing of James Dinnan, a University of Georgia professor who refused on principle to disclose under oath how he'd voted on a tenure decision behind closed doors. "Women's groups welcomed the decision" to jail the don, according to news reports.

———

A very common tactic is to sue managers, supervisors, owners, or company directors as individuals. As one federal court put it in a 1990 bias case, current law permits the imposition of personal liability on everyone who "participated in the decision making process that forms the basis of the discrimination." Naming managers as defendants is now standard in California wrongful-firing suits, according to the *San Francisco Recorder,* the city's legal newspaper. Sometimes a complaint will name outside consultants or even ordinary co-workers said to have conspired against a worker's interests by, say, accepting a promotion they knew should have gone to him.

Personal damages get folks' attention. In one early harassment case a federal judge levied personal fines on workers at a Western Electric plant, including supervisors who'd engaged in no harassment themselves but failed to prevent "boisterous" underlings from doing so; to make sure the fines achieved their deterrent effect, the court forbade the company to reimburse the workers for them. Some employment plaintiffs have successfully tagged owners of incorporated businesses who had not expected their personal assets to be at risk. In housing cases, courts have ruled that individual property owners can be held personally liable for the bias sins of agents or managers even if the owners specifically ordered them not to discriminate—even, as one admirer of this trend puts it, "in the absence of any wrongdoing, negligence, knowledge, or ratification."

Some courts use personal liability to settle defendants' hash for failing to show proper remorse. In one of the first big cases under the Americans with Disabilities Act, a judge approved levying punitive damages of $150,000 against owner Ruth Vrdolyak personally as well as her security-investigations company; Vrdolyak had insisted that a longtime employee dying gruesomely of brain cancer take retirement at full pension instead of continuing to come in to the office. The judge approved the personal damages as the best way to make the owner bow her head suitably: "It is clear from the testimony of Vrdolyak that she still believes that her conduct was proper."

Personal targeting of managers and owners can raise a suit's settlement value not only because of the threat and nuisance value but as a way to trigger coverage from additional insurance policies; indeed, it is often done for this reason alone. If the employer offers to pick up the tab for a crew of individual defendants, it may have to hire a small army of separate lawyers to cover the possible conflicts of interest among them; in one tenure suit the university picked up the tab for twenty attorneys of record, one for each trustee and administrator. At other times, employers refuse to defend the named individuals: if the charge is sexual harassment or something else with a flavor of turpitude, they may even feel it legally hazardous to do so. At that point the individually sued worker may suddenly be on the hook for $300-an-hour fees that come out of his own savings, quite aside from the risk of an eventual judgment.

One case that reached the Seventh Circuit was unfair enough on its face to draw a protest from noted appeals judge Richard Posner: the owners of a small business had granted maternity benefits to its female employees but not to the wives of its male employees, acting in part on the basis of a court decision upholding that policy. When that court decision was later overturned, the EEOC demanded retroactive payment. To pay the back fines and damages, the owners had to come out of retirement and restart the business. Posner called attention to the unfairness but said the court's obligation to enforce the law as written left no choice but to approve the verdict.

———

It is a truism that litigation is an adversary process, but it often turns out to be a good deal more adversary than its novice participants were expecting.

Take a case charging disparate treatment or unequal pay. The complainant may expect to denounce management, hear its response, and let a jury decide. Or, if he is more familiar with the process, he may be prepared for the employer's lawyers to search out every bit of evidence suggesting that he was a poor performer, interview all his co-workers in search of the most damaging such bits, and assemble the whole into a coherent (if one-sided) narrative to his discredit. What he may not anticipate is the case his own side will have to make. That case may require focusing legal scrutiny on the shortcomings of a co-worker against whom he may have no particular grudge—"chosen," as one pair of commentators put it, "because he has some weakness that will make the plaintiff look good by comparison." This "comparator" will be shown to have been given higher pay or a faster promotion, or to have survived a downsizing where the plaintiff didn't. The case may then turn on how effectively the lawyer can assemble evidence of this person's incompetence, personality flaws, and so forth.

Nancy Ezold sued the big law firm of Wolf, Block, Schorr and Solis-

Cohen for turning down her partnership bid, arguing that eight men had made partner over the same period. She eventually lost, but the resulting airing of the eight men's dirty laundry in the judge's opinion became the talk of the Philadelphia legal community. "People knew which associate had offended the father-in-law of which senior partner," ran the *New York Times*'s account. "They knew which associate had 'disappeared without notice, sometimes for a couple of days, and sometimes on extended vacations,' and who had said that about him. They knew which lawyer's 'lack of judgment' almost cost a client $1 million. They knew whose writing skills were seen as not being up to par, and who was perceived as 'more sizzle than steak.'"

Even if people have not chosen up sides at the start, the process is likely to lead in that direction. "You become an enemy," said one professor at City University of New York. "You're not a colleague and not accepted as you were before." The more collegial the workplace had been, the greater the scar tissue. "Institutions that have been through a full-scale legal battle really know it," Princeton University counsel Thomas H. Wright, Jr., has observed. "Class action and tenure disputes can just rip the department and even an institution apart in ways that take years and years to rebuild."

Nor is the damage confined to fancy institutions. In the town of Montrose, New York, a controversy over whether the school board properly removed principal Joanne Falinski, two years into the legal process, "has split parents into pro- and anti-Falinski camps," according to another *New York Times* report. "Children from families on opposing sides no longer have play dates. Former friends silently push their grocery carts past each other at the local A & P. 'There are deep-seated animosities here, and feelings in these cases tend to last for years, like the Hatfields and the McCoys,' said Robert Saperstein, Dr. Falinski's lawyer. 'It will probably go on until all the children and parents involved have graduated from the school system.'"

In *The Girls in the Balcony*, her history of women at the *New York Times*, Nan Robertson tells the story of an early landmark sex-discrimination case that charged the newspaper with paying its female employees less than their male counterparts. Robertson wears on her sleeve her sympathy for the premises and goals of *Boylan* v. *New York Times,* making it all the more noteworthy that she recounts the course of its events with such evident ambivalence.

The suit was big and messy. Plaintiffs deposed eighteen executives and successfully demanded ten years' worth of payroll records for the paper's entire workforce. They also demanded—and had to be given— reams of private correspondence, memos, and confidential personnel evaluations written by the paper's bigwigs. So as to allow proper comparisons, the paper had to turn over confidential evaluations of its male as well as female reporters.

Among the highlights was the deposition of managing editor (and later columnist) Abe Rosenthal, which went on for three days and produced a 571-page, six-pound transcript. Rosenthal was apparently outraged at the demands for confidential in-house memos and the like; he did not realize the law armed plaintiffs with such powers, though his paper had consistently editorialized in favor of conferring the broadest procedural rights on bias complainants. As lawyers grilled him under oath about the reasons why one named reporter was paid more than another, they elicited the kind of opinions that might have been set forth in a particularly salty memoir. "I recall people saying that she had a foul temper; that she shouted at people; that she used obscenities and was very difficult to get along with; cried rather too much," he said of one plaintiff, describing the work of others as, in the opposing lawyer's paraphrase, "puerile, simplistic, poor, uninspiring, [or] merely competent." Defending the paper's compensation policies, Rosenthal argued that—in Robertson's paraphrase—he "had also given some men jobs at lower salaries than they were worth."

The lawyers for the newspaper could dish it out as well, conducting a "brutal . . . painful and lacerating and bruising" deposition of leading reporter Eileen Shanahan to extract damaging admissions about ways her work had fallen short of perfection. By the time a few months of this process had gone by, the atmosphere had become "poisonous." Attorney Harriet Rabb, who represented the women employees as part of a string of high-profile feminist cases and then quit the field, put it bluntly: waging a lawsuit against one's employer is a "long, slow, painful, difficult, and ego-destroying process."

By the time going to trial became a possibility, Robertson writes, the very thought loomed as a "vision of horror" to all involved. Rabb kept imagining "two huge ships . . . on a collision course." *New York Times* lawyer Kathy Darrow thought it would be "like the worst divorce that ever happened"—worse, in a way, because the parties would "have to live with each other afterward. . . . How will they get a newspaper out?" "We knew that people were going to get up on that stand and say terrible things about each other in public. . . . Even taking the depositions, people cried, people were devastated, and there was nobody there but the lawyers to hear them."

"If they were going to say something rotten about one of our women, we'd say something rotten about their men," Rabb recalled. "We knew vile things, and they knew vile things. We'd wave papers with damning facts at each other. We had a vast pile of shared, accumulated knowledge—it would wreck not just individuals, men and women alike, but the *Times*." What bothered her most was not the dirt on who was a drunk or adulterer, but the attacks on competence. "To strike at somebody's conception of his or her standards of professionalism is devastating. The thought of having it dragged to the light scared the socks off me. The lawyers on the other side would ask, 'Are you really prepared to do this?' Or we'd say, 'Is this what you are prepared to do to win?'

"We never answered each other."

The vast new self-help literature for disgruntled employees is rather skimpy on warnings about the downside of the process. No less a pillar of respectability than *Fortune* is not above a little sharp-elbow advice. "Never quit. Make the company fire you," offers a self-help article for fired executives by managing editor Marshall Loeb. "Reject management's first offer. If you cave, the company will say thanks a lot and figure you're a wimp." Hire a lawyer, and tell the company you've done so; you want to "send a signal" that "the company had better prepare to deal with you." Happily, "the higher your rank, the more you can get." Don't worry about stepping on the little people, either: when handed over from a senior exec to an HR person, "You can be as pushy with that bureaucrat as you wish."

Loeb says little about the possible practical or psychological benefits of being content to squeeze less than every last drop out of your employer if your goal is to get out of a failing relationship, proceed with your life, and find out what to do next—even if it should mean being nice to an HR person. Most startling is his advice to execs already covered by written agreements that may specify what severance is due: "If you have a contract, view it only as a floor, and negotiate for richer terms." Loeb seems either not to realize or not to care that ignoring a contract you've signed, and instead sending in your lawyers to rip more money out of the other side, is the kind of conduct that gives business a bad name.

In passing, Loeb concedes that "even if you prevail, you may badly hurt your chances of getting a new job. Not many companies want to hire someone who has sued his previous employer." Perhaps the trick is to use the threat but never follow through, especially since one danger is that the case will actually get to trial. *Lieberman* v. *Gant*, a 1980 denial-of-tenure suit against the University of Connecticut, absorbed fifty-two days of court time, the evidence filling nearly 10,000 pages including almost 400 exhibits. The shaken department head declared that the case had "cost him at least one book," but the losing plaintiff fared worse: she declared bankruptcy after being hit with a bill for more than $14,000 just for copying costs. Some trials, like the six-week televised harassment trial arising from Rena Weeks's fifteen-day stint with law-firm boss Martin Greenstein, go on considerably longer than the job itself. By the time the courts resolved a bias suit by black workers at DuPont's Louisville plant, twenty years had elapsed; all of the workers had retired, and more than a third of them had died.

———

Both camps in the job wars complain a lot about retaliation. Personnel managers tell of treating complainants with kid gloves, of jumping at their beck and call and having to give them more than the loyal workers who never complain. Lawyers for complainants tell of the many indignities that can't be proved in court: the silent treatment, the ways of freezing someone out from training and collegiality. All complain of the enormous pettiness to which the wrangling can descend.

Both are right—and sometimes in the same cases. There's no inconsistency between overpoliteness and the psychological equivalent of setting tacks on the other guy's chair, between a careful doling out of equal (or more than equal) material rewards and a withholding of the spirit of cooperation. The mix of signals can come from different colleagues, or from the same colleague on different days. Once again, the law runs into the intractable difficulty of ordering incompatible parties to cohabit under the same roof.

LaNoue and Lee's study of faculty litigation found that although a few complainants found the experience "exhilarating," many more suffered lasting harm to "their finances; their relationships with family, friends, and colleagues; their attitudes toward lawyers and the legal process in general; and most of all [to] their careers." Once upon a time, "May your life be filled with lawyers" was considered a pretty fair curse. It took our age to imagine that by tempting restless workers into this fate we were doing them a favor.

Chapter 13

WHY BUSINESS WILL MISS UNIONS

Despite its reputation for being tough on employers, Europe is not a place where individual litigants tend to strike it rich by suing their bosses. One typical scholar describes European industrial tribunals that handle individual cases of wrongful firing or mistreatment as dispensing "very modest awards that serve principally as a balm to the employee's wounded pride." (Mandated automatic severance—which applies across the board with no allegation of fault—is a different matter, and can be substantial.) British workers who won individual firing complaints won a few weeks' pay on average, studies found. Japan, which perhaps surprisingly has allowed suits over layoffs violating "socially accepted standards," again reports smallish cash figures; a sixty-year-old engineering manager got $22,000. In the new Russia, cleaning women Tamara Yashchina and Larisa Gubareva contested the Radisson-Slavyanskaya Hotel's refusal to renew their work contracts, invoking a "jobs for life" law held over from the previous Soviet regime. A Moscow judge reinstated them but with an award of only $94 each, not the $10 million they had hopefully asked for (perhaps with an eye to the fact that the partners in the hotel venture were Americans).

In many of these countries, awards Americans might dismiss as rounding errors make headlines as record-breakers. Thus a British debate broke out over runaway awards when Samantha Phillips, who had complained of sexual harassment after being subjected to egregious come-ons by her insurance-broker boss, was awarded what was seen as the extravagant sum of £18,000 ($28,000). In New York City, by contrast, the average sexual harassment verdict has been reported to stand at $250,000.

Not a few foreign observers goggled at our televised San Francisco case of *Weeks* v. *Baker & McKenzie,* where a legal secretary at the nation's largest law firm sued after a two-week stint assigned to a partner who had, among other crude behavior and overtures, slipped M & Ms down the front pocket of her blouse. The jury voted Weeks compensatory damages of $50,000, a remarkable enough sum given that the insulting conduct had caused little if any apparent damage to her finances (she had jumped to a better job shortly after the episode). Then it added punitive damages of $7 million, a figure representing a tenth of the firm's capital—a juror later explaining that since the firm claimed to have "gotten religion" on the subject of stopping harassment, it should "do a little tithing." The judge knocked this figure down to an equally arbitrary $3.7 million.

Around this point the case ended for purposes of most public attention, the Court TV cameras having moved on. But some of its most revealing moments were yet to come, in a post-trial struggle before the judge on the question of attorneys' fees.

Federal law entitles winning harassment complainants to recover reasonable attorneys' fees and expenses from their opponents. But how much should Baker & McKenzie have to pay Rena Weeks's lawyers for the privilege of being beaten by them? According to her lawyers' petition, the amount should be a cool $3.8 million. That figure included a $1.8 million subtotal for direct fees, including not only standard high hourly fees but also an explicit $650,000 bonus to reward them for doing such a good job in extracting much more money from the jury than many had expected. Expenses (photocopying, expert witnesses, exhibit preparation, travel, and so forth) came to another million or so. Wonderfully, the legal team also demanded more than $600,000 in "fees on fees": money to compensate other lawyers it had hired to help devise the most persuasive arguments for why it deserved a huge fee award. One of these outside lawyers was to get $1,080 an hour.

Judge John E. Munter approved most of the $3.8 million, although he did slash the fees-on-fees request to a paltry $166,000. This still left the outside lawyers brought in to make the case for high fees receiving more than three times as much as the jury's estimate of Weeks's own personal losses.

The judge also dismissed one last argument the defendant had tried to make. Baker pointed out that Weeks's lawyers had taken her case on contingency; that is to say, they would charge no fee if she lost and would pocket a share of the award if she won. Because they had won big, this arrangement was going to pay off big for them, guaranteeing them an estimated million or more in fees. Shouldn't they be content with that fee, or at least offset it from the statutory fee award so they wouldn't get paid twice? This argument was doomed from the start, though, since such double-dipping is a routinely accepted perk for employment litigators. The judge rejected out of hand the idea of any offset, remarking without apparent irony that it would result in giving Baker a "windfall."

———

Until roughly the 1970s, liberal workplace reformers tended to hang their hopes on unions (with help from government agencies) as a way to vindicate workers' interests against management's. But the new employment law has handed power over to a group of actors with profoundly different interests, powers, and incentives: lawyers representing individual workers. Coincidental or not, the trend has for years run broad and consistent; while the power of the union movement has waned, the power of the freelance employment bar has mounted. Employers stand up to union demands, but pull out their checkbooks for the individual complainant who shows up with an attorney. Leading plaintiff's lawyer Judith Vladeck has noted the irony: "It's a hell of a lot easier to get $100,000 than to get five cents an hour for blue-collar workers."

Union leaders themselves have appeared to view these developments with ambivalence. Common interest gives them some occasions to cooperate with private employment lawyers, as when both are fighting the same management. But other new legal developments let the same plaintiffs' lawyers sue unions themselves, as they do with some frequency. While supporting most of the new laws in principle, many union leaders uneasily sense that each new right-to-sue law strengthens the tendency for the private bar to compete with them in providing the service of extracting concessions from management.

Much of the literature makes this shift explicit. Yesterday it was the union shop steward who was expected to listen to workers' grievances, decide which were strong enough to present to management, and then present them in their strongest light and negotiate for redress. Now, increasingly, it is the private employment lawyer at the other end of a telephone who performs these functions. The parallel is almost too neat, and yet the differences between the two cases go to the heart of the contrast between the new employment law and the old labor law.

First and foremost, unionism is *collective* bargaining. Unions assist individual members, but they are supposed to keep in mind their responsibility to represent the membership as a whole. When weighing individual workers' complaints and deciding how to press them, it is thus natural for them to give priority to those that are confirmed by the general sentiment of co-workers. Part of the union's mission is also to keep special deals from being cut either for or against individual members: if one member is asking to be let out of tough assignments or demanding schedules, the shop steward will have to consider whether the result will be to make other members shoulder a heavier burden.

Most of the new employment law, on the other hand, makes a point of *not* consulting general sentiment among co-workers. ADA and harassment manuals stress that failure to accommodate a complainant must never be rationalized on grounds of damage to office morale. An individual right is an individual right, and it doesn't matter whether anyone else approves of your asserting it. Management can easily lose even though co-workers troop through by the dozen to testify in favor of its position. Besides, the co-workers may themselves be the problem: they may harbor bias, or be the ones who put up the cheesecake calendars. Paradoxically, the lawyer whose client is the target of anger (or even the cold shoulder) from many others in the office will sometimes boast a more lucrative case than the one whose client is widely popular, simply because such attitudes can serve as bankable evidence of harassment, infliction of emotional distress, interference with the carrying out of job functions, and so forth.

With their continuous presence in the workplace, unions are also in a far better position to keep themselves informed about its workings, history, and personalities. They are likely to start off with a fund of information—What's this supervisor's reputation? This worker's? What's this shop's standard operating procedure?—that can help to decide where the problem lies and whether workers in a similar position are getting the same shake. Union representation also confers the power to make and keep pledges of future action ("We intend to challenge A, but you'll be allowed to do B") and stick by them with a certain amount of future credibility at stake. Expecting to be around for the long haul, a union may also hesitate to make demands that endanger the shop's long-term market viability.

Grievance-pressing by lawyers is different on all these fronts. With no direct eyes on the shop floor, lawyers will find themselves more dependent on the story the grievant brings them, with its possible biases, omissions, and distortions. Many will prudently refuse to take cases that do not check out as strongly grounded, but there are all sorts of lawyers out there, and a persistent client need not take no for an answer—five lawyers may turn down a case, but a sixth may be willing to give it a shot. And even a conscientious outside lawyer will have little material incentive to care overmuch what life is like in the workplace after the case is over, or indeed whether it continues at all.

———

Equally profound are the differences in how grievances get resolved. Union grievances get handled through in-house procedures that occasionally culminate in outside arbitration. Legal complaints, unless the parties agree otherwise, will proceed through formal litigation in a public court that occasionally culminates in a trial. In both cases, the great majority of cases are settled short of formal conclusion.

All agree that litigation is slower and more expensive than arbitration; its pretrial procedures, such as the "discovery" stage in which lawyers demand access to company files, are considerably more costly and menacing to management interests. The prospect of trial also casts a different kind of shadow on settlement negotiations than the prospect of arbitration. Judges and juries will tend to sit at a greater distance from the events at issue, both temporally and psychologically, than an arbitrator. Indeed, while professional arbitrators hired in union settings are selected in part for their specialized feel for the "law of the shop," judges are more often generalists who may be trying an assault case the week before and a copyright-infringement suit the week after. And juries, under modern American techniques of selection, are often screened by lawyers precisely for their lack of expertise in the issues likely to arise.

Grievance arbitration awards are often substantial, especially when management has attempted to fire a worker and a long period of back pay has mounted up. But court awards in similar cases run systematically higher. Arbitrators generally decline to order compensation for open-ended categories such as emotional and punitive damages; for reputational damages in cases where workers claim that the company has defamed them; or for "consequential" damages (for example, claims of lost pay in future jobs at other workplaces). According to the literature, they "almost never" award interest on back pay, a major add-on to many court awards.

By contrast, employment litigation is part and parcel of America's culture of personal injury litigation. This culture's shoot-the-moon dollar amounts always astound overseas visitors: the million-dollar coffee spill, the $4.8 million awarded to a fleeing mugger shot by police, the $1.2 million voted to a would-be suicide who jumped in front of a subway train. "We can't electrocute him, so let's put him in the poorhouse," said a San Diego juror after one $7.5 million award. "If we were to calculate the real back pay in this case, they'd have to take

Brooklyn College and City College and auction them off to pay the damages," said attorney Judith Vladeck of a case against the City University of New York. A pioneering Rand Corporation study found that half of California workers who won common-law wrongful-firing actions got punitive damages, and that these damages averaged more than $500,000.

Lawmakers help things along; for instance, the Civil Rights Restoration Act of 1991 greatly boosted the damages payable in many kinds of suits. "If you have turned down any discrimination suits recently because you didn't think they would pay for themselves, you should reconsider," advised the newsletter *Lawyers' Alert* after the law passed, explaining that it "makes these suits much more economically worthwhile than they were previously." Along with raising damages, the 1991 act allowed claims to be decided by juries, which few if any other countries employ for such purposes. "Higher damages, plus a jury; that makes a huge difference," Detroit attorney Deborah Gordon told the *New York Times*. "If you have a sympathetic case, you don't want a crusty old judge deciding what you could get. You want a nice empathetic jury."

A final difference—how the advocates get paid—is of the utmost importance. Unions, of course, commonly draw on either volunteer effort or resources paid for by members' common dues. Some lawyers, especially in situations such as reasonably amicable negotiations over severance packages, charge hourly fees or flat retainers. But in cases that are filed as lawsuits, the more common practice is for them to take a share in their grievants' winnings through a contingency fee set at 30, 33, or 40 percent of the recovered amount ("no fee unless successful"). Most nations ban the lawyers' contingency fee as unethical, holding that to let lawyers become participants in their claims gives them too sharp an incentive to overpress their cases. The United States does not.

All by itself, the contingency fee makes it considerably more lucrative to be a reasonably successful freelance employment lawyer than to be a staff lawyer for a union. As the case of *Weeks* v. *Baker & McKenzie* showed, however, we sweeten the pot still further by the way we create separate entitlements for the award of attorneys' fees and expenses.

———

Our legal system, unlike virtually every other advanced country's, does not in general require losing litigants to compensate their vindicated opponents, a divergence that helps explain a great many of the differences between our experience and theirs. Discrimination claims, as well as some other categories, are exceptions, but *one-way* exceptions: the courts' creative reading of statutory language has meant that winning plaintiffs in such cases have a right to demand fees and expenses from losing opponents, but winning defendants do not.

To follow up on this lopsided policy, courts have proceeded to adopt extraordinarily generous fee-shift calculations. Other countries, in making losers pay, insist on tough judicial oversight of fee levies to make sure lawyers destined to win a case do not get a chance to go on a spree paid for by their opponent. Our courts do no such thing; their explicit aim has been to reward plaintiff's attorneys richly enough to attract more of them to take these admirable cases. Thus they have permitted prevailing attorneys to demand fees far higher than they in fact would have charged the client at hand or any other client for the work, then added routine "bonus" multipliers over ordinary fee levels for successful results. Lawyers have asked for customary hourly rates for holding press conferences, squiring clients to movies, birthday parties, and other social events, and much more.

One result is to permit small underlying damage awards to serve as the basis of big fee entitlements. A Gotham attorney quoted in *New York* says it's "not a problem" for an age bias case worth $10,000 in itself to support a six-figure fee demand on the opponent. In a Florida case whose bizarre facts attracted notice in the national press, a woman claimed that post-traumatic fear of black men, contracted after a mugging, had disabled her from continuing to work at her employer's integrated workplace. The resulting workers' compensation claim brought her a negotiated settlement of $50,000 along with $450,000 as a fee to her law firm, a representative of which proceeded to complain that the figure was too low: "I think we were really entitled to $800,000 [or] $900,000 in attorneys' fees."

———

Sharing as they do the sharp incentive of personal-injury lawyers to blow up the size of awards, the contingency-fee employment bar has refined highly effective techniques toward that end. One is the creative use of hired experts, such as psychologists to testify to the client's severe emotional trauma or economists and accountants to testify to the enormous lost potential of his derailed career. Courts in other advanced countries generally appoint their own experts, but we allow each side to bring in its own hired partisans and then invite juries to guess which is right. Thus a thirty-four-year-old Montana engineer won $1.7 million in purportedly economic damages after being fired from a $63,000-a-year job. Psychiatric testimony is commonly introduced to buttress demands for six- and even seven-figure sums for emotional distress.

Recruitment has been systematized as well. In hot states like Michigan, New Jersey, and California, personal injury lawyers soon began listing wrongful firing, discrimination, and harassment as specialties in their yellow-pages advertisements (along with dog bites, birth defects, and accidental falls). California, which began allowing cash-for-stress through both common law and workers' compensation, found itself a particular hotbed. Employment-law classifieds in the *Los Angeles Times* have gone on for half a page, while television ads fill the airwaves at hours when the laid-off are likely to tune in. ("Every injured worker in the country" watches *Wheel of Fortune,* one cynic notes, because "it's the only game show you can play on painkillers.") One California plant was set to close after due notice and with severance pay; on the last day of work, lawyers swooped down in vans and whisked workers to offices where 230 of the total payroll of 300 filed injury claims. A California ad described by Charles Oliver in *Reason* "ends with a stressed-out secretary and a warehouse worker with a back injury clinking champagne glasses on a yacht."

More idealistic groups got into the act, too, as when the Disability Rights Education and Defense Fund trained five thousand "Barrier

Busters" to search for violations of the new Americans with Disabilities Act. Oakland lawyer Peter Lomhoff got $50,000 from a hotel for two clients who couldn't have lunch comfortably in wheelchairs. "These are good, quick, simple cases where there are good damages available," he told the *San Francisco Recorder*. "It's amazing to me that more people are not doing them." Sometimes the fee shift itself seems to be the central attraction; one Texas freelancer in concert with an attorney relative had sued fifteen businesses over a few weeks. "The legal system was not designed to allow someone to sue and collect attorney's fees when they haven't even asked someone to do it (make renovations)," protested a Texas Association of Business spokesperson. "I can't believe you go sue Eckerd to lower a telephone without talking to them." Activist Chuck Weir was unapologetic. "They've been put on notice. It's been in the news," he said when asked why he didn't contact the stores first. "We're not going to play games anymore." Another South Texas operation was reported filing three to five ADA suits a week against local restaurants, video stores, convenience stores, gas stations, and retailers.

A West Coast outfit called Documented Reference Check hires itself out to call former employers and find out what kind of references they're giving. A federal appeals court has ruled that the giving of a bad reference to an ex-employee's paid agent counts as enough "publication" of defamatory statements to support a suit. An even more controversial way of generating a caseload is carried out under the label of "testing." Pairs of confederates are sent out to pose as job seekers, with made-up resumes and prepared false answers to interview questions; if the white applicant gets treated better than the black one, or the able better than the disabled, it's off to court. Fond of shooting fish in barrels, the Massachusetts Commission Against Discrimination sent young and elderly testers to apply for jobs as salesclerks at Boston clothing stores with a clientele dominated by fashion-conscious teenagers; substantial settlements from store owners followed.

Until lately, courts tended to frown on litigation trumped up this way—worrying about the various undocumentable reasons that might account for differential treatment in any one case, the evils of allowing lies to become the basis for legal process, and indeed the credibility of parties who'd already shown themselves willing to lie boldly at least once. Now they began to view it as a public-spirited activity, and in order to encourage more of it they began awarding substantial damages for testers to pocket personally. Thus a court in Washington, D.C., awarded $79,000 to two women who posed as job applicants to verify that a local employment agency interviewer was getting fresh with clients. Such incentives help guarantee a ready supply of private groups eager to conduct testing, and even quite respectable groups now carry on the practice with blessing from a legal establishment that would never think of calling it entrapment.

In a 1983 housing case the Seventh Circuit acknowledged that testing might involve a "regrettable" dimension of "deception," but said this was "a relatively small price to pay" to enforce bias laws. "Indeed," it added, "tester evidence may receive *more* weight because of its source" [emphasis added]. The court explained that testers "seem more likely to be careful and dispassionate observers" than sincere applicants who might take rejection personally because they had genuinely wanted what they were applying for. Revealingly, repeated testing has been reported to produce numerous results in the "wrong" direction—that is, in which the minority applicant turns out to advance farther in the process; again, these may be the result of random factors in any individual case. But a testing operation can simply discard the anomalous results, go to court to trade in the cases with opposite fact patterns for cash, pick more ads from the classifieds, and start again.

———

Employment suits are increasingly run as a sophisticated business. The *Wall Street Journal*'s news columns profiled Guy Saperstein of Oakland, California, who was making civil rights law "profitable—embarrassingly so, in the eyes of some of his colleagues"; Saperstein personally owns more than 75 percent of the twenty-four lawyer firm of Saperstein, Mayeda, Larkin & Goldstein, which is known for suits against supermarket chains and other large West Coast employers. The firm has collected fees totaling a reported $100 million from just four of the many cases it has handled; one, on behalf of women not hired as agents by the State Farm insurance company, brought in a re-ported $65 million fee. (Single-case fee hauls reaching tens of millions are by no means unheard of in employment class actions.) Saperstein, who got his start defending Black Panthers on a murder rap, "seems to owe his success largely to his insistence on treating civil-rights law as a business, while many of his competitors view it more as a mission." For example, he builds a file on companies he plans to sue, then arranges to be quoted in news articles flaying their policies; a suitable client often steps forward. And his own practices as an employer stand in amusing contrast to those favored by progressive authorities. He is said to pile on newly hired lawyers to get through a big case, then dump them when it ends; the happy result for his firm is "record prof-its *and* layoffs."

The Civil Rights Restoration Act of 1991 symbolizes, and itself has advanced, this transformation of bias complaints from the turf of ide-alists to a high-rolling legal specialty. Backers of the CRRA sold it to editorial boards and polite opinion as a needed reversal of several re-cent Supreme Court rulings that were said to have upset the delicate balance of fairness achieved by previous civil rights law—most promi-nently the 1989 *Wards Cove* v. *Atonio,* which had somewhat relaxed "disparate impact" scrutiny of employers' hiring practices. Rising to the bait, conservative critics agreed in treating the *Wards Cove* reversal as by far the most important aspect of the bill. They countered with their own "quota" issue: it was wrong to restore the earlier and tougher disparate-impact standard because it had led employers, fear-ing such suits, to hire by the numbers to stay out of legal trouble. While denying that employers ever had behaved this way, the bill's backers agreed to insert language disavowing quotas as such. This was good enough for President George Bush, who signed the measure af-ter vetoing an earlier version.

For many practicing lawyers, a far more important provision in the bill was comparatively neglected in the public debate. This provision sharply boosted the money damages payable in most suits charging "garden-variety" individual discriminatory treatment (as distinct from disparate-impact suits). In particular, it allowed claimants suing over discrimination on the basis of sex, disability, national origin, and so forth to demand punitive damages, compensation for emotional distress and other intangibles, and trials before juries. Previously these perks had been available only to plaintiffs charging race bias, who had obtained them via the Supreme Court's fancy footwork on Section 1981, the Reconstruction-era law.

You'd think these provisions would have received particularly close scrutiny. After all, unlike the reversals of *Wards Cove* and several smaller Supreme Court decisions, they hardly fit the stated purpose of "restoring" rights cut back by an unsympathetic majority of justices. Nor was it appropriate to view them as measures that simply resumed policies the nation had been pursuing for almost eighteen years, and therefore couldn't hold many surprises. Employer groups, which disliked and feared the damages expansion, asked for it to be taken off the main bill and considered separately on its merits. Curiously, backers flatly refused to consider any such thing: though they were selling the "restoration" package as an urgent national priority, they refused to let it go forward unless the damage enrichment went with it. This strategy worked—the damages expansion stayed in the final bill, its only significant modification being a ceiling on the award of punitive damages. Conservative critics put up little resistance on the damages expansion; some even endorsed it, saying that so long as quotas or preferences weren't at issue, they were all in favor of enforcing bias laws with the utmost vigor.

Once the CRRA became law, something very odd happened. From both sides' pronouncements, one would have expected the sweeping away of *Wards Cove* to be followed by a renewed surge of hiring suits under the disparate-impact doctrine. But that didn't seem to happen at all. Instead, it was the garden-variety suits over disparate treatment (firings, harassment, and refusals to accommodate) that boomed. Astonishingly, if anything there seemed to be a mild *drop* in disparate-impact litigation.

Had lawyers gone crazy? Hardly. In fact, they'd been perfectly rational. The substance of the law may have been reliberalized in the case of disparate-impact suits, but the rewards had not; the new damage provisions did not apply to them. In the case of disparate-treatment suits the pattern was the reverse: the rewards had been liberalized, even though the law had not. And in a sort of controlled experiment—will the flow of litigation respond more to monetary incentives, or to high-flown rhetoric about the country's civil rights needs?—the lawyers had followed the money, investing talent in the more remunerative claims even though that left less attention for the kind that had been the centerpiece of the campaign for the law.

Civil rights groups carried the banner in the vanguard of the successful CRRA campaign, but other interested parties were not far behind. Nelson Lund, now a law professor and at that time an official with the Bush administration, recalls that the negotiators sent by civil rights groups to hammer out a compromise were themselves actively practicing employment lawyers; in fact, the practicing lawyers and the civil rights groups "were a little hard to distinguish" from each other. This left him less surprised when the negotiators went out of their way to protect provisions securing attorneys' fees, even when this meant trading off provisions of more direct benefit to individual complainants. He was left less than impressed with their idealistic credentials: "They had their own interests at heart from the very start."

Chapter 14

WORKPLACE CLEANSING

———

When the Dairy Mart convenience chain promoted Dolores Stanley to store manager it assigned her to a store near Steubenville, Ohio. One of the first things she did when she got there was banish the copies of Playboy *that had been sold from behind the counter in brown paper sleeves. When word reached management, it said that sort of decision wasn't up to her; company policy had to take precedence over managers' own views.*

The company offered to transfer Stanley to a store that didn't stock men's magazines (because of slow local demand for them), but instead she filed a complaint with the EEOC. The magazine's presence constituted sexual harassment by creating a "hostile environment," she said, and also subjected her to religious discrimination. "It goes against everything I believe in as a Christian. . . . There's nothing more damaging to the image of women than pornography," she said, touching on both themes.

Stanley turned for legal representation to the American Family Association, the antipornography group headed by Rev. Donald Wildmon of Tupelo, Mississippi. Its attorney, Benjamin Bull, said he planned to cite the recent Jacksonville Shipyards *case in which attorneys from the National*

*Organization for Women Legal Defense and Education Fund had success-
fully argued that it constituted sexual harassment for men to be allowed to
bring sexually explicit magazines, pin-ups, or books to the workplace. "If
it's a hostile environment in a [shipyard], it's a hostile environment in a
Dairy Mart," Bull said. "It may be even more so because a female is being
forced to actually pick up and handle the material."*

*The case provoked press comment back in Hartford, Connecticut, where
Dairy Mart had its headquarters. The editorial in the daily* Hartford
Courant *didn't see where it would all end, speculating that "Muslims
could get jobs in liquor stores and demand that the entire stock be eliminated." But a spokeswoman for the state commission on the status of
women endorsed Stanley's argument: for a store to sell the magazine, she
said, could constitute harassment of its women employees.*

---

*The harassment literature often describes women as having to "run a
gauntlet" of jeering or leering men in order to do their jobs. This was no
exaggeration as regards what Barbara Lawler faced as an executive at a
local plant of the Georgia Kraft forest-products company. Day after day as
Lawler arrived at work, she had to walk past a line of male workers who
would accost her with what a federal court later found to be "crude and
obscene," "lewd and insulting" epithets; "ugly bitch" was among the more
printable. The company was willing to discipline the men, but the
Eleventh Circuit ruled it couldn't: their speech enjoyed legal protection.*

*This was not a case from the benighted ages before anyone thought up
sexual harassment law; the date was 1983. The explanation for what
might otherwise be a baffling mystery is that the rule to be applied came
from the old labor law, not the new employment law. The gauntlet was a
picket line, and the men were on strike.*

*For the student of contemporary harassment law, the realm of legally
protected strike speech is the world turned upside down. In the one, awkward compliments on hairstyles may be the object of mandatory discipline; in the other, death threats can get a free pass. During the Georgia
Kraft strike, according to court opinions, strikers who "reeked of liquor"
showed up at the home of nonstriker William Walker, stood in his door-
way, and (with his expectant wife and small daughter looking on) vowed,*

KID GLOVES AND BRASS KNUCKLES

"We'll take care of you," punctuating the remark with the twelve-letter epithet often reckoned the most obscene in the English language. Though Walker asked them to leave, they hung around for some time. This too was legally protected speech, ruled the National Labor Relations Board, being "ambiguous and unaccompanied by violence or physical gestures." Walker had no reasonable fear for his safety, a court later ruled in upholding the board, because although the strikers had indeed committed acts of violence, "the acts were directed only at company property." Ruled as protected speech in another case were the actions of strikers who followed a nonstriking worker's car home and confronted her: "You'd better watch it, Debbie. We know where you live."

————

In Seattle, John Dill dragged Bryan Griggs before the city human rights commission, charging him with two counts of creating a hostile working environment for himself as a gay man. One of the charges was that Griggs had aired conservative talk radio shows in the office, and the other was that he'd posted a letter from a local congresswoman endorsing the ban on gays in the military. Griggs said he hadn't known Dill was gay at all, and Dill admitted he'd never told Griggs he was offended by the radio, but a spokeswoman for the city commission agreed that both acts could in principle create a hostile environment. After Griggs had spent $5,000 on legal defense, Dill dropped his complaint, explaining that his point had been made; the Seattle Times *called it a "scary assault on the First Amendment."*

According to the U.S. Supreme Court, the Constitution guarantees that Americans will never suffer the imposition of any official line as to what is permissible for them to say or think on sensitive matters of political or religious opinion. "If there is any fixed star in our Constitutional constellation," wrote Justice Robert Jackson in a leading pronouncement on the subject, "it is that no official, high or petty, can prescribe what shall be orthodox in politics, nationalism, religion, or other matters of opinion or force citizens to confess by word or act their faith therein."

This principle is a bit hard to square with recent developments in harassment law. Today's law routinely suppresses verbal comments, literature, and other expression of political, nationalist, and religious views in the workplace, and it does so very much on the basis of their content—as opposed to, say, the crudity with which they are couched. It is relentless in prescribing orthodoxy, throwing its full weight behind the advancement of some controversial views and the suppression of others. And as Barbara Lawler learned, it is not even consistent in minimally protecting women from personal verbal outrage; even on that core goal, it all depends on whose ox is being gored.

———

In retrospect, it seems astounding that one of the leading motifs of the early push for employment law was the allegedly pressing need to assure workers that they could speak out on controversial topics at work without fear of any consequences.

It was the 1960s, and the press featured numerous accounts of "whistleblowers" fired or persecuted for criticizing the organizations for which they worked or reporting them to government agencies or activist groups. Law professors painstakingly assembled these stories as evidence of the need for new measures giving workers a right to sue over bad-cause firings. Under employment at will, a private employee might be fired just for wearing a controversial button to work, or for being a liberal or conservative. New court rulings were giving public employees a constitutional right not to be treated that way. Why not everyone?

The lack of protection for controversial views, commentators explained, was just the most visible symptom of a wider problem. *Harvard Business Review* managing editor David Ewing, who brought the new ideas to a popular audience in several books, called it the need for "Freedom Within the Organization." Some employers snooped into their employees' affairs, keeping track of their hobbies, where and with whom they lived, and so forth. They enforced arbitrary dress codes and discouraged personal eccentricities. They put employees through psychological tests and even manipulated their attitudes, piping Muzak onto the factory floor and assembling the staff for motivational pep talks. Didn't this add up to near-Orwellian mind control?

Employees of big companies "for all practical purposes" resemble the subjects of totalitarian states, Ewing declared. Such arguments could be made to provide a seeming libertarian gloss to highly un-libertarian proposals; Lawrence Blades entitled his influential 1967 proposal for wrongful-firing law "Employment at Will vs. Individual Freedom."

The framers of the Bill of Rights, of course, had not seen fit to equate employer pressures with government controls on opinion. The First Amendment had directed that "Congress shall make no law" abridging free speech, suggesting that framers saw the police knock on the door in the middle of the night as a threat to speech markedly more serious than the fear of alienating one's boss. One important difference was that while we are stuck with the government, employers and jobs offer a choice: if you feel constrained in one kind of post, there are others where such pressure is absent. In short, a free society offers a wide choice of which socializing incentives to submit to. People hold their tongues on politics or religion for many reasons, of course: for most, fear of offending bosses may be a weaker motive than fear of alienating spouses, neighbors, and the operators of local printing presses and pulpits. These others are often in a stronger position to disapprove simply because, of these relations, employment is by far the most thoroughly driven by the almighty dollar. Most bosses rationally will put up with all sorts of disagreement on how someone votes if they think they are making money from his talents.

Ah, said the opponents of employment at will, but times have changed. Employers have grown huge; they're really a lot more like authoritarian governments in themselves, not private associations. Some of the rest of us found it far from obvious that our local hamburger stands, garden centers, and galvanized-steel fabricators really bore all that close a resemblance to the Stroessner regime of Paraguay, but the analogy was good enough for the American Civil Liberties Union, which was steadily refocusing its efforts so as to promote steps that would expand rather than curb the power of government. "It does not make sense to say we live in a free country" if employers may cut us off their payroll any time they wish, declared ACLU executive director Ira Glasser. "Unjust termination is not only a social and economic evil, but a violation of basic civil liberties," agreed project director Lewis Maltby.

———

At the end of *Iolanthe,* Gilbert and Sullivan's Lord Chancellor saves the day for the ladies' chorus, who are being inconvenienced by the language of a contract, by inserting into its text the single word *not.* Something similar happened to the large reformist literature on the need for perfectly untrammeled rights of workplace speech when some prominent feminists cleared their throats and announced that the men didn't seem to get it; speech was the *problem.*

The skid marks were so short they could barely be seen on the pavement; all anyone could tell was that the vehicle was now speeding in the opposite direction. One moment reformers—as if fresh from local productions of *The Crucible*—were citing chapter and verse about the dangers of conformist pressures and groupthink, and calling for new infusions of workplace due process that would make New York City teacher-removal rules look impetuous and peremptory. The next moment it was clear to all concerned that joking about, criticizing, or eyeing women simply had to be suppressed, and that the most humane course might be to separate offenders from the workplace cleanly (after perhaps one warning).

Management does well to err on the side of suppressing speech before it gets out of hand, after all. "Conduct considered harmless by many today may be considered discriminatory in the future," a court pointed out in one leading harassment case. A Los Angeles Police Department official said the department was moving against a range of "inappropriate" male doings even though "very, very few" of them "would rise to the level of true sex harassment," because "we certainly want to nip them in the bud before they rise to harassment." Perhaps in this spirit, two male Los Angeles Police Department officers with otherwise sterling records were given punitive reassignments after publicly complaining that women were getting undeserved promotions; the authorities did not resort to some other pretext to punish them for this speech, instead citing it as open grounds for discipline.

KID GLOVES AND BRASS KNUCKLES

In the case of *Davis* v. *Monsanto,* a federal appeals court observed that current doctrines "require that an employer take prompt action to prevent" employees who harbor erroneous racial or sexual views "from expressing their opinions in a way that abuses or offends their co-workers." Then it went on to salute the law's role in correcting those disfavored opinions: "By informing people that the expression of racist or sexist attitudes in public is unacceptable, people may eventually learn that such views are undesirable in private, as well." In 1992 a federal court ordered that workers in a government office be made to "refrain from any . . . remarks" that are "contrary to their fellow employees' religious beliefs," though remarks contrary to other peoples' religious beliefs had until lately counted as a core concern of the First Amendment.

Again and again, employers have been hit with painful financial exactions because they have allowed managers or staff to express opinions on the wrong side of controversial topics of the day. A production manager at WUSA-TV in Washington, D.C., came out with a Rush Limbaugh-style crack about how, to quote the *Washington Post,* he'd "like to smoke a cigar but the 'Nazi feminists' wouldn't let him." Local jurors hit the station with a $500,000 verdict, telling the press afterward that station employees "seemed to feel it was partly okay to make jokes about women." "[N]egative comments about women who work versus women who stay at home" helped prove fatal in another suit.

It would be far too optimistic to hope that universities would rally the resistance to these trends in line with their tradition of free thought. For one thing, there are precedents like the 1981 Ninth Circuit case of *Lynn* v. *Board of Regents,* where faculty stood accused of too readily dismissing the credentials of a women's studies specialist. Judge Stephen Reinhardt pronounced that "a disdain for women's issues, and a diminished opinion of those who concentrate on those issues, is evidence of a discriminatory attitude toward women." The message, apparently, is as follows: treat identity studies as being just as rigorous as molecular biochemistry, or have your checkbook ready. A Modern Language Association newsletter has defined "anti-feminist harassment" to include "easy dismissal of feminist writers, journals and presses" and "automatic depreciation of feminist work as 'narrow,' 'partisan' and 'lacking in rigor.'" A Harvard law professor wrote that it creates a hostile environment to treat women's "work as insignificant, their fears as trivial, their ideas as unworthy."

The harassment literature urges managements to act boldly. As the *9 to 5 Guide* announces airily, "no employee is indispensable"; it adds that unfounded accusations are "rare." It also offers one of those confident little tables separating "fact" from "myth" ("Myth: A man's career can be destroyed by an accusation of sexual harassment, while the woman who accuses him suffers no consequences.") One institution in the forefront of attitude control is the military, where toleration of public dissent has never been a high priority. Several congresswomen spearheaded an official Committee on Women's Issues, which called in 1990 for the "immediate dismissal of senior officers who question the role of women in the military" and said harassment at the service academies should be "punishable by expulsion in most instances"—a noteworthy demand since, according to the General Accounting Office, harassment charges at the academies are most commonly filed against cadets who express the opinion that standards have been lowered for women's benefit. The superintendent of the U.S. Naval Academy pledged speedy adoption of the panel's recommendations. In her sympathetic account of military women, *Mixed Company,* Helen Rogan nonetheless expresses unease about how "people who speak out too freely on the subject can ruin their careers," while Brian Mitchell (who takes a critical view of the same general subject in his book *Weak Link*) recounts considerable evidence that quite a few careers have indeed been ruined this way.

The EEOC seemed surprised in 1994 when the biggest volume of protest mail it had ever received on any issue forced it to back down from formal rules prohibiting speech or conduct that "denigrates" or shows "aversion" to any religion. The rules would "have a chilling effect on religious expression," predicted Forest D. Montgomery of the National Association of Evangelicals. Many leading religions, of course, inculcate as a matter of doctrine a moral obligation to try to persuade others, which can mean advancing the most pointed arguments as to the fallaciousness of the target's existing beliefs. Yet the formal withdrawal of the rules meant less than appeared on the surface, since to a large extent they simply codified what EEOC staffers (and many courts) already regarded as settled doctrine—and that prevailing doctrine persists, whether codified or not.

Nor is harassment law the only new law to chill speech. Courts have traditionally been cautious about construing someone's expression of opposition to a law as evidence that he will be inclined to break it, given the obvious danger of chilling dissenting opinions; mature citizens are also thought capable of the complicated feat of disliking yet obeying a law. But a New Hampshire college lost after plaintiffs discovered a private letter from one of its officers calling bias charges a "form of anarchy" that he feared "may creep north into our virgin territory." One early federal case premised a finding of liability in part on a manager's comment *before* the Equal Pay Act was enacted that "Congress would never pass such a foolish law as that." A 1977 editorial column in *Forbes* magazine by Malcolm Forbes, Jr., advised Congress to "think long and hard before axing the practice of mandatory retirement at age 65, at least in the private sector"; the passage was thrown back at him in an age bias suit a decade and a half later.

Criticizing judges and their orders is another ticket to regret, as mayor Emory Folmar and police chief John Wilson of Montgomery, Alabama, found in a 1987 case. "The only person who thinks she's qualified to be a captain is Judge Thompson," Folmar told the press, referring to a policewoman whom a federal judge had ordered promoted. "If we sneeze in front of her she'll be back in federal court," added Wilson. "Who is going to be responsible for her misjudgments and actions? Is it going to be Judge Thompson? No. It will be me. I will be legally responsible for what she does." The comments earned the two officials a personal $3,500 fine for contempt, the court citing a provision in its earlier order requiring them to treat the complainant with "respect, support and encouragement."

An employee bull session at a large Chicago law firm about whether the legal rights of blacks compare favorably to those of Jews became a ground of complaint in a black employee's suit. Someone at a Minnesota construction firm posted a leaflet criticizing Indian claims to unlimited fishing rights in local waters, which were highly unpopular among local conservation and sporting groups; the leaflet was cited in

WORKPLACE CLEANSING

an Indian worker's later constructive-discharge suit. Texas law professor Douglas Laycock told a Senate panel in 1994 that he for one "would not be seriously troubled" at a workplace ban on profane or blasphemous expressions such as "Jesus Christ!" or "Goddammit"—after all, such "speech of little First Amendment value" makes for "an uncomfortable working environment for many believers."

Far from enjoying any special exemption, press outlets were a favorite target. After a complaint from a Los Angeles city councilman, the federal Civil Rights Commission launched a publicized crackdown on seven southern California television stations focusing not only on treatment of minority staffers—who, as one informant complained, had been getting "negative memos criticizing their performance"—but also charges that the stations were failing to give favorable enough coverage to minorities. EEOC chairman Evan Kemp told the *National Journal*'s John Moore that he slapped Baltimore broadcaster WBAL-TV with a complaint "because I wanted TV to be more sympathetic to the cases we are bringing, and I thought this would do it." Not long ago there might have been an outcry at a government official's use of the club of official enforcement to reshape news coverage on controversial topics, but by now there was none: we'd all become too sensitized, or perhaps too numb.

The other half of a regime of orthodoxy is required showings of assent to the approved line of thought, and these too are much in evidence. Sensitivity training is increasingly becoming mandatory—as is the case, for example, for private-company managers in Connecticut. To be sure, there has been some public reaction against the more extreme "shame-and-blame" seminars, in which captive attendees have been reduced to tears by probing for racist thoughts or browbeating about their privileged status. A *New York Times* report on the Seattle municipal ferry system's million-dollar, compulsory training program ("shock therapy . . . a sort of cultural boot camp") found the training had left ferry workers "more polarized than before," with a "huge backlash. Tons of anger," to quote one supporter. "We used to be all ferry workers, but now everyone's divided up into little groups," a supervisor said. Complaints of harassment had soared; at least a dozen pending cases would soon cost the state $800,000 in settlements. "Dozens of

KID GLOVES AND BRASS KNUCKLES

workers interviewed at the ferry system said they were afraid to talk to each other, and some supervisors said they hesitated to give orders." Trainers, however, were unrepentant. "We have moved them from denial to resistance," said one. "We consider that a healthy move."

———

It might be nice to imagine that the new repression is still an exceptional matter confined to a few do-everything-to-excess employers. Unfortunately, there are plenty of signs that it's coming soon to a company near you. Attorney Ellen Wagner, quoted in *Fortune,* was critical of the trend: "Accusers are believed on the basis of very little evidence or none at all," she said. "And the ultimate punishment, termination, is a first resort rather than a last one."

A business professor at a prominent university in the East tells of running into a surprise when he gave his students a case study meant to illustrate the handling of a modern workplace conflict. The example involved a genteel older man who has been with the company for many years; he persists in calling younger women "honey" and "dear," a habit that a few newer female hires have mentioned they find annoying. How should the company handle things?

The professor had expected classroom discussion to revolve around diplomatic, perhaps humorous ways to send the fellow a message without stepping on his feelings. Instead, his students' reaction was prompt, emphatic, and the same among males and females alike—get this guy out pronto before the company lands in real trouble. The only debate was over such questions as whether it was better to offer him an immediate buyout or build a paper trail to nail him.

A *New York Times* business article on March 27, 1994, followed similar format, asking various sexual harassment specialists how they would handle cases drawn from real life. In one case, a female employee who had sought a promotion but received a poor review filed a complaint against her supervisor; it seems she'd observed him locked in an embrace with his secretary in her cubicle. What the company discovers in its investigation throws quite a new light on the report: when the executive embraced her, the secretary had just received word of her mother's death.

The facts in this example might seem so utterly one-sided that only a decision in favor of the accused manager would make sense, but it's presented as a close case. None of the panelists proposes counseling (or, as an older generation might have put it, "telling off") the complainant about the strong advisability of minding her own business, lest she get innocent people in trouble. Nor has the real-life company done anything of that sort. Instead it has put a letter of warning in the *manager's* file saying, in the best organizational weasel-speak, that he may have exercised poor judgment—not saying that he did or didn't, just that he *may* have. Far from putting the matter to rest, this decision has sent the office into an uproar, with an angry staff taking the manager's side and ostracizing the complainant, who is now proceeding to charge retaliation based on her exercise of rights. The manager himself has expressed reluctance to handle her performance review for fear of further retaliation charges.

Even a slow student might by this point see that the company might have made a mistake in reprimanding the supervisor, and should now start going to bat for him rather than letting him absorb further damage. But none of the *Times* panelists go on to express any recorded second thoughts about the company's handling of the situation. One timidly suggests it might consider offering the complainant a transfer to another department, but that is all.

———

Defending the new developments in harassment law against a small but growing band of First Amendment critics, many in the law schools have resorted to what is perhaps their most amazing argument yet, set against its historical context. They triumphantly haul out the banner—for this one occasion only—of employment at will.

Traditional employment-at-will doctrine always upheld an employer's right to set whatever standard for decorum it wished, so that it could dismiss a thirty-year veteran for telling a single off-color joke if it wanted. All companies were doing now was exercising such rights— so what could the First Amendment problem be? This was strictly private action; it's not as if big companies were anything like governments. A widely cited *William and Mary Law Review* treatment agrees that it would be fallacious to compare workplace interactions with any sort of "dialogue among autonomous self-governing citizens." The same law reviews that not long before were full of articles asserting that private workplaces needed "bills of rights" now began running laborious proofs that since taking a job is totally voluntary, all employees can reasonably be deemed to have waived any right to object to an employer's antiharassment policy.

These arguments have already been picked up by lawyers and courts. After a Massachusetts court ruled that obscene satirical collages about an opposing candidate (which would almost certainly have counted as protected speech had they been circulated in a city council race) were unlawful when circulated in a campaign for union office, winning lawyer Nancy Gertner said the ruling disposed of the view that "people should be allowed to speak as freely in the workplace as they are outside." A Michigan federal court blandly noted that everyone would recognize a private employer's right to demand that its workers take down a pinup, so how could anyone think a question of free speech was involved if the government simply ordered the employer to exercise that right?

Easily. Under First Amendment law, private newsstand owners have an absolute right to refuse to carry a controversial publication, but that doesn't smuggle in a right for government to order them not to carry it. It is amusing, after three decades of efforts in legal academia to blur the distinction between private and public action, to see it suddenly revived for tactical purposes. But harassment law and discrimination law are not private matters. They are distinctly public and governmental sanctions enforced at the point of the government's guns. No doubt harassment law sometimes directs employers to suppress opinion that they would have suppressed anyway. Even so, the action still offends First Amendment values, just as it would if newsstands were forbidden to carry a publication that they weren't planning to carry anyway.

———

When faced with what it concedes to be "real" speech, the Supreme Court has developed a body of jurisprudence wildly at odds with the premises of the new harassment law. It protects language that is meant to inflame and wound—even, sometimes, if it is followed in short order by an actual outbreak of violence. As the Court found in a 1982 case involving an NAACP boycott, "extemporaneous rhetoric cannot be nicely channeled in purely dulcet phrases." Other courts have found constitutional protection even for some speech that is specifically intended to harass; for instance, the Montana supreme court in 1993 struck down a state law banning harassment of hunters by animal-rights activists.

The Supreme Court has also, of course, long and properly recognized the "chilling effect" of vague or overbroad prohibitions on speech and association. Thus it struck down a vague loyalty oath on the grounds that it would give oath-takers reason to "steer far wider of the unlawful zone" than if it were well defined, thus "restricting their conduct to that which is unquestionably safe" by shutting up on all sorts of controversial topics. It also has struck down otherwise rational restrictions on speech for "overbreadth" if they curb or chill a substantial amount of protected along with unprotected speech.

Sometimes the Court has upheld curbs on the possibly disruptive time, place, and manner of speech, as when trucks equipped with loudspeakers are driven through residential neighborhoods. But it is then careful to enforce "viewpoint neutrality," making sure such regulations are not enforced against dissidents when they are waived for friends of the ruling orthodoxy. As Eugene Volokh of UCLA points out, it remains perfectly within the law to dismay and upset co-workers, rendering them too angry to do their jobs, by the use of inflammatory speech of most kinds. Harangues by the unpatriotic can create a "hostile working environment" for loyal Americans and the government will not move to stop them—happily so, since we would never trust it with the power to attach liability to speech in those circumstances.

But harassment law is hopelessly, unfixably biased according to viewpoint. Dozens of reported cases involve liability claims based on antifeminist statements that are frequently not at all obscene but often highly political and analytic in content; an exhaustive search fails to uncover a single case in which feminist assertions have been ruled to contribute to a hostile environment.

Some harassment-law advocates appear willing to accept the equivalent of "reverse discrimination" concepts into harassment law and order the exclusion from the workplace of feminist or black-nationalist ideas that make males or whites feel uncomfortable. Another large faction, though, is perfectly happy to embrace a double standard. Law professor Mari Matsuda calls for speech to come under legal proscription only when it is "directed against a historically oppressed group." The *9 to 5 Guide,* a bit more cryptically, notes that while jokes about the "powerless" are to be condemned, jokes about "those in power" are fine—a paradox, you might say, since the prerogative of suppressing jokes inimical to one's interests is traditionally a sign of being very powerful indeed.

Matsuda, Catharine MacKinnon, and other influential legal academics go one perhaps inevitable step farther. Scorning to resurrect the public-private distinction, they instead argue that the time is at hand to cleanse not just the workplace but the wider culture of published or spoken materials that might offend women and minorities. Various so-called critical race theorists have proposed to criminalize what they deem racist and sexist speech—which they often define in such a way as to take in a great deal of political discussion, including many comments critical of affirmative action. Dozens, indeed scores of law review articles have taken up the subject of the legality of unprogressive speech in the public square and private publications, and most have taken a firm stand for suppressing a lot more of it. Many of these articles, seizing on harassment law as exactly the precedent they had in mind, argue that the success of recent efforts to suppress speech in the workplace shows that government can and should order undesirable speech to be punished in the wider society.

———

Not many free-speech advocates would care to cure the harassment-law problem by going to the opposite, appalling extreme of the protected-strike-speech cases like Barbara Lawler's, where employers are forbidden to exercise discipline against threats and obscenities. But an entirely different strand in federal labor law, dating back to the New Deal, offers a far better approach: it simply directs the government not to interpret the expression of views as a labor violation. "The expressing of any views, argument, or opinion, or the dissemination thereof, whether in written, printed, graphic, or visual form, shall not constitute or be evidence of an unfair labor practice under any of the provisions of this subchapter, if such expression contains no threat of reprisal or force or promise of benefit." Thus reads the National Labor Relations Act, and note its careful language: protected speech not only will not constitute an unfair labor practice in itself, but cannot be introduced as evidence as such.

Perhaps it's time to introduce a similar principle into harassment and discrimination law.

Part V

THE TERMS OF COOPERATION

Chapter 15

OUR SCOFFLAW BOSSES

It was a case of "a basic lack of human decency," a "sickness in the organization." The Exxon company knew its captain had a history of alcoholism, yet it chose to let him command a tanker, accepting his story that his problems were behind him. And the result? The *Exxon Valdez* had run aground in Alaska's Prince William Sound, causing one of history's worst oil spills. And it happened because the giant company had taken a "callous, cold-hearted business risk."

So went the closing arguments of the plaintiff's attorney suing Exxon in the main damage case resulting from the spill. To reflect the uncomplicated nature of the moral issues at stake, he even quoted from the best-selling book of homilies *Everything I Know I Learned in Kindergarten* as he urged a punitive damage award of $20 billion for his clients. (Contingency fees for plaintiff's lawyers commonly run at around a third of total damages.) The jury, doubtless thinking itself moderate, responded by awarding $5 billion.

In other courtrooms, meanwhile, other lawyers were suing Exxon on other grounds—in particular, on behalf of workers with drinking pasts whom the company had taken off safety-sensitive positions. By the mid-1990s at least a hundred challenges to the company's substance abuse policies had been filed, and dozens of cases were pending around the country. Lawyers citing handbook language had already won one big verdict for an officer in Portland, Maine, whom Exxon had transferred with no cut in pay. "Public perception of the Valdez incident as having been caused by a recovering alcoholic," declared a Department of Labor administrative law judge in 1992, "does not justify discrimination against all recovering alcoholics."

It became a standing joke: after the lawyers were done suing you up one side of the street, they'd sue you down the other. They would sue when you gave a bad reference, then sue for failure to warn—in other words, failure to give a bad reference—when your old employee committed some atrocity in his new job. They would sue when you turned away a job applicant with a violent or criminal past, or sue if you did take him and he hurt someone. A landmark California case allowed a negligent-hiring suit against a laundromat owner who had taken on an unstable halfway-house graduate, even though the man had no criminal record.

Rules on dating and nepotism are another sued-if-you-do, sued-if-you-don't favorite. Letting officemates get romantically involved invites suits by other workers charging favoritism or a sexualized environment—or, more commonly, by the junior-ranking participant in the affair charging a hostile environment or retaliation after it ends. Even third parties may have claims: for example, a Texas court ruled in 1994 that the spouse of an employee carrying on an adulterous affair could sue the company for letting it happen. But clamping down runs into claims of privacy invasion, interference with off-hours conduct, defamation, and so forth. Companies have been sued both for carrying on nepotism (because it is unfair to minorities who aren't in the family) and for enforcing rules against it (a practice that was deemed unfair to married couples.)

Litigators have targeted employers over "English-only" rules that prevent workers from speaking among themselves in the language with which they're most at home. Yet New York's Bellevue Hospital lost a suit to an English-speaking nurse who charged that co-workers' casual use of the Filipino language Tagalog kept her from doing her job by depriving her of critical information about patients. Federal law and fear of accident liability push companies to carry on employee drug testing even where they might not wish to do so, but guessing wrong about which employees may be subjected to such tests has led to six-figure verdicts. Then there is the perennial puzzle of how to find out about employees' protected-group status—so as to file all the proper reports and the like—without seeming to take an interest in the topic. "We're not supposed to ask, but we are supposed to know" is how more than one businessperson has put it.

Disparate-impact doctrine leads to compliance jams, too. Courts have generally held it unlawful for companies to accord hiring preference to U.S. war veterans, since such policies have adverse impact on women. Some laws on the books, though, *require* many private employers to observe such a preference. To resolve the issue, it was ruled that veterans' preferences would be forbidden everywhere they weren't mandatory and mandatory everywhere they weren't forbidden—the truly unthinkable alternative, of course, being to allow employers to follow their own wishes on the subject.

The discipline of misbehaving workers is a constant source of double binds. The sheriff of Suffolk County, New York, tried to fire two white officers he considered responsible for taunting minority workers in the county prison system, but civil service appeals gave them their jobs back; the county proceeded to lose a huge harassment case filed by the outraged workers. Civil service and union protections often led to reinstatement of sex harassers as well.

———————

To hear many descriptions of the new employment law, you'd think its main challenge for employers was simply to summon the force of character to behave properly. "It is as simple as requiring everyone on the job to treat everyone with decency and respect," the *Washington Post* editorialized after a harassment ruling. "The law simply codifies courtesy," said an advocate quoted in a *New York Times* account announcing that employers "need not fret" about compliance with the new ADA. Another proponent agreed, saying, "This isn't rocket science." Several academics writing in the *Law and Society Review* reproach employers for wasting effort on defensive management measures when it would be so much easier for them just to treat workers "more fairly" and "avoid discharging employees without good cause."

Employers found liable in court verdicts, or sometimes even just those taken to court in the first place, are often assumed to have acted in defiance of clear legal dictates. "Managers who follow generally accepted principles of management, and keep in mind the general dictates of the law, do not get sued," contends the author of the self-help guidebook *Your Rights at Work*. Any litigation that may arise under the ADA, declared a *Wall Street Journal* letter writer, "will occur solely because . . . civil rights . . . have been ignored."

No more absurd view could be imagined. Employers cannot knowingly and fully comply with the new employment law the way a wage earner can be sure he has filed his income taxes by April 15. The new law is voluminous; much of it is vague, so that employers cannot tell exactly what is asked of them but must find out after the fact when courts or regulators rule; it changes constantly and often retroactively; it assigns liability to common workplace interactions that are bound to come up every day; and its dictates are often in what lawyers diplomatically call tension with one another. No degree of good faith can keep employers from being taken to court and sometimes losing. Nor can they ensure victory by sinking a fortune into compliance efforts, although this does not keep them from trying.

Employers react to this state of uncompliability in various ways, all unsatisfactory to one degree or another. Some paddle ever more frantically in hopes of reaching the fabled shores of compliance. Some document personnel decisions obsessively, while others put as little on paper as they can get away with. Many hire squadrons of personnel and compliance specialists, as well as in-house lawyers, often yanking authority from front-line managers and professionals in the process. Some adopt clever subterfuge, others resolve to live dangerously and hope they don't get sued, and yet others cultivate ultra-progressive reputations for overcompliance that they hope will count in their favor if they are ever put in the dock. The result is a varied culture of compliance whose one consistent feature may be its propensity to usher in personnel practices no one would have thought of adopting for any other reason.

———

One of the most obvious problems with the new law is its sheer size. The criminal code Macaulay drafted for India was said to be so clear and concise that ordinary Indians might keep a copy rolled in the lining of their cap and pull it out to resolve a dispute on the road. Any manager who tried such a thing with the new employment law would risk spinal compression. One survey found federal personnel managers were bound by 850 pages of directly pertinent law and 1,300 pages of regulations, aside from rooms full of commentary and case law. Private managers are not far behind. Policies on race and sex and age, disability, harassment, family leave, common-law wrongful termination, and employee privacy and defamation each generate volumes of laws, regulations, and court interpretations analyzed in commercially available manuals and case reporters. Former IRS official Alvin Lurie has observed that though employers have spent scores of billions trying to comply with the federal pension law he once oversaw, "even experts cannot understand" it, with the result that there "continues to be massive noncompliance"—the law operating on two levels, an incomprehensible "official" version and a "vulgate." Companies that do as much as $10,000 worth of business with the government come under thousands of pages of distinct additional rules for contractors.

The American with Disabilities Act, Civil Rights Restoration Act, and Family and Medical Leave Act all hit within a few years in the early 1990s. But at least those laws were the outcome of a conventional legislative process, published in official records and widely publicized before becoming effective at a stated future date. Much employment law was never preannounced or published as such at all, instead taking the form of judicial innovations fastened on unsuspecting employers who hadn't a clue that the law's interpretation was going to change. (In fact, flying in the face of very old ideas about the rule of law, advocates have repeatedly endorsed the idea that newly passed discrimination statutes should also get retroactive application.) Regulators, too, periodically redefine as prohibited vast swaths of formerly accepted behavior.

Even more corrosive is the law's vagueness. How is an employer supposed to tell which of its employees count as legally disabled (and thus covered by the ADA), how much accommodation for them is reasonable, when the costs of compliance finally amount to undue hardship, when a boisterous or tense working environment reaches the point of being hostile, or when a suspension or failure to promote will count as having been for good cause? The answer is that it frequently does not and cannot know. Complying with laws of this sort is not like stopping for red lights or staying within a speed limit; one would wait forever for the light to turn green, and being an employer is unsafe at any speed. Instead you must act first and then learn later whether you've acted lawfully—when a lawyer hauls you before a jury to demand a fortune.

Constant jeopardy is inevitable as well because the law takes so many commonplace work situations and turns them into potential suits. Not only is every firing open to challenge; so is every failure to hire or promote, as well as an endless array of problematic working conditions, pay disparities, and criticisms or other remarks that might have given pain. (As Camille Paglia puts it, every workplace is hostile.) Pretty much all employee selection and evaluation methods, very much including the subjective and word-of-mouth methods most in use, show disparate impact or are legally suspect for some other reason. "Absent discrimination," the EEOC has proclaimed in one of its baldest defiances of reality, "one would expect a nearly random distribution of women and minorities in all jobs." Absurd though that standard may be, it guarantees the commission a full docket till doomsday.

Shrewd enforcers know they do *not* want regulated parties to achieve definite compliance; that would badly undercut the basis of their power. When the EEOC issued its landmark rules on the use of employment tests, a Justice Department official observed that "the thrust of the proposed Guidelines is to place almost all test users in a posture of noncompliance" while giving "great discretion to enforcement personnel to determine who should be prosecuted." That discretion suited enforcers just fine, since it meant their inspectors met a very obliging if not obsequious reception. Professor Alfred Blumrosen, who directed the EEOC's enforcement operations for many years, has described the agency's periodic inspection visits to large employers during his years as a "nibbling" approach in which "the government will take an arm this year and come back next year for an ear or a leg." At each visit, inspectors could add new demands "where the violations appear clearest or where the resistance to change might be less." (Uniroyal got an unpleasant surprise this way in one early case; an inspector had observed and let go its practice of maintaining separate seniority lists by department, a then-common practice; later, officials decided it ought to be against the law, costing the tire company an estimated $15 to $20 million in resulting contract-debarment proceedings.) An important point, in Blumrosen's view, is that "the government does not give the regulated institution a clean bill of health" at any point in the process.

———

Almost by necessity, staying abreast of legal obligations now tends to become a specialized function within companies. Line managers simply cannot assimilate the whole mass of new law—even if they each took a sabbatical year to study their legal obligations, the flow of new laws, regulations, and court rulings would soon render their knowledge dangerously obsolete. Increasingly, therefore, all large employers and many smaller ones maintain ongoing and formal efforts devoted to compliance. Even if they can't bring full compliance within reach, these departments can make a valuable contribution by improving the employer's odds.

A serious compliance effort can be expensive even for an employer facing no unusual compliance issues. Some internal inspection process will be advisable to check on whether far-flung offices have followed company policy. The government has provided a steady diet of new responsibilities for personnel specialists: harassment and sensitivity training and complaint hotlines, disability and language accommodation issues, "family-friendly" policies (with their growing legal component), and on and on. Since staying current on the ever-changing law is of the essence in all these areas, one soon tends to become a customer of the sprawling industry of seminars and conferences, looseleaf services, newsletters, and hotlines on new developments.

Compliance incentives often point in the direction of standardizing company policy on personnel practices, which can involve both formalization and centralization. One reason is that in many situations foolish consistency is legally safer for an employer than provable inconsistency. Suppose the job specifications for a certain position have always called for an MBA, but a dream candidate shows up who isn't one: bending the rules to take him gives both past and future disgruntled applicants ammunition to portray the requirement as a mere sham. The problem often comes up in employee discipline cases, where it is often legally hazardous for managers to be lenient in overlooking employees' infractions of company rules. "Uniform application" of a rule against resumé inaccuracies is "critical," warns Detroit attorney George Mesritz, lest the employer lose the right to press the matter in more urgent cases. An *Investor's Business Daily* account likewise advises the employer to resist the temptation to ignore absenteeism rules in the case of an employee with an otherwise fine record, because it could find itself losing all right to enforce such rules. "Compassionate leave" policies governing such matters as time off when a family member dies are nowadays enmeshed in equally dismal complications; lawyers for other workers may seize on the granting of one variance as a precedent when their own clients are denied leave in less sympathetic situations.

The results are as perverse as anyone could have imagined. Fear of the leniency-for-one, leniency-for-all rule leads some companies to discipline or even fire workers they'd rather have retained. Compassionate leave is doled out with an eyedropper on advice of counsel. At the extreme, the totally rule-bound company begins timing people's bathroom breaks.

Many courts and regulators construe inconsistent or informal policies as evidence of a cavalier attitude toward compliance or even as violations in themselves. If a company hasn't kept written records of requests for permission to vary from vacation policy, for example, it may not notice a pattern in which women have fared worse than men at getting such permission—which in turn suggests it doesn't *care* whether that happens. The Automobile Club of Michigan lost a case after a court cited its lack of "consistent and public standards" in personnel decisions, including its failure to maintain a "systematic job description and evaluation system." In harassment law and increasingly in other legal areas, failure to maintain a formal policy on a topic can lead to payouts even if it is not clear that such a policy would have prevented anyone's misbehavior on matters of substance.

The pressure for formal consistency and against managerial discretion has helped encourage one of the policies most irritating to ordinary employees, the across-the-board drug test. When companies institute such tests, the most frequent question from employees is why they aren't just testing workers who have shown some performance problem suggesting impairment. The answer is that singling out an employee this way invites a suit for defamation, infliction of emotional distress, and other atrocities. Across-the-board testing intrudes on a far larger class of employees, but it is paradoxically safer for most legal purposes because it is freer from the taint of individualized manager discretion.

The threat of companywide punitive damages is another legal pressure strongly encouraging centralization. Prevailing doctrines allow juries that discover a violation at any of a huge company's far-flung subsidiaries to levy punitive damages based on the parent enterprise's wealth—just as if that parent enterprise were a single brooding intelligence rather than, perhaps, a bunch of fairly autonomous enterprises responding to the center mostly on matters of finance and capitalization. Once higher-ups realize that the off-the-wall personnel decisions of the tiniest operating unit in the smallest town can anger some jury into lopping off a third part of the parent company's assets, though, many will resolve to make sure nothing of the sort happens. They will back up this determination by hiring headquarters staff to start issuing central personnel policies, thus becoming (self-fulfillingly) something measurably closer to the lawyer-portrayed octopus of unitary brain and intention.

Another inevitable result of the compliance culture is the growing number and clout of attorneys within organizations of all sorts. Lawyers, both in-house and hired from the outside, are needed to vet employee communications, hover in the background during dismissals, individual reprimands, or warnings, monitor the keeping and timely destruction of personnel records, plan downsizings and buy-outs, and much more.

———

Many of the compliance issues arising from the Americans with Disabilities Act provide case studies in how the new employment laws tend to abet centralization and bureaucratization in the workplace.

In one of its least-noted but most disturbing effects, the ADA gives employers a powerful new motive to devise and adhere to formal job descriptions. The law provides that a disabled worker turned down for a job because he can perform only some of its functions can sue on the grounds that the other duties are not truly essential. Aware that this doctrine opens up formidable scope for messy factual disputes, the law provides that courts should grant some deference to the employer's own ideas on which functions are essential—but on the condition that the company put a job description in writing *before* being faced with the disabled person and his particular shortcoming. The rationale for requiring prior written descriptions is that otherwise employers might tailor job requirements to exclude a particular applicant who has begun raising a fuss.

The drawing up of legally robust job descriptions for this purpose is no light undertaking. To begin with, a job's most fundamental aspects will be among the easiest to overlook: forget to stipulate that applicants be able to read handwriting, or show up on time, or remain quiet when unattended, and there may be no time for second thoughts later. It will be highly dangerous to rely on the language of job descriptions prepared earlier without legal implications in mind; in any case, these are notoriously inaccurate and incomplete at many companies. An *Employee Relations Law Journal* article advises that descriptions be worded by persons seasoned in ADA issues. These should draw on "behavioral profiles of successful incumbents" prepared with input from expert psychologists, but at the same time they must not demand traits found in uneven proportions among different demographic groups. All but the largest businesses will think of hiring an outside consultant to meet this tall order, at great expense. The city of Baytown, Texas, found it would cost $81,000 to have a consultant prepare ADA job descriptions for its 270 job titles, though it managed to reduce the outlay by collaborating with a consortium of similar-sized towns.

For many organizations, though, the real cost of ADA job descriptions will go far beyond a consultant's fee. To begin with, many will rightly sense that the description on paper is to an extent legally binding on them, even when it begins to seem unrealistic. There will also be a reluctance, common in bureaucracies, to create new job classifications freely or to reassign duties among incumbents. For reasons like these, many employers would not want fixed and obligatory job descriptions even if they came drafted with great skill for free. Newer, fast-growing companies in fluid industries are especially prone to disparage the "job-description mentality" in favor of shifting talent around ("forget what you were doing, come over here and help with this"). It's hardly as if the free-form entrepreneurial model is somehow always better than the highly structured model; different forms appear best for different tasks. But a distinctive strength of the American economy has been its compatibility with both models. Economies like those of Germany and Canada, which generate some successful bureaucratically organized companies, have had far more trouble nurturing the entrepreneurial kind. Laws like ADA tilt our playing field toward the organizationalists as well.

Companies maintain centralized personnel departments for many reasons other than legal compliance. Still, business historians note that the authority and prestige of such departments have taken big jumps during three distinct periods during this century—World War I, the New Deal and World War II, and the period beginning in the mid-1960s—and each expansion wave has coincided with a period of increased pressure on companies by government, unions, or both.

———

A special and painful case of bureaucratization is that of the university. The governance of academic life, traditionally and proudly the province of the faculty itself, has for twenty-five years been steadily moving into the hands of central university administration. Many more department decisions than before must be vetted in advance by the head office, often by its lawyers. A survey reported in the *Chronicle of Higher Education* found lawyers had taken a steadily increasing role in governance: between 1972 and 1984, the percentage of colleges keeping full-time attorneys in-house doubled to nearly half. And no wonder, since a slip by one department can bring down a lawsuit that damages the entire institution. Inconsistencies between the practices of different departments also spell trouble, since tenure complainants can seize on them (arguing, for example, that because one department has waived publication requirements, another is being arbitrary by refusing to do so).

As lawyers and compliance experts have advanced, faculty themselves have beaten a retreat. A *Journal of Higher Education* article found "it is more and more difficult to get them to serve on personnel and grievance committees." At one of the first colleges to face a tenure lawsuit, reported LaNoue and Lee, "the faculty is reluctant to record positive and negative votes or to associate names of committee members with certain viewpoints about the candidate under consideration." "Faculty members threatened by lawsuits often develop a new wariness . . . shying away from hard decisions," Princeton counsel Thomas H. Wright, Jr., has observed. "These are not healthy instincts in a university."

Collegiality? Esprit? The great enterprise of learning? George LaNoue and Barbara Lee, summarizing the views of administrators at a state university traumatized by tenure litigation, say one lesson learned was: "Don't be too nice to borderline or mediocre faculty members," since "overly positive evaluations" can make it hard to deny tenure later. Departments were advised to let the university's lawyers vet all correspondence with faculty.

———

An entire corps of "diversity professionals" has by now sprung up in larger organizations. Federal regulations, it may be noted, do not leave this process to chance; contract compliance regulations covering virtually all the nation's largest companies require them to name equal employment opportunity/affirmative action (EEO/AA) officers and vest in them a long list of functions. Many of these tasks might not otherwise be united in a single job description: investigating employee complaints; designing "systems that will . . . indicate need for remedial action"; developing goals, timetables, and "policy statements" on group hiring; providing "interpersonal relations awareness and EEO compliance training and other staff development"; and providing "[c]areer counseling for all employees." These officers must also be given access to line management, the regulations specify.

These regulations go far beyond any plausible concern with ensuring compliance as such. They appear rather more like an effort to install a beachhead of EEO culture within each company and guarantee it a substantial amount of turf by annexing such functions as career counseling. Surveys indicate that EEO staffs are apt to differ to some extent from the executives around them—for example, they appear to view numerical hiring goals more favorably. They are still hired by and answerable to their employers, however, so they are more likely to feel torn by conflicting expectations than they are to live up to the hopes of outside grievance-organizers.

Still, widely held views of the EEO function encourage these officers to depart in some rather dramatic ways from prevailing norms of organizational loyalty. Seattle attorney Patricia Rose has written that an EEO officer commonly may, along with investigating an employee complaint impartially, offer the complainant "emotional support and counseling. . . . If her mediation and informal resolution efforts fail, the EEO officer routinely helps the aggrieved employee file a complaint with a government enforcement agency." The EEOC has even taken the view in court that giving "aid and comfort" to the employer's legal adversaries is part and parcel of an EEO officer's job, against which the company must not retaliate.

Whether out of sincere belief or simply to improve what lawyers call the atmospherics on future suits, many employers make a big show of enthusiastic support for the new law's spirit as well as its letter. A "history of progressive attitudes regarding the advancement of women" makes it easier to prevail as a defendant, observes an *Ohio*

THE TERMS OF COOPERATION

State Law Journal writer. Most large companies have ventured into not only compliance and antiharassment training but more elaborate diversity sessions designed to instill correct attitudes in workers. These training sessions commonly feature the trappings of a law-driven effort, such as mandatory attendance and checkoffs so the company can later document that everyone was there. At the same time, an underlying purpose of the sessions is to demonstrate that the company is really smitten with the new law in the full beauty of its spirit, not just dragging itself into compliance with the crabbed letter.

———

Other managers (or, sometimes, managers at the same firms) at some point simply give up trying to comply, reasoning that they can't keep from being sued anyway and may as well run a rational business. Not many bosses refrain from word-of-mouth hiring until they get a validation study, or pay the slightest heed to the rules against criminal-record discrimination, or make sure to advertise in the minority press if they are in the want ads of a big city's daily newspaper. The "dirty little secret" of job interviewers, a *Wall Street Journal* reporter breathlessly announced, is that lots of them knowingly violate the law on forbidden inquiries and the like. Headhunter searches specifying female candidates are on the rise, though the practice is blatantly unlawful. And although age bias law keeps producing big verdicts for complainants in court, it is among the most routinely ignored parts of the law, especially in hiring. Ad agencies, entertainment companies, and other trend-chasers make few bones about preferring young staffs. A *New York Times* account of September 25, 1995, credits NBC's dominance in network programming to its success to reaching 18-to-34-year-olds (the "viewers most sought after by advertisers") and lauds its strategy of hiring programming executives in that age bracket, including a 31-year-old and two 29-year-olds: "They're the right age," says an NBC executive. No one is quoted saying that this is the employment-law equivalent of announcing in a U.S. Customs inspection line what a good living you've been making as a smuggler.

Short of deliberate violation there is subterfuge, as managers learn how to elicit information without asking, or raise their eyebrows just so when asked about an ex-employee. Where restrained from firing they also learn the knack—familiar in civil service settings—of making subordinates' lives unpleasant enough that they think of leaving voluntarily.

———

Presumably no one has access to better advice on how to stay out of legal trouble than the nation's biggest law firms. Yet big law firms have not only been sued repeatedly by their employees but have paid large amounts in a long series of notable verdicts and settlements. Targets include Baker & McKenzie (the record harassment verdict), King & Spalding (a landmark ruling establishing that denial of partnership could be sued over), Cadwalader, Wickersham & Taft (removal of partner), Coudert Brothers ($500,000–$700,000 settlement of pregnancy discrimination suit), Katten, Muchin & Zavis ($2.5 million award over race), and White & Case ($500,000 settlement). All these firms are known for representing large institutional clients, and some are famous for their employment-law-defense departments.

Law firms are renowned as particularly egregious offenders on the age issue, hiring fresh grads to fill their associate ranks, then ejecting those who fail to make partner ("up or out") to make way for more young faces. "It wouldn't be easy for an older attorney to come in and pick up the firm's style," explained a lawyer at Winthrop Stimson. Retaining senior associates would "create a hardening of the arteries by removing an opportunity for a younger person," declared one at Morrison & Foerster. Big-firm recruitment ads have called for grads of specified law-school classes, or set a maximum number of years' experience—belatedly prompting an EEOC probe that might have come a decade or two earlier had the practices been noted in any other line of work.

Nearly every pressure group known for championing the cause of protected groups in the workplace has run into compliance woes of its own. The National Association for the Advancement of Colored People has faced major sex bias and harassment claims. Consumers Union, which has pushed for harsher liability laws in close cooperation with trial lawyer lobbyists, has been bedeviled by labor unrest on its own staff. "Nearly everyone [at its Mount Vernon, N.Y., headquarters], including members of the public-relations staff, wears buttons that say 'Don't Buy *Consumer Reports,*' " according to a *New York Times* report. Vassar, of all colleges, managed to lose a tenure case charging it with bias against women. The Gay Men's Health Crisis, the chief lobby for antibias laws covering those with the HIV virus, was itself sued by a former volunteer coordinator on those very grounds, notwithstanding that 20 percent of its staff is HIV-positive. Leading publications that have ardently supported the new law, from the *New York Times* on down, have all faced their own suits.

Among federal agencies, those concerned with employment bias have been targeted with many more complaints from their own staffs than other agencies. Both the Civil Rights Commission and the EEOC have been hit repeatedly, while the Department of Labor agreed to pay $5 million to settle a bias suit by its employees. In 1995 a jury found the New York City Department for the Aging liable for age discrimination, awarding $1 million to a $51,000/year social worker who blamed her job dismissal on age. If even the enforcers and experts can't stay out of legal trouble, what can the rest of us expect?

———

Most business managers yearn for legal safe harbors; they wish to know, as James DeLong has put it, "that their organizations are in compliance, not that they are out of compliance but that the agency probably will not treat the matter seriously." Our legal system denies them that chance, and its denial is effectively deliberate. As programmers might put it: it's not a bug, it's a feature. The ACLU, campaigning to overturn the employment-at-will principle, has called for the content of good cause in dismissal *not* to be specified in legislation, but to be left up to shifting judicial discretion. Sexual-harassment-law advocates have consistently preferred keeping the law "fluid"—keeping employers guessing about what is permitted—to codifying by statute what is required. ADA advocates successfully fought off any set definition, however high, on how much "reasonable accommodation" would be enough.

If we gave employers any definite safe harbor, after all, some of them might reach it. And then, for advocates and lawyers and enforcement agencies, a train of unwelcome consequences would follow. They might feel their moral high ground beginning to slip away, along with the practical leverage—in the form of threats to call down the law—that goes with it. It would not be so easy to depict the enemy as a bunch of scofflaws or to list the unmet promises, stretching out unending to the horizon, on which the existing law has still not delivered. The rest of us might cease feeling guilty and turn our attention to other deserving needs, issues, causes, and groups, and even the most burningly felt aspiration of identity politics might recede to the status of just one more private grievance among many, rather than a legal right being denied.

Many a hands-on manager has been tempted to cry out to the heavens in frustration: "Do they really expect us to comply with all these laws?" To which the appropriate answer is a question in turn: Whatever made you think they did?

Chapter 16

SECURE IN WHAT?

"The Temping of America," gasped a 1993 *Time* cover story. The magazine proclaimed the scary rise of something called "contingent employment," exemplified by temp work but also including such things as staff "outsourcing." These offered arm's length work relationships, sparse benefits, and tenuous commitment. But we had better get used to them, because they were the coming thing: "In 1988 contingent workers were about a quarter of the labor force. By 2000, they are expected to be half of it." In fact, it seemed that Manpower, Inc., the leading temporary personnel firm, now counted as the world's largest private employer: it sported a payroll of 600,000, ahead of General Motors with 375,000. The trend invited moody journalistic ruminations on the modern age—why, every year things are getting more transient! More rootless! More impersonal! The familiar Warholism might get a new twist: in the future, we could spend fifteen minutes apiece working for each different employer.

There was a kernel of genuine news in the contingent-employment scare, but to get at it one had to strip away layer after layer of hype. To get the count of total "contingent" workers up to 25 percent of the la-

bor force, for example, the trendmongers had to count such large categories as self-employed and part-time workers. Yet neither of these
groups has grown especially rapidly in recent years as a share of the
workforce. Surveys also indicate that most workers in both categories
are there by choice; many part-timers are semi-retired, for example.
There is little reason to think voluntarily self-employed or part-time
workers feel markedly more insecure as a general matter than those
who depend on a single employer for a full-time paycheck.

Given the general stability of the self-employed and part-time sectors, it soon became apparent that the wild prediction that half of all
workers would be contingent by 2000 was an utter fiction; the overall
numbers were growing slowly if at all. The scare, it turned out, had
been fed by union leaders and their allies in government seeking to
rouse concern about the supposed economic insecurity of the American workforce and employers' maltreatment of their "throwaway,"
"disposable" workers. It was in fact a dress rehearsal for the even more
successful "downsizing" scare of 1996, in which trendmongers ea-
gerly seized on the idea that a few highly publicized layoffs signaled
the end of middle-class life.

And what of temporary work? In fact, when *Time* ran with its story,
such work accounted for a mere 1.5 percent of the labor force—hardly
a "Temping of America." Because most workers temp for relatively
brief periods rather than through the year, simply counting the number that pass through in any given year overstates the size of the sector by a factor of perhaps five to seven times. Only by this sort of
method can Manpower, Inc., be portrayed as more important to the
economy than GM. (In shouldering responsibility for the contingent-
employment scare, temp firms' promotional efforts must share blame
with union activists.) It was as if an airport with a million passengers
a year were considered akin to a city with a million residents.

Yet here one did approach the kernel of truth. Though starting from
a low base, temp work was indeed enjoying a boom: by one estimate,
it had quadrupled between 1980 and 1993. The rise of "outsourcing"
and staff leasing were also genuine trends, again from what had been
a low base. Notably, too, despite the widespread image of tempwork as
primarily consisting of routine clerical or blue-collar assignments,

some of the most impressive growth had come in highly skilled, even prestigious white-collar areas. One survey found that temping by professionals such as accountants and physicians had doubled in four years, and significant amounts were being seen among such groups as lawyers and software experts. Some scattered reports also indicated that the composition of such groups as the self-employed and part-time had tilted more toward highly skilled workers and older men.

Temporary, contract, and part-time work had previously boomed in various European countries, one of the chief driving forces being the weight of burdensome government controls on conventional work relationships. Might something similar be going on here? "Costs of termination have become a major contributor to the growing use of a contingency work force," says Michael Losey of the Society for Human Resource Management. Such workers have fewer rights to sue, often maintaining a direct relationship with only a relatively anonymous intermediary firm with shallow pockets. "The best thing about it," a consultant told *Time*, "is that you never have to face firing people—because you never really hire them in the first place."

———

Markets are a moving target. They react to controls by adjusting—often slowly at first, then more and more fully in the long run. And time and again, when attempts are made to impose artificial job security, markets adjust in ways that gradually undercut that goal.

Employment-security buffs used to point with pride to the example of Europe, where employers have long operated under tenure laws that by American standards are fabulously stringent. "Dismissal [in Italy is] considered practically impossible except for criminal acts," observes economist David Henderson. Mandated severance payments in Germany can run many tens of thousands per worker; Portugal does not consider incompetence good cause for termination, and so forth. Where was the employment crisis that some labor economists warned about? Standards of living were high, and official European jobless rates through the 1960s and 1970s generally stayed below the U.S. level.

To all appearances, the laws had indeed contributed to—as well as reflecting—what one might call a culture of tenure in Europe. Statistics suggest European workers are much likelier than their American counterparts to stay with a single employer for many years, both because layoffs and dismissals are less frequent and because workers there quit their jobs at a much lower rate. As of roughly the end of the 1970s the share of employees in the EEC who were relatively new to their workplace (having spent two or fewer years on the job) stood at 19 percent, as opposed to 39 percent in the United States. "My great-grandfather walked 200 miles in his clogs to get here, and I'm damned if I'm going to move out now," said a Welsh coal miner, with no irony intended, during a 1984 strike.

At the same time, certain serious problems were apparent in the European job market even at its greatest flush of success. By American or Japanese standards the European economy was extraordinarily poor at creating new jobs, and its rate of labor force participation fell well below American or Japanese levels—one reason official jobless rates could remain low. For example, European women were much slower than American women to move into paid jobs outside the home, pensioners were less likely to stay in the official labor force on even a part-time basis, and newly graduated students found it considerably harder to land first jobs in their chosen careers, a perennial sore spot in European cities (which tended to contain a large, alienated class of educated but unemployed young persons at loose ends). It was as if most of the desirable seats had been taken in the economy's great game of musical chairs, resulting in a much tougher scramble for the few that opened up.

There were further distress signs relating specifically to legal burdens on employment, such as the shift toward less-regulated temporary work. A substantial share of European hiring is also done "off the books"; underground hiring reportedly makes up a large part of the small-business economy even in famously law-abiding Sweden.

Still, until roughly the 1980s, the European economies did seem to muddle through. Then the bills came due with a vengeance.

Modern methods allow all sorts of old-line industrial activities to be run with far fewer employees than previously. American and Japanese employers, unionized or not, had mostly found ways to make the appropriate payroll cuts. But Europe had postponed the day of reckoning, often plowing subsidies into industry to simulate competitiveness. When the crunch finally hit, the long-delayed layoffs were all the more severe, and unemployment rates shot up to distress levels; Spain's hit a ghastly 24 percent. The aftermath was even worse. The U.S. economy, which suffered sharp periodic recessions, also tended to recover quickly because it did so well at creating new jobs. But the pain in Europe went on and on—by 1996 its jobless rate of about 11 percent was double the U.S. level, and its rate of long-term joblessness was several times ours. Economists dubbed the crisis "Eurosclerosis" and pointed to one overwhelming cause: the continent's abysmally low pace of new job creation.

The figures, indeed, became a standing embarrassment. Over a period when America was adding tens of millions of net new jobs, Europe added at most a few million, and the prime suspect was the continent's punitive employment laws. "Obstacle No. 1 to hiring new employees is the difficulty in terminating workers," an American consultant in Frankfurt told the *Wall Street Journal.* "Once you have to invest in cutting a job, you think three or four times before you create one again," agreed a German machinery executive. In a survey of British heavy-industry firms, more than half said that wrongful-dismissal law had been a "significant inhibiting factor" for them in hiring new workers. An influential 1994 report from the Organization for Economic Cooperation and Development called for member countries to relax labor-market controls. The need for reform, the *New York Times* reported, was widely accepted not just by conservatives like Britain's Margaret Thatcher but "even among Socialists such as Prime Minister Felipe Gonzalez of Spain."

––––––

Here, too, there were signs, though far more scattered and preliminary, that our much more recent ventures into labor-market control were beginning to backfire.

To begin with, there are the small businesses that resolve to stay small. OSHA kicks in at 10 employees, the ADA and Civil Rights Act at 15; age bias and the COBRA health-insurance-continuation law at

20; plant-closing-notification and family-leave mandates at 50; ERISA and EEOC reporting at 100. Press reports confirm that many businesspeople are well aware of these thresholds. "Many businesses are taking pains to keep their payrolls under 50," reported the *Wall Street Journal* when the family-leave law went into effect. "Fifty is the magic number," agreed the president of an Arizona packaging firm. A gathering of the Virginia restauranteurs' association found several were forgoing expansions into catering and carryout services so as to keep head counts below legal thresholds.

Do employers hesitate when thinking of hiring a member of a legally protected group, aware of the extra potential for litigation should things not work out? Nearly every business manager will stoutly deny for the record being swayed by any such considerations, but there have been exceptions—especially among women entrepreneurs, who may feel freer to speak out on the issue than some men. "I am a feminist, but the law has made me fearful of hiring women," writes Pittsburgh restauranteur Sarah McCarthy. "You have made women into china dolls that if broken come with a $300,000 price tag." New Yorker Tama Starr, whose family business ArtKraft Strauss builds many of the signs in Times Square, caused fainting fits among editorialists with similar remarks on the Family and Medical Leave Act: "If you're an employer, you will look at a young woman and say, 'Can we really entrust her to do crucial responsibilities that no one else can do because she's going to take three months off?'" In fact, women's groups did report an upsurge in complaints of firings around the law's effective date. A National Federation of Independent Business survey of 1,000 small businesses found that half admitted some reluctance to hire women of childbearing age due to leave concerns.

For many employers, of course, affirmative action requirements and other fears of numerical scrutiny provide strong countervailing legal pressures that cut in favor of hiring minorities and women. These may balance or outweigh any reluctance based on fear that a particular hiring decision will be hard to undo. But that leaves a distinctive bind for groups like the elderly, which are only partially protected. Older workers are among the most successful groups in individual firing claims, but by and large they are not covered by rules mandating affirmative action in hiring. (Nor do they do well at individual lawsuits over hiring bias, one reason being the trouble they have, unlike minorities and female applicants, in getting low overall hiring numbers accepted as evidence of bias against their group.) This situation tilts the balance of incentives against hiring the middle-aged manager: he is old enough to be a dangerous prospect for an age bias suit or (more likely) an expensive buyout, but the legal pressure in his favor is minimal. After the lifting of the exception allowing for automatic faculty retirement, Harvard history department chair Thomas Bisson was quoted as saying that the law had worsened age bias in hiring because universities were afraid that older hires would be unwilling to depart gracefully.

Not all jobs are affected equally. In a widely noted *Washington Post* piece, *American Lawyer* editor and Court TV founder Steven Brill has warned that discrimination law has become a deterrent to hiring protected-group members for "high-pressure, high-turnover" jobs. Hiring that takes a chance on people for demanding positions is especially discouraged.

———

As for firing, subterfuge and careful lawyering can go far in neutralizing the intent of the law. Given enough time, skill, and luck to build a file without making missteps, most employers probably can eventually succeed in ousting not only a problem employee but also a talented employee on the wrong side of a personality conflict. If hirers "keep their noses procedurally clean, they can get away with murder," observed a college dean in LaNoue and Lee's study of tenure litigation.

There is one other simple step many employers can take to reduce exposure, and that is to depersonalize dismissals by couching them as part of a purely economic layoff that in no way reflects discontent with the particular workers being let go. To be sure, layoffs are themselves the subject of mounting litigation risks, especially if managers have failed to balance them demographically or have made age-related remarks. But it's harder for any one worker to claim that his dismissal is pretextual if the company is giving pink slips to a thousand others at the same time. Hence the familiar pattern in which companies hold off taking action against problem employees, then make sure their positions are included when a reduction in force comes along—deadwood elimination by way of forest fires.

Employees are naturally angry if they suspect that their firing is being grounded on a tactical or insincere pretext, and the technique has other unhappy results as well. Firing via RIF typically sends the ex-employees onto the labor market en masse, often during the recessionary times that are worst for finding new jobs. Even more perversely, the need to preserve appearances may lead managers into wider dismissals than they might otherwise have chosen. Selectively canning all the underperformers and disruptive personalities may be far too obvious, but things will look reasonably neutral if a bunch of clearly competent employees get axed at the same time. Hence the sometimes-heard tale in which a company shuts down a whole branch office, innocent staff and all, rather than sack its out-of-control manager. It's a paradox: the law discourages firing *for cause,* but is more lenient with firms that make a show of firing good and bad workers alike.

Which leads to the "downsizing" panic of 1996. The issue had been smoldering in the press for years; in 1996 it finally burst into flame. Editorialists and commentators everywhere began to ask: why were American businesses—even highly profitable ones—continuing to slash away at their payrolls, cutting jobs by the thousand in round after round of layoffs? It was a catastrophe for the middle class and also a moral and ethical abomination. Business was turning its back on loyalty and community in search of short-term bottom line results.

This panic was, if nothing else, oddly timed. It came not during a recession but at a time of at least normal prosperity: the jobless rate was at 6 percent and falling, the lowest level in twenty years. New jobs were being created at a rapid clip, and such customary indicators of consumer well-being as housing starts and auto sales were doing fine. True, some firms continued to announce big layoffs and downsizing plans, as they had during the recession of the early 1990s; but these were heavily concentrated in fields being transformed by new technology, firms facing competitive reverses, and those with a reputation for past overstaffing. The most prominent downsizing case, AT&T, fell into all three categories.

Some of the more elaborate downsizing critiques told of the decline of a "deal." Clinton labor secretary Robert Reich made himself a leading promoter of this theme, citing a supposed "unwritten contract" that "if you did your job conscientiously, you could count on having that job as long as the company stayed in business." Since companies were letting employees go while staying in business, it was clear they had reneged somewhere along the line. It was in effect a wrongful-termination complaint based on an implied-contract theory, on behalf of not one single worker but the entire workforce.

The realities of business history told a starkly different story. Mass layoffs, even during prosperity and even at big companies, have been common since the dawn of American industry. To be sure, there have been some periods of unusually sunny career prospects for ambitious workers, such as the sustained expansion that followed World War II. For a while, a matter of decades, there had even been a small number of companies—unusual enough that business professors could tick off their names—that sustained a policy of never laying anyone off. These companies, which generally had a reputation as followers of paternalistic policies on many fronts, were concentrated in highly stable consumer markets (meat packer Hormel, shoemaker Nunn-Bush) or in a few cases were wildly successful growth companies (IBM). But one by one, even these companies abandoned the no-layoff policies when their markets turned out to be not so stable after all. That only confirmed what most street-level workers already knew: the American economy was no haven of guaranteed lifelong employment.

A look at wider statistics also tended to dispel the panic. Although different researchers came up with varying figures, the most widely cited study (by a National Bureau of Economic Research team) found that the number of years most workers had spent working for the current employer had remained reasonably stable over decades. Some critics noted that while some old-line companies were shrinking their workforce, many others were growing fast: AT&T had laid off hordes of long-distance telephone workers, but MCI had sprouted from nowhere to create a similar number of jobs. Scott Paper was shrinking, but companies no one had heard of till recently—like Sun Microsystems—had vaulted into the ranks of major employers.

And yet, as with the contingent-employment scare, there was clearly some kernel of truth wrapped deep within the layers of hype. Management-watchers generally concurred that by past standards employers really were pushing very hard to hold down the number of jobs on their payrolls, and that they had kept up these efforts in prosperity as well as recession. "One Company After Another Redesigns Tasks to Curb Its Need for Employment" ran the heading over a *Wall Street Journal* account. Factory overtime reached a postwar high in 1994, a trend attributed in part to companies' reluctance to add employees even when capacity was tight. Some firms were reported turning away sales in periods of heavy demand rather than bring on newcomers.

The structure of the job market was also changing in unexpected ways. The rise of the corporation a century or so ago had brought with it a trend toward labor-market concentration: big firms employed a larger and larger share of the nation's workforce. Many social critics, including early advocates of the new employment law, had portrayed this trend as unstoppable and deplored its effects—workers would have less real choice about where to take their skills, would feel more pressure to knuckle under to the organization-man model, and so on. But now the trend began to reverse itself. In place of earlier management buzzwords like *vertical integration, diversification,* and *synergy* came new themes like *core competencies, outsourcing,* and the *virtual corporation.* Companies scrambled to sell peripheral subsidiaries, shed extraneous functions and product lines, and close in-house departments from data processing to travel in favor of outside contractors. In part because of such trends, the share of jobs provided by the largest companies began dropping. Significantly, contractors sprang up to handle the personnel function itself, offering staff leasing and similar schemes by which an outside contractor assumes payroll burdens (including, in many cases, benefit administration and regulatory compliance).

Everyone agreed about one further effect of downsizing: managers were being hit hardest, especially veteran managers at big companies. This contrasted with the usual recessionary pattern, in which marginal workers (such as new graduates and part-timers) and workers in highly cyclical businesses (such as production workers in capital goods industries) bore the brunt of cutbacks. According to Eric Greenberg of the American Management Association, middle managers make up something like 18 to 22 percent of those ousted in downsizing but only 5 to 8 percent of the relevant workforces. Doubtless the computer revolution made many managerial jobs obsolete by flattening information pyramids, but few believed that accounted for the full trend. Was it coincidence that managers at big firms were the very group that had obtained the most effective protection under the new employment law—or, to put it differently, the group that had become most dangerous to employers?

————

One of the most remarkable studies so far of the effects of the new laws was conducted by a research team led by James Dertouzos of the Rand Corporation. Its results suggest that the laws may already have measurably hurt the level of hiring. The team examined trends in employment levels in each state and compared them with the extent to which each state had moved away from traditional employment-at-will law toward new wrongful-firing doctrines. (Discrimination, harassment, and other non-common-law claims were not part of the study.) The apparent effects were surprisingly large: total employment ran between 2 and 5 percent lower in states where the legal climate had turned most hostile toward employers, such as California, compared with states that had stayed closest to the old rules. States where dismissed employees could sue for pain and suffering showed more harm to employment levels than those where they could sue only for back pay. Hardest hit was service and financial employment, while manufacturing was least affected—a finding consistent with the wide perception that managers file wrongful-termination cases more often than machinists (who are more likely to turn to union procedures or none).

Averaged over the whole universe of employment, the Rand researchers found that the direct, countable costs of the new common-law wrongful-firing doctrines did not seem all that high: perhaps only a tenth of 1 percent of the nation's total wage bill, averaging out to $100 per dismissed worker nationwide. Yet in practice, Dertouzos estimates, California employers behaved as if the indirect costs of being sued were 100 times as important to them as the direct costs. Numbers of this sort can be little better than guesswork, but a survey of British employers found the total economic costs to employers of that country's dismissal law, given lost managerial time and the like, to run six times the direct cost of awards. Reputation costs and general unpleasantness would boost the multiplier further. If Dertouzos and colleagues are anywhere near correct, then wrongful-firing law casts a chill on employers far in excess of its likely effect in transferring money to lucky workers, and that chill may already have seriously hurt the employment climate in the most litigious states.

Another study, by Edward Lazear in the August 1990 *Quarterly Journal of Economics,* found significant negative effects from mandated severance payments, a close cousin to tenure notions. Lazear analyzed data from labor markets in twenty-two countries over three decades and found on average that a mandate of three months' severance pay could be expected to reduce the ratio of employment to population by 1 percent. If implemented in the United States, he estimates, such a policy would raise the unemployment rate by more than 5 percent; it would also turn 9 million full-time jobs into part-time ones.

Mandated severance as a benefit would also be self-defeating in another way: mainstream economics suggests that workers commonly wind up "paying for" their own benefit packages in the form of lower wages. Studies have found that once the market adjusts, more than 80 percent of the incidence of workers' compensation costs winds up coming out of workers' wage packets. Where they can, as MIT economist Jonathan Gruber has shown in a series of studies, employers will target the offsetting cuts on the particular classes of worker likely to use the benefit in question; thus Gruber found mandated pregnancy coverage to have been accompanied by a slowdown in wage gains for workers in the age group likely to draw the benefits.

This research has important implications for the question of who will wind up paying the cost of buyouts and exit settlements in a lawyer-driven job market. The first time an employer finds itself shelling out for a $100,000 buyout, it may take a painful hit on profits; as the risks become foreseeable, though, it will begin to factor them into the original terms of hiring. Since age is the most success-ful right-to-sue theory against employers (a fact reflected in buyouts that track age and length of service), one may predict that the new law will also depress salaries of older workers—whether by flattening what economists call the wage-age curve, so that longevity brings fewer raises than it once did, or perhaps by causing employers to cut back on growth in pensions. A leading report on faculty retirement proposes a different way to target offsetting exactions on the benefi-ciary group: universities could end their current practice of allowing senior professors lighter teaching loads.

———

In short, as time goes on, workers can be expected to shoulder the bulk of the costs of a right to sue over things that go wrong in the workplace. Those costs are likely to be substantial, and in fact to far exceed the valuation most rational workers would put on the benefits being paid for. In short, faced (as indirectly they are) with both the costs and the benefits of a system allowing easy litigation, there's every reason to think very many workers would decline to buy the product.

For one thing, no one trying to design a workplace fringe benefit—or, for that matter, a government relief program—would ever have de-vised the features of today's employment litigation. Such litigation pays off, when it does at all, with lottery-like randomness (similarly situated workers fare quite differently, depending on who gets a clever lawyer or a sympathetic court district or jury) and commonly after a long wait (the Rand researchers found that workers received final pay-ments on their claims an average of six years after originally filing their cases). The overhead is phenomenal (Rand studies found the av-erage involved a $25,000 payout and $15,000 in defense legal fees), and the process inflicts extraordinary injury on workers' as well as employers' privacy and reputation. It also tends to inhibit the process by which displaced workers find suitable new jobs: the plaintiff wait-ing for trial may withdraw from work, or be frozen out of a small in-dustry in ways that are hard to reverse afterward. And the process inflicts innumerable distortions on employment practice in ways that harm workers as well as employers.

Relatively successful workplace insurance programs, such as disability coverage, consciously avoid each of these features; so do relatively successful government-mandated benefits, such as workers' compensation and unemployment insurance. Both aim to provide prompt, standardized, and predictable compensation with minimal scope for fights over eligibility. Rather than engage in guessing games for unlimited damages over intangible and emotional distress, both settle for benefits that can be looked up in tables. Benefits can also be tailored beforehand to ideas of deservingness, rather than left to the theorizing of juries whose ideas vary greatly one from the next. Both systems allow administrators, when they see fit, to arrange incentives so as to encourage diligence in looking for work.

Conceivably, unemployment insurance might offer special optional "fault" coverage that would pay additional benefits if a worker's dismissal was found to be wrongly motivated after exhaustive adversary investigation. It is unlikely, though, that such insurance would find many takers. Unlike ordinary unemployment claims, such claims would almost always be contested vigorously by the employer, leading to high overhead and a poor payout ratio. A benefit that is much more costly for employers to provide than it is valuable to workers is the kind of benefit that will probably not develop of its own accord, even in periods of brisk labor demand when employers are competing for talent by inventing new benefits.

As Mayer Freed and Daniel Polsby of Northwestern University point out in an *Emory Law Journal* article, even employees who obtain individual work contracts with their employers (such as especially talented managers or entertainers) seldom negotiate for open-ended promises of lifelong tenure based on "good cause." This is true even when they enjoy very strong bargaining positions; rather than tenure, they are more likely to ask for and extract fixed-term salary guarantees, severance payouts, "golden parachutes," and so forth. Rationally enough, they'd rather go after knowable and definite benefits than take their chances on a commitment that would be extraordinarily hard to define or enforce, and that could skew later incentives on both sides to conduct the relationship responsibly. Just as rationally, employers would rather offer more money than offer tenure. In short, if allowed freedom to contract, both sides have every reason to contract vigorously out of today's employment law.

––––––––

In recent years, the organized employment bar has been beating the drums over what it characterizes as an intolerable new workplace outrage: employers are actually getting workers to sign contracts agreeing not to sue them.

The timing of these attempts seems to make a big difference in how outrageous they are considered to be. It is acceptable—indeed, it helps the world go round—for an employer to escape litigation by forking over a settlement once one of its workers has hired a lawyer to press a claim. But waivers signed before any dispute arises (and maybe buyout offers where the worker did not hire a lawyer) are a threat to everyone's birthright. The main employment laws currently on the books generally forbid any pre-waiver of the rights they create, but usually do permit workers to agree that disputes should be sent to arbitration rather than court, which often cuts out the chance for a lawyer to be involved. The arbitrators hired to hear such disputes are generally less oriented toward a presumption of tenure than the union and civil service arbitrators described in Chapter 9. In addition, arbitration involves less investment in discovery and other legal fencing, is less likely to call forth shoot-the-moon damage demands, and does not take place before juries. Detroit lawyer Joseph Golden favors trials over arbitration because of the jury feature: "You can make a more emotional appeal . . . and have a lot more impact."

Another big push is to give temporary, contract, and part-time workers wider rights to sue. (Unions have also favored steps to mandate benefits and regulatory coverage for these workers, which would curb their competitive threat to union members.) Of course, the idea of giving temporary employees permanent tenure suggests that someone is being, as they say, unclear on the concept. In Europe, some countries have allowed temp work to develop as a safety valve, while Italy and Sweden have effectively banned it, spurring the rise of what economist David Henderson describes as "large black markets in temporary employment." Germany allows fixed-term contracts. In Spain, employers who renew such contracts risk having them become permanent, and as a result some companies make a practice of cutting loose jobholders when their contracts expire even when they have done a fine job.

In this country, scattered court decisions have extended various employment laws to cover contingent workers. One court rattled business observers by ruling than an agency temp who had lasted sixteen days could sue for bias just like a regular employee. Workers who take jobs on an explicit independent-contractor basis have nonetheless successfully asked courts to reinterpret the relationship as one of employment for purposes of letting them sue.

Other suits have sought to get temps redefined as permanent employees, a trend that has already had unintended consequences. To avoid blurring the distinction, attorney James Prozzi has warned against supervising temps too closely or letting them attend general staff meetings. Instead, he cites a company that made a point of never requesting or rejecting any temp by name. "If a temp is unhappy with the working conditions at your company," he adds, "do not attempt to resolve the problems yourself. Instead, refer the worker to the temporary agency" (a process less charitably called the run-around). Similarly, attorney John Wymer III advises that since companies risk being designated the "real" employer if they try to send back a temp whose performance is unsatisfactory, they should consider switching temp firms entirely—though, of course, this will mean more disruption for other workers who had been doing a good job. And because another source of legal risk is the practice of offering permanent-employee jobs to some but not all temps, Wymer hints that companies might be better off not offering permanent slots to temps at all: another triumph for the gentle art of compliance.

———

As markets go, employment markets are reasonably fluid. Hiring is still a basically voluntary process, and each time it happens the terms can be reordered from scratch. As a result, the new employment law faces an endless struggle against an insidious enemy: choice. Both employers and workers tend to make choices that defeat the law's intent,

THE TERMS OF COOPERATION

substituting a rationally paid bird-in-the-hand for a lawsuit-obtained two-in-the-bush a decade later. Such choices help advance the kind of security most of us prefer—that of an open economy and society, where there will be many places to take our talents—however incompatible they may be with the Old World style of security, where we know our place and everyone else's.

But it would be hasty to count out the forces of legal coercion: they are good at what they do. Already it is unlawful to escape most of the new laws by simply contracting out of their coverage, no matter how voluntary and well-informed such consent might be. Bans on contractually agreed-to arbitration may be next. It is characteristic of a bad product that it must be forced on unwilling users. And it is increasingly clear that today's employment litigation is just such a bad product.

Chapter 17

THE TERMS OF COOPERATION

In their text *Human Behavior in Organizations*, Leonard R. Sayles and George Strauss cite a case study in which nursing stations on different floors of a hospital were observed to be run under very dissimilar management styles. One floor was known as a tight ship, with no nonsense and strict professionalism. The other was warmer, more relaxed and informal. Which style proved more popular with the participating nurses? Which proved more successful in patient outcomes?

The questions might have been posed as a knock-down test pitting wet against dry views of human nature. And yet for those who would have framed it that way, the actual answers must have been rather anticlimactic. It seems that both floors were popular with their nursing staffs, who could and did transfer from one floor to the other in search of a working style better matched to their inclinations. And both floors were considered successful in patient care.

There is a lesson here for anyone who'd try to forge a grand theory of what makes a job satisfying. The problem isn't so much that experts can't agree on such a theory; it's that workers themselves can't agree. "They seem to think we all want the same thing," said an insurance-company clerk (quoted in Louise Kapp Howe's *Pink-Collar Workers*) in criticizing a "job enrichment" program. "I don't think that's true. I think some women, some people, want more responsibility and some don't. Some like to work slow and careful and some quick and forget it. Some want to be with other people. Then there are those like me who prefer to work alone. But they act like we're all alike."

As Sayles and Strauss point out, many of the job-satisfaction nostrums favored among outside reformers and management gurus are in fact popular with only *some* workers. Teamwork and participatory techniques aimed at giving workers a say in management succeed nicely at some shops while falling flat at others, where they are seen as an effort to evade managerial responsibilities ("Running this place is supposed to be your job"). At one textile mill in the South, the last straw came when the president's wife, trying to make things homier, put potted geraniums in the factory windows; workers went on strike.

In surveys, most working Americans express reasonably high levels of contentment with our particular jobs; even so, we wonder how all those other people put up with jobs we know we couldn't stand. Young women who punch in at a noisy factory every morning can't picture what motivates others to accept a pittance for long hours in *au pair* work, and vice versa. Some of us loathe the idea of high pressure, others most fear getting in a rut.

Hence the difficulty of distinguishing dream from nightmare jobs. "Oh my God," ran an account of team members at one enterprise, "they've got ulcers, high blood pressure, allergies, a divorce . . . it's one thing after another. . . . We've all been physically run down." Grist for a lawsuit under many new employment-law theories, no doubt, and yet the workplace being described here—the airline People Express—was one of the winners singled out for commendation in Robert Levering's 1988 *A Great Place to Work*. Many of the companies praised in Levering's book, including People Express, were start-ups, a type of business often associated with intense and demanding atmospheres, long hours with little or no overtime, and not coincidentally a dire lack of job security. (Though it was fondly remembered by many early employees, People Express went out of business after only a few years.)

Over the history of American enterprise, only hindsight separates some of the fabulous, get-in-at-the-ground-floor opportunities from some of the wretched sweatshops. The Chicago headquarters of Sears, Roebuck at the turn of the century, one historian notes, was "a room on the middle floor of a building housing a steam laundry on the lower level and a carpenter's shop above. Steam permeated the place and sawdust regularly showered down over the room . . . little light came through the dirty windows." Overtime till nearly midnight was common. The story differs only in particulars in accounts of early Hollywood moviemaking, of pioneer aviation, or of presidential campaigns. The Haloid Corporation, plowing every spare cent into the development of its novel copying process, offered a virtually amenity-free workplace, with the vice president for sales using orange crates for shelving. New employees, "upon being hired, were typically told that their first task would be to build themselves a desk to work on," observe David Kearns and David Nadler in their account of the company that was to become Xerox.

———

The new employment law typically proceeds on the assumption that certain types of job and workplace—those with arbitrary job insecurity, few gestures toward internal due process, a lack of accommodative attitudes, or hurtful levels of psychological stress—are simply unacceptable, and can safely be ordered either to turn into something else or just to go away. But official presumptions along these lines are likely to have at least two long-term effects. One will be to lop off many jobs and workplaces that are in some way extreme or unusual. A second effect, among the jobs that remain, will be to slow down the natural circulatory sorting process by which people switch (or are switched) from job to job to discover (or be discovered by) the ones to which they are best suited.

One kind of job likely to come under legal pressure is what has been called the high-commitment workplace. In part because the tenure idea has been slow to take hold, America still excels at generating the software "skunk works" full of whiz kids trying to deliver on deadline, the messy ad agency where creative types yell at each other, the go-getting sales force that gets so caught up in team spirit that it takes on the air of a religious cult. Not many of these places can cope well with a newcomer, fully imbued with workplace-rights ideology, who demands a precise job description from day one, construes hazing as infliction of emotional distress and defamation, insists that office policies be preannounced and enforced to the letter, and plans on taking full advantage of legal scheduling rights (including overtime and every last bit of allowable family and sick leave).

Paradoxically, legally prescribed tenure also poses a threat to many low-commitment jobs whose attractions include what they do *not* demand. If employers must regard each job offer in the light of a marriage proposal, they will withhold many casual labor opportunities, including many well suited to actors and musicians looking for day jobs, footloose workers who want to be free to quit at short notice, and many others whose prime motivation is something other than forging a "career." (Don't call them less ambitious; they may just be ambitious in different ways.) As the European experience shows, the widespread job lock caused by entrenchment of incumbent workers tends to create pressure for an outright two-tier system, in which casual workers and new graduates are shunted into whatever exceptional categories the law happens to tolerate—temp work, independent contracting, and so forth—that provide employers with some margin of room to maneuver.

In short, sweeping rules suppress many jobs. The worst thing isn't that some of those jobs were tolerable, but that some of them—for some of us—approached the ideal.

———

One reason to doubt the practicality of the new employment law is that its own advocates find it so hard to live with its precepts. Without exception, the institutions that have pushed the new agenda—government agencies and courts, law firms and advocacy groups—have been loath to give up their own freedom to choose their associates and the terms on which they work.

Congress, of course, until recently exempted itself in blanket fashion from the employment regime it prescribed for the rest of the country. "The need is not so great in the congressional employment field as it may be in some others," allowed Rep. Claude Pepper when his Age Discrimination in Employment Act explicitly excepted lawmakers' own staffs. "It is absolutely essential," agreed Sen. Warren Rudman during consideration of the 1991 civil rights law, "that, as to our legislative employees, we have an absolute right without outside review by anyone of what we do." Otherwise, warned the widely praised New Hampshire moderate, the Senate might fall prey "to the whims of a U.S. district-court judge" who "would have the power to overrule the considered judgment of 100 members of this body." Eventually the hypocrisy became a campaign issue, and one of the most popular planks in the 1994 Republican Contract with America was the one requiring Congress to obey federal laws of general application, a measure that became law the next year.

The higher levels of the executive branch still work this way. No matter how strenuously top officials of the Department of Labor deplore private-sector dismissals, they themselves still serve strictly at the pleasure of the president, and there is no record that they have demanded (nor that any president has offered to award them) permanence in office against his future displeasure. Even as Congress moved to require cities to keep elderly firefighters and police officers on the job, it was careful to arrange for continued automatic retirement at 55 of the firefighters and other public safety officers who guard many *federal* installations.

Presidents of both parties, whatever their declared enthusiasm for laws banning age and handicap bias, openly tilt their judicial selection toward young and vigorous appointees so as to heighten their long-term influence over the development of the law. Thus President Clinton personally consulted two physicians to check on the prognosis of a possible Supreme Court nominee who had been ill; his staff confirmed that the judge's life expectancy had been a factor in the president's calculations. As newsletter editor Milton Bordwin pointed out, Clinton would hardly have dared make this admission had he been hiring for a private position, since he "would have been hauled into court and forced to pay damages."

What about the legal profession, which has taken such a prominent role in developing the new rules and imposing them on the rest of us? Longstanding rules of legal ethics encourage a pure at-will relationship on both sides of the lawyer-client relationship. In particular, clients are supposed to have an absolute right in principle to change lawyers—for good reason, bad reason, or no reason at all. (Lawyers on staff at big organizations, to be sure, can sometimes invoke the new laws' protection in their role as employees.) The guarantee of clients' freedom to end a relationship with a lawyer is correctly seen as encouraging more clients to engage lawyers in the first place, since it spares them fear of being locked into a potentially permanent relationship.

Judges? Although federal judges, for sufficient if peculiar reason, are among the few dignitaries in America who have long enjoyed tenure, they wouldn't think of granting it to those who work for them—their clerks, for instance. No examples are on record in which jurists have offered to guarantee a continued berth for all existing clerks who would like to stay on; nor have they volunteered to be sued by older lawyers who might like to snag one of the prestigious clerkships that usually go to the young.

The American Civil Liberties Union, which has led the crusade against employment at will, is nonetheless in no hurry to institute tenure principles in its own operations. "Please leave the building and take only personal possessions with you," then-executive director Ira Glasser is reported to have ordered Janet Benshoff, head of the group's reproductive-rights project, after relations soured. "Get rid of dead wood," advises a newsletter for unions in a piece on revitalizing locals. "This will be painful, but it has to be done to enable the union to meet today's challenges." Lefter-than-thou magazine *Mother Jones* unceremoniously sacked editor and documentary filmmaker Michael Moore.

A piquant case is that of Mr. Litigation himself, Ralph Nader. "Because Nader's activities are funded partially by labor organizations, he was asked whether he would welcome unionization of his employees," one newspaper reported. But his groups "have a mission," came the negative reply. "Missionary movements cannot be organized [by] unions. . . . The problem with organized labor in this city is that their employees are unionized so they quit work at five o'clock." Nor has he been afraid to back up his words with deeds. "You shouldn't think of this as a job," editor Tim Shorrock says Nader told him. Shorrock's Nader-backed, small-circulation *Multinational Monitor* had flayed companies for such misdeeds as failing to pay overtime, freezing workers' pay, and retaliating against "whistleblowers"; it publicized resulting lists of the year's "ten worst employers" in the companies' home towns. Perhaps intoxicated by such ideas, Shorrock and two other staffers decided they wanted to bargain collectively over such matters as pay (he was getting $13,000 a year), sixty-to-eighty-hour work weeks, and lack of grievance procedures. Before they knew what hit them, the locks had been changed and Nader had transferred the operation's ownership to a new company that, as the *Washington Post* put it, "chose not to continue their employment."

Perhaps such thinking comes naturally to many who see themselves as social reformers. We have a mission, it's easy to imagine, and so of course we need the right to select the most highly motivated and talented and eject those who show themselves unworthy of our crusade. Giving up our right to choose associates in our mission would be a lot like giving up our right to choose the mission itself; certainly it is vastly harder to accomplish a mission of any sort if one must work at cross purposes with an unwanted staff.

Should such logic apply to the rest of the world? Of course not; that's only the materialist realm of commerce, goods and services. All it does is cure disease, pave roads into the desert, feed, clothe, shelter, defend, entertain, discover, invent, teach, organize, calculate, electrify, and comfort. How could it have a mission? Surely, then, the jobs it offers are a socially generated patchwork of sinecures ready for redistribution along fairer lines.

At their extreme, there is hardly doubt that the quest for socially provided "job security" fails conclusively. In one of history's most misguided experiments, half of Europe spent much of this century attempting to achieve absolute job security, and it was left with only an economic joke: "We pretend to work, and they pretend to pay us."

Of all the ways of redistributing wealth in a modern society, employment lawsuits must be among the most costly and distracting. In New York City, where good apartments are scarce, some divorce courts refuse to order either party out of a unit, insisting instead that they go on cohabiting with a curtain down the middle of the living room. Such arrangements, as can be imagined, often come at an excruciating cost in tension and acrimony, yet even they pale compared with today's workplace "divorce-in-place," where the two sides in the broken-down relationship must not only encounter each other daily at close range but cooperate (or pretend to) in producing some complicated thing of value, perhaps with clients or customers present. When this happens at other people's workplaces, it merely sounds grim; when it arrives at our own—when it keeps us from pursuing *our* mission—we see it as the disaster it is.

The new employment law makes scarcely a single promise that it does not break. It promises a fairer sharing of the blessings and burdens of work, but doles out its rewards capriciously, giving most to those who already are doing the best. It promises economic security, but sets up a host of arbitrary new discouragements and uncertainties that hinder any rational planning of hiring, career development, and retirement for both sides. It promises a renewed focus on merit, but creates a hundred new openings for the incompetent, the slacker, and the scheming player of office politics. It promises to protect reputation, earning power, privacy, and emotional equilibrium, yet winds up launching its own assault on all these values. And though it pretends to ensure a dignified, respectful, and humanized workplace, it in fact leaves one that is divided, bureaucratic, and adversarial.

Yet here in America, each year witnesses a further advance for the forces of litigation and legal regimentation, and a further retreat for the forces of—of what, exactly? We do not even have a good word for what we are giving up when we invite courtroom wrangling over everything that happens to us at our jobs, with the outcome to be decided by strangers remote from the actual places and relationships. "Employment at will" is a dry and unsympathetic way of describing what is lost. Perhaps the best term for what we give up is "freedom of association."

"Freedom of association" retains plenty of currency at the ground level as a commonsense assessment of the terms on which people accept work. "No one was holding a gun to anyone's head," writes riveter-essayist Ben Hamper, describing why he didn't resent the stream of indignities that went along with his high pay when he decided to take a job on the GM assembly line. "I was still relatively raw, but I assumed a deal was a deal."

And yet the concept holds very little sway in our jurisprudence. The few circumstances in which the Supreme Court has lately recognized rights of free association have concerned associations for political purposes; the right to associate for productive, commercial, or social purposes appears to have no particular standing as a liberty worth guarding. It is true that many thoughtful Supreme Court justices, including no less a liberal than Arthur Goldberg, formerly considered it self-evident that the U.S. Constitution must protect many private rights of association, including a private club's right to determine its own membership and a business partnership's right to merge personal liabilities with partners of its own choice. Since Goldberg cited those examples, unfortunately, various levels of government have indeed proceeded to order private clubs and partnerships to admit unwanted new members and partners, and elite legal opinion has ceased to think that any important private rights could be at stake when such orders are handed down.

Gradually, as freedom of association has decayed, we have begun to miss it. "We live in fear of someone reporting us for discrimination," said the proprietor of a London service that offers female drivers to women who need rides late at night. Similar policies tripped up the Women's Transit Authority of Madison, Wisconsin, a two-decade-old feminist venture. "I serve people in their seventies and eighties who have lost loved ones," fumed Santa Cruz mortician Eric Bianco when the city council of that California town brought up its bill to prohibit discrimination on the basis of appearance. "The last thing wives want

THE TERMS OF COOPERATION

to see at their husband's funeral is a punk with a pin through his nose." It turned out the misgivings ran the other way, too. "I don't want to be forced to hire clean-cut people who come here in a suit and tie," declared the owner of a shop called Anubis Warpus, which stocks bondage accessories and satanic knickknacks. "They can sue if they want to."

Ironically it is diversity, that great shibboleth of our day, that suffers most when association is compelled. Surely the most inane modern fallacy is the one about how each place of work should resemble a microcosm of all human nature and all demographic variety, with exact proportions of guys and gals, introverts and gladhanders, old and young, hedonists and prudes, Scots and Hottentots, boors and sensitivity buffs, with the radio in the background shuttling every few minutes from pop to classical to talk to reggae to big band to silence. A nation that truly cared about diversity would allow the flourishing of both bawdy calendars at some workplaces and Bible readings at others, rather than insist on some homogenized middle ground in which no one could have either. The genuine diversity of freedom and pluralism—not the ersatz diversity of government compulsion—is the best way to make sure the job we really want is there when we start looking for it, whether that job is one of ruthless self-discipline toward a creative goal or one full of kidding and gentle camaraderie; one in which to bear witness to our deepest beliefs or to enjoy the routine of accomplishing useful tasks; one in which to find romance or solitude; one in which to appreciate manners or to match wits.

For all its risks and disappointments, liberty—the simple policy of refusing to force others to deal with us against their will and without their consent—turns out to be the best method to elicit the greatest willingness and enthusiasm to cooperate from those who might do us good. No wonder that until recently, free association was considered the crowning glory of a liberal and civilized society. It can be again.

ACKNOWLEDGMENTS

The Manhattan Institute once again provided steadfast and patient support for this book, as it did for *The Litigation Explosion*. My thanks especially to Bill Hammett and his successor Larry Mone, whose confidence in the work never faltered, and to the staff of the Institute, who handled countless logistical details and research requests, especially Andrew Hazlett and Alan Fenster.

Two of the finest editors in American publishing, Erwin Glikes and Martin Kessler, believed in the book and helped it get under way; neither lived to see its completion. They set high standards, and I hope the results would have pleased them. David Bernstein ably saw the project to completion, assisted by Adam Bellow, John Ekizian and the rest of The Free Press staff, and my agents on the book, Lynn Chu and Glen Hartley.

The librarians at Yale Law School, Quinnipiac College School of Law (at that time affiliated with the University of Bridgeport), and the Wilton and Westport public libraries were helpful. Lucy Shockley kindly arranged to provide me with access to the extensive General Electric law library in Fairfield (as opposed to the Internet's 'Lectric Law Library, which I also visited). Of the many who commented on chapters or directed my attention to topics, cases, or useful materials, I will offer special thanks to Charles Shanor, Eugene Volokh, Gene Meyer, Jeremy Rabkin, Chris Powell, and Terry Teachout. And as before Steve Pippin was indispensable.

SOURCE NOTES

Introduction

Page

1 How-to-fire seminars: Andrea Gerlin, "Seminars Teach Managers Finer Points of Firing," *Wall Street Journal,* April 26, 1995.

2 Midwest store chain: Bob Davis, Peter Gumbel, and David P. Hamilton, "To All U.S. Managers Upset by Regulations: Try Germany or Japan," *Wall Street Journal,* December 14, 1995.

2 Bringing loaded gun to work: *Hindman* v. *GTE Data Services,* 1994 U.S. Dist. LEXIS 9522 (M.D.Fla., June 24, 1994). Occasional nap: "Court Revives Discrimination Claim Filed by EPA Worker with Depression," *Government Employee Relations Report* (BNA), November 2, 1992.

2 Fewer than 5 percent very candid: Robert Half, *Robert Half on Hiring* (Crown, 1985), p. 203 (citing Burke Marketing Research survey of Fortune 1,000 firms). Whole thing has broken down: Tim Weiner, "Fearing Suits, Companies Avoid Giving Job References," *New York Times,* May 8, 1993 (quoting former Touche Ross personnel director Cornelia Eldridge).

3 Fastest growing: Deborah Shalowitz Cowans, "Liability for Employment Practices Growing Problem for Public Entities," *Business Insurance,* December 11, 1995 (quoting Chicago attorney Jeffrey Goldwater). "By far" leading risk for nonprofit boards: Mark Hofmann, "Nonprofit Groups Find D&O Capacity," *Business Insurance,* May 25, 1992 (quoting Phillip Norton of the Wyatt Co.). Wyatt surveys have found employee claims making up 80 percent of claims against board members of

313

hospitals and private colleges, and average payouts in such claims (which are apt to be larger than employee claims in general) rising from around $450,000 in 1990 to $700,000 in 1991 and $2,000,000 in 1992. Other quotes: Sally Roberts, "With Employment Claims Up, Prevention Is Order of Day," *Business Insurance,* June 5, 1995 (quoting state of Nebraska risk manager Yvonne Norton-Leung and New York City environmental official).

4   Tripling of requests: "20 Hot Job Tracks," Katherine Beddingfield et al., 1996 Career Guide, *U.S. News & World Report,* October 30, 1995.

6   Every time you open your mouth: Martha Middleton, "Employers Face Upsurge in Suits Over Defamation," *National Law Journal,* May 4, 1987 (quoting Chicago lawyer Michael Leech).

8   Unlawful law-firm questions: Marc Hequet, "The Intricacies of Interviewing," *Training,* April 1993 (quoting attorney Laura Cooper).

9   Rather substantial, go for it: Marilyn Webb, "How Old is Too Old? In the Nineties Business World, 'Middle-Aged' Can Mean 'Obsolete,'" *New York,* March 29, 1993 (quoting attorney Jeffrey Bernbach).

9   Award out there with your name on it: Lewin G. Joel III, *Every Employee's Guide to the Law* (Pantheon, 1993), pp. 158. Vast sums: E. Richard Larson, *Sue Your Boss* (Farrar, Straus & Giroux, 1981), preface, pp. ix, xx.

9   Far greater than any severance package: Stephen Pollan and Mark Levine, "How to Survive Getting Fired," *New York,* September 7, 1992. $200,000 estimate: Anne Fisher, "Sexual Harassment: What to Do," *Fortune,* August 23, 1993 (quoting New York attorney Bettina Plevan).

10   Privacy, harassment, and defamation averaged $375,000: Ira Shepard, Paul Heylman, and Robert Duston, *Without Just Cause: An Employer's Practical and Legal Guide on Wrongful Discharge* (Bureau of National Affairs, 1989.) Surveys of wrongful-firing cases come up with various numbers, but reports of a half-million dollars on average are common. See, e.g., "Labor Letter," *Wall Street Journal,* May 12, 1992 (quoting Lewis Maltby of American Civil Liberties Union, who says that jury verdicts in wrongful-firing cases nationwide now average more than $500,000); Michele Himmelberg, "On Working," *Orange County Register,* June 24, 1996 (average wrongful-firing jury award now $442,000 in California, per San Francisco law firm of Orrick, Herrington); Mark Pulliam, *Los Angeles Daily Journal,* July 7, 1993 (survey of 110 California jury awards in employment cases in early 1990s found average verdict in excess of $1.5 million.)

10   Top verdicts often exceeded lottery payouts: Alan B. Krueger, "The Evolution of Unjust-Dismissal Legislation in the United States," 44 *Ind. & Labor Rel's Rev.* 644, 650 (1991). La Guardia manager: "American Airlines Must Pay $7 Million in Discrimination Suit," *Wall Street Journal,* January 27, 1992. Credit manager: "Woman Wins a Bias Suit Against Texaco" (Associated Press dispatch), *New York Times,* September 28, 1991. Garbage-truck driver: Margaret Cronin Fisk, "Notable Verdicts," *National Law Journal,* August 9, 1993 (*Decker* v. *Browning-Ferris,* Colorado); OTB handyman: Peg Tyre, "Handyman Wins $2.5M from OTB," *Newsday,* June 16, 1995. Managers do better: This conclusion is widely agreed on in the literature. See, e.g., James Dertouzos, Elaine Holland, and Patricia Ebener, "The Legal and

Economic Consequences of Wrongful Termination" (Rand, 1988), p. 21 (most wrongful-termination claimants from middle management or higher); and Paul Weiler, *Governing the Workplace: The Future of Labor and Employment Law* (Harvard, 1990), pp. 28 and 82.

11 Few who are fired: "Preparing for a Recession," *Consumer Reports,* February, 1991 (quoting Washington, D.C., attorney Robert Fitzpatrick).

Chapter 1. Hiring Hell

Page

17 Martin K. case: *Martin K. v. Police Commissioner of Boston,* 571 N.E. 2d 380 (Mass. 1991).

18 Ads in the big local newspaper: Guidelines from federal regulators on the closely related issue of housing advertisements warn against the "use of English language media alone or the exclusive use of media catering to the majority population in an area, when, in such area, there are also available non-English language or other minority media." Higher ad rates: see, e.g., "G. Kindrow," "The Candidate: Inside One Affirmative Action Search," *Lingua Franca,* April 1991 (author finds minority media outlets for academic recruitment charge five times going rate).

18 Hazardous to ask whether applicant has friends at the company: Junda Woo, "Job Interviews Pose Rising Risk to Employees," *Wall Street Journal,* March 11, 1992 (quoting Maury Hanigan).

19 Community Coffee case: "Big Day[s] for the ADA," *Texas Lawyer,* July 10, 1995.

19 Probably safe to say this is a nice place to work: Alan M. Koral, *Conducting the Lawful Employment Interview: How to Avoid Charges of Discrimination When Interviewing Job Candidates,* revised edition (New York: Executive Enterprises Publications Co., 1986), p. 72.

19 Firing "for cause" presents jury question on defamation: *Carney v. Memorial Hospital,* 475 N.E. 2d 451 (N.Y. 1985). Malice = conscious indifference: Annotation, 24 *ALR 4th* 144, 161 (1991). Railroad intentional interference: this case is described in Tim Weiner, "Fearing Suits, Companies Avoid Giving Job References," *New York Times,* May 8, 1993.

19 Caveat here and there: see, e.g., Claudia H. Deutsch, "Managing: Psst! References Are Sneaking Back, for Real" and "A 'Catch 22' in Honesty," *New York Times,* December 2, 1990 (many companies discourage giving positive references because lawyers could seize on "a mildly negative remark used to temper effusive praise"). Silence seen as tantamount to negative reference: William L. Kandel, "Employee Dishonesty and Workplace Security: Precautions About Prevention," *Employee Relations Law Journal,* September 22, 1990, p. 85. Company that gives positive reference just begging to be sued: Lewin G. Joel III, *Every Employee's Guide to the Law* (Pantheon, 1993), p. 35. See also *Wall Street Journal,* Labor Letter, May 10, 1994 (poll by Robert Half staffing firm finds widespread lack of honesty in references; "lies were blamed on fear of lawsuits").

20 Few reference suits win big at trial: Ramona L. Paetzold and Steven L. Willborn,

"Employer (Ir)Rationality and the Demise of Employment References," 30 *American Business Law Journal* 123 (1992). Court orders employer to falsify references: see, e.g., *Ackerman* v. *Western Electric,* 643 F. Supp. 836, at 857 (company ordered to tell all inquirers that complainant left voluntarily).

20 Wandering in a wasteland: Tim Weiner, "Fearing Suits, Companies Avoid Giving Job References," *New York Times,* May 8, 1993 (quoting Alan Schonberg).

20 Adverse impact on blacks: see *EEOC* v. *National Academy of Sciences,* 12 FEP Cases 1690, 12 EPD #11,010 (D.D.C. 1976).

21 Approved by the Supreme Court: see *Griggs* v. *Duke Power,* 401 U.S. 424 (1971). Uniform Guidelines on Employee Selection Procedures: 29 C.F.R. s. 1607.4D.

22 Gerrymandering: *Hammon* v. *Barry,* 813 F. 2d 412 (D.C. Cir. 1987), 826 F. 2d 73 (D.C. Cir. 1987). See Mikva dissent, p. 435 (arguing that racial statistics for in-city workforce alone relevant though fire department had hired extensively from suburbs). According to Herman Belz, federal contract-compliance regulators have taken the view that "the labor market meant the SMSA, county, city or recruitment area, or some combination thereof which reflected the highest minority population and work force." Herman Belz, *Equality Transformed: A Quarter Century of Affirmative Action* (Transaction, 1991), p. 101. On applicant pools as "an endlessly manipulable sample," see Barbara Lerner, "*Washington* v. *Davis:* Quantity, Quality, and Equality in Employment Testing," 1976 *Sup. Ct. Rev.* 263, 272–273.

23 Employers reluctant to ask for transcripts or diplomas: see C. Boyden Gray and Evan J. Kemp, "Flunking Testing: Is Too Much Fairness Unfair To School Kids?" *Washington Post,* September 19, 1993 (quoting Cornell labor economist John Bishop). Credit for previous job experience seen as unfair: Peter T. Kilborn, "New York Police Force Lagging in Recruitment of Black Officers," *New York Times,* July 17, 1994.

23 Overweight flight attendants: *Independent Union of Flight Attendants* v. *Pan Am* (N.D. Calif. 1981). See also Gail Diane Cox, "Comparable Weight," *National Law Journal,* November 27, 1989.

24 Commonwealth Edison case: Patricia Moore, "Edison Settles Hiring-Bias Suit for $3.3 Million," *Chicago Sun Times,* December 30, 1993. Daniel Lamp: James Bovard, "The Latest EEOC Quota Madness," *Wall Street Journal,* April 27, 1995.

24 Crusade against word-of-mouth hiring: see cases cited at *Thomas* v. *Wash. Cty. Sch. Board,* 915 F. 2d 922, 925 (4th Cir. 1990) ("Courts generally agree that, whatever the benefits of nepotism and word-of-mouth hiring, those benefits are outweighed by the goal of providing everyone with equal opportunities for employment.") An isolated Supreme Court decision on the other side, finding such references adequate in hiring casual bricklayers, has not prevented continued attacks on the practice: *Furnco Construction* v. *Waters,* 438 U.S. 567 (1978). On its prevalence, see Corcoran, Datcher, and Duncan, "Most Workers Find Jobs Through Word of Mouth," 103 *Monthly Labor Review* no. 8, 33 (August 1980). World's Finest: James Bovard, "Job-Breakers: The EEOC's Assault on the Workplace," *American Spectator,* March 1994. Too many Hispanics: Mary Wisniewski, "Court Reverses Discrimination Ruling," *Chicago Daily Law Bulletin,* November 12, 1991 (Chicago Miniature Lamp Works).

25   Korean janitors: *EEOC* v. *Consolidated Services Systems,* 989 F. 2d 233 (7th Cir. 1993, Posner). Joseph B. Cahill, "Taking on the EEOC: Fighting Agency Not for Faint-Hearted," *Crain's Chicago Business,* June 5, 1995.

25   Fourteen arrests: *Gregory* v. *Litton Systems,* 316 F. Supp. 402, 5 FEP Cases 267 (1972) (appeal). Blanket rule on criminal records unlawful: *Green* v. *Missouri Pacific,* 523 F. 2d 1290 (8th Cir. 1975).

26   Crane operator paroled after serving six years for first-degree murder: EEOC decision #80-17, August 12, 1980, Empl. Prac. Guide (CCH) Para. 6809; shoplifting conviction job-related but unlawful not to hire because items taken were of small value: EEOC Decision #80-8, March 25, 1981, Empl. Prac. Guide (CCH) Para. 6791; portrait photographic studio and convicted forger: #80-17, August 12, 1980, Para. 6808. Minor losses from pilfering: Mack A. Player, *Employment Discrimination Law, Student's Edition* (West, 1988), p. 384.

26   They should stop stealing: *EEOC* v. *Carolina Freight Carriers,* 723 F. Supp. 734 (S.D. Fla. 1989).

26   Little evidence employees with records are safety risks: Note, 54 *Fordham Law Review* 563, 572, footnote 71 (1986); Comment, "Employers' Use of Criminal Records Under Title VII," 29 *Catholic University Law Review* 597, 602 (similar language), 600 (unfair that persons without criminal records should have an advantage on job market), 607 (no greater tendency to drink or abuse drugs apparent), 611 (violence-prone inmate and embezzler to be forced on factory), and 623 (employer should have to demonstrate criminal propensity) (1980).

27   Looks-ism: "Facial Discrimination," 100 *Harvard Law Review* 2035, 2049 (employer should have to reconsider "prejudicial process" of face-to-face interview), 2050 (screens and Chinese walls) (1987). See also Margaret Carlson, "And Now, Obesity Rights," *Time,* December 6, 1993.

27   "A picture of the person": Robert Hamburger, *A Stranger in the House* (Macmillan, 1978) (interview with domestic referral manager Irene Larsen).

28   Expressed opinions that were less representative: see studies cited at Cornelius Peck, "Employment Problems of the Handicapped: Would Title VII Remedies Be Appropriate and Effective?" 16 *U. Mich. J. L. Ref.* 343, 352 (1983). Cues of "affective retreat": see studies cited at Mari Matsuda, "Public Response to Racist Speech: Considering the Victim's Story," 87 *Mich. L. Rev.* 2320, 2339, n. 93 (1989).

28   They assume the worst: Carl Quintanilla, "Disabilities Act Helps—But Not Much: Disabled People Aren't Getting More Job Offers," *Wall Street Journal,* July 19, 1993 (quoting Kathi Pugh).

28   Right to fail on the job: Bernard R. Gifford, ed., *Test Policy and the Politics of Opportunity Allocation: The Workplace and the Law* (National Commission on Testing and Public Policy, 1989), p. 17. See also, e.g., Mark Kelman, "Concepts of Discrimination in 'General Ability' Job Testing," 104 *Harvard Law Review* 1158, 1204 (1991) (rather than test to predict performance, employers should have to hire less carefully "and discharg[e] those who prove to be inadequately competent"); Jon Bible, "When Employers Look for Other Things than Drugs . . .", 41 *Labor Law Journal* 195, 210 (April 1990).

29   New York bans interviewers from asking about organizational memberships: see

Michael W. Miller, "Privacy: Equifax Agrees To Alter Tactics in Job Inquiries," *Wall Street Journal,* August 10, 1992.

29   Interview software: Suzanne Oliver, "Slouches make better operators," *Forbes,* August 16, 1993.

Chapter 2. Tenure Track

Page

31   Veronica Stone case: *Stone* v. *Mission Bay Mtge. Co.,* 672 P. 2d 629 (Nevada 1983) (emphasis added in phrase "could have been").

32   Manifest encroachment on liberty: Adam Smith, *The Wealth of Nations* (1776), Cannan ed. (U. of Chicago Press, 1976), p. 136.

33   Takes the employment on the terms offered: *McAuliffe* v. *New Bedford* (Mass. 1892) (Holmes, J.).

33   Not within the functions: *Adair* v. *U.S.,* 208 U.S. 161, 174–75 (1908). Not a liberty to procure: *Coppage* v. *Kansas,* 236 U.S. 1 (1915); fundamental and vital, *Coppage* at 14. The Wisconsin Supreme Court observed that "free will in forming and continuing" the employment relationship was "entitled to be held sacred" as specifically (and ironically, given later redefinitions in usage) among each citizen's *civil* rights. "Hardly any of the personal civil rights is higher," it added. *State* v. *Kreutzberg,* 114 Wisc. 530, 546 (1903), cited at Sanford M. Jacoby, "The Duration of Indefinite Employment Contracts in the U.S. and England: An Historical Analysis," 5 *Comparative Labor Law* 85, 123 (1982). Another classic statement regarding the proper functions of government in a free society came in *Payne* v. *Western & Atlantic Railway,* 81 Tenn. 507 518–19 (1884): "[M]en must be left, without interference to buy and sell where they please, and to discharge or retain employees at will for good cause or for no cause, or even for bad cause without thereby being guilty of an unlawful act per se. It is a right which an employee may exercise in the same way, to the same extent, for the same cause or want of cause as the employer." Cited at Richard Epstein, "In Defense of the Contract at Will," 51 *University of Chicago Law Review* 947, footnote 3 (1984).

During the 1970s a literature arose advancing the claim that employment at will had not in fact been traditional American practice but had instead been foisted on an unsuspecting nation in the late nineteenth century by Horace Wood, author of a leading treatise on the law of master and servant, and then adopted by activist courts whose goal was to protect employers. See, e.g., Jay M. Feinman, "The Development of the Employment at Will Rule," 20 *Am. J. of Leg. Hist.* 118 (1976). These assertions found their way into much of the new literature hostile to employment at will: see, e.g., Lewis Maltby, "An Unjust Workplace," in *Liberty at Work: Expanding the Rights of Employees in America* (American Civil Liberties Union Public Policy Report, 1988), p. 18 (employment at will doctrine "created by the courts in the late 19th century . . . the courts seized upon the concept of employment at will, which a writer named Horace Woods [sic] had advocated in a 1877 treatise, and elevated it to the law of the land") and "Why Courts Are Always

Making Law," by Harvard Law professor and Critical Legal Studies exponent Jerry Frug, *Fortune*, September 25, 1989 ("the conservative interpretation of employment-at-will itself became part of the law only through judicial activism [and] was first articulated by courts only in the late 19th century"). They even crept into court decisions, such as *Wagenseller v. Scottsdale Memorial Hospital,* 710 P. 2d 1025, 1030 (Ariz. 1985). Recent scholarship has decisively laid these contentions to rest, demonstrating that employment at will had been the prevailing American practice with regard to free labor since colonial times. See Deborah A. Ballam, "Exploding the Original Myth Regarding Employment-at-Will: The True Origins of the Doctrine," 17 *Berkeley Journal of Employment and Labor Law* 91 (1996); Deborah A. Ballam, "The Traditional View on the Origins of the Employment-at-Will Doctrine: Myth or Reality?" 33 *American Business Law Journal* 1 (1995).

33   Court submits to show of force: *NLRB v. Jones & Laughlin,* 301 U.S. 1 (1937), overturned constitutional protection of employment at will.

36   Daring idea: Lawrence E. Blades, "Employment at Will Vs. Individual Freedom: On Limiting the Abusive Exercise of Employer Power," 67 *Columbia L.R.* 1404 (1967) (rustic simplicity, 1416; ever-increasing, even more easily oppressed, 1405; great majority easy prey, 1413; practical difficulties conceded, 1428; courts should act because legislatures won't, 1434).

36   Suing is good for America: Walter Olson, "Make the Loser Pay," *Reader's Digest,* May 1992 (quoting Alan Dershowitz). Put the blame where it will do the most good: cartoon by Bernard Schoenbaum, *New Yorker,* issue of December 26, 1994–January 2, 1995.

38   A maverick or two: Richard Epstein's writings on the subject include "In Defense of the Contract at Will," 51 *University of Chicago Law Review* 947 (1984); "A Common Law for Labor Relations," 92 *Yale Law Journal* 1357 (1983); and *Forbidden Grounds: The Case Against Employment Discrimination Laws* (Harvard, 1992). Also see Mayer G. Freed & Daniel D. Polsby, "Just Cause for Termination Rules and Economic Efficiency," 38 *Emory L.J.* 1097 (1989); and other work by Freed and Polsby. Virtually self-evident: Paul Weiler, *Governing the Workplace: The Future of Labor and Employment Law* (Harvard, 1990), pp. 49–50. On the near-unanimity of other contemporary academic literature in opposing employment at will, see the list of articles compiled at Note, 96 *Harvard Law Review* 1931, footnote 3 (1983).

39   Always a first time: *Toussaint v. Blue Cross & Blue Shield of Michigan,* 292 N.W. 2d 880 (Mich. 1980).

40   A 1990 survey: see *Sanders v. Parker Drilling Co.* 911 F.2d 191, 200, footnote 10 (9th Cir. 1990).

40   Future opportunities jeopardized: "Sued if You Do" (editorial), *Wall Street Journal,* February 3, 1992; and letter to the editor, *Wall Street Journal,* February 18, 1992, from attorneys Daniel W. Bates and Peter Bennett.

40   Stay and grow: *Forman v. BRI Corp.,* 532 F. Supp. 49 (1982). Stretch on "permanent" as opposed to temporary worker: Darien McWhirter, *Your Rights at Work* (Wiley, 1989), p. 12. So much the first year and so much the second: Judy Greenwald, "Tips for Minimizing Employer Liability," *Business Insurance,* May 6, 1991 (quoting attorney Eleanor Acheson of Boston's Ropes & Gray).

40   Palefsky speech: Cliff Palefsky, "Wrongful Termination Litigation: 'Dagwood' and Goliath," 62 *Mich. Bar J.* 776, 778 (1983). Margins of a memo: Lewin G. Joel III, *Every Employee's Guide to the Law* (Pantheon, 1993), p. 208.

41   Same day as *Toussaint: Ebling* v. *Masco,* 292 N.W. 2d 880 (1980). Last job: *McKinney* v. *National Dairy Council,* 491 F. Supp. 1108 (D. Mass. 1980).

42   Most firms announce right to fire at will: see "Labor Letter," *Wall Street Journal,* May 12, 1992 (citing survey).

42   Like cases treated alike: *Rulon-Miller* v. *IBM,* 162 Cal. App. 3d 241, 248 (Cal. App. 1984).

43   Becoming unlawful while they slept: *Payne* v. *Rozendaal,* 520 A. 2d 586 (Vt. 1986). On "public policy" absent particular law or constitutional provision see, e.g., *Cloutier* v. *Great A & P Tea Co.,* 436 A. 2d 1140, 1144 (N.H. 1981).

43   Second thoughts in Michigan: see *Rowe* v. *Montgomery Ward & Co.,* 473 N.W. 2d 268, 289 (Mich. 1991), where Justice Cavanagh's dissent charges that his colleagues have virtually overruled *Toussaint.*

43   At the will of either party: California Labor Code, s. 2922 ("An employment, having no specified term, may be terminated at the will of either party on notice to the other.") Lack of criticism: *Gardner* v. *Charles Schwab,* 267 Cal. Rptr. 326 (1990). Sun Life of Canada case: Anne Kruéger, "Jury awards fired manager for Sun Life $3.5 million," San Diego *Union-Tribune,* December 5, 1992.

43   True allegations count as defamation: William L. Kandel, "Employee Dishonesty and Workplace Security: Precautions About Prevention," *Employee Relations Law Journal,* September 22, 1990. Spread the word: Martha Middleton, "Employers Face Upsurge in Suits over Defamation," *National Law Journal,* May 4, 1987 (quoting Paul Tobias).

44   False imprisonment: Kandel, "Employee Dishonesty and Workplace Security."

44   Diner case: "Ex-Schering Salesman Gets $8.4 Million in Bias Suit," *Wall Street Journal,* October 31, 1994 ($425,000 compensatory, $8 million punitive damages). An executive with the defendant, Schering-Plough, said the company had often chosen locations away from the workplace to break the news of a firing.

44   Nationwide legal ferment: see Alan B. Krueger, "The Evolution of Unjust-Dismissal Legislation in the United States," 44 *Industrial and Labor Relations Review* 644 (1991), for a table showing the rapid state-by-state advance of the new theories in the 1980s.

44   High California verdicts: see Craig A. Horowitz, "Righting the Wrongs of Employment Termination," *San Francisco Recorder,* July 9, 1992 ("The median verdict for 1991 was $500,000. Since May 1989, there have been at least 33 verdicts awarded in the amount of $1 million or greater—or more than one million-dollar verdict per month.")

45   Few better settled: 62 *A.L.R. 3d* 271 (1975); ("few legal principles would seem to be better settled than the broad generality that an employment for an indefinite term is regarded as an employment at will which may be terminated at any time by either party for any reason or no reason at all.") By 1985 a completely refurbished commentary was needed: "Discharge of At-Will Employees," 12 *A.L.R. 4th* 544 (1985).

45   Experts differed on how many: see, e.g., Jack Steiber and Michael Murray, "Protection Against Unjust Discharge: The Need for a Federal Statute," 16 *U. Mich. J.L. Reform* 319, 322–324 (1983), estimating that unfair-dismissal rule would generate 150,000 cases a year; David Ewing, *Justice on the Job: Resolving Grievances in the Nonunion Workplace* (Harvard Business School Press, 1983), p. 10 (expert estimates range from 70,000–200,000); Lorne Seidman, Robert J. Aalberts, and Jolie R. Gaston, "The Model Employment Termination Act," *Cornell Hotel & Restaurant Administration Quarterly,* December 1993 (2 million at-will nonprobationary employees dismissed each year, of whom an estimated 150,000 to 200,000 are fired without good cause.)

45   On the ACLU's redefinition of its mission away from concentration on traditional civil-liberties concerns and toward new concepts of "economic rights," see Charles Oliver, "The First Shall Be Last?" *Reason,* October 1990. Embarrassing relic: Maltby, "An Unjust Workplace," p. 18.

46   Even if the employee gets her way: Ewing, *Justice on the Job,* p. 5.

Chapter 3. All Protected Now

47   *Muldrew* v. *Anheuser-Busch,* 728 F. 2d 989 (8th Cir. 1984).

48   Up 2,166 percent: John Donohue III and Peter Siegelman, "The Changing Nature of Employment Discrimination Litigation," 43 *Stanford Law Review* 983 (1991), 985–986.

51   "May" = "must": *Albemarle Paper* v. *Moody,* 422 U.S. 405 (1975). State university: *Carpenter* v. *Stephen F. Austin State University,* 706 F. 2d 608 (5th Cir. 1983). Ambulance service: *Hodgson* v. *A-1 Ambulance Service,* 455 F. 2d 372 (8th Cir. 1972).

52   Discretionary two-way = mandatory one-way: *Christiansburg Garment* v. *EEOC,* 434 U.S. 412, 422–24 (1978); *Newman* v. *Piggie Park Enterprises, Inc.,* 390 U.S. 400 (1968).

52   Most amazing creative flight: the Court's misreading was accomplished in a series of cases construing the Civil Rights Act of 1866's parallel Sections 1981 and 1982; the latter guaranteed all citizens the same right as whites "to inherit, purchase, lease, sell, hold, and convey real and personal property." In *Jones* v. *Mayer,* 392 U.S. 409 (1968) the Court said Section 1982 had not simply nullified the legal incapacities by which some states had prevented blacks from buying and owning property—as had previously been thought—but actually had forbidden private property owners to treat black buyers differently from white, on penalty of being sued for damages. Similar inventions applying Section 1981 to employment (*Johnson* v. *Railway Express,* 421 U.S. 454 [1975]), and private schools (*Runyon* v. *McCrary,* 427 U.S. 160 [1976]) followed.

      Legal academics, sympathetic to the Court's objectives, generally spared its reasoning close scrutiny, but there were some exceptions. Gerhard Casper of the University of Chicago ("*Jones* v. *Mayer:* Clio, Bemused and Confused Muse," 1968 *Supreme Court Review* 89) examined the Court's reading of the Reconstruction-era legislative history and dismissed it as "impossible or contrived . . . one loses whatever belief there may have been in the possibility of communication." Having come up with its new reading by an arbitrary act of will, the Court proceeded to decree equally arbitrary limits confining Section 1981 to cases of intentional discrimination and to commercial contracts rather than those deemed "personal"—thus sparing from liability risk, for example, lemonade-selling kids and adults who spurned proposals to engage in the "contract" of marriage. See Note, 90 *Harvard LR* 412 (1976); *Gen. Bldg. Contractors Assn v. Pennsylvania,* 458 U.S. 375 (1982). Commenting on such difficulties of interpretation, the Fifth Circuit commented that if the "natural construction" of Section 1981 (that is, as not being meant to restrain voluntary private action at all) were to be rejected, "another is not easily found, much as though a student had been told that any answer was acceptable as the sum of two plus two except four and directed to find another suitable one." See *Bhandari v. First National Bank of Commerce,* 808 F. 2d 1082 and later proceedings, 829 F. 2d 1343 (both 5th Cir. 1987).

Some justices later appointed to the Court agreed that the line of cases had been erroneously decided but declined to disturb it. Lewis Powell found "quite persuasive" the view that the 1866 act "was not intended to restrict private contractual choices" but accepted the new doctrines as *stare decisis.* John Paul Stevens noted that the Court's interpretation "would have amazed the legislators who voted for" the original act, but cheerfully added that it "accords with the prevailing sense of justice today." Other justices continued to deny that any mistake at all had been made—as if, years after printing the famous stamp with the upside-down aircraft, postal commissioners had continued to swear that this was the way biplanes actually fly. In its 1987 *Bhandari* cases, the Fifth Circuit described *Jones* and *McCrary* as "part of our marching orders," but added that Justice Byron White's *McCrary* dissent is "echoed by most observers who take the view that words have an ascertainable meaning."

53 Back pay doubts resolved against employer: *Johnson v. Goodyear Tire & Rubber,* 491 F. 2d. 1364, 1379–1380 (5th Cir. 1974). By mid-1995 a search in Shepard's Citations showed *Goodyear* had been cited more than seven hundred times in later cases (not always on the back-pay-uncertainty issue). Another notable element of the *Goodyear* ruling was that it brushed aside as "totally irrelevant" to the amount of back pay owed any questions of the company's "motive or intent"—in particular, its contention that it had adopted its diploma and testing policy in good faith with no discriminatory intent; until the Supreme Court's recent *Griggs* decision, such policies had widely been considered lawful.

54 "Raises an inference . . . we presume": *Furnco Construction Corp. v. Waters,* 438 U.S. 567, 577 (1978). Prima facie case: *McDonnell-Douglas Corp. v. Green,* 411 U.S. 792, 802 (1973).

55 Anyone who could read was qualified: Patricia Moore, "Edison Settles Hiring-Bias Suit for $3.3 Million," *Chicago Sun-Times,* December 30, 1993. Prima facie case stands even if eventual applicant hired was more qualified: see, e.g., *Mitchell v. Baldrige,* 759 F. 2d 80 (D.C. Cir. 1985). Having hired another member of same pro-

tected group for job no defense: see, e.g., *Jones* v. *Western Geophysical,* 669 F. 2d 280 (5th Cir. 1980).

55 "Clear and reasonably specific" justification needed under *McDonnell: Texas Dept. of Community Affairs* v. *Burdine,* 450 U.S. 248 (1981). Target to shoot at: Mack A. Player, *Employment Discrimination Law* (West, 1988), p. 336. "Poor voice quality," "poor personality," "bad attitude," "showed no interest" are insufficient: same. "Personality," "attitude," "grooming," "motivation," etc.: Alan M. Koral, *Conducting the Lawful Employment Interview: How to Avoid Charges of Discrimination When Interviewing Job Candidates,* revised edition (New York: Executive Enterprises Publications Co., 1986), p. 20. Courts "consistently" object to long list of personality and attitude indicators: Barry R. Nathan and Wayne F. Cascio, "Technical and Legal Standards," in Ronald A. Berk, ed., *Performance Assessment: Methods and Applications* (Johns Hopkins, 1986), p. 17 (performance appraisals of incumbent employees). See also Robert Gelerter, "Uniform Guidelines and Subjective Selection Criteria and Procedures," in Bernard R. Gifford, ed., *Test Policy and the Politics of Opportunity Allocation: The Workplace and the Law* (National Commission on Testing and Public Policy, 1989), pp. 122, 131 (cautioning against job selection based on workers' "attitudes").

56 Ageism is as odious: Irwin Ross, "Retirement at Seventy: A New Trauma for Management," *Fortune,* May 8, 1978 (quoting Rep. Claude Pepper). For similar comments, see, e.g., Richard G. Kass, "Early Retirement Incentives and the ADEA," 4 *Hofstra Labor L.J.* 63, 66 (1986); age bias "should be treated the same way under the law" as race bias. Every bit as pernicious: Robert Pear, "$2.4 Million Awarded in Housing Case," *New York Times,* July 16, 1992 (quoting attorney John Relman). Discrimination against pets: "In Brief," *Regulation,* January/February 1984.

57 Won't look down on us: Terry Wilson, "For the Disabled, It's 'Independence Day,'" *Chicago Tribune,* July 27, 1990 (quoting Alfred Gillespie). Empowering kind of thing: Laura Muha, "'Civil-Rights Bill' for Disabled" *Newsday,* July 27, 1990 (quoting Bruce Blower).

58 Toni Linda Cassista case: Maura Dolan, "Job Bias Ruling Gives the Obese Limited Rights," *Los Angeles Times,* September 3, 1993. After the dispute was under way the health food store offered to hire Cassista, but she refused on the grounds that (as the *Los Angeles Times* put it) the store "had not adequately 'educated' itself about the problems of overweight people."

58 Wooden post: *Los Angeles Times,* January 24, 1992. Expected to wear teeth daily: "Toothless Chambermaid Gains Trial on Claims of Sex and Handicap Bias," BNA *Daily Labor Report,* November 27, 1992 (*Hodgdon* v. *Mt. Mansfield*).

59 Contrary to policies: "Witch Wins Lawsuit Against Salvation Army," *St. Louis Post-Dispatch,* January 16, 1989.

59 UFO lid to be blown any day now: T. Layley Hapgood, "UFO Believer Wins Dispute Over Job," Gannett News Service (from *Tucson Citizen*), March 17, 1992; Junda Woo, "Ex-Workers Hit Back with Age-Bias Suits," *Wall Street Journal,* December 8, 1992.

59 Pilot training: *Smallwood* v. *UAL,* 661 F. 2d 303 (4th Cir. 1981). The court pointed out that although the FAA required pilots and co-pilots to retire at age sixty, the airline could keep the employees on in other positions.

60 Mere pleasant environment: *Diaz* v. *Pan Am,* 311 F. Supp. 559 (1970).

61 Never say bad for morale: Sara J. Harty, "Anticipating the Impact of ADA Requirements," *Business Insurance,* April 13, 1992 (quoting Brian McMahon, rehabilitation expert affiliated with University of Wisconsin-Milwaukee).

61 "Bankruptcy out": The story is told in several places, including Jeffrey O. Cooper, "Overcoming Barriers to Employment: The Meaning of Reasonable Accommodation and Undue Hardship in the Americans with Disabilities Act." 139 *U. Pa. L.R.* 1423, 1448 (1991) and Bonnie P. Tucker, "The Americans with Disabilities Act: An Overview," 1989 *U. Ill. L. Rev.* 923, 927, citing Hearings Before the Committee on Labor and Human Resources and the Subcommittee on the Handicapped, 101st Cong., 1st Sess. 64–65 (1989), p. 90.

61 Firing claims boomed: see Donohue & Siegelman, 43 *Stanford Law Review* 983 (1991) at 1016 (hiring and firing claims ran about equal through 1973, then diverged so that by 1984 firing charges outnumbered hiring by six to one; rates of lawsuit-filing in federal court followed the same pattern with a lag of a couple of years). Ten discharge cases for every firing: David Frum, "The Right to Fire," *Forbes,* October 26, 1992 (quoting Los Angeles attorney Paul Grossman of Paul, Hastings, Janofsky & Walker and Paul Tobias, founder of National Employment Lawyers Association).

62 Every decision discharging a woman subject to fairness scrutiny: Paul Tobia62Robert Fitzpatrick and David Torchia, *Litigating Wrongful Discharge Claims* (Wilmette, Ill.: Callaghan, 1987) ch. 1. p. 5. Call a lawyer immediately, increased leverage whether or not firing is discriminatory: Stephen Pollan and Mark Levine, "How To Survive Getting Fired," *New York,* September 7, 1992. As many laws as are available, chances are you're a victim, so assume the worst: E. Richard Larson, *Sue Your Boss* (Farrar, Straus & Giroux, 1981), p. 194.

63 Jury likely to look at issue of overall fairness, not discrimination alone: Judith McMorrow, "Retirement and Worker Choice: Incentives to Retire and the Age Discrimination in Employment Act," 29 *Boston College Law Review* 347, 376 (1988), writing in the context of age discrimination.

Chapter 4. Fear of Flirting

64 Joyce Capelle case: The account here is based on *Los Angeles Times* coverage, including Martin Miller, "Sex Harassment Alleged in O.C. School District," *Los Angeles Times,* Orange County edition, December 2, 1993; Dana Parsons, "Accusers May Be the Real Harassers at Orange Unified," December 8, 1993; Greg Krikorian, "A Rare Look in Files on Sex Harassment in L.A.P.D.," March 27, 1994 (quoting Judith Kurtz comments on another harassment case); Dana Parsons, "Behavior May Not Be What School District Was Targeting," August 9, 1995.

65 Not complicated to define: Ellen Bravo and Ellen Cassedy, *The Nine to Five Guide to Combating Sexual Harassment* (Wiley, 1992), p. 15. Almost anything employee finds offensive: Tamar Lewin, "Law on Sex Harassment Is Recent and Evolving," *New York Times*, October 8, 1991 (quoting Claudia Withers). Things that make people uncomfortable: Nicole Wise, "Connecticut Q & A: On Line with the Sexual Harassment Law," *New York Times*, Connecticut weekly edition, October 18, 1992 (quoting Lorna Brown Flynn).

66 Cleansing the workplace: *Robinson* v. *Jacksonville Shipyards,* 760 F. Supp. 1486, 1536 (M.D. Fla. 1991).

66 Annoying or distracting, humorous or insignificant: see Kingsley Browne, "Title VII as Censorship: Hostile-Environment Harassment and the First Amendment," 52 *Ohio State L.J.* 481, 507 (1991) (quoting Civil Rights Commission's Massachusetts advisory panel). I am indebted at several points to Browne's pioneering analysis. "Sweetheart," "hon": *Magnuson* v. *Peak Technical Svcs.,* 808 F. Supp. 50 (E.D. Va. 1992).

66 Chicago Board of Education rules: Rosalind Rossi, "Sexual Harassment Ban Spelled Out," *Chicago Sun-Times*, June 23, 1994. *Boston Globe* writer case: Barbara Matusow, "Baby, What'd I Say?" *Washingtonian*, August 1993 (quoting EEOC's Susan Reilly). Need not have been the target of any conduct: Rocco Cammarere, "Court defines new sex harassment test," *New Jersey Lawyer*, July 19, 1993 (*Lehmann* v. *Toys 'R' Us*).

66 Federal guidelines on negative stereotyping: Tamar Lewin, "Dispute Over Computer Messages Raises Questions on Free Speech," *New York Times*, September 22, 1994 (federal civil rights enforcers sought ban on college computer bulletin-board comments, "slurs, negative stereotypes, jokes or pranks" that "denigrate or show hostility toward" protected groups). Women don't belong in the mines: *Jenson* v. *Eveleth Taconite Co.,* 824 F. Supp. 847 (D. Minn. 1991). Blatantly sexist computer messages at LAPD: Jim Newton, "Sexual Harassment a Tough LAPD Problem," *Los Angeles Times*, March 3, 1994.

66 "Broad": *Materson* v. *La Brum & Doak,* 846 F. Supp. 1224, 1233 (E.D. Pa. 1993). Not funny: *Lipsett* v. *Univ. of Puerto Rico,* 864 F. 2d 881, 906 (1st Cir. 1988).

67 "Trust your instincts": Bravo & Cassedy, *The 9 to 5 Guide*, p. 68. More than half of offenders didn't realize it was harassment: Sameera Khan, "Reducing Harassment Exposure: Employers Turning to Liability Cover, Prevention Efforts," *Business Insurance*, July 4, 1994 (quoting Victor Schachter). Excessive male handwringing, coping strategy: William Petrocelli & Barbara Kate Repa, *Sexual Harassment on the Job* (Nolo Press, 1992), pp. 3/9, 2/24. In some cases by not responding: Tamar Lewin, "Law on Sex Harassment is Recent and Evolving," *New York Times*, October 8, 1991 (quoting Claudia Withers). Who decides: Bravo and Cassedy, p. 15. Gut-check: Maureen O'Brien, "Publishing's Best-Kept Secret," *Publisher's Weekly*, April 25, 1994 (quoting William Petrocelli).

67 Exert a good influence: James Schouler, *A Treatise on the Law of Domestic Relations*, 5th ed. (1895), quoted in Mary Ann Glendon, *The New Family and the New Property* (Butterworths, 1981), p. 147.

68 Supreme Court struck down: *Brown* v. *Oklahoma,* 408 U.S. 914 (1972), remanding

a conviction for using obscene language in public in the presence of women in light of *Cohen* v. *California,* 403 U.S. 15 (1971), and *Gooding* v. *Wilson,* 405 U.S. 518. On inconsistent handling of obscenity and related issues, see Kingsley Browne, "Title VII as Censorship," 52 *Ohio State L.J.* 481, 529 (1991).

68 Sleeping with boss = prostitution: *Lucas* v. *Brown & Root,* 736 F. 2d 1202 (8th Cir. 1984).

69 Savonarola of Ann Arbor: Catharine MacKinnon, *Sexual Harassment of Working Women:* A Case of Sex Discrimination (Yale, 1979). The index of this founding manifesto of harassment law contains no entry for "free speech" or "First Amendment."

69 Dictionary definition: *The American College Dictionary* (Harper, 1948).

70 U.S. Supreme Court accepted: *Meritor Savings Bank* v. *Vinson,* 477 U.S. 57 (1986).

71 T-shirts with offensive mottoes: *Cohen* v. *California,* 403 U.S. 15 (1971). An even more remarkable case on the need to avert eyes was *Erznoznik* v. *Jacksonville,* 422 U.S. 205 (1975), upholding a Constitutional right to display nudity at a drive-in theater visible from nearby roads.

71 Office radio or TV: see Browne, "Title VII as Censorship," 546, n. 388 (complaint of "pornographic radio shows" in one case based on co-workers' habit of listening to sex adviser "Dr. Ruth").

72 Real claim is that atmosphere did not change: Browne, "Title VII as Censorship," 487.

72 Male employee's religious objections to nudie photos: see, e.g., *Lambert* v. *Condor Mfg.,* 768 F. Supp. 600 (E.D. Mich. 1991). Bachelorette parties thrown by other women: see, e.g., Jennifer Oldham, "Same-Sex Charges of Harassment Filed," *Los Angeles Times,* Valley edition, April 27, 1994. Cartoons without women in them: *Cardin* v. *Via Tropical Fruits, Inc.,* 1993 U.S. Dist. LEXIS 16302 (S.D. Fla. July 9, 1993). Jenny Craig case: Jane Gross, "Now Look Who's Taunting. Now Look Who's Suing," *New York Times,* February 26, 1995. See also Barbara Carton, "At Jenny Craig, Men Are Ones Who Claim Sex Discrimination," *Wall Street Journal,* November 29, 1994.

73 No more tangible or serious injury needed: Rocco Cammarere, "Court Defines New Sex Harassment Test," *New Jersey Lawyer,* July 19, 1993. Peggy Kimzey case: 907 F. Supp. 1309 (W.D.M.O. 1995).

73 Long Beach policewoman $1.7 million, no-touch case: "Female Police Officers Awarded $3.1 Million," Associated Press, September 27, 1991. Chevron settlement: Tamar Lewin, "Chevron Settles Sexual-Harassment Charges," *New York Times,* February 22, 1995. On "beer is better" gag, see also Alex Markels, "Managers Aren't Always Able to Get the Right Message Across with E-Mail," *Wall Street Journal,* August 6, 1996.

74 California hot tub case: Julia Lawlor, "Women Gain Power, Means to Abuse It," *USA Today,* January 17, 1994.

74 Religious harassment: John Moore, "Possibly One 'Thou Shalt Not' Too Many," *National Journal,* May 21, 1994; complaints filed with EEOC jumped from 196 in 1989 to 319 in 1993. Religious "advances": *Meltebeke* v. *Bureau of Labor and Industries,* 852 P. 2d 859, 862 (Ore. App. 1993), upholding the general regulation but overturning the penalty in the case at hand on the grounds that unwelcomeness

had not been made clear enough. See Virginia Postrel, "Persecution Complex," *Reason,* Aug/Sept. 1994. Disparaging remarks about weight: Kara Swisher, "Overweight Workers Battle Bias on the Job," *Washington Post,* January 24, 1994.

74   University of Nebraska case: Nat Hentoff, "A 'Pinup' of His Wife," *Washington Post,* June 5, 1993. Cartoon at library: Cheryl Johnson, "The Latest in Offensive Workplace Items? A New Yorker Cartoon," *Minneapolis Star-Tribune,* January 18, 1994. Polish-joke mugs: *State Div. of Human Rights* v. *McHarris Gift Center,* 418 N.E.2d 393 (N.Y. 1980), *aff'g* 419 N.Y.S. 2d 405 (1979). Even pigs need love: *Rabidue* v. *Osceola,* 805 F. 2d 611, 624 (Keith, J., dissenting).

75   Europeans arriving in New World: "Vermont Censors Painting," *Newsday,* May 3, 1992. Oglesby, Ill., post office mural: Wes Smith, "The Mural Minority: Janitor Drives 'Pornographic' Public Art Under Cover in Illinois Town," *Chicago Tribune,* July 29, 1993 (more scantily clad Indians); Fig leaves of the 1990s: "Aphrodite Can't Fight City Hall," *Chicago Tribune,* reprint of *San Francisco Examiner* report, April 11, 1993 (woodcuts by artist Zoravia Bettiol). For a list of other art-as-harassment cases, see Mark Schapiro, "The Fine Art of Sexual Harassment," *Harper's,* July 1994.

75   Japanese competitors pictured as samurai: Eugene Volokh, "Freedom of Speech and Workplace Harassment," 39 *U.C.L.A. Law Review* 1791, 1795 (1992) (Hyster Corp).

75   No Sexual Harassment or Innuendos: *Ross* v. *Double Diamond,* 672 F. Supp. 261 (N.D. Tex. 1987).

76   Suppress more speech: Bravo and Cassedy, *The 9 to 5 Guide,* pp. 92 (need to squelch jokes told by men among themselves), 94–95 (no disrespectful jokes about policy itself).

76   Maximize options via different channels, Bravo and Cassedy, pp. 103–104.

76   Weil, Gotshal on discipline: Jeffrey Klein and Nicholas Pappas, "Responding to Claims of Sexual Harassment," *New York Law Journal,* August 18, 1994. DuPont beepers: Bravo and Cassedy, *The 9 to 5 Guide,* p. 103.

76   Use two investigators, type everything themselves: James J. Oh, "Internal Sexual Harassment Complaints: Investigating to Win," *Employee Relations Law Journal,* September 22, 1992, pp. 227, 229, 232. On hazards in interviewing complainant, see Donald H. Weiss, *Fair, Square and Legal* (AMACOM, 1991), pp. 160–161. Among questions that shouldn't be asked of a complainant during an investigation, Weiss says, are why she didn't complain earlier or whether she would like a transfer.

77   Separate complainant from target: *Intlekofer* v. *Turnage,* 973 F. 2d 773 (9th Cir. 1992).

77   Cornell lock-box: Michael S. Greve, "Sexual Harassment: Telling the Other Victims' Story," 23 *No. Ky. L.R.* 523, 533 (1996); Craig Hymowitz, "The Locked Box," *Heterdoxy,* May 1995.

77   Must be of disciplinary nature: *Intlekofer* v. *Turnage,* 973 F. 2d 773, 777–779 (9th Cir. 1992); p. 780 notes that "counseling is sufficient only as a first resort." Demotion found sufficient in case of single bestowal of unwanted hugs and kisses: *Hirschfeld* v. *New Mexico Corrections Dept.,* 916 F. 2d 572 at 574. Slurs and humor:

Snell v. *Suffolk County*, 611 F. Supp. 521 at 531, 782 F. 2d 1094, 1100 (2d Cir. 1986) ("sanitizing the workplace"). Some form of discipline: Jeffrey Klein and Nicholas Pappas, "Responding to Claims of Sexual Harassment," *New York Law Journal*, August 18, 1994.

78   Should have fired him the first time: *Ewald* v. *Wornick Family Foods Corp.*, Corpus Christi, reported in Tessie Borden, "Definition Has Changed as Litigants Push Limits," Houston *Post*, September 4, 1994. See Kingsley Browne, "Title VII as Censorship," 52 *Ohio State L.J.* 504, note 155 (1991) (listing many cases where employers lost because their discipline of a miscreant was not prompt or severe enough).

78   NOWLDEF, phone numbers posted: Dana S. Connell, "Effective Sexual Harassment Policies: Unexpected Lessons from *Jacksonville Shipyards*," 17 *Employee Relations Law Journal* 191 (1991). Connell says employers might wish to emulate the court-ordered JSI policy, which offers "protection" because it was "designed in substantial part by NOW's Legal Defense and Education Fund." Not many places different from Jacksonville Shipyards: Arthur S. Hayes, "Pinup Case Splits Free-Speech Activists," *Wall Street Journal*, April 29, 1992 (quoting Deborah A. Ellis).

79   Any tone that feels right to you: Bravo & Cassedy, *The 9 to 5 Guide*, p. 69. Series of escalating steps, confiscate cartoons, look for link in joke chain, "What a Lawyer Wants to Hear": William Petrocelli & Barbara Kate Repa, *Sexual Harassment on the Job* (Nolo Press, 1992), pp. 1/25, 2/15, 3/31, 9/5. Forget counseling: Nicole Wise, "Connecticut Q & A: On Line with the Sexual Harassment Law," *New York Times*, Connecticut weekly, October 18, 1992 (quoting Lorna Brown Flynn).

80   Plaintiff's profanity fitting into environment at hand: *Morris* v. *American National Can*, 730 F. Supp. 1489 (E.D. Mo. 1989), (egregious co-worker misconduct); see also *Swentek* v. *USAir, Inc.*, 830 F. 2d 552 (4th Cir. 1987), for a plaintiff's own staging of serious pranks. Quit while they're ahead: "Title VII as Censorship," 52 *Ohio State L.J.* 481, 542–3 (1991).

80   Psychological fringes: *Rogers* v. *EEOC*, 454 F. 2d 234, 238 (5th Cir. 1971), *cert. denied*, 406 U.S. 957 (1972).

80   Maryland disability harassment: *Davis* v. *York International*, November 22, 1993, U.S. Dist. LEXIS 17649.

81   Would never date anyone in the office: Sally Jacobs, "Sexual Chill Hits the Office," *Boston Globe*, August 30, 1992 (quoting Alex McLaren). He could ask once, carefully: Tamar Lewin, "Law on Sex Harassment is Recent and Evolving," *New York Times*, October 8, 1991 (quoting Alison Wethersfeld).

81   New York sanitation sensitivity training: Jane Gross, "Two Women Welcomed (By Some)," *New York Times*, August 26, 1986. The reporter interviewed both male and female workers, with colorful results. One, Frank Gasparo, said: " 'No talking about different subjects. And, God forbid you should call them broads.' 'It's like the three monkeys,' Mr. Gasparo concluded. 'You know, the ones with their hands over the mouth. It's make-believe.' " The reporter said the mandatory training classes "seem to teach more sensitivity than the women require. 'I'm sure there's nothing I haven't heard before,' said Ms. Sanderson, who could barely contain her laughter when asked if she would be able to tolerate off-color language."

SOURCE NOTES

82   "Machine mode," Freada Klein quote: Sally Jacobs, "Sexual Chill Hits the Office," *Boston Globe*, August 30, 1992.

Chapter 5. Mistaken Identity

Page

85   Forced to go on welfare: Joseph Shapiro, *No Pity: People With Disabilities Forging a New Civil Rights Movement* (Times Books, 1993), p. 27 (quoting Sandra Swift Parrino). Appears largely due to discrimination: Robert L. Burgdorf, Jr., "The A.D.A.: Analysis and Implications of a Second-Generation Civil Rights Statute," *Harvard Civil Rights–Civil Liberties Law Review* 413, 421 (1991).

86   Pay for themselves, solve by throwing money at it: Frank Bowe, *Rehabilitating America* (Harper & Row, 1980), pp. xi, 7. Give up $60 billion: Leslie Phillips, "Access: Bill Would Guarantee Equality for Disabled," *USA Today*, May 15, 1990. More than repay the cost: "Dismantling the Barriers" (editorial), *Boston Globe*, May 25, 1990. Such arguments crucial: "A Law for Every American" (editorial), *New York Times*, July 27, 1990. Helping solve labor shortages: "An Enabling Law for the Disabled" (editorial), *Business Week*, June 11, 1990.

86   Effects on employment: Carl Quintanilla, "Disabilities Act Helps—But Not Much: Disabled People Aren't Getting More Job Offers," July 19, 1993 (survey by National Center for Disability Services found that percentage of disabled employed didn't rise in first year of law); Steven Holmes, "In 4 Years, Disabilities Act Hasn't Improved Jobs Rate," *New York Times*, October 23, 1994. Later study: Jay Mathews, "More Disabled Hired, Census Study Shows," *Washington Post*, July 26, 1996.

89   Unconscious, unthinking discrimination: Tom Kenworthy, "House Votes New Rights for Disabled," *Washington Post*, May 23, 1990 (quoting Rep. Steny Hoyer).

90   Fall in voc-rehab placements: see Paul G. Hearne, "Employment Strategies for People with Disabilities: A Prescription for Change," in Jane West, ed., *The Americans with Disabilities Act: From Policy to Practice* (Milbank Memorial Fund, 1991), p. 119 (placements fell to 220,000 annually from 325,000 in 1975). Social Security disability outlays soared: figures are from Budget of the U.S. Government, fiscal year 1997, historical tables (GPO, 1996)

92   Welfare trap: see Cornelius Peck, "Employment Problems of the Handicapped: Would Title VII Remedies Be Appropriate and Effective?" 16 *U. Mich. J.L. Ref.* 343, 374–376 (1983) (citing evidence that incentives operate strongly in disability program, and that expansion of benefits had caused massive drop in work effort). See also Thomas N. Chirikos, "The Economics of Employment," in West, *The Americans with Disabilities Act*, p. 164 ("virtually all economists who have studied the issue take as given the likelihood that disability transfers will impel individuals to leave the work force," with the only dispute being how big the effect is).

92   Oppression, systematic oppression: John Gliedman and William Roth, *The Unexpected Minority: Handicapped Children in America* (Harcourt Brace Jovanovich, 1980), pp. 3–4, 25, 264–266.

SOURCE NOTES

93 Not what God wrought: Phillips, *USA Today,* May 15, 1990 (quoting Gov. Lowell Weicker).

94 Fewer than half agree in polls: 1986 Harris poll for International Center for the Disabled and National Council on the Handicapped, cited in Shapiro, *No Pity,* p. 25.

94 No good or bad members of oppressing class: Harlan Lane, *The Mask of Benevolence* (Knopf, 1992), p. 87. Pervaded by ignorance: Jeffrey O. Cooper, "Overcoming Barriers to Employment: The Meaning of Reasonable Accommodation and Undue Hardship in the Americans with Disabilities Act," 139 *U. Pa. L.R.,* 1423, 1467 (1991). American people insensitive: Senate Report No. 93-1297, p. 50 (1974).

94 Bristling at generalizations: Sara J. Harty, "Etiquette Tips Fight Discrimination," *Business Insurance,* July 13, 1992 (quoting National Easter Seals Society literature).

95 92 percent felt admiration: "Public Attitudes Toward People with Disabilities," Harris poll, 1991, cited at Shapiro, *No Pity,* p. 328. Halo effect: see Peck, 16 *U. Mich. J.L. Ref.* 343, 377 (1983), footnote 171 (citing studies).

95 Widely viewed as oppressive: Shapiro, *No Pity,* p. 16. Sympathetic atmosphere must be overcome: Cooper, 139 *U. Pa. L. Rev.,* p. 1467.

95 FDR's status widely known: see, e.g. Rosanne Klass, letter to the editor, *American Spectator,* February 1995.

96 Porky Pig always shown as victim: Kevin Goldman, "From Witches to Anorexics, Critical Eyes Scrutinize Ads for Political Correctness," *Wall Street Journal,* May 19, 1994 (quoting Ira Zimmerman of National Stuttering Project).

96 Hand signals: Edward D. Berkowitz, *Disabled Policy: America's Programs for the Handicapped: A Twentieth Century Fund Report* (Cambridge University Press, 1987), p. 188. Nothing regrettable, deaf identity to be adopted with pride: Shapiro, *No Pity,* p. 224.

97 Malleability of estimated number of disabled: see, e.g., Peck, 16 *U. Mich. J.L. Ref.* 343 at 346, citing M. Berkowitz, W. Johnson, & E. Murphy, *Public Policy Toward Disability* 14 (1976); 1973 estimates ranged from 7.7 million to 31 million.

97 Definition depends on what you want the numbers to do for you: Heather Mac Donald, "Welfare's Next Vietnam," *City Journal,* Winter 1995 (quoting John Kiernan). Inclusion of everyone over age 65: Edward L. Hudgins, "Handicapping Freedom: The ADA," *Regulation,* 1995, no. 2 ("In order to get to 43 million, the act assumed that everyone over 65 years old, 31 million at the time the act passed, was disabled.")

98 San Francisco federal building occupation: Richard K. Scotch, *From Good Will to Civil Rights: Transforming Federal Disability Policy* (Temple University Press, 1984), p. 115. Welcomed the poignancy: Joseph A. Califano, Jr., *Governing America* (1981), pp. 260–261.

98 Orchestrated demonstrations: Scotch, *From Good Will to Civil Rights,* pp. 36–37 (origin of groups), 86 *et seq.* (ACCD and federal grantee National Center on Law and the Handicapped), 92 (OCR staff encouraged outside groups to pressure HEW head and fed them information, which "culminated in a demonstration"), 115 (OCR and congressional committees involved in planning sit-ins).

98 No grass-roots pressure: see, e.g., Scotch, *From Good Will to Civil Rights,* p. 57 (staffers agree "it was an initiative of liberal congressional staff and not done at the

request, suggestion or demand of outside groups"); Gliedman and Roth, *The Unexpected Minority,* p. 267 (section 504 "not the result of grass-roots pressure from the disabled and their able-bodied allies").

99 Network of federally supported centers: see Berkowitz, *Disabled Policy,* p. 205 ("One goal of the ILCs was to help a handicapped person secure all the welfare benefits to which he was entitled"; counselors "coached" people on how to appear and tried to "destigmatize" the receipt of welfare.) See also Shapiro, *No Pity,* p. 72, on ILCs' "fervor of advocacy."

99 Delegating to ACLU: Susan Mandel, "Disabling the GOP," *National Review,* June 11, 1990 (both Bush administration and Judiciary Committee members referred decisions on amendments to ACLU's Chai Feldblum and Disability Rights Education and Defense Fund).

100 Potentially the most expensive in history: Louis Richman, "Report Card on Bushonomics," *Fortune,* November 4, 1991 (citing National Association of Manufacturers analysts). Surprisingly muted: Shapiro, *No Pity,* p. 116; Shuster office takeover, p. 138.

100 Unabashed venture into social engineering: Peter T. Kilborn, "Major Shift Likely as Law Bans Bias Toward Disabled," *New York Times,* July 19, 1992. Rorschach test: 136 *Cong. Record* S9694 (July 13, 1990) (remarks of Sen. Armstrong). Congress so seldom does something wonderful: Mary McGrory, "For the Disabled, a Capital Day," *Washington Post,* May 27, 1990.

101 President Bush compares ADA enactment to fall of Berlin Wall: Christopher Connell, "Bush Signs Landmark Legislation," Associated Press, July 26, 1990. Will change the way we live forever: Robert Greene, "Senate OKs Disabilities Act," Associated Press, July 13, 1990 (quoting Sen. Tom Harkin).

Chapter 6. The Age of Accommodation

Page

102 Two widely cited surveys on cost: One was a 1982 survey of federal contractors conducted by Berkeley Planning Associates for the Department of Labor; the other was a 1987 report by the Job Accommodation Network, a federally supported group that offers advice to employers seeking ways to accommodate disabled workers.

102 Nothing that should be terribly threatening: "Bush Signs Law on Disabled," *St. Louis Post-Dispatch,* July 27, 1990 (quoting Jim Tuscher). Cost concerns highly exaggerated: "An Enabling Law for the Disabled" (editorial), *Business Week,* June 11, 1990. Shouldn't fear large lawsuits: "Opening Doors—Disabled Persons Need Anti-Bias Protection" (editorial), *Seattle Times,* May 19, 1990.

103 Some journalistic naysayers: Janet Reno and Dick Thornburgh, "ADA—Not a Disabling Mandate," *Wall Street Journal,* July 26, 1995.

103 Clear and narrowly crafted: Walter Kendall, letter to editor, *American Spectator,* September 1995.

103 Section 504: This account of the law draws heavily on two excellent books, Richard

K. Scotch, *From Good Will to Civil Rights: Transforming Federal Disability Policy* (Temple University Press, 1984), and Robert A. Katzmann, *Institutional Disability* (Brookings, 1986).

104 Door-to-door paratransit: Cornelius Peck, "Employment Problems of the Handicapped: Would Title VII Remedies Be Appropriate and Effective?" 16 *U. Mich. J.L. Ref.* 343, 346 (1983); taxis could serve nearly four times as many seriously disabled persons as the legislation actually passed, at one-fifth the cost per ride, according to a 1979 Congressional Budget Office study. See also Roger Starr, "Wheels of Misfortune," *Harper's,* January 1982, and Katzmann, *Institutional Disability.*

104 No public comment or debate: Edward D. Berkowitz, *Disabled Policy: America's Programs for the Handicapped: A Twentieth Century Fund Report* (Cambridge University Press, 1987), p. 212. Could not even have imagined: Katzmann, *Institutional Disability,* pp. 46–50 (quoting Ohio Democratic Rep. Charles Vanik).

104 Frame of mind we all had: Scotch, *From Good Will to Civil Rights,* pp. 47–48 (quoting Nik Edes, staffer with New Jersey Democratic Sen. Harrison Williams).

105 OCR retroactive legislative history: see Katzmann, pp. 53–54. This ploy eventually failed to impress the Supreme Court, which scathingly dismissed the ersatz history in a later case, but meanwhile it helped activists at the agency win at least one important lower court ruling; see Katzmann, p. 163 (*Cherry v. Mathews*).

106 Major tenet of faith: Scotch, p. 77. Does not take into account, cost officially a nonissue: p. 75. Nice things to do for Easter Seal children: p. 88 (quoting Martin Gerry). Party line in our office: p. 76 (quoting Sally Foley).

107 Draconic character of philanthropic legislation: E. F. Benson, *As We Were* (1930; reprinted Hogarth Press, 1985), p. 192 (quoting Lord Salisbury). Disabled education: see, e.g. Stuart Anderson, "Why Schools Don't Dare to Discipline the Disabled" *The Weekly Standard,* February 19, 1996. Drug addicts in elderly housing: see, e.g., Cynthia Durcanin, "Elderly cringe as danger becomes next-door neighbor." *Atlanta Journal and Constitution,* April 28, 1991.

109 Low burden of accommodation: Thomas N. Chirikos, "The Economics of Employment," in Jane West, ed., *The Americans with Disabilities Act: From Policy to Practice* (Milbank Memorial Fund, 1991), pp. 161–162 (detailing selection bias and other problems with surveys). Even after the law took effect, advocates had much success in the press portraying compliance costs as low: see, e.g., Udayan Gupta, "Disabilities Act Isn't as Burdensome as Many Feared," *Wall Street Journal,* April 20, 1992; Timothy L. O'Brien, "An Industry Emerges to Exploit the Disabilities Act: Companies Use Fear to Sell Unneeded Goods and Services, Critics Say," *Wall Street Journal,* December 1, 1992. "ADA Compliance Comes Cheap, a Survey Finds," roundup item, *Wall Street Journal,* September 16, 1994 (reporting updated number finding two-thirds of accommodations under $500). Also see Stephen L. Percy, *Disability, Civil Rights, and Public Policy: The Politics of Implementation* (U. of Alabama Press, 1989), p. 210 (on Berkeley Planning Associates study).

110 Hotel and hospital expenditure plans: Carolyn Lochhead, "New Law on the Disabled to Make a Huge Impact," *San Francisco Chronicle,* November 14, 1991. Stepfordization of street environment: see, e.g., Gupta, "Disabilities Act Isn't as Burdensome as Many Feared," *Wall Street Journal,* April 20, 1992; and Claudia

Deutsch, "Commercial Property/The Multilevel Concept; New Stores Make Shopping a Many-Tiered Experience," *New York Times,* August 28, 1994 (ADA has slowed trend toward retail space off grade level).

111 Not just near aisles and exits: Robert P. O'Quinn, "The Americans with Disabilities Act: Time for Amendments," Cato Institute Policy Analysis, August 9, 1991.

111 Goods shipped in smaller packages: Gupta, *Wall Street Journal,* April 20, 1992.

000 Lighting, carpet patterns, unusual fonts, large type: John C. DeWitt, "The Role of Technology in Removing Barriers," in West, ed., *The ADA: From Policy to Practice,* p. 323.

112 Memory aids & color-coding, etc.: Gary Eisler, "Attention Deficit Disorder Can't Be Ignored," *Wall Street Journal,* June 27, 1994.

112 Paper-averse letter sorter: BNA *Daily Labor Report,* December 24, 1992 (*James v. Runyon,* E.D. Pa., December 9, 1992). Our basic premise: Victoria Slind-Flor, "The Smell of Success," *National Law Journal,* October 14, 1991 (quoting Julia Kendall). Kendall coordinates a group called the Chemical Injury Litigation Project. See Carl Nolte, "Perfume Protest at Fairmont Hotel: Mask-Wearing Demonstrators Say Scents Make Them Sick," *San Francisco Chronicle,* October 25, 1994; James Bovard, "Olfactory Correctness," *Heterodoxy,* November 1995.

113 Texas ophthalmologist: Susan Lee, "That Can't-Do Spirit," *Reason,* March 1996. Personal assistance new top-of-the-line issue, technology no longer a luxury: Joseph Shapiro, *No Pity: People With Disabilities Forging a New Civil Rights Movement* (Times Books, 1993), pp. 236, 251.

114 Kemp on deliberate vagueness: Steven A. Holmes, "Advocates of Disabled Workers Say New Rules Don't Do Enough," New York *Times,* July 26, 1991. Toileting and eating not ruled out: EEOC press conference on ADA final regulations, July 25, 1991, transcript by Federal News Service, available on Nexis (comments of Chris Bell).

115 Morning stiffness: Edward Yelin, "History and Future of Employment," in West, ed., *The ADA: From Policy to Practice,* p. 142.

115 Third bite of apple: *Business Insurance,* May 29, 1995, roundup item (quoting Douglas W. Poole). Judge Samuel B. Kent cited the "audacity" and "obvious bad faith exhibited by the plaintiff and his counsel," calling the move a "blatant attempt to extort additional money from the defendant" that left an "uncomfortable inference of outright fraud" (*McNeill v. Atchison, Topeka and Santa Fe Railway Co.,* S.D. Tex.).

115 Low-dust: *Ackerman v. Western Electric,* 643 F. Supp. 836 (N.D. Calif. 1986), *aff'd* 860 F. 2d 1514 (9th Cir. 1988).

116 Halt the interview so union rep can step in: Barbara A. Lee, "Reasonable Accommodation Under the ADA: The Limitations of Rehabilitation Act Precedent," 14 *Berkeley Journal of Employment and Labor Law* 221–2 (1993) (former NLRB general counsel says the two acts are "directly opposed," and NLRB clashes with EEOC on interpretation).

117 Tried to draft regulations: Jules L. Smith, "Accommodating the ADA to Collective Bargaining Obligations Under the NLRA," *Employee Relations Law Journal,* September 22, 1992.

117 Family and Medical Leave Act: see Joann S. Lublin, "Family-Leave Law Can Be Ex-

cuse for a Day Off," *Wall Street Journal,* July 7, 1995. Sign language and pictographs: Mari Matsuda, "Voices of America: Accent, Antidiscrimination Law and a Jurisprudence for the Last Reconstruction," 100 *Yale Law Journal* 1329 (1991), text accompanying note 180.

Chapter 7. Accommodating Demons

Page

119   The Northwest pilot case is drawn from published accounts including David Carr, "Drinking and Flying: Former Northwest Captain Norman Lyle Prouse Tells His Story in an Exclusive Interview," *Corporate Report Minnesota,* February 1991; Glenn Kessler, "Three Pilots Guilty of Flying Jetliner While Intoxicated," *Newsday,* August 21, 1990; Eric Weiner, "Northwest Pilots Are Found Guilty of Drunken Flying," *New York Times,* August 21, 1990; "Keep the 'Alcohol Problem' in Perspective" (editorial), *Aviation Week,* August 27, 1990; Dennis Cassano, "Northwest Crew's Convictions Upheld," *Minneapolis Star-Tribune,* September 21, 1991; David Phelps, "Pilot Who Flew Drunk Will Rejoin NWA; Prouse Initially to Work as Ground School Trainer," *Minneapolis Star-Tribune,* October 13, 1993; and other Associated Press, *Minneapolis Star-Tribune, Newsday,* and *New York Times* articles.

122   Viewed in a negative light: Stephen L. Percy, *Disability, Civil Rights, and Public Policy: The Politics of Implementation* (U. of Alabama Press, 1989), p. 5. Legally no different: Amy Stevens, "Boss's Brain Teaser: Accommodating Depressed Worker," *Wall Street Journal,* September 11, 1995 (quoting Chris Bell).

122   Errors in judgment, quick temper: Margaret Hart Edwards, "The ADA and the Employment of Individuals with Mental Disabilities," *Employee Relations Law Journal,* December 22, 1992, p. 354.

123   Sleeping security guard: The case was *Ruzek* v. *General Services Administration* (Aug. 20, 1981). See Walter F. Scanlon, *Alcoholism and Drug Abuse in the Workplace* (Praeger, 1986), p. 106 (quoting MSPB opinion) and T. R. Reid, "Uncle Sam's Alcoholic Nephews Get a Break Under Law," *Washington Post,* August 28, 1981. Relapse is predictable: *Whitlock* v. *Donovan,* 598 F. Supp. 126, 131 (D.D.C. 1984), 790 F. 2d 964 (D.C. Cir. 1986). Must be permitted some opportunity for failure: *Rodgers* v. *Lehman,* 869 F. 2d 253 (4th Cir. 1989). Another case in this series was *Callicotte* v. *Carlucci,* 698 F. Supp. 944, 950 (D.D.C. 1988), which significantly refers to the government/defendant's having "conceded" that an employee's poor performance was due to alcoholism.

124   Volitional acts of dissipation: *Walker* v. *Weinberger,* 600 F. Supp. 757, 762 (D.D.C. 1985).

124   Charlotte F. case: cited at 687 F. Supp. 1214 (S.D. Ohio 1988).

125   Great show of precision: Milt Freudenheim, "New Law to Bring Wider Job Rights for Mentally Ill," *New York Times,* September 23, 1991.

126   No fear we are imposing: Rep. Steny Hoyer, 136 *Cong. Rec.* H2637 (May 22, 1990).

126   Standard Gravure case: see Minority Views, House Energy & Commerce Committee Report, #101-485 (May 15, 1990). Joseph Wesbecker's rampage took place on

September 14, 1989; on his long trail of belligerent and irrational behavior, see Jim Adams, Cary Willis, and Leslie Scanlon, *Louisville Courier-Journal*, October 1, 1989.

126   Women's restroom: "High Court Upholds Ruling in Boeing Firing of Transsexual," Associated Press, March 4, 1993.

127   David Shaw case: Based on published sources including Gary Libow, "Hamden Schools Chief Will Fight for His Job," *Hartford Courant*, May 14, 1994; Robert Frahm, "Removing Hamden Superintendent May Pose Legal Tangle," *Hartford Courant*, May 25, 1994 (quoting Lillian Clayman and DeWitt Jones); Lawrence Van Gelder, "Little Town Faces a Big Dilemma," *New York Times*, May 22, 1994 (quoting Hugh Keefe); Lucinda Harper, "Mental-Health Law Protects Many People But Vexes Employers," *Wall Street Journal*, July 19, 1994 (quoting Hamden attorney Jeffrey Pingpank).

128   See a lawyer before taking any adverse action: McNair law firm, *South Carolina Employment Law Letter*, August 1995. Not just a day's pay, it's the principle: Phinjo Gombu, "Arbitrator Orders Pay for Hangover Book-Off," *Toronto Star*, January 26, 1994 (quoting Emmerson Phillips). Same number of days for binge as for coronary: *Simpson v. Reynolds Metals Co.*, 629 F. 2d 1226 (7th Cir. 1980) at 1231, n. 8 (defendant wins on other grounds).

128   Positive duty to confront: *Ferguson v. U.S. Dept. of Commerce*, 680 F. Supp. 1514, 1518 (M.D. Fla. 1988). "Does [this decision] mean we have to look at everyone who's lurching in the hallway and accuse them of being an alcoholic?" Ferguson's supervisor, Dan Furlong, asked a reporter. "Because the flip side of all this is they'll sue us and say we're invading their privacy." Milo Geyelin, "Experts See Trouble over Federal Ruling," *St. Petersburg Times*, March 6, 1988. The parties later settled out of court, and at the request of both sides' lawyers Judge Elizabeth Kovachevich vacated the ruling. See 694 F. Supp. 1541 (M.D. Fla. 1988); "Judge Rescinds Ruling on Alcoholics," United Press International, August 2, 1988. $100,000 punitive damages after mistaken confrontation of employee who was depressed, not drunk: *Wangen v. Knudsen*, 428 N.W. 2d 242 (S.D. 1988).

129   Not even mention drinking: William C. Symonds, "How to Confront—and Help— an Alcoholic Employee," *Business Week*, March 25, 1991.

130   Climactic confrontation scene: On the threat of job loss as way of getting alcoholics to confront their problem, see, e.g., John B. Miner and J. Frank Brewer, "The Management of Ineffective Performance," in Marvin D. Dunnette, ed., *Handbook of Industrial and Organizational Psychology* (Wiley, 1983), pp. 1015–1016.

130   Coca-Cola Dallas verdict: "Jury Sets $7.1 Million in Damages Against Firm That Fired Alcoholic Worker," *Disability Compliance Bulletin*, August 3, 1995.

131   Judges may adopt the *Whitlock* analysis: Barbara A. Lee, "Reasonable Accommodation Under the ADA: The Limitations of Rehabilitation Act Precedent," 14 *Berkeley Journal of Employment and Labor Law* (1993) 201, 248, footnote 317.

131   Theft, bringing loaded gun to work: *Hindman v. GTE Data Services*, 1994 U.S. Dist. LEXIS 9522 (M.D. Fla.; June 24, 1994); see also *Kupferschmidt v. Runyon*, 827 F. Supp. 570 (E.D. Wis. 1993), involving death threats by an employee.

132   Medical and other licensing boards: Iver Peterson, "New Jersey and New York Want to Monitor Doctors' Past Problems," *New York Times*, August 27, 1992 (cit-

ing estimates that more than 10 percent of New Jersey doctors may have abuse problems); Thomas Scheffey, "Local Cases Bolster ADA-Based Challenges to Bar Examiners," *Connecticut Law Tribune,* December 6, 1993; and *Wall Street Journal* news coverage, including "Bar Application Can't Ask Mental Health History, Group Claims," roundup item, January 16, 1992; "ADA Ruling," October 8, 1993; and Wade Lambert, "Bar Debates Screening Out Mentally Ill," March 10, 1995. A British study based on liver cirrhosis mortality found the medical profession had more than its share of alcoholism, closely trailing the notoriously besotted ranks of "authors, journalists, and related workers." In further confirmations of folk wisdom, the groups with highest indications of alcoholism were tavern proprietors, sailors, and various occupational groups who travel a lot; among the lowest were schoolteachers, construction workers, and farm workers. See Martin A. Plaut, *Drinking Careers* (Tavistock, 1979), pp. 24–25, 33.

133   So-called mental illness: letter by Peter Ross, *Wall Street Journal,* March 28, 1995.

134   Staying on medication: see Freudenheim, "New Law to Bring Wider Job Rights for Mentally Ill" (citing case of business owner trying to determine his rights in dealing with mentally ill worker who refuses to take prescribed medication).

134   Manic-depressive crane operator: Joanne Cleaver, "Lengthening Arm of the ADA: Law's Broad Scope Covers Not-So-Obvious Conditions," *Crain's Chicago Business,* June 13, 1994.

134   One rubric or another: Richard E. Vatz, "Blanket Mental Health Coverage—Crazy," *Wall Street Journal,* April 14, 1993 (quoting Jay Katz). Oppositional Defiant Disorder, etc.: Stuart A. Kirk and Herb Kutchins, "Is Bad Writing a Mental Disorder?" *New York Times,* June 20, 1994. Personality disorders: James J. MacDonald, Jr., Francine B. Kulick, and Myra K. Creighton, "Mental Disabilities under the ADA: A Management Rights Approach," *Employee Relations Law Journal,* March 22, 1995.

135   Get into power struggles: Gary Eisler, "Attention Deficit Disorder Can't Be Ignored," *Wall Street Journal,* June 27, 1994. ADD diagnostic difficulties: Richard E. Vatz, "Attention Deficit Delirium," *Wall Street Journal,* July 27, 1994. Salesman: "Bill Clinton and the ADA" (editorial), *Wall Street Journal,* May 20, 1994. Steve Howe case: John Leo, *Two Steps Ahead of the Thought Police* (Simon & Schuster, 1994), p. 27.

136   Narcolepsy: "Court Revives Discrimination Claim Filed by EPA Worker with Depression," *Government Employee Relations Report* (BNA), November 2, 1992 (*Overton* v. *Reilly,* 7th Circuit, October 22, 1992). Employers setting aside nap space: Edwards, "The ADA and the Employment of Individuals with Mental Disabilities," p. 381. Detroit surgeon case: Daniel Seligman, "Keeping Up," *Fortune,* April 11, 1988.

137   Sensitivity training as reasonable accommodation: MacDonald, Kulick, & Creighton, "Mental Disabilities Under the ADA," citing *Kent* v. *Derwinski,* 790 F. Supp. 1032 (E.D. Wash. 1991). Slightest hint of rejection or criticism: *Pesterfield* v. *TVA,* 941 F. 2d 437 (6th Cir. 1991). May respond better in a supportive environment: Stevens, "Boss's Brain Teaser: Accommodating Depressed Worker."

137   Habit of throwing furniture: *Mozzarella* v. *United States Postal Service,* 849 F. Supp.

89 (D. Mass. 1994) (Rehab Act claim). Postal worker in Portland: *Lussier* v. *Runyon,* D. Me., March 1, 1994; the case then proceeded to extended litigation on the question whether Lussier's front-pay damage award, which totaled in the hundreds of thousands of dollars, should be offset by the amount of the disability payments he would instead be collecting from the government.

137   Florida judge failed: "Supreme Court Rejects Appeal, Ousts Garrett," *Fort Lauderdale Sun-Sentinel,* March 10, 1993. Maine prof's addiction: David G. Savage, "Fired 'Sexual Addict' Loses His Bid to Get Teaching Job Back," *Los Angeles Times,* May 3, 1994. BU prof's loosened inhibitions: "Court Rejects Fired Professor's Claim," *Massachusetts Lawyers Weekly,* June 24, 1996. Northwestern prof's procrastination: George Papajohn and John Lucadamo, "Prof Says He's Not Dishonest, Just Disabled," *Chicago Tribune,* February 19, 1993.

138   Golden age of exoneration, Pete Rose, Richard Berendzen, caffeine, steroids cases: John Leo, *Two Steps Ahead of the Thought Police,* pp. 24–28. Failure-to-file syndrome: James W. Wetzler & Scott Wetzler, "Enforcement, Not Prozac, for Nonfilers," *New York Law Journal,* March 7, 1994. Weight gain and depressed mood: "Judge Reduces Sentence for FBI Agent-Turned-Spy," Reuters, May 5, 1994. A crime to have epileptic spells: John Money, "Law and Order Is No Cure for Sex 'Crimes,'" *Newsday,* November 24, 1992. Brain shrinkage: Rajiv Chandrasekaran and Bill Miller, "Aramony's Defense Strategy Called Creative but Risky," *Washington Post,* March 8, 1995. Attack on chauffeur: Robin Estrin, "Judge Acquits Man Who Stopped Medication," Associated Press, March 16, 1995.

139   Duxbury firefighter: see Don Aucoin, "MCAD Reverses Itself, Overturns Bias Ruling," *Boston Globe,* April 6, 1993 (quoting Jerrold Levinsky and Jane Alper); Don Aucoin, "After Battering, Woman Fights Fears, Reclaims Her Life," *Boston Globe,* April 8, 1993 (quoting Carol Zoroya); Susan Roberts Boyle, "Appeal Taken of Handicap Ruling," *Massachusetts Lawyers Weekly,* October 28, 1991.

Chapter 8. Surprise Farewells

Page

141   Even in their thirties: see Ruth Simon, "When to Accept—or to Reject—an Early-Retirement Deal," *Money,* February 1993 (profiling IBM employee who took "early retirement" buyout at age 39). One survey found average lump sum $38,000: Charles Brown, "Early Retirement Windows: Windows of Opportunity? Defenestrations?" (University of Michigan and National Bureau of Economic Research working paper, November 1993.)

142   General Motors voucher: Fran Hawthorne, "Rigging the Early-Retirement Game," *Institutional Investor,* May 1993.

142   Some people complain: Author's interview with Judith McMorrow, Boston College Law School.

143   Decline of longevity awards: Alex Markels and Joann S. Lublin, "Longevity-Reward Programs Get Short Shrift," *Wall Street Journal,* April 27, 1995.

143 Not a suspect class needing extraordinary protection: *Massachusetts Board of Retirement v. Murgia,* 427 U.S. 307 (1976); the case challenged a law on judges' retirement.

144 It would be mad: Richard Posner, *Aging and Old Age* (Chicago, 1995), p. 320.

145 Age not given proper consideration: *Kyriazi v. Western Electric,* 476 F. Supp. 335 (D. N.J. 1979), (citing inconsistent employer practice). Pay cut, reporting to junior: *Guthrie v. Tifco Industries,* 941 F. 2d 374 (5th Cir. 1991).

146 Most older workers not subject to mandatory retirement policies: Malcolm H. Morrison, "Changes in the Legal Mandatory Retirement Age: Labor Force Participation Implications," in Rita Ricardo-Campbell and Edward P. Lazear, eds., *Issues in Contemporary Retirement* (Hoover Institution Press, 1988), p. 378 (citing Department of Labor study that predicted no significant increase in labor force participation from banning such private policies).

147 Japanese practice: see Steven G. Allen, "Discussion," in Ricardo-Campbell and Lazear, eds., *Issues in Contemporary Retirement,* p. 301 (employment rates for older men in Japan unusually high by world standards, though "almost all firms in Japan have mandatory retirement between the ages of 55 and 60"). Link between high pay and abbreviated tenure: Ezra Vogel, *Japan as Number One* (Harvard, 1979), p. 140. On the Japanese contract-after-55 system, see also Edward P. Lazear, "Why Is There Mandatory Retirement?" 87 *Journal of Political Economy* 1261 (1979), citing an unpublished paper by M. Hashimoto, 1977, University of Washington.

147 An individual option: S. Rep. No. 493 on the Age Discrimination in Employment Act Amendments of 1978, PL 95-256, 95th Congress, reprinted in 1978 U.S. *Code Cong. & Ad. News* 504, 506.

148 Something to get up for: Jill Lawrence, "House Votes to End Mandatory Retirement," Associated Press, September 24, 1986 (quoting Rep. Claude Pepper). Necessity for collective survival: Rod Angove, Associated Press, September 19, 1977 (quoting Gov. Jerry Brown).

149 Deluge of cases: Thomas J. Lueck, "Job-Loss Anger: Age Bias Cases Soar in Region," *New York Times,* December 12, 1993 (quoting Leonard Flamm).

149 Ernst & Young case: Mike Boyer, "Court Upholds Claim Against Ernst & Young," *Cincinnati Enquirer,* September 27, 1994. McDonnell-Douglas case: Mike Dorning, "Fired Older Workers Sue on Bias, and Win: More Cases and Richer Awards," *Chicago Tribune,* May 29, 1994. IDS case: Barbara Dewey, Financial Firm to Pay $35 Million to Settle Age Discrimination Suit," Associated Press, August 27, 1992. Most dangerous to take to trial: Thomas J. Piskorski, "The Growing Judicial Acceptance of Summary Judgment in Age Discrimination Cases," *Employee Relations Law Journal,* September 22, 1992.

149 Juries of older persons: E. Richard Larson, *Sue Your Boss* (Farrar, Straus & Giroux, 1981), p. 95. Plays well to younger jurors, too: see, e.g., Milo Geyelin, "Age-Bias Cases Found to Bring Big Jury Awards," *Wall Street Journal,* December 17, 1993.

150 Typical to say they would have worked till they drop: Allen Fagin, attorney with Proskauer, Rose, Goetz & Mendelsohn, interview with author.

150 Five years difference enough for prima facie case: *Douglas v. Anderson,* 656 F. 2d

528, 533 (9th Cir. 1981); but even replacement by an older employee is not necessarily a safe harbor.

151 "Get up and go": *Blackwell* v. *Sun Electric,* 696 F. 2d 1176 (6th Cir. 1983). Wasn't keeping up with the times: "Million-Dollar Verdict Slapped on Kodak," *Iowa Employment Law Letter,* August 1996. "Wavelength": *McCoy* v. *WGN Continental Bdctg. Co.,* 957 F. 2d 368, 372, fn 3 (7th Cir. 1992). "New blood," "deadwood," etc: *Buckley* v. *Hospital Corp. of America,* 758 F. 2d 1525 (11th Cir. 1985); *Karlen* v. *City Colleges of Chicago,* 837 F. 2d 314 (7th Cir. 1987). See Judith McMorrow, book review, 12 *Industrial Relations Law Journal* 197 (1990) at footnote 21 (such phrases "almost guarantee that a defendant will be unable to get summary judgment"). "Overqualified" as code word: *Taggart* v. *Time, Inc.,* 924 F. 2d 43 (2d Cir. 1991). Later decisions limited the damage somewhat for employers: see *Binder* v. *LILCO,* 933 F. 2d 187 (2d Cir. 1991), where a rule against overqualified applicants is ruled OK if adopted in good faith and enforced consistently, but the employer is denied summary judgment in the case at hand; *Bay* v. *Times Mirror Magazines,* 936 F. 2d 112 (2d Cir. 1991), where a rejection as overqualified is held suspect if "conclusory" and unsupported by evidence. Van Gordon Sauter episode: "Veteran Reporter Sues Fox for Age Discrimination," Reuters, August 15, 1994. "Dynamic," "aggressive" as code words: see Brian Bulger and Carolyn Gessner, "Sign of the Times: Implementing Reductions in Force," *Employee Relations Law Journal,* December 22, 1991. Employers may find themselves in equally hot water, though, if they appear to count "aggressiveness" against an employee. See "Goldman Sachs Trial Begins," roundup item, *Wall Street Journal,* October 8, 1993; (the lawyer in a sex bias case whose client had been termed "aggressive" charges that such are "gender words").

151 Higher cost of older worker no excuse: see *Geller* v. *Markham,* 635 F. 2d 1027 (2d Cir. 1980); *cert. denied,* 451 U.S. 945 (1981). Supreme Court casts doubt: *Hazen Paper Co.* v. *Biggins,* 506 U.S. 604 (1993). Lower-cost replacements: "LCI Ex-Executives Awarded $7.2 Million in Discrimination Suit," *Wall Street Journal,* October 28, 1993. Ordinary businessman trying to save a buck: Geyelin, "Age Bias Cases Found to Bring Big Jury Awards" (quoting Leonard Flamm).

151 The main action shifted: One survey found two-thirds of age cases arose from terminations and only 10 percent from hirings (Posner, *Aging and Old Age,* p. 330–31.) Other surveys have found even more lopsided margins.

152 Age-balancing the RIF: *Matras* v. *Amoco,* 424 Mich. 675, 686 (1986).

152 Frustrating humanitarian layoff policies: *EEOC* v. *Altoona,* 723 F. 2d 4 (3d Cir. 1983); *EEOC* v. *Borden's,* 724 F. 2d 1390 (9th Cir. 1984).

153 Ought to weed out incompetents: press release from office of Rep. Claude Pepper, October 11, 1977, quoted in Matthew Finkin, "Tenure After an Uncapped ADEA: A Different View," 15 *Journal of College and University Law* 43, 51 at footnote 32 (1988).

154 Elite professors: Eliot Marshall, "NRC Panel: Abolish Mandatory Retirement," *Science,* May 31, 1991. Steady-state projections: Richard E. Epstein and Saunders MacLane, "Keep Mandatory Retirement for Tenured Faculty," *Regulation,* Spring 1991. Academic criticism: William H. Honan, "New Law Against Age Bias on Cam-

pus Clogs Academic Pipeline, Critics Say," *New York Times,* June 15, 1994 (quoting Oscar Handlin and Jeremy Knowles).

155   Stanford's buyout plan: Paul Wallich and Elizabeth Corcoran, "The Analytical Economist: Golden Handshakes, Golden Handcuffs," *Scientific American,* April 1991.

155   Polaroid "pandemonium": Thomas Watterson, "Bills May Threaten Early-Retirement Plans," *Chicago Tribune,* April 22, 1990 (reprinted from *Boston Globe*). Driving out more than planned: Wallich and Corcoran: "The Analytical Economist." Chicago post office: Jonathan Franzen, "Lost in the Mail," *New Yorker,* October 24, 1994. NYC teachers: Sarah Kershaw, "New York Buyouts Could Leave Gaps In Teaching Ranks," *New York Times,* July 26, 1995, and Jacques Steinberg, "Buyouts Leave School Board Racing to Fill 3,000 Jobs," *New York Times,* July 29, 1996.

155   Need to rehire after buyout: see, e.g., Fran Hawthorne, "Rigging the Early-Retirement Game" (Lockheed).

156   We're actuaries: Author interview with William Miner, consultant, Wyatt Company. Cosmic waiver: *EEOC* v. *American Express Publ. Co.,* 681 F. Supp. 216 (S.D.N.Y. 1988).

156   Almost anything you say: author interview with Allen Fagin, attorney, Proskauer, Rose, Goetz & Mendelsohn. On the incentives for supervisors to withhold information and candid advice, see Judith McMorrow, "Retirement and Worker Choice: Incentives to Retire and the Age Discrimination in Employment Act," 29 *B.C.L. Rev.* 347, 376–367 (1988).

156   Permanent fixture: Neil H. Abramson, "Early Retirement Incentives Under the ADEA," 11 *Industrial Relations Law Journal* 323 (1989). Built into employee expectations: Author interview with economist Finis Welch, Texas A & M. Jim Mullins case: Jonathan Rabinowitz, "Connecticut Man Who Missed Buyout Prevails in Court," *New York Times,* October 22, 1995.

157   All retirement is "early": Wallich and Corcoran, "The Analytical Economist."

Chapter 9. The Excuse Factory

Page

161   New Haven case: Robert A. Frahm, "Penalty Reduced for Teacher in Mastery Test Cheating Case," *Hartford Courant,* July 27, 1994 (quoting arbitrator Tim Bornstein, Lorraine Aronson, and Patricia McCann-Vissepo).

162   Teacher that no one has been able to fire: James Litke, "Teacher Admits to Being 'Part of Problem' in Beleaguered Public Schools," Associated Press, May 20, 1988 (quoting principal Dyanne Dandridge-Alexander).

162   New York City cases: Sam Dillon, "Teacher Tenure: Rights Vs. Discipline," *New York Times,* June 28, 1994.

162   Overview of arbitration: Adolph Koven and Susan L. Smith, *Just Cause: The Seven Tests* (Coloracre, 1985); (hereafter "K & S").

163   Waterbury principal: AP dispatch, *Norwalk Hour,* December 23, 1994. Ridgefield teacher: "There's Still Safety in the Blackboard Jungle," *Connecticut Law Tribune,*

July 31, 1995; *Sekor v. Capwell,* 889 F. Supp. 34 (D. Conn. 1995). The other cases were covered in the *Manchester Journal-Inquirer* and assembled by its managing editor, Chris Powell, as follows: South Windsor police: Karen A. Gleason, "Fired Police Officer to Get Job Back," April 30, 1994. Ticket-fixing: "O'Neill Lets State Workers get away with a lot" (editorial), April 26, 1982. Police dispatcher: Andrew P. Nelson, "Dispatcher Charged with Padding Hours," June 27, 1991; "Police Ordered to Reinstate EH Dispatcher," February 24, 1992; and "Kniep Challenges Dispatcher's Reinstatement," February 26, 1992. Dumbwaiter injury: John Pallato, "Veterans Home Guards Reinstated," April 23, 1982. Toll-taker and orphanage bookkeeper cases: "Even Stealing is OK" (editorial), October 5, 1988; Mary Darby, "DOT's Burns Defends Late Theft Report," October 17, 1988; and "Firing DOT Employee Might Have Failed," letter to the editor from transportation commissioner J. William Burns, October 12, 1988.

165   Fundamental assumption that employee owns the job: Clyde Summers, "Unjust Dismissal," 62 *Virginia Law Review* 481, 506 (1976).

165   Bouncing the sleeper: R. M. Kaus, "The Trouble with Unions," *Harper's,* June 1983, pp. 30–31.

165   Friend called in a bomb threat: *Eastern Associated Coal Co.,* 66 LA 1063 (1976), cited at K & S, p. 224.

165   Transit indecency: *Phila. Transportation Co.,* 49 LA 606 (no date given), cited at K & S, p. 376. Should have confronted on-the-job drinker: *Industrial Plastics Corp.,* 58 LA 546 (1972), cited at K & S, p. 348. Hardline arbitrators unwilling to permit firing unless all intermediate steps have been tried and are sure to be futile if tried again: K & S, pp. 349–350. Various colorful arbitration fact patterns can be found in Roger I. Abrams and Dennis R. Nolan, "Towards a Theory of 'Just Cause' in Employee Discipline Cases," 1985 *Duke Law Journal* 594, including *Central Soya,* 74 LA 1084, 1090 (1980), involving a death threat against a foreman; *Ralston Purina,* 75 LA 313 (1980), a bomb threat; *Allied Aviation Service,* 77 LA 455, 458 (1981), a threat to blow up aircraft; and *ITT Continental Baking,* 75 LA 764, 768–70 (1980), verbal abuse and spraying the supervisor with a high-pressure water hose.

166   Looked upon the lots as sanctuaries: *Lockheed,* 75 LA 1081, cited at K & S, p. 65.

166   Reasonableness as determined by labor relations community: K & S p. 74. Social Security TV sets: K & S, pp. 86–87. Wisconsin cemetery case: *City of Racine,* 68 LA 473 (1977), cited at K & S, p. 94.

167   Fire driver and boating fatality: *City of Shawnee, Okla.,* 91 LA 93 (Allen, 1988), cited in Daniel H. Kruger and Michael McEachern, "An Analysis of Arbitration Decisions Involving Off-Duty Conduct of Public Employees," 14 *Government Union Review* 29 (Fall 1993).

167   Completely unrelated to his job: "Court Ruling Helped Pilot Avoid FAA Scrutiny," Associated Press, March 25, 1990.

168   Failure to make progress over substantial period of time: see Janet Maleson Spencer, "The Developing Notion of Employer Responsibility for the Alcoholic, Drug-Addicted or Mentally Ill Employee: An Examination Under Federal and State Employment Statutes and Arbitration Decisions," 53 *St. John's Law Review* 659, 701 (1979), quoting arbitrator Lewis Kesselman. Spencer writes (p. 697) that "It has

been well established that arbitration decisions tend to reverse discharges of mentally ill and alcoholic employees." Study found only a quarter of reinstated alcoholics improved: John B. Miner and J. Frank Brewer, "The Management of Ineffective Performance," in Marvin D. Dunnette, ed., *Handbook of Industrial and Organizational Psychology* (Wiley, 1983), pp. 995, 1015–1016.

168   "Compassionate" arbitrators recognize worker is not responsible: Marcia Greenbaum, "The 'Disciplinator,' the 'Arbichiatrist' and the 'Social Psychotrator,'" 37 *Arbitration Journal* 51 (December 1982) Sara Lee case, helpless to prevent what he did: *Consolidated Foods,* 58 LA 1285 (1972), involving threats, slander, insubordination, and "vulgar and abusive language"; cited in George T. Roumell, Jr., "Mental Illness, the Workplace and Grievance Arbitration," *Michigan Bar Journal* 758 (September 1983). Some hope of recovery: Roumell, "Mental Illness," p. 763. Paranoia, reinstated in hopes treatment would be successful: *Amoco Oil,* 61 LA 10 (1973), cited at K & S, p. 217. Schizophrenic remission: *National Steel,* 66 LA 533 (Traynor 1976), cited in Roumell, "Mental Illness."

168   Roughhousing with a jackknife, etc.: *Standard-Knapp,* 50 LA 833 (1968). Telephone operator outbursts: *Jamestown Telephone,* 61 LA 121 (1973).

168   Seized substance, lab technicians: *Babcock & Wilcox,* 60 LA 778 (1972), cited at K & S, p. 235. Shooting bartender: *Par Beverage Co.,* 35 LA 77 (1960), cited at K & S, p. 242–243. From the *Par Beverage* arbitrator's opinion at p. 80, on a review of earlier arbitrations: "The one consistent factor in almost all of the cases reviewed was that the arrest and/or indictment for the commission of a crime was not sufficient to justify discharge."

169   Back pay awarded despite theft conviction because management had charged only obstruction of investigation: *Hollytex Carpet Mills,* 79-1 ARB para. 8181 (1979), cited at K & S, p. 205.

169   East Bay sick leave: *Alameda/Contra Costa Transit,* 76 LA 770 (1981), cited at K & S, p. 211.

169   Triumph of analogy: K & S, p. 328, quoting arbitrator Benjamin Aaron, "Some Procedural Problems in Arbitration," 10 *Vanderbilt Law Review* 740 (1957), calling "economic capital punishment" notion "the historic conquest of common sense by rhetoric." Ten going free: K & S, p. 231 (quoting William Blackstone). Arbitrators at pains to deny analogy with criminal due process: K & S, p. 159.

170   Alcohol level 0.14: *Northrop Worldwide Aviation Services,* 64 LA 742 (1975), cited at K & S, p. 63. Second offense, not first: *Zapata Industries,* 76 LA 467, 472 (1981), cited at K & S, p. 339.

170   Union shop steward hadn't been present: *NLRB v. J. Weingarten,* 420 U.S. 251 (1975). Tricked, coerced, or misled into confessions: Julius Getman, "What Price Employment? Arbitration, The Constitution, and Personal Freedom," in Alan F. Westin and Stephan Salisbury, *Individual Rights in the Corporation: A Reader on Employee Rights* (Pantheon, 1980), p. 282. See also Eva Robins, "Unfair Dismissal: Emerging Trends in the Use of Arbitration as a Dispute Resolution Alternative for the Nonunion Workforce," 12 *Fordham Urban Law Journal* 437 (1984); a list of 15 arbitration just-cause standards includes "Was the employee provoked into adverse

behavior?" Reinstating employee though misconduct was established: K & S, p. 162.

171 Didn't snap a photo: K & S, p. 162. Too many warnings in brief span improper "building of record": K & S, p. 369.

171 Every job handled high explosives: *Silas Mason Co.,* 59 LA 200 (1972), cited in Roumell, "Mental Illness." Outburst in cardiac wing: *Connecticut Law Tribune,* January 24, 1994, p. 8A. Even after he slugged a foreman: Richard Vigilante, *Strike: The Daily News War and the Future of American Labor* (Simon & Schuster, 1994), p. 64 (quoting Jerry Cronin).

172 Eighty-four steps to fire Chicago park worker: "Work Week," *Wall Street Journal,* December 6, 1994. Boston's four stages in the 1970s: Harry Wellington and Ralph Winter, *The Unions and the Cities* (Brookings, 1971), p. 158.

172 High cost of ousting teachers in New York and New Jersey: Dillon, "Teacher Tenure: Rights Vs. Discipline." Michigan investigation: Joan Richardson and Margaret Timer-Hartley, "Shielding Bad Teachers," *Detroit Free Press,* March 25–27, 1992 (quoting Dansville principal Roger Pollock) and related coverage by Brenda Gilchrist (quoting Eileen Rodak and Linda Stewart). This investigative series was the source for numerous Michigan examples cited in this chapter.

172 100 D.C. cops reinstated a year: Tucker Carlson, "D.C. Blues: The Rap Sheet on the Washington Police," *Policy Review,* Winter 1993. Endless maze, may go on forever: Judy Rakowsky, "Bad Apples' Sour Police Commissioner; Calls Cambridge Discipline Too Slow," *Boston Globe,* January 31, 1993 (quoting Perry Anderson).

173 Pleaded guilty to possession of child pornography: Larry Oakes, "UMD Paid Prof in Pornography Case $75,000 As He Left," *Minneapolis Star-Tribune,* November 29, 1989, quoted in Ian Maitland, "How the University of Minnesota Was Subverted by Litigation," *Academic Questions,* Winter 1992–93.

173 Practice of civil service law more onerous than letter: Gerald Frug, "Does the Constitution Prevent the Discharge of Civil Service Employees?" 124 *University of Pennsylvania Law Review* 942, 943–946 (1976).

174 Alaska oil rigs: *Sanders* v. *Parker Drilling Co.,* 911 F. 2d 191 (9th Cir. 1990).

176 Not civil service or Europe yet, but might look that way: Christopher Farrell et al., "The Scary Math of New Hires," *Business Week,* February 22, 1993 (quoting Gary Burtless).

Chapter 10. Dropping the Stretcher

Page

177 Houston test saga: Eric Hanson, "Firefighters See Red as Scores on Promotion Exam Changed," *Houston Chronicle,* October 3, 1991. See also John Williams, "Council Settles 18-Year-Old Lawsuit: City Boosts HPD Minority Promotions," *Houston Chronicle,* February 4, 1993 (Houston police department agrees in settlement to discard questions with more than 20 percent differential.)

179 A scrap of paper: Specific language in the 1964 act (42 USC s. 2000e-2[h]) declared

it lawful for employers "to give and to act upon the results of any professionally developed ability test provided that such test, its administration or action upon the results is not designed, intended, or used to discriminate because of race, color, religion, sex or national origin." See *Guardians Association* v. *New York,* 630 F. 2d 79, 89–90 (2d Cir. 1980) (*Guardians IV*), doubting that Congress could have intended sweeping ban on all testing for any but the most rudimentary skill, as plaintiffs' experts had requested.

180 Uniform Guidelines, "acceptable" job proficiency: 29 CFR s. 1607.H. New York City cutoff still too high: *Guardians IV* at 105. Pass-fail versus ranking: 29 CFR s. 1607.5G.

180 Opponents defeat tests by showing they fall short of perfect predictive power: see also Mark Kelman, "Concepts of Discrimination in 'General Ability' Job Testing." 104 *Harvard Law Review* 1158, 1217 (1991) (test should be unlawful if it has a significant chance of ranking any two candidates incorrectly with respect to each other).

181 Exceedingly difficult: Barbara Schlei and Paul Grossman, *Employment Discrimination Law* (Bureau of National Affairs, 1976), p. 102. *Walls* v. *Miss. State Dept. of Public Welfare,* 542 F. Supp. 281 (N.D. Miss. 1982). *aff'd* 730 F. 2d 306 (5th Cir. 1984) (testing of grammar, spelling, punctuation for clerk typist jobs not validated despite substantial study). Agility of police applicants: *Blake* v. *Los Angeles,* 595 F. 2d 1367 (9th Cir. 1979). Tests have generally failed to survive when courts apply EEOC guidelines: A. Larson and L. Larson, *Employment Discrimination,* s. 75.32 (Matthew Bender, 1981), quoted at Thomas O. McGarity and Elinor P. Schroeder, "Risk-Oriented Employment Screening," 59 *Texas Law Review* 999, 1034 (1981). In 1973 a federal court observed that so far as it could determine, EEOC had never actually given its approval to any employer's use of any test anywhere in the country: *Henderson* v. *First National Bank,* 360 F. Supp. 531, 545 (M.D. Ala. 1973).

181 Extreme factual skepticism: Kelman, "Concepts of Discrimination," 104 *Harvard Law Review* 1158, 1190 (1991).

181 Women's upper-body strength: Charles Moskos, "Army Women," *The Atlantic,* August 1990.

182 Hot-button comparison with literacy tests: Susan Blank, "Women Firefighters: Can They Do the Job?" *Civil Liberties,* Summer 1984, pp. 7–8 (quoting Isabelle Katz Pinzler).

182 Ann Brunet case: *Brunet* v. *Columbus,* 642 F. Supp. 1214 (S.D. Ohio 1986). The city's use of multiple-choice testing as an important component of scoring might itself had fallen victim to a disparate-impact challenge from black applicants had a court not already ordered the city to set aside half its firefighting jobs for blacks. On courts' rejection of ranking, see also Patrick O. Patterson, "Employment Testing and Title VII of the Civil Rights Act of 1964," in Bernard R. Gifford, ed., *Test Policy and the Politics of Opportunity Allocation: The Workplace and the Law* (National Commission on Testing and Public Policy, 1989), p. 120 (courts and enforcement agencies "nearly unanimous" in requiring pass-fail when disputes have arisen).

183 Heart or kidney failure: When Boston put firefighting recruits through a test designed to push them to the edge of their physical capacities, twelve were hospitalized with kidney failure, and two nearly died.

184   Some say speed is critical, some not, Lauren Howard quote: Anne Zusy, "For
      Women Who Fight Fires, Acceptance and Frustrations," *New York Times*, October
      12, 1987. After Kinneary's decision Columbus settled with Brunet's lawyers, agree-
      ing to adopt pass-fail and hire women proportionally among those who passed.
      Four men then sued charging reverse discrimination, and they fared better than
      men usually do in such suits; in 1992 a federal court struck down the settlement.
      But the city had still not received (and might never be sure of receiving) the go-
      ahead to use any particular test. See 1 F. 3d 390 (6th Cir. 1993).

185   Los Angeles testing: Zusy, "For Women Who Fight Fires." New York exam passed
      by "nearly everyone": E. R. Shipp, "Ruling Could Curtail Hiring More Women in
      Fire Department," *New York Times*, April 14, 1987. On other cities' exams, see K. L.
      Billingsley, "Status Quota," *Heterodoxy*, February 1995, and Paul Ciotti, "Backdraft
      in the S.F.F.D.: The Fire This Time," *Heterodoxy*, February 1996.

185   Out-of-shape cops: John Connolly, "New York's Fattest," *New York*, June 13, 1994.
      See also Associated Press, AP Online, January 9, 1995 (citing *New York Post* report
      that more than one in five city cops are seriously out of shape.) Tearing down LAPD
      wall: Michelle Malkin, "Lowering Barriers, Literally," *American Experiment* (Center
      for Equal Opportunity), Summer 1995.

185   Bad aim: Wendell Jamieson, "No Cop Bullseye: Cops Shot More, Hit Less Last Year,"
      Newsday, June 23, 1994; Daniel Seligman, "Keeping Up: Target Practice in Pitts-
      burgh," *Fortune*, July 4, 1988 (quoting report in *Pittsburgh Post-Gazette*).

186   NYC sanitation-job lottery: Deirdre Carmody, "Two Female Sanitation Workers
      Earning High Marks," *New York Times*, January 31, 1987; Shipp, "Ruling Could
      Curtail Hiring"; William Murphy, "Sanitation's Perfect Quiz; 98 percent pass phys-
      ical test," *Newsday*, March 25, 1992 (quoting Edward Ostrowski).

186   Collapsing in stages: The tension between female and minority candidates' de-
      mands turned up in many cases. Thus in a leading firefighting case feminist litiga-
      tors alleged that a written test had been made too *easy: Berkman* v. *City of New York*,
      536 F. Supp. 177 (1982); 580 F. Supp. 226 (E.D.N.Y. 1983); 626 F. Supp. 591
      (E.D.N.Y. 1985).

186   Foreign Service flounderings: James Workman, "Gender Norming," *New Republic*,
      July 1, 1991. Arithmetic and algebra among first topics pitched from federal civil
      service exam: Nathan Glazer, *Affirmative Discrimination* (Basic Books, 1975), pp.
      54–55.

187   Part credit for guessing right the second time: William Murphy, "Firefighter Test
      Has Union Burning," *Newsday*, May 30, 1992. Whipsawed: Selwyn Raab, "City
      Aide Calls Police Test Too Easy," *New York Times*, July 12, 1985 (quoting Juan Or-
      tiz). Dart-throwing sufficed: *Hammon* v. *Barry*, 813 F. 2d 412 (D.C.Cir. 1987).

187   Psychological stability of security guards: *Soroka* v. *Dayton Hudson*, 235 Cal. App.
      3d 654 (1991).

188   New York bar exam accommodation: Gary Spencer, "Appeals Rules Required for
      Bar Applicants," *New York Law Journal*, August 5, 1992. Learning-disabled teacher-
      to-be: *Pandazides* v. *Virginia Bd. of Educ.*, 946 F. 2d 345 (4th Cir. 1991).

188   SAT accommodation demands: Tamar Lewin, "For Learning Disabled, New Help
      With College," *New York Times*, Education Life, January 8, 1995.

189   No longer federal typing tests: C. Boyden Gray and Evan J. Kemp, "Flunking Testing: Is Too Much Fairness Unfair To School Kids?" *Washington Post,* September 19, 1993. Santa Cruz secretaries: Robert F. Adams, "Economic Models of Discrimination, Testing, and Public Policy," in Gifford, ed., *Test Policy and the Politics of Opportunity Allocation,* p. 191, at p. 204.

189   Supreme Court decisions upholding: A key case was *U.S. v. South Carolina,* 434 U.S. 1026 (1978), summarily approving the use of the National Teachers' Examination and rebuffing the position of federal enforcers that the state should give no test at all and instead accept anyone who had made it through a teacher training program. The decision cast doubt on a string of 1970s cases in which lower courts had struck down use of the NTE. See Michael A. Rebell, "Disparate Impact of Teacher Competency Testing on Minorities: Don't Blame the Test-Takers—or the Tests," 4 *Yale Law & Policy Review* 375 (1986). Another decision signaling a changed mood came when the Second Circuit upheld a reformulated New York test for firefighters, an earlier one having been struck down; the court sent advocates into a tizzy by pronouncing the need for strength and speed in firefighting to be obvious and self-evident. Courts in other circuits, of course, were not bound by the ruling. See Shipp, "Ruling Could Curtail Hiring."

190   Flunking teacher reinstated: *Richardson* v. *Lamar County Board of Education,* 729 F. Supp. 806 (M.D. Ala. 1989).

191   Flipping a coin: Darien McWhirter, *Your Rights at Work* (Wiley, 1989), p. 85.

Chapter 11. The New Meaning of Competence

Page

192   Sources on police woes include extensive *Washington Post* coverage: Tucker Carlson, "D.C. Blues: The Rap Sheet on the Washington Police," *Policy Review,* Winter 1993 (murder cases dropped for paperwork deficiencies, "routine" hiring of those with misdemeanor records, "Hire them now" [quoting then-police chief Isaac Falwood, Jr.]); Harry S. Jaffe and Tom Sherwood, *Dream City* (Simon & Schuster, 1994); William McGowan, "The Corrupt Influence of Policy Diversity Hiring," *Wall Street Journal,* June 29, 1994 (10 percent of Miami force accused); Daniel Seligman, "Keeping Up—Only in America (Cont'd)," *Fortune,* April 20, 1992 (reprinting *Boston Globe* account quoting Robert Healy); Judy Rakowsky, "'Bad Apples' Sour Police Commissioner; Calls Cambridge Discipline Too Slow," *Boston Globe,* January 31, 1993.

193   Improve the total national economy: On the history of arguments that Title VII advances efficiency and productivity, see Paulette M. Caldwell, "Reaffirming the Disproportionate Effects Standard of Liability in Title VII Litigation," 46 *U. Pitt. L.R.* 555, 580–583 (1985); for an attempt to salvage the theoretical case, see John J. Donohue III, "Is Title VII Efficient?" 134 *U. Pa. L. Rev.* 1411, 1423–31 (1986).

194   University of Minnesota: George R. LaNoue and Barbara A. Lee, *Academics in Court: The Consequences of Faculty Discrimination Litigation* (Michigan, 1987), p.

184 (citing exhibit in *Rajender* trial). Cases from federal hiring: ABC-TV "20/20," Nov. 18, 1994.

195　Early deference on safety: see, e.g., *Spurlock* v. *United Airlines,* 475 F. 2d 216, 219 (10th Cir. 1972), ruling a college degree requirement OK when hazards of unqualified applicant are obvious. Deaf nurse: *Southeastern Comm. Coll.* v. *Davis,* 442 U.S. 397 (1979). Hesitance on applying the new doctrines to high-level jobs can be found in such early articles as Lawrence E. Blades, "Employment at Will Vs. Individual Freedom: On Limiting the Abusive Exercise of Employer Power," 67 *Columbia L.R.* 1404, 1428–9 (1967), arguing that more employer discretion must be granted in case of high-level executives; and in pioneering decisions such as *Pugh* v. *See's Candies,* 116 Cal. App. 3d 311, 330 (1980) (Grodin, J.: when employee holds a "sensitive managerial or confidential position, the employer must of necessity be allowed substantial scope for the exercise of subjective judgment"). Parallel ideas can be observed in labor law (excluding managerial and some professional workers) and civil service rules exempting "policymaking" positions.

195　High-level jobs: Elizabeth Bartholet, "Application of Title VII to Jobs in High Places," 95 *Harvard L.R.* 945 (1982). Inexplicable deference on public safety: Thomas O. McGarity and Elinor P. Schroeder, "Risk-Oriented Employment Screening," 59 *Texas Law Review* 999, 1042 (1981).

195　Must prove substantial risk: *Sch. Bd. Nassau County* v. *Arline,* 480 U.S. 273 (1987).

196　Existing back condition cases: *Sterling Transit Co.* v. *Calif. Fair Empl. C.,* 121 Cal. App. 3d 791, 798 (1981); *Johnson* v. *Civil Service Commission,* 153 Cal. App. 3d 585, 591 (1984); *E.E. Black, Ltd.* v. *Marshall,* 497 F. Supp. 1088 (D. Haw. 1980).

196　Safety defense very difficult in any but most extreme cases: Barbara A. Lee, "Reasonable Accommodation Under the ADA: The Limitations of Rehabilitation Act Precedent," 14 *Berkeley Journal of Employment and Labor Law* 1993, p. 230. Not just elevated risk, but substantial, direct, case-by-case only, etc.: see, e.g., Laurence O. Gostin, "Public Health Powers: The Imminence of Radical Change," in Jane West, ed., *The Americans with Disabilities Act: From Policy to Practice* (Milbank Memorial Fund, 1991), p. 278, and sources cited there; Stephanie Simon, "Warning Patients of HIV-Positive Doctor," *Wall Street Journal,* August 2, 1991.

197　Bank officers must be severable at will: Paul Tobias, Robert Fitzpatrick, and David Torchia, *Litigating Wrongful Discharge Claims* (Callaghan, 1987) 2:96 (2, 271–2), citing National Bank Act.

197　UCLA surgeon: Lawrence Altman, "The Doctor's World; Investigating a Medical Maze: Virus Transmission in Surgery," *New York Times,* March 22, 1994. Seen through the lens: Gostin, "Public Health Powers," in West, ed., *The ADA: From Policy to Practice,* p. 269.

197　No issue has broader or more passionate support: Frederick Nesbitt, testimony before Senate Labor and Human Resources Committee, April 19, 1994.

198　New York buses: Lawrence Goodman, "Bus Drivers with a License to Kill," *New York Post,* May 8, 1995.

199　American Eagle crash: Matthew L. Wald, "Board Blames Pilot for Commuter Crash," *New York Times,* October 25, 1995 (quoting James E. Hall).

199 *Detroit Free Press* investigation: Joan Richardson and Margaret Trimer-Hartley, "Shielding Bad Teachers," *Detroit Free Press*, March 25–27, 1992.

200 Two-thirds of crimes at fast-food restaurants: Laurie Grossman, "Fast-Food Industry Is Slow to Take Action Against Growing Crime," *Wall Street Journal*, September 22, 1994. Survey on crimes by guards themselves: "Risky Business," roundup item, *Wall Street Journal*, September 13, 1994, p. 1. Employee theft costs $120 billion a year. "Work Week," *Wall Street Journal*, February 6, 1996. See also John R. Emshwiller, "Small Business Is the Biggest Victim of Theft by Employees, Survey Shows," *Wall Street Journal*, October 2, 1995 (Association of Certified Fraud Examiners survey of 2,600 firms finds fraud inflicts $120,000 loss in median case).

200 Ames case: Tim Weiner, "Jailed, Turncoat at CIA Tells of a Long Betrayal," *New York Times*, July 28, 1994 (quoting R. James Woolsey).

200 Federal hiring: Judith Havemann, "Employee Survey Reports a Drain in Quality," *Washington Post*, June 26, 1990 (reporting on MSPB survey of 16,000 randomly sampled federal workers as "fresh evidence that federal workers see an accelerating decline in the quality of the young people coming into their agencies"); David Segal, "What's Wrong with the Gore Report: Poor Quality of Civil Service," *Washington Monthly*, November 1993 (quoting Pat Ingraham); Judith Havemann, "New Federal Job Exams Set for June: Competitive Process Revived After Gap of Nearly a Decade," *Washington Post*, April 22, 1990 (quoting Constance Horner). According to Havemann, "The hiring process is almost universally blamed for at least part of the problem described as the 'quiet crisis.'" "Widespread sense" is from Volcker report.

201 Can't really cut the mustard: Scott Shuger and Daniel Kaufman, "How to Cut the Bureaucracy in Half," *Washington Monthly*, June 1990. Unemployable elsewhere: James Lardner, "Worth a Raise?" *New York Times*, February 16, 1996 (quoting Michael Julian, NYPD).

201 Few D.C. teachers get low ratings: "D.C. Schools' Numbers Game" (editorial), *Washington Post*, February 21, 1992. Brooklyn teacher strikes student so as to return to administrative job: Sam Dillon, "Teacher Tenure: Rights Vs. Discipline," *New York Times*, June 28, 1994.

202 Five incompetent teachers: Louis Fischer, David Schimmel, and Cynthia Kelly, *Teachers and the Law* (1981), p. 22. "Can the person do the job" analysis = illegality: Lee, "Reasonable Accommodations Under the ADA," p. 204. Supposedly same performance standards for disabled: 29 CFR s. 1630 (EEOC regulations on ADA). Soothing language and second-guessing: Lee, "Reasonable Accommodation Under the ADA."

203 Fluency in English must not affect decision: see Bill Piatt, *Language on the Job* (New Mexico, 1993), p. 55 (quoting ad in Lubbock *Avalanche-Journal*, May 19, 1991, placed by the Office of the Special Counsel for Immigration-Related Unfair Employment Practices, U.S. Department of Justice, and similar ad running in New York subways at around the same time). Stop, don't, look out: Alan M. Koral, *Conducting the Lawful Employment Interview: How to Avoid Charges of Discrimination When Interviewing Job Candidates*, revised edition (New York: Executive Enterprises Publications Co., 1986), pp. 12–13.

203   Customer whims: Mari Matsuda, "Voices of America: Accent, Antidiscrimination Law and a Jurisprudence for the Last Reconstruction," 100 *Yale Law Journal* 1329, 1376–1378 (1991). The article gets off to a hot start with a poem by a Hispanic activist describing the United States as a "fanged monster." See also Bill Piatt, *¿English Only?* (New Mexico, 1990), p. 187 (avoiding customer annoyance no excuse for English-on-job rule, citing *Diaz*). Customers will ultimately adjust: Mark Kelman, "Concepts of Discrimination in 'General Ability' Job Testing," 104 *Harvard Law Review* 1158, 1178–1179 (1991). Manner of speaking reflects Caucasian norms: Koral, *Conducting the Lawful Employment Interview,* p. 39.

204   Westfield controversy: see Philip Bennett, "Voices Rise on Plan to Bar Teacher Accents," *Boston Globe,* July 2, 1992, and other coverage. A pioneering federal court decision is *Gutierrez* v. *Municipal Court,* 838 F. 2d 1031 (9th Cir. 1988), ruling that court employees have right to speak Spanish on the job; if supervisors want to understand what's being said, let them learn that language. 861 F. 2d 1187 (refusal of *en banc* review; see Kozinski dissent), *dism'd as moot,* 109 S. Ct. 1736 (1989).

204   Very carefully reconsidered: Milt Freudenheim, "New Law to Bring Wider Job Rights for Mentally Ill," *New York Times,* September 23, 1991 (quoting Kenneth Collins of Chevron).

205   Abolish heavy lifting by law: McGarity and Schroeder, "Risk-Oriented Employment Screening," p. 1020. The same article at p. 1067 complains that there is no "empirical verification" for the proposition that business necessity requires any degree of disparate treatment of the disabled at all.

205   Illegitimacy of mainstream judgments of merit: Kelman, "Concepts of Discrimination," p. 1188; p. 1243 (by hypothesis, not obvious); p. 1161 (politically progressive deny legitimacy); p. 1176 (static and formal). On "ever-shifting social needs," the article cites Kenneth L. Karst & Harold W. Horowitz, "Affirmative Action and Equal Protection," 60 *Va. L. Rev.* 955, 961–963 (1974)

205   Meritocratic myth: Bartholet, "Application of Title VII to Jobs in High Places," p. 955 (Meritocratic Myth), p. 958 (essentially political); p. 1021 (good ratings from big shots).

205   Music is music: Isabel Wilkerson, "Discordant Notes in Detroit: Music and Affirmative Action," *New York Times,* March 5, 1989 (quoting David S. Holmes, Jr.). James Blanton, "A Limit to Affirmative Action?" *Commentary,* June 1989. Whole peculiar matter of "qualifications": Ellen Goodman, column, April 2, 1987, reprinted in Nicolaus Mills, ed., *Debating Affirmative Action* (Delta, 1994). Pure merit, whatever that might be: Brent Staples, "Editorial Notebook: The 'Scientific' War on the Poor," *New York Times,* October 28, 1994.

206   Math and science weight biased: Heather Mac Donald, "The Diversity Industry," *New Republic,* July 5, 1993 (quoting Ann Morrison, Andrea Cisco, Tom Nelson). Do your part: Koral, *Conducting the Lawful Employment Interview,* pp. 64–65.

Chapter 12. Kid Gloves and Brass Knuckles

Page

211 The account of *Rajender v. University of Minnesota* is drawn from published accounts and case records with a particular debt to George LaNoue and Barbara Lee's pioneering study, *Academics in Court: The Consequences of Faculty Discrimination Litigation* (U. of Michigan, 1987), henceforth "L & L." The main reported decisions can be found at 24 FEP Cases 1045 (D. Minn. 1978), 24 FEP Cases 1051 (D. Minn. 1979); 546 F. Supp. 158 (D. Minn. 1982), 563 F. Supp. 401 (D. Minn. 1983). Newspaper accounts include regular *Minneapolis Star-Tribune* coverage and E. R. Shipp, "The Litigious Groves of Academe," *New York Times,* November 8, 1987. For details on Judge Lord, see Steve Berg and Doug Stone, "The Lord of Federal Court and His Life of Intrigue," *Minneapolis Tribune,* December 9, 1976; Larry Millet, "Champion of the Underdog or Misguided Judicial Zealot?" *St. Paul Pioneer Press,* September 14, 1980; and *Reserve Mining v. Lord,* 529 F. 2d 181 (8th Cir. 1976). My attorney talks to their attorney: Robert Ingrassia, *Minnesota Daily,* November 12, 1990 (quoting Prof. Charlotte Striebel); compare Vladimir Nabokov, *Pale Fire* (Vintage International, 1989), p. 257 ("Do not try to explain to me what your lawyer tells you but have him explain it to my lawyer, and *he* will explain it to me"). Anything bad and wasteful: *Minneapolis Tribune,* June 5, 1982 (quoting Phyllis Freier). Both are cited in Ian Maitland, "How the University of Minnesota Was Subverted by Litigation," *Academic Questions,* Winter 1992–93. A disaster: L & L, p. 215. Erosion of peer review: William Broad, "Ending Sex Discrimination in Academia," *Science,* June 6, 1980 (quoting Sheldon Steinbach, general counsel of American Council on Education).

214 Job versus marriage: Mary Ann Glendon, *The New Family and the New Property* (Butterworths, 1981).

215 Deliberately made conditions intolerable: *NLRB v. Tennessee Packers Inc.,* 339 F. 2d 203, 204 (6th Cir. 1964). Told she wasn't being fired: *Young v. Southwestern Savings & Loan,* 509 F. 2d 140 (5th Cir. 1975). Predictable humiliation and loss of prestige: *Clark v. Marsh,* 665 F. 2d 1168, 1175 (D.C. Cir. 1981).

215 Pressure cooker: *Hunio v. Tishman Construction,* 14 Cal. App. 4th 1010 (1993). Inferior sales territory: *Goss v. Exxon Office Systems,* 747 F. 2d 885 (3rd Cir. 1984). Transfer to another store: *Moniodis v. Cook,* 494 A. 2d 212 (Md. App. 1985); the award was $1 million plus punitive damages. Smelly cigar: David Ewing, *"Do It My Way or You're Fired!"* (Wiley, 1983), p. 137.

217 Rebecca F. case: *Francis v. AT&T,* 55 FRD 202 (D.D.C. 1972).

219 Telling a caller that an employee filed a complaint: Mack A. Player, *Employment Discrimination Law, Student's Edition* (West, 1988), p. 270; Lewin G. Joel III, *Every Employee's Guide to the Law* (Pantheon, 1993), p. 33.

219 Justify an inference of retaliatory motive: *Couty v. Dole,* 886 F. 2d 147, 148 (8th Cir. 1989).

220 Employees do go public: Robert P. Dwoskin, *Rights of the Public Employee* (American Library Association, 1978), p. 102. As a practical matter, filing safety complaint can add to job security: Joel, *Every Employee's Guide to the Law,* pp. 305–306. Pre-

emptive strike by federal transferee: Scott Shuger and Daniel Kaufman, "How to Cut the Bureaucracy in Half," *Washington Monthly,* June 1990.

221 Stand alone: see, e.g., *Pantchenko v. C.B. Dolge Co.,* 581 F. 2d 1052 (2d Cir. 1978), in which an employer won on the merits of the original claim, but a failure to give a reference letter was ruled attackable as retaliation.

221 Highly adversarial, complex, and costly: Stephen M. Kohn, *The Whistleblower Litigation Handbook: Environmental, Health and Safety Claims* (Professional Education Systems, Inc., 1990), p. 235.

221 Avoid expression of negative opinions: Mary E. Reid, "Words That May Later Haunt You," *Wall Street Journal,* December 20, 1993; "be certain personnel files contain only that which can be substantiated."

222 If you receive verbal praise: Ellen Bravo and Ellen Cassedy, *The Nine to Five Guide to Combating Sexual Harassment* (1992), p. 72. Contest the new handbook: Darien McWhirter, *Your Rights at Work* (Wiley, 1989), p. 20; something stupid like admitting guilt, p. 240.

222 Critical internal assessments: *Brandt v. Board of Cooperative Educational Services,* 820 F. 2d 41, 43–45 (2d Cir. 1987), (citing public employee's constitutional liberty interest despite lack of disclosure).

222 Biggest pile of papers wins: Joel, *Every Employee's Guide to the Law,* p. 6; other quotes, pp. 6, 65, 148, 293, 296.

223 One in five have secretly taped: Junda Woo, "Secret Taping of Supervisors Is on the Rise, Lawyers Say," *Wall Street Journal,* November 3, 1992 (quoting San Francisco attorney Mark Rudy). Wired for success: *Heller v. Champion International,* 891 F. 2d 432 (2d Cir. 1989). While content to countenance Mr. Heller's choice of tactics, the *Champion* judges did muster indignation at a co-worker who learned of the taping and told the company, calling him an "unfaithful confidant." See also Jay W. Waks, "Taping Raises Legal, Practical Questions," *National Law Journal,* September 7, 1992.

223 Forgo any gloating: *Snell v. Suffolk County,* 611 F. Supp. 521 at 532. Healthy but natural: *Adcock v. Board of Education,* 513 P. 2d 900, 905 (Calif. 1973). Almost every form "disloyal": *EEOC v. Crown Zellerbach,* 720 F. 2d 1008, 1014 (9th Cir. 1983). Staying for future banquets: McCoy, Arb., in *Forest City Publishing Co.,* 58 LA 773 (1972).

224 Nothing has changed, but I avoid them at all costs: L & L, p. 224 (quoting unnamed interview subject).

224 Relation has become intolerable to one of the parties: Robert S. Stevens, "Involuntary Servitude by Injunction: The Doctrine of *Lumley v. Wagner* Considered," 6 *Cornell Law Quarterly* 235 (1921). After confidence and loyalty are gone: Mark Rothstein, Andria S. Knapp and Lance Liebman, *Employment Law* (Foundation Press) p. 798. See also *Beverly Glen Music v. Warner Comm.,* 224 Cal. Rptr. 260 (1986); Christopher T. Wonnell, "The Contractual Disempowerment of Employees," 46 *Stanford Law Review* 87, 99 (1993).

224 Animosity so intense: *Whittlesey v. Union Carbide Corp.,* 35 FEP Cases 1085 (S.D.N.Y. 1983).

225 James R. Ryan/Equitable Life case: *Wall Street Journal,* March 13, 1992.

225 State every single reason: Cliff Palefsky, "Wrongful Termination Litigation: 'Dag-

wood' and Goliath," 62 *Michigan Bar Journal* 776, 778 (1983). Nothing better to do than attend depositions: Joseph B. Cahill, "Taking on the EEOC: Fighting Agency Not for Faint-Hearted," *Crain's Chicago Business,* June 5, 1995 (quoting Mark Kaminsky of Koch Poultry Co.). The story was a sidebar to a larger investigative piece: Joseph B. Cahill, "Why EEOC Can Spell Trouble," *Crain's Chicago Business,* June 5, 1995.

225 Everyone who had recommended promotions: *EEOC* v. *Citicorp Diner's Club,* 985 F. 2d 1036 (10th Cir. 1993).

226 It was devastating: Cahill, "Taking On the EEOC" (quoting Edward Stein). Cleaning out Sears: Steve Weiner, "Sears' Costly Win in a Hiring Suit," *Wall Street Journal,* March 18, 1986; "the transcript of the 10-month trial in the last case alone is 15 feet high." Women's groups welcomed jailing of Dinnan: *New York Times,* January 9, 1983. See *In re Dinnan,* 661 F. 2d 426 (5th Cir. 1981).

226 Participated in the decision-making process: *Wanamaker* v. *Columbian Rope Co.,* 740 F. Supp. 127, 134–136 (N.D.N.Y. 1990).

226 Naming individual supervisors: Craig A. Horowitz, "Righting the Wrongs of Employment Termination," *San Francisco Recorder,* July 9, 1992 ("most" California complaints now do so). Sue co-workers: see, e.g., *Lyon* v. *Bennington College,* 400 A. 2d 1010 (Vt. 1979).

227 Court forbids company to reimburse supervisors who failed to prevent harassment: *Kyriazi* v. *Western Electric,* 476 F. Supp. 335, 340-1 (D. N.J. 1979). Even absent any wrongdoing, negligence, knowledge, or ratification: Note (Alex S. Navarro), "Bona Fide Damages for Tester Plaintiffs: An Economic Approach to Private Enforcement of the Antidiscrimination Statutes," 81 *Georgetown Law Journal* 2727, 2760 (1993), citing *Chicago* v. *Matchmaker Real Estate Sales Center,* 982 F. 2d 1086 (7th Cir. 1992) and *Walker* v. *Crigler,* 976 F. 2d 900 (4th Cir. 1992).

227 Ruth Vrdolyak case: *EEOC* v. *AIC Sec. Invtgtns. Ltd.,* 823 F. Supp. 571 (N.D. Ill. 1993).

227 Small army of separate lawyers: the example in the text comes from L & L, p. 141.

228 Had to come out of retirement: *EEOC* v. *Vucitech,* 842 F. 2d 936 (7th Cir. 1988). Judge Posner characterized the action (p. 938) as "a protracted effort by the EEOC to fix personal liability on an employer's officers for a practice not authoritatively determined to be discrimination until years after they committed it." See also Barbara Marsh, "Suits Go After Personal Assets of Firm Owners," *Wall Street Journal,* August 13, 1993; Gary W. Florkowski, "Personal Liability Under Federal Labor and Employment Laws," *Employee Relations Law Journal,* March 22, 1989, p. 593.

228 Look good by comparison: L & L, p. 230.

228 Wolf, Block dirty laundry: Unsigned, "Victory in Sex-Bias Suit Would Only Do So Much," *New York Times,* August 21, 1992. Plaintiff Ezold lost on appeal: 983 F. 2d 509 (3d Cir. 1992).

229 You become an enemy: Robert McFadden, "U.S. Court Rules Against City U. in Sex-Bias Suit," *New York Times,* March 19, 1983 (quoting Lilia Melani). Rip the institution apart: LaNoue & Lee, p. 245 (quoting Thomas H. Wright, Jr.).

229 Until all of them have graduated: "Attempt to Oust School Principal Drags On," *New York Times,* September 24, 1995.

229 Most details on *Boylan* v. *New York Times* are taken from Nan Robertson, *The Girls in the Balcony* (Random House, 1992). On plaintiffs' loss of privacy, see also Ellen Schultz and Junda Woo, "Plaintiffs' Sex Lives Are Being Laid Bare In Harassment Cases," *Wall Street Journal*, September 19, 1994.

231 Make the company fire you: Marshall Loeb, "What to Do If You Get Fired," *Fortune*, January 15, 1996.

232 *Lieberman* v. *Gant*, 630 F. 2d 60, 67 (2d Cir. 1980). Details on impact: L & L.

232 DuPont workers' endless case: Bureau of National Affairs *Daily Labor Report*, August 16, 1993.

233 Effects of faculty litigation: L & L, p. 226.

Chapter 13. Why Business Will Miss Unions

Page

234 Balm to wounded pride: Richard W. Power, "A Defense of the Employment at Will Rule," 27 *St. Louis U.L.J.* 881, 887 (1983). Small British awards: see Sam Estreicher, "Unjust Dismissal Laws: Some Cautionary Notes," 33 *Am. Journal of Comparative Law* 310 (1985); Paul Weiler, *Governing the Workplace: The Future of Labor and Employment Law* (Harvard, 1990), p. 83, citing Linda Dickens, Moira Hart, Michael Jones, and Brian Weekes, "The British Experience Under a Statute Prohibiting Unfair Dismissal," 37 *Industrial and Labor Relations Review* 497 (1984). Japan: "The Employees Strike Back," *Nikkei Weekly*, August 15, 1994. Moscow hotel: Michael Hetzer, "Foreign Firms Wrestle With Jobs-for-Life Law," *Moscow Times*, April 6, 1994; "This just shows that the market economy isn't here yet," said a hotel official. Marya Fogel, "Pro-Worker Bias of Russian Law Fuels Foreign Worries About Doing Business," *Wall Street Journal*, May 11, 1994 (quoting Vladimir Draitser).

235 Samantha Phillips case: Allan Massie, "Is Compensation Culture the New Curse of Britain?" *Daily Mail* (London), August 13, 1994. New York City harassment average $250,000: Sameera Khan, "Reducing Harassment Exposure," *Business Insurance*, July 4, 1994 (citing EEOC New York enforcement supervisor Nancy Boyd).

235 A little tithing: "Turmoil and Turnabout," *San Francisco Recorder*, December 27, 1994.

235 Rena Weeks case: *Weeks* v. *Baker & McKenzie*, Opinion and Order Awarding Attorney's Fees and Expenses to Plaintiff, California Superior Court, filed May 2, 1995.

237 Hell of a lot easier: Susan Antilla, "Workplace Discrimination? Don't Try It Around Her," *New York Times*, February 13, 1994 (quoting Judith Vladeck).

237 Never rationalize on grounds of co-worker morale: See 29 CFR s. 1630.15(d), Appendix: Interpretive Guidance.

239 We can't electrocute him: Anne Krueger, "Four on Spital Jury Criticize Other Jurors," *San Diego Union-Tribune*, April 28, 1993 (quoting unnamed juror).

240 Auction them off to pay the damages: Antilla, "Workplace Discrimination?" (quoting Judith Vladeck).

240 Much more economically worthwhile: *Lawyers Alert*, January 1992 issue, quoted in

Barbara Matusow, "Baby, What'd I Say?" *Washingtonian,* August 1993. Don't want a crusty old judge: Steven A. Holmes, "Lawyers Expect Ambiguities in New Rights Law to Bring Years of Lawsuits," *New York Times,* December 27, 1991 (quoting Deborah Gordon).

241 Fees for press conferences: "Civil Rights Lawyers May Be Awarded Fees for Press Conferences," roundup item, *Wall Street Journal,* October 12, 1992 (*Davis* v. *San Francisco,* 9th Circuit). Birthday party: Steven Lerman, "A King's Ransom: Excerpts from Rodney King's Attorney's Bill," *Harper's,* April 1995.

241 Not a problem: "Workplace Warrior" (interview with Jeffrey Bernbach), *Folio,* March 15, 1993. Bizarre Florida case: "Race-Phobia Case Settled," *Wall Street Journal,* December 23, 1992.

242 34-year-old Montana engineer: *Farrens* v. *Meridian Oil,* cited in Alan B. Krueger, "The Evolution of Unjust-Dismissal Legislation in the United States," 44 *Industrial and Labor Relations Review* 644 (1991).

242 *Wheel of Fortune:* Rodd Zolkos, "Avoiding Charges of Bias," *Business Insurance,* July 18, 1994 (quoting Richard Pimentel). Clink of champagne glasses: Charles Oliver, "No Pain, No Gain? Why Workers' Comp is Out of Control," *Reason,* January 1993.

242– Barrier Busters: "Disabling America" (editorial), *Wall Street Journal,* July 24, 1992.
43 Good, quick, simple cases: Jorge Aquino, "No Gold Rush for ADA Bar," *San Francisco Recorder,* August 15, 1994. You go sue Eckerd: "Barrier Buster: San Antonio Official Suits Are Tool to Gain Compliance on Act for Disabled." Denise Gamino, *Dallas Morning News,* December 11, 1992, reprinted from *Austin American-Statesman* (quoting Jeff Londa, Texas Association of Business). Other Texas group: "Disability Group Launches ADA Litigation Campaign in Texas," *Daily Labor Report* (BNA), July 23, 1993.

243 Documented Reference Check (L.A. reference-testing service): L. M. Sixel, "Service Lets Applicants Check Their Own References," *Houston Chronicle,* March 18, 1996.

243 Massachusetts commission's testers: BNA *Daily Labor Report,* January 20, 1994; Diane E. Lewis, "Employment Testing: Useful Tool, or Entrapment?" *Boston Globe,* April 11, 1993; "Diversity Lending," editorial, *Wall Street Journal,* May 14, 1993.

244 $79,000 to two D.C. sex-harassment testers: "Verdict in 'Testers' Case," roundup item, *Wall Street Journal,* August 16, 1993. But see Jay Mathews, "Court Limits Whom Job Bias 'Testers' Can Sue," *Washington Post,* July 30, 1994, where the D.C. Circuit ruled in a separate case that under pre-1991 law only the testing group, and not individual testers, could sue for a monetary award. Testing advocates said, however, that the Civil Rights Act of 1991 may have given individuals as well as groups standing to sue.

244 More weight to tester evidence: *Richardson* v. *Howard,* 712 F. 2d 319, 321 (7th Cir. 1983).

244 Saperstein profile: Benjamin Holden, "Doing Well: A Law Firm Shows Civil Rights Can Be a Lucrative Business," *Wall Street Journal,* June 10, 1993. See also "Safeway Inc. Agrees to Settle A Suit on Sex Discrimination," *Wall Street Journal,* April 4, 1994 (three northern California supermarket chains have paid at least $141 million in Saperstein cases); Gay Jervey, "Runaway Train," *American Lawyer,* July/August 1992.

247 A little hard to distinguish: Author interview with Nelson Lund, George Mason University Law School.

Chapter 14. Workplace Cleansing

Page

248 Dolores Stanley case: *Hartford Courant* coverage, January 1992.

249 Barbara Lawler case: *Georgia Kraft* v. *NLRB,* 696 F. 2d 931 (11th Cir. 1983). Watch it, Debbie: *MP Ind's Inc.,* 227 NLRB 1709, 1710–11 (1977).

250 Dill/Griggs case: John Carlson, "When Political Correctness Becomes Political Coercion," *Seattle Times,* June 21, 1994, and other *Seattle Times* coverage.

250 Fixed star in our Constitutional constellation: *West Virginia Board of Education* v. *Barnette,* 319 U.S. 624, 642 (1942).

252 For all practical purposes employees are like subjects of totalitarian regimes: Max Ways, "The Myth of the 'Oppressive Corporation'," *Fortune,* October, 1977 (quoting David Ewing).

252 Ira Glasser, Lewis Maltby quotes: ACLU: *Liberty at Work: Expanding the Rights of Employees in America* (American Civil Liberties Union, 1988).

253 Harmless today, may be considered unlawful in the future: *Ellison* v. *Brady,* 924 F. 2d 872, 879 (1991). Nip in the bud before they rise to harassment: Greg Krikorian, "A Rare Look in Files on Sex Harassment in LAPD," *Los Angeles Times,* March 27, 1994 (quoting LAPD's Karen Kimball). LAPD punitive reassignments: Jim Newton, *Los Angeles Times* coverage, August 25, 1993, and February 18, February 22, and March 3, 1994.

254 Teaching workers that such views undesirable in private as well: *Davis* v. *Monsanto,* 858 F. 2d 345, 350 (6th Cir. 1988) (liability was not imposed because the employer had taken strong remedial steps). No remarks contrary to religious beliefs: *Turner* v. *Barr,* 806 F. Supp. 1025 (D.D.C. 1992).

254 Like to smoke a cigar: Ellen Edwards, "Channel 9 Guilty of Sex Bias; Jury Notes Hostile 'Climate'; Awards Female Editor $500,000," *Washington Post,* May 27, 1994. Comments favoring women who stay at home: *Parker* v. *Burnley,* 693 F. Supp. 1138, 1152 (N.D. Ga. 1988).

254 Disdain for women's issues: *Lynn* v. *Board of Regents,* 656 F. 2d 1343 (9th Cir. 1981) (remanded on other grounds). "Anti-feminist harassment": see Richard Bernstein, *Dictatorship of Virtue* (Knopf, 1994), p. 123. Their work as insignificant: Eugene Volokh, "Freedom of Speech and Workplace Harassment," 39 *U.C.L.A. Law Review* 1791, 1802, at n. 54 (1992), citing letters to faculty by Elizabeth Bartholet and Duncan Kennedy on Mary Jo Frug incident. See also, e.g., Maureen O'Brien, "Publishing's Best-Kept Secret," *Publishers Weekly,* April 25, 1994 (roundup on sexual harassment in the publishing business).

255 No employee indispensable: Ellen Bravo and Ellen Cassedy, *The Nine to Five Guide to Combating Sexual Harassment* (1992), p. 99; false accusations rare, p. 22; fact versus myth, p. 20. Naval bombardment: Lisa Leff, "Sex Bias Study Takes Naval Academy to Task," *Washington Post,* October 10, 1990 (quoting Rear Admiral Vir-

gil L. Hill, Jr., who said some recommendations had already been put into effect and pledged speedy adoption of the others). Most frequent harassment charge at academies: Jack Kammer, "Recovering from a Tailspin," *Reason,* January 1994. Speaking out can ruin careers: Helen Rogan, *Mixed Company: Women in the Modern Army* (Putnam, 1981), p. 19; Brian Mitchell, *Weak Link: The Feminization of the American Military* (Regnery Gateway, 1989).

255 Chilling effect on religious expression: W. John Moore, "Possibly One 'Thou Shalt Not' Too Many," *National Journal,* May 21, 1994 (quoting Forest D. Montgomery).

256 Form of anarchy creep north into our virgin territory: *Sweeney* v. *Keene State College,* 569 F. 2d 169, 179 (1st Cir. 1978). Congress would never pass such a foolish law as that: *Wirtz* v. *Basic, Inc.,* 256 F. Supp. 786, 787 (D. Nev. 1966). *Forbes* retirement editorial: Douglas Frantz, "Forbes Settled a Bias Suit Before Start of Candidacy," *New York Times,* January 28, 1996.

256 If we sneeze in front of her: *Jordan* v. *Wilson,* 662 F. Supp. 528 (M.D. Ala. 1987).

256 Employee bull session comparing Jewish to black rights: *Williams* v. *Katten, Muchin & Zavis,* 837 F. Supp. 1430 (N.D. Ill. 1993). Leaflet on fishing-rights controversy: Jim Parsons, "Indian Sues, Alleging Racial Harassment," *Minneapolis Star Tribune,* April 14, 1994. Blasphemy of little value: Douglas Laycock, University of Texas School of Law, prepared testimony, Senate Judiciary Committee, Subcommittee on Courts, June 9, 1994.

257 Federal probe of Los Angeles TV stations: Greg Braxton, "L.A. Stations Under Civil Rights Scrutiny," *Los Angeles Times,* March 17, 1994. Baltimore TV complaint: John Moore, "On the Case" (interview with Evan Kemp, Jr.), *National Journal,* March 2, 1991.

257 Connecticut's mandatory sensitivity training: Walter Olson, "When Sensitivity Training Is the Law," *Wall Street Journal,* January 20, 1993. Shame and blame: see, e.g., Bravo & Cassedy, *The Nine to Five Guide,* p. 103 (conceding that most participants walked out on one training session when the trainer treated them as guilty by nature); Kathleen Murray, "The Unfortunate Side Effects of 'Diversity Training,'" *New York Times,* August 1, 1993. Seattle ferry woes: Timothy Egan, "Teaching Tolerance in Workplaces: A Seattle Program Illustrates Limits," *New York Times,* October 8, 1993. See also Richard Seven, "Ex-Ferry Oiler Awarded $105,000—Gay Plaintiff Charges He Was Harassed, Forced to Go on Unpaid Leave," *Seattle Times,* November 13, 1993 ($800,000 in settlements).

258 Believe accuser, fire as first resort: Anne B. Fisher, "Sexual Harassment: What to Do," *Fortune,* August 23, 1993 (quoting attorney Ellen Wagner). On suicides by men facing questionable charges of harassment, see Christopher Byron, "The Joke That Killed," *Esquire,* January 1995 (AT&T employee, Guilford, N.C.); Barbara Matusow, "Baby, What'd I Say?" *Washingtonian,* August 1993 (Fairfax County, Va., math teacher).

258 Business professor's case study: Personal communication to author.

258 Embrace in cubicle as "close case": Margot Slade, "Sexual Harassment: Stories from the Field," *New York Times,* March 27, 1994.

260 Dialogue among autonomous citizens: Robert C. Post, "Free Speech and Religious, Racial, and Sexual Harassment: Racist Speech, Democracy, and the First Amendment," 32 *Wm. & Mary L. Rev.* 267, 289 (1991). For an example of the "before" view, see C. Edwin Baker, "Free Speech," in *Liberty at Work* (employer's interest in avoiding disruptive speech should be interpreted "narrowly," and employer must not be allowed to suppress speech just because it "puts a strain on office routine or relations"); David Ewing, *"Do It My Way or You're Fired!"* (Wiley, 1983), pp. 68–75, praising *Holodnak* v. *Avco,* 514 F. 2d 285 (2d Cir. 1975), an atypical decision in which a private defense contractor-employer was treated as equivalent to a government employer.

260 Disposed of the view that people should speak as freely: Indira A. R. Lakshmanan, "Judge Declares Election 'Satire' Sex Harassment," *Boston Globe,* July 10, 1993, quoting Nancy Gertner (*Bowman* v. *Heller*). How could anyone think free speech was at stake?: *Lambert* v. *Condor Mfg.,* 769 F. Supp. 600 (E.D. Mich. 1991).

260 "Real" speech jurisprudence: see *NAACP* v. *Claiborne Hardware,* 458 U.S. 886, 928 (1982), ruling that even threats to "break [someone's] neck" may be protected; "U.S. Judge Strikes Down Texas Picketing Laws," *New York Times,* August 9, 1985, about a law against "insulting, threatening, or obscene language" used to hinder people from working.

261 Chilling effect: *Baggett* v. *Bullitt,* 377 U.S. 360, 372 (1964) (loyalty oath struck down because of vagueness).

262 Suppress speech directed against historically oppressed group: Mari Matsuda, "Public Response to Racist Speech: Considering the Victim's Story," 87 *Mich. L. Rev.* 2320 (1989), p. 2357. Jokes about those in power vs. powerless: Bravo and Cassedy, *The Nine to Five Guide,* p. 92.

262 Calls for criminal prosecution of speech: Matsuda, "Public Response to Racist Speech," 2320, 2334 (alleging that criticism of affirmative action serves same social function as violence against minorities). For other opposition to free speech, see Post, "Free Speech and Religious, Racial, and Sexual Harassment," at 267, n. 5 (1991), citing 26 articles dealing with racist speech, most favoring more suppression; Suzanne Sangree, "Title VII Prohibitions Against Hostile-Environment Sexual Harassment and the First Amendment: No Collision in Sight," 42 *Rutgers L.R.* 461 (1995), pp. 475, 548 ("sexist speech" in workplace).

263 National Labor Relations Act free-speech clause: 29 USCA s. 158 (c).

Chapter 15. Our Scofflaw Bosses

Page

267 Valdez lawyer's closing argument: contemporaneous trial reports. Exxon sued 107 times, administrative law judge quote: Daniel Seligman, "Keeping Up," *Fortune,* November 28, 1994.

268 Failure to give bad reference: Claudia Deutsch, "A 'Catch 22' in Honesty," *New York Times,* December 2, 1990 (companies sued for negligently hiring a worker "often"

turn around and sue the worker's former firm for failing to pass on damning information). Laundromat case: *Nigg* v. *Patterson*, 233 Cal. App. 3d 171 (1990).

268   Sued-if-you-do on dating: see Alex Markels, "Employer's Dilemma: Whether to Regulate Romance," *Wall Street Journal*, February 14, 1995. Third-party claims: Tessie Borden, "Definition Has Changed As Litigants Push Limits," *Houston Post*, September 4, 1994 (state appeals panel rules in case of *Snyder* v. *Helena Laboratories* that, in reporter's words, "the spouses of two adulterous employees could sue the company for allowing the affair to occur." The report quotes Richard Carlson, a professor at South Texas College of Law, as saying that since the *Snyder* case "a lot of employers are adopting no-dating rules for their employees.") Nepotism unfair: see, e.g., *Thomas* v. *Wash. Cty. Sch. Bd.*, 915 F. 2d 922 (4th Cir. 1990). Anti-nepotism unfair: see, e.g., *EEOC* v. *Roth Packing*, 787 F. 2d 318 (8th Cir. 1986) ("no-spouse" rule).

268   Bellevue Hospital language case: Junda Woo and Milo Geyelin, "Lawsuit Claiming Language Bias in the Workplace Heads to Court," September 24, 1993 (*McNeil* v. *Aguilos*, S.D.N.Y.). "We are not supposed to ask, but we are supposed to know": Susan Lee, "That Can't-Do Spirit," *Reason*, March 1996 (quoting Tennessee candy maker James Spradley, Jr.). Also see Tama Starr, "So Sue Me," *Washington Post*, April 11, 1993.

269   Veterans' preference: on the topic generally, see John H. Fleming and Charles Shanor, "Veteran's Preference in Public Employment: Unconstitutional Gender Discrimination?" 26 *Emory L.J.* 13 (1977).

269   Suffolk prison officers: *Snell* v. *Suffolk County*, 782 F. 2d 1094 (2d Cir. 1986). Reinstatement of harassers: One of the better known cases is *Chrysler Motors* v. *Local 793 Int'l Union Allied Indus'l Workers of America*, 959 F. 2d 685 (7th Cir. 1992); see Bureau of National Affairs, *Daily Labor Report*, April 10, 1992. See also *Matter of NYC Transit Authority (Transport Workers Union of America)*, reported in *New York Law Journal*, October 28, 1993. In *Ellison* v. *Brady*, 924 F. 2d 872 (9th Cir. 1991), a widely noted harassment case, the Internal Revenue Service had responded to a female worker's complaints about unwelcome overtures from a male co-worker by transferring him to another office; he filed a successful grievance to win reinstatement in the old office, and her successful complaint of hostile work environment followed. See Alex Kozinski, "The False Protection of a Gilded Cage," *San Francisco Recorder*, May 27, 1992.

269   It is as simple: "When the Boss is a Boor" (editorial), *Washington Post*, November 14, 1993. Not rocket science: Barbara Presley Noble, "At Work: When Businesses Need Not Fret," *New York Times*, June 7, 1992. So much easier to treat "more fairly," avoid discharging without good cause: Lauren B. Edelman, Steven E. Abraham, and Howard S. Erlanger, "Professional Construction of Law: The Inflated Threat of Wrongful Discharge," 26 *Law and Soc. Rev.* 47 (1992).

270   Managers who follow generally accepted principles: Darien McWhirter, *Your Rights at Work* (Wiley, 1989), p. 240. Solely because rights have been ignored: letter to the editor, *Wall Street Journal*, August 20, 1992.

271   Federal personnel managers were bound: See Ron Fournier, "White House An-

nounces Plan to Overhaul Government," Associated Press, September 7, 1993 (following National Performance Review headed by Vice President Gore, Clinton holds press conference to vow action, citing 10,000-page personnel manual for federal managers, "which the report says should be phased out to give managers more freedom to hire, fire and promote employees"). Pension law "vulgate": Alvin D. Lurie, "Reform Pension Reform," *Wall Street Journal,* December 8, 1993.

271   Supreme Court declined to read retroactivity into Civil Rights Act of 1991: *Landgraf* v. *USI Film Prods.,* 511 U.S. 244 (1994); *Rivers* v. *Roadway Express,* 511 U.S. 298 (1994). For a view deploring the Court's failure to impose the higher penalties retroactively, see "Another Barrier to Simple Justice" (editorial), *New York Times,* April 28, 1991. A case in which the Supreme Court upheld retroactive enforcement of an employment law was *Nachman* v. *PBGC,* 446 U.S. 359 (1980); it ruled that the Employment Retirement Income Security Act could declare certain benefits "nonforfeitable" even though a private pension plan had explicitly disclaimed making them so, and even though plan administrators had sought to abolish the plan entirely before the law's effective date.

272   Need to guess as to legality: see, e.g., Paul Weiler, *Governing the Workplace: The Future of Labor and Employment Law* (Harvard, 1990), p. 156 ("the price of guessing wrong . . . may well be a huge monetary damage award") and a similar passage on p. 28.

272   Every workplace is hostile: Camille Paglia, "No Law in the Arena," in *Vamps and Tramps* (Vintage, 1994), p. 48. "Absent discrimination": EEOC language intervening in AT & T rate hike case, quoted by Nathan Glazer, *Affirmative Discrimination* (Basic Books, 1975), p. 62. The Supreme Court adopted similar language in a 1977 decision where it declared that "absent explanation, it is ordinarily to be expected that nondiscriminatory hiring practices will, in time, result in a work force more or less representative of the racial and ethnic composition of the population in the community from which employees are hired." *Teamsters* v. *U.S.,* 431 U.S. 324, 340, n. 20 (1977).

272   Thrust of the proposed guidelines to place test users in posture of noncompliance: Herman Belz, *Equality Transformed: A Quarter Century of Affirmative Action* (Transaction Books, 1991), p. 127 (quoting memo by Department of Justice official David Rose from *Congressional Record,* 94th Cong., 2d Sess, 1976, p. 22589). Nibbling during periodic inspections: Alfred W. Blumrosen, *Modern Law: The Law Transmission System and Equal Employment Opportunity* (Wisconsin, 1993), pp. 221–222 (and details of Uniroyal case).

274   Uniform enforcement on resumé accuracy: George Mesritz, " 'After-Acquired' Evidence of Pre-Employment Misrepresentations: An Effective Defense Against Wrongful Discharge Claims," 18 *Employee Relations Law Journal* 215, 223 (1992). On attendance: Michelle Laque Johnson, "Executive Update: Is Now a Good Time to Unload the Staff Deadbeats?" *Investor's Daily* (now *Investor's Business Daily*), June 21, 1991.

274   On employer's argued obligation under civil rights law to monitor workers' leave requests and maintain definite policy, even before passage of the Family and Med-

ical Leave Act, see Mack A. Player, *Employment Discrimination Law, Student's Edition* (West, 1988), p. 243. Lack of consistent and public standards: see *Greenspan* v. *Automobile Club of Michigan,* 495 F. Supp. 1021 (E.D. Mich. 1980); *Chrisner* v. *Complete Auto Transit,* 645 F. 2d 1251, 1262 (6th Cir. 1981), characterizing facts of *Greenspan.*

275   Managers impose across-the-board drug testing because "for-cause" tests get them sued: see, e.g., Tim Ferguson, "Motorola Aims High, So Motorolans Won't Be Getting High," *Wall Street Journal,* June 26, 1990.

276   Job descriptions notoriously inaccurate: see, e.g., Robert Half, *Robert Half on Hiring* (Crown, 1985), pp. 9–10. Behavioral profiles of successful incumbents: Margaret Hart Edwards, "The ADA and the Employment of Individuals with Mental Disabilities," 18 *Employee Relations Law Journal* 347 (Winter 1992–93), p. 361.

277   Job descriptions in Baytown, Texas: Meg Fletcher and Sara J. Harty, "Steps to Manage ADA's Impact," *Business Insurance,* January 27, 1992. Real cost far beyond consultant's fee: see, e.g., Robert Half, *Robert Half on Hiring,* p. 62 (advises trying to hire workers who are not locked into job-description mentality).

277   Rise of formal company personnel departments: Sanford M. Jacoby, *Employing Bureaucracy: Managers, Unions and the Transformation of Work in American Industry, 1900–1945* (Columbia University Press, 1985), p. 233. On observation of timing of waves of personnel centralization, see his book generally. Third wave during our own day: According to Herman Belz, *Equality Transformed: A Quarter Century of Affirmative Action* (Transaction Books, 1991), p. 83, the EEOC's 1972–74 campaign of "big" suit-filing precipitated a shift in compliance responsibilities within large employers away from personnel departments toward legal departments. In the campaign, the commission filed massive complaints against many large companies that had previously been considered to have good EEO records; many of these companies wound up disbursing tens of millions in resulting back-pay settlements.

278   Rise in college use of attorneys: Cheryl Fields, "Academics' Increased Reliance on Legal Advice Documented by College Attorneys' Association," *Chronicle of Higher Education,* July 17, 1985.

278   More and more difficult to get professors to serve on personnel and grievance committees: Helen Gouldner, "The Social Impact of Campus Litigation," 51 *J. of Higher Ed.* 329, 331 (1980), quoted by George R. LaNoue and Barbara Lee, *Academics in Court: The Consequences of Faculty Discrimination Litigation* (hereafter referred to as L & L), pp. 21–22. Reluctant to record positive and negative votes: L & L, p. 111. Shying away from hard decisions: Fields, "Academics' Increased Reliance" (quoting Thomas H. Wright, Jr.), cited in L & L, p. 245. Overly positive evaluations, don't be too nice: L & L, pp. 81–82. See also L & L, p. 214, on how one institution felt legally impelled to abandon the "German" academic model, in which the most senior scholar was given wide latitude to run a department.

279   List of EEO functions: Patricia S. Rose, "Going Too Far or Just Doing Their Job: The Double Bind Facing EEO and AA Officers," 6 *The Labor Lawyer,* 421 (1990) at 456; Rose is with the Seattle law firm of Frank & Rosen. On functions of EEO officers, also see Lee Bowes, *No One Need Apply: Getting and Keeping the Best Workers* (Harvard Business School Press, 1987), p. 165.

279   EEO staffs differ in their views from other managers: see, e.g.: Ann Tickamyer, Susan Scollay, Janet Bokemeier, and Teresa Wood, "Administrators' Perceptions of Affirmative Action in Higher Education," in F. A. Blanchard and F. J. Crosby, eds., *Affirmative Action in Perspective* (Springer, 1989), pp. 125, 131 (survey finds gulf between views of college administrators and of AA/EEO officers at their colleges).

279   May help others file complaints: Rose, "Going Too Far or Just Doing Their Job." EEOC aid and comfort: This view did not convince the Fifth Circuit in one case where the issue came up; see *Jones* v. *Flagship Int'l.*, 793 F. 2d 714, 724–5 (5th Cir. 1986)

279   History of progressive attitudes: "The Application of Title VII to Law Firm Partnership Decisions: Women Struggle to Join the Club," Note (Jeffrey Horst), 44 *Ohio St. L.J.* at 888. See also, e.g., Denise L. Hummel, "Anatomy of an ADA Case," 19 *Employee Relations Law Journal* 103 (1993); plaintiff's attorney Hummel advises employers that their most important task in defending discrimination suits is to keep before the court at all times the message that "Our Business Supports Diversity."

280   Law widely ignored: see, e.g., Julie C. Janofsky, "Whoever Wrote ADA Regs Never Ran a Business," *Wall Street Journal,* March 15, 1993; Junda Woo, "Job Interviews Pose Rising Risk to Employees," *Wall Street Journal,* March 11, 1992; William Berkeley, "Job Interviewers' Dirty Little Secret," *Wall Street Journal,* March 20, 1989. Female-only headhunter searches: Joann S. Lublin, "Firms Designate Some Openings for Women Only," *Wall Street Journal,* February 7, 1994. They're the right age: Andy Meisler, "To Reach Generation X, Hire Generation X," *New York Times,* September 25, 1995 (quoting NBC executive Warren Littlefield).

281   Big law firms lose verdicts: see Karen Dillon, "The Cadwalader Paradox," *American Lawyer,* September 1996; "When David Takes On Goliath," *American Lawyer,* September 1996 (Coudert, Baker & McKenzie); *Hishon* v. *King & Spalding,* 467 U.S. 69 (1984). Margaret A. Jacobs, "Law Firm Loses Race Discrimination Case," *Wall Street Journal,* March 25, 1996 (Katten Muchin & Zavis); Amy Stevens and Benjamin Holden, "How Bigotry Charges Rocked White & Case," *Wall Street Journal,* August 19, 1994.

281   Wouldn't be easy for older lawyer to pick up style: Wade Lambert, "EEOC Investigates Law-Firm Hirings," *Wall Street Journal,* May 26, 1993 (quoting Jane Stein of Winthrop Stimson). Create hardening of arteries: Amy Stevens, "Lawyer With Six Years of Experience, Top Credentials, Seeks Job, Any Job at All," *Wall Street Journal,* July 22, 1994 (quoting Robert Loeffler of Morrison & Foerster). See also Amy Stevens, "Graying Attorneys Aim More Suits at Own Law Firms," *Wall Street Journal,* December 9, 1994.

281   NAACP woes: see, e.g., Dorothy Gaiter, "Limits Imposed in NAACP Sex-Bias Case," *Wall Street Journal,* April 16, 1996. Consumers Union labor strife: Michael DeCourcy Hinds, "Consumer's World: How Consumers Union Puts Teeth into 'Let the Seller Beware,'" *New York Times,* June 11, 1988. Vassar unfair to women: *Fisher* v. *Vassar College,* reported in *Wall Street Journal,* May 17, 1994. The Second Circuit overturned the plaintiff's victory on appeal. Gay Men's Health Crisis: Mireya Navarro, "Worker Claims Discrimination by AIDS Group," *New York Times,* Feb-

ruary 5, 1994. The *New York Times,* on down: Nan Robertson, *The Girls in the Balcony* (Random House, 1992).

282   Labor Department pays $4.9 million to settle: Asra Q. Nomani, "Labor Department Settles Bias Suit by Black Workers," *Wall Street Journal,* September 30, 1994. NYC Department of Aging: Don Van Natta, Jr., "Department for the Aging Loses Age-Bias Lawsuit," *New York Times,* November 2, 1995.

282   Want to know they are in compliance: James DeLong, "The Criminalization of Just About Everything," *American Enterprise,* March/April 1994.

282   Deliberate vagueness in ADA language: This is widely agreed in contemporary news reports, including, for example, Peter T. Kilborn, "Major Shift Likely as Law Bans Bias Toward Disabled," *New York Times,* July 19, 1992; Carolyn Lochhead, "New Law on the Disabled to Make a Huge Impact" and "Many Rules in New Law Left Vague on Purpose" (sidebar), *San Francisco Chronicle,* November 14, 1991.

Chapter 16. Secure In What?

Page

284   Expected to be half of workforce: Janice Castro, "The Temping of America: Disposable Workers." *Time,* March 29, 1993. Corrective and revisionist stories appearing over the next year or two included Jaclyn Fierman, "The Contingency Work Force," *Fortune,* January 24, 1994; Ida L. Walters, "Temping Fate," *Reason,* April, 1994; and Janet Novack, "Is Lean, Mean?" *Forbes,* August 15, 1994. The deflation of the relative importance of Manpower, Inc. relies on Walters.

285   On growth in temp services, see, e.g., Roger Ricklefs, "Worker Staffing Becomes a Hot Entrepreneurial Field," *Wall Street Journal,* June 4, 1996 (National Association of Temporary and Staffing Services says average daily employment of temp services nearly doubled from 1990 to 1995, to 2.2 million; staff leasing said to be growing at 30 percent a year.) Rise of share of temp dollar going to professionals: Margaret O. Kirk, "The Temps in the Gray Flannel Suits," *New York Times,* December 17, 1995.

286   Major contributor to growth of contingency work force: William Tucker, "The Changing Face of America's Work Force," *Insight,* March 14, 1994 (quoting Michael Losey). "Family leave, mandated health benefits—anything that scares a permanent employer has a tendency to help the temp industry," John Larson, a Milwaukee securities analyst who follows the temp industry, told Tucker. Never really hire them: Castro, "The Temping of America" (quoting Robert Uhlaner).

286   Dismissal considered practically impossible: David Henderson, "The Europeanization of the U.S. Labor Market," *The Public Interest,* Fall 1993. Credo of dug-in miner: Stephen D. Barber, "U.K. Class Barriers: Pure Codswallop," letter to the editor, *Wall Street Journal,* February 25, 1992.

288   Obstacle No. 1: Greg Steinmetz, "Americans, Too, Run Afoul of Rigorous German Rules," *Wall Street Journal,* February 2, 1996 (quoting consultant Michael Hoerner and chairman Heinrich Weiss of Duesseldorf-based machinery builder SMS Schloemann-Siemag AG). For a sampling of reports from other countries, see Alix

Christie, "Restructuring Is Common for the French," *San Francisco Chronicle,* December 26, 1992; Richard W. Stevenson, "Spanish Economy Picking Up, but Many People Still Suffer," *New York Times,* September 27, 1994; Lawrence Ingrassia, "Out of Work, But Not Out of Luck, in Spain's Cadiz," *Wall Street Journal,* November 30, 1995; Peter Gumbel, "Western Europe Finds That It's Pricing Itself Out of the Job Market," *Wall Street Journal,* December 9, 1993 (European labor rules are a "major disincentive to job-creation—and a powerful incentive to moving production elsewhere.")

For a summary of research indicating that U.S. employers are faster in adjusting to shifting market conditions in both adding and in removing workers, see Daniel S. Hamermesh, "Employment Protection: Theoretical Implications and Some U.S. Evidence," in C. Buechtemann, ed., *Employment Security and Labor Market Behavior* (Cornell, 1993). Survey by British heavy-industry group: see Jack Stieber in Alan F. Westin and Stephan Salisbury, *Individual Rights in the Corporation: A Reader on Employee Rights* (Pantheon, 1980), p. 62. On the far higher rate at which the U.S. economy created jobs 1970–90 compared with Europe, see figures from Todd Godbout in *Monthly Labor Review,* October 1993.

289   Fifty is the magic number: Jeanne Saddler, "Small Firms Try To Curb Impact of Leave Law," *Wall Street Journal,* August 5, 1993 (quoting Ruth Stafford). For more examples, see Christopher Farrell *et al.,* "The Scary Math of New Hires," *Business Week,* February 22, 1993 (steel-service center stays below 50); Clark S. Judge, "Thresholds of Pain," *Wall Street Journal,* August 10, 1994 (founder of Schonstedt Instruments Inc. took care to stay below 50); Tucker, "The Changing Face" (Pittsburgh restauranteurs stay under 50 by refraining from opening additional outlets).

289   China dolls: Sarah McCarthy, "Cultural Fascism," *Forbes,* December 9, 1991. You will look at a young woman: "Women's Work—and Men's, Too" (editorial), *New York Times,* August 17, 1993; Susan Chira, "Family Leave Is Law: Will Things Change?" *New York Times,* August 15, 1993 (quoting Tama Starr). Surge in firing complaints before FMLA effective date: "Do Some Firms Try to Skirt Family Leave?" roundup item, *Wall Street Journal,* October 25, 1993. NFIB survey: "Job Destruction Bill No. 1" (editorial), *Wall Street Journal,* February 8, 1993. See also William Berkeley, "Job Interviewers' Dirty Little Secret," *Wall Street Journal,* March 20, 1989 (reporting "skittishness" about hiring women of childbearing age).

290   Worsened age bias in faculty hiring: William H. Honan, "New Law Against Age Bias on Campus Clogs Academic Pipeline, Critics Say," *New York Times,* June 15, 1994 (quoting Thomas Bisson).

290   Backfiring on high-pressure, high-turnover jobs: Steven Brill, "Paula Jones: There Ought to Be a Law," *Washington Post,* June 5, 1994.

290   Get away with murder: George R. LaNoue and Barbara A. Lee, *Academics in Court: The Consequences of Faculty Discrimination Litigation* (Michigan, 1987), p. 82 (quoting Dean Julius Elias).

290   Depersonalizing dismissals via layoffs: see, e.g., Sara Marley, "Age-Related Suits Increase," *Business Insurance,* January 17, 1994 ("Legitimate business purpose may be easier to prove when an entire department is being eliminated, rather than a percentage of the overall workforce"). See also Sanford M. Jacoby, *Employing Bureau-*

cracy: Managers, Unions and the Transformation of Work in American Industry, 1900–1945 (Columbia, 1985), p. 276; and Theodore St. Antoine, "A Seed Germinates: Unjust Discharge Reform Heads Toward Full Flower," 67 Neb. L.R. 56, 76 (1988). "European experience indicates that protections against unjust discipline will inevitably force inquiries into an employer's handling of 'redundancies.'"

291 Downsizing scare of 1996: an analysis generally debunking the scare is John Cassidy, "All Worked Up," *The New Yorker,* April 22, 1996.

292 A leading promoter of the unwritten contract: Robert B. Reich, "Companies Are Cutting Their Hearts Out," *New York Times Magazine,* December 19, 1993.

292 Realities of business history: Paul Pigors and Charles Myers, *Personnel Administration* (McGraw-Hill, 1961), p. 397 (citing Hormel, Nunn-Bush).

292 The most widely cited study: see Albert B. Crenshaw, "So Much for the Myth of a Mobile Work Force," *Washington Post National Weekly Edition,* January 2–8, 1995, and other coverage (reporting on NBER working paper by Francis X. Diebold, Daniel Polsky, and David Neumark finding no decline in average length-on-job for most workers). In the summer of 1995 economist Stephen Rose of the Clinton-appointed National Commission for Employment Policy issued a study drawing contrasting conclusions: see G. Pascal Zachary, "Sharp Decline in Job Stability Is Found in New Study, Contradicting Prior Data," *Wall Street Journal,* June 6, 1995. See also "Security Check" (editorial), *Wall Street Journal,* December 27, 1993 (citing study by John Haltiwanger and Stephen Davis of NBER and Scott Schuh of the Federal Reserve, which found the widely talked-of decline of job security in manufacturing much exaggerated).

293 "One Company After Another": Al Ehrbar, "'Re-Engineering' Gives Firms New Efficiency, Workers the Pink Slip," *Wall Street Journal,* March 16, 1993 (citing American Management Association annual survey showing more companies planning to cut work forces despite economic recovery: "Downsizing preceded the recession and it will continue after the recession," said Eric Greenberg, survey director). Very high rates of overtime: "Labor Letter," *Wall Street Journal,* May 10, 1994 (record factory overtime blamed on reluctance to conduct new hiring); "The Outlook," *Wall Street Journal,* January 17, 1994; Joan E. Rigdon, "Some Workers Grip Bosses Are Ordering Too Much Overtime," *Wall Street Journal,* September 29, 1994.

296 Ending practice of allowing senior professors lighter teaching loads: Albert Rees and Sharon B. Smith, "The end of mandatory retirement for tenured faculty," *Science,* August 31, 1991.

296 Final payments an average of six years after filing: James Dertouzos, Elaine Holland, and Patricia Ebener, "The Legal and Economic Consequences of Wrongful Termination" (Rand, 1988), p. 35.

297 Individual talents seldom negotiate lifelong tenure contracts: Mayer G. Freed and Daniel D. Polsby, "Just Cause for Termination Rules and Economic Efficiency," 38 *Emory L.J.* 1097 (1989).

298 Arbitration more emotional appeal: Joann S. Lublin, "Companies Try to Prevent Fired Executives from Suing," *Wall Street Journal,* June 28, 1995 (quoting Detroit lawyer Joseph Golden).

299 Large black markets in Europe: Henderson, "The Europeanization of the U.S. La-

bor Market." On shift in Germany toward fixed-term contracts, see Steinmetz, "Americans, Too, Run Afoul of Rigorous German Rules."

299 An agency temp who had lasted sixteen days: *Amarnare* v. *Merrill Lynch*, 611 F. Supp. 344 (S.D.N.Y. 1984), *aff'd*, 770 F. 2d 157 (2d Cir. 1985) (defense won on merits). In *Magnuson* v. *Peak Technical Services*, 808 F. Supp. 500 (E.D. Va. 1992), a temporary worker referred to as "hon," "too cute," and "Fahrvergnügen girl" was allowed to sue both her temp agency and the auto dealership where she had been placed in temporary work.

299 Avoiding tag as employer: "Temporary Employees Bring Big Benefits to Business . . . Big Legal Problems, Too" (based on interview with James A. Prozzi, Jackson, Lewis, Schnitzler & Krupman, Pittsburgh), *Bottom Line Business* (newsletter), February 15, 1996; John F. Wymer III, "Contact Employees: Yours, Mine, or Ours?", 19 *Employee Relations Law Journal* 247 (1993) at 254.

Chapter 17. The Terms of Cooperation

Page

301 Nursing stations case study: Leonard R. Sayles and George Strauss, *Human Behavior in Organizations* (Prentice-Hall, 1996), p. 142.

302 They act like we're all alike: Louise Kapp Howe, *Pink-Collar Workers* (Avon, 1977), p. 160 (quoting Chicago insurance clerk), quoted in Robert Levering, *A Great Place to Work: What Makes Some Employers So Good (and Most So Bad)* (Random House, 1988), p. 179. Potted geraniums: Sayles & Strauss, p. 179.

302 Most of us like our jobs: see, for example, Tamar Lewin, "Working Women Say Bias Persists," *New York Times*, October 15, 1994 (a national survey by the Labor Department's Women's Bureau found "nearly four out of five women said that they liked or loved their jobs—and only 4 percent said they disliked their work or found it 'totally miserable'"). Confirming commonsense tradeoffs, the same study found higher pay correlated quite strongly with less flexible hours of work and less enjoyment of co-workers' company. On different criteria of what makes a job good, see also Glenn Garvin, "America's Economic Refugees," *Reason*, November 1993, quoting sociologist Patricia Fernandez-Kelly, who studied a Mexican border *maquiladora* plant. Fernandez-Kelly conceded that "one of the constant pains to left-of-center observers" is that workers do not always feel the expected discontents, and quoted one of her own interview subjects, a young woman who worked at the factory: "I love it! I want to keep working here forever! It's more money than my parents ever made in their whole lives!"

302 Ulcers, run down: Levering, *A Great Place To Work*, p. 167.

303 Steam laundry below, carpenter's shop above: Boris Emmet and John E. Jeuck, *Catalogues and Counters* (University of Chicago Press, 1950), p. 137.

303 Orange crates for shelves: David T. Kearns and David A. Nadler, *Prophets in the Dark: How Xerox Reinvented Itself and Beat Back the Japanese* (HarperCollins, 1992).

305 The need is not so great: Jill Lawrence, "House Votes to End Mandatory Retirement," Associated Press, September 24, 1986 (quoting Claude Pepper). Absolutely

essential right to act without outside review, whims of judge: "Civil-Rights Exemption" (editorial), *Wall Street Journal*, July 25, 1990 (quoting Warren Rudman). Contract with America popular plank applying laws to Congress: Stephen Glass, "Do As They Do," *New Republic*, April 15, 1996 (on Congressional Accountability Act). On the history of attempts to apply the Americans with Disabilities Act to Congress, see also Daniel Seligman, "Keeping Up," *Fortune*, June 15, 1992. Iowa's Charles Grassley offered an ADA amendment to cover Congress that, according to an October 23, 1989 Heritage Foundation report quoted by Seligman, "sparked a heated debate in the Senate chamber, much of it unreported in the official *Congressional Record* . . . . Grassley was surrounded by angry Democrats warning of the grave consequences should his amendment pass. One Senator, a chief sponsor of the bill, warned Grassley that his amendment would torpedo [it]. Another Senator was even more candid in his off-the-record remarks, saying that the amendment would be enormously costly, forcing Congress to construct additional office buildings to accommodate all the new facilities required." As Seligman observes, "This was a bill whose requirements were being sold to business as no big deal." While Senators were apparently unwilling to vote down Grassley's amendment openly, it later got eliminated in conference, the classic location for the disposal of such things without fingerprints.

305   Municipal versus federal firefighters: *Johnson* v. *Mayor and City Council of Baltimore*, 472 U.S. 353 (1985). A unanimous Supreme Court held that Congress was free to be inconsistent in imposing mandates on state and city but not on federal officials given the principle known as federal supremacy, which in this case might be paraphrased with reference to the child-rearing maxim, "Because I'm the Mommy, that's why."

305   Supreme Court nominee: "Bill Clinton and the ADA," editorial, *Wall Street Journal*, May 20, 1994 (quoting Milton Bordwin). On longevity of presidential candidates, see also a letter to the editor, *New York Times*, December 8, 1992, from Charles F. Glassman, M.D.

306   Please leave the building: *New York*, August 3, 1992 (quoting Ira Glasser). See also Daniel Wise, "ACLU Battles with Ex-Unit Over Breakup," *National Law Journal*, June 29, 1992. Get rid of dead wood: *Wall Street Journal*, roundup item, February 20, 1996, p. 1 (quoting Economic Notes, "a monthly newsletter for unions"). Mother Jones case: Alex S. Jones, "Radical Magazine Removes Editor, Setting Off a Widening Political Debate," *New York Times*, September 27, 1986. Such cases could be catalogued at almost any length: see, e.g., "Pinko Is the Man," *New York*, May 27, 1996 (allegations of high-handed management at left-wing Pacifica radio chain).

306   Mr. Litigation: Thomas Love, "Nader Hits Firms, Unions in Explaining 'Business Day,'" *Washington Star*, April 15, 1980. *Multinational Monitor* case: Peter Perl, "Editors Claim Firing by Nader Based on Unionization Attempt," *Washington Post*, June 28, 1984. Nader's comments quoted in the *Post* story resembled those reported in the earlier story: "I don't think there is a role for unions in small nonprofit 'cause' organizations any more than . . . within a monastery or within a union," he

said, with a jab at how "people come here and say they want to fight polluters and unresponsive agencies, but not after 5 o'clock and not on weekends."

309   Deal was a deal: Ben Hamper, *Rivethead* (Warner, 1992), p. 49.

309   Freedom of association: see *Bell v. Maryland,* 378 U.S. 226 (1964) (Goldberg, J., concurring at 313): "Prejudice and bigotry in any form are regrettable, but it is the constitutional right of every person to close his home or club to any person or to choose his social intimates and business partners solely on the basis of personal prejudices including race." Quoted by Judge Avant Edenfield in *Hishon v. King & Spalding,* 24 FEP Cases 1303 (N.D. Ga. 1980). "In a very real sense," Judge Edenfield went on to observe, "a professional partnership is like a marriage . . . a 'business marriage' for better or worse," adding that the use of legal force "to coerce a mismatched or unwanted partnership too closely resembles a statute for the enforcement of shotgun weddings." Unfortunately, the Supreme Court proceeded to reverse him unanimously.

309   "Women Taxi Drivers Demand Fair Deal to Prevent Attacks," We live in fear: Barbara Lewis, *London Sunday Telegraph,* August 30, 1992 (quoting Barbara Haroon). Women's Transit Authority: "Campus Life: Wisconsin; Ride Service to Avoid Rape Is Ruled Biased," *New York Times,* April 19, 1992. Santa Cruz business comments: Peter Sheridan, "I'm Ugly, Hire Me," *London Daily Mail,* May 28, 1992 (quoting funeral director Eric Bianco and Anubis Warpus owner Brian Friedman).

INDEX

INDEX

Mesritz, George, 274
Metzenbaum, Howard, 198
Michigan Blue Cross and Blue Shield, 38–39, 40
Michigan Supreme Court, 39–41, 43
Milbank Memorial Fund, 112
Miller, Richard, 138
Miner, William, 156
Minnesota, University of, 194, 211–13
Mission Bay Mortgage Company, 31–32, 42
Mitchell, Brian, 255
Montgomery, Forest D., 255
Moore, John, 257
Moore, Michael, 306
Muldrew, Finley, 47–48, 49
Mullins, Jim, 157
Munter, John E., 236

NAACP, 261, 281
Nader, Ralph, 100, 306–7
Nadler, David, 303
narcolepsy, 2, 136
National Education Association, 204
National Federation of Independent Business, 100, 289
National Foundation for Depressive Illness, 133
National Labor Relations Act, 263
National Labor Relations Board, 50, 215, 250
National Organization for Women, 78, 81, 249
national origin, 2, 4, 56, 58, 203
National Stuttering Project, 96
National Teachers Examination, 188
National Transportation Safety Board, 199
Naval Academy, U.S., 255
Nebraska, University of, 74
nepotism, 268
Nesbitt, Frederick, 198
New Deal, 7, 8, 33, 262, 277
New Haven, Ct., 161–62
New York, 9–10, 62, 185, 241
New York City, 155, 162, 181, 195, 198–99, 282, 308
New York Police Department, 185, 187, 192, 193, 201
New York Times, 86, 184, 206, 258–59, 269, sued as employer, 229–31, 282

9 to 5 Guide to Combating Sexual Harassment (Bravo and Cassedy), 65, 67, 76, 79, 222, 255, 262
No Pity (Shapiro), 95, 96, 114
Northwest Airlines, 119–22, 167

obesity, 4, 23, 58, 74, 113, 136
Occupational Safety and Health Administration, 50, 288
off-job misconduct, 130, 134, 166–167, 169
Office of Civil Rights (OCR), 98, 105–6, 123
Oh, James J., 77
Oliver, Charles, 242
Oliver, Suzanne, 29
Orange Unified School District, 64–65, 82
Organization for Economic Cooperation and Development, 288
Ortiz, Juan, 187
Ostrowski, Edward, 186
outsourcing, 37, 284, 285

Paglia, Camille, 272
Palefsky, Cliff, 40, 46, 225
Pam Am, 60
Parker Drilling, 174–75
Parrino, Sandra Swift, 85
Peck, Louis, 43
People Express, 302
Pepper, Claude, 56, 148, 153, 305
personal-appearance discrimination, 58–59
personal attendants, 113–14
personal liability of managers, 226–28
Petrocelli, William, 67, 79
Pfizer, 157
Phillips, Emmerson, 128
Phillips, Samantha, 235
photocopier humor, *see* jokes
pilots, 59, 119–22, 167, 199
Playboy, 65, 248–49
police departments, 66, 81, 166, 172–73, 198, 253
hiring by, 17–18, 23, 180, 185, 187, 192–93, 201
Polsby, Daniel, 297
Poole, Douglas, 115

INDEX

INDEX